COLUMBIA COLLEGE
973.923J67R   C1   V2
LYNDON B. JOHNSON   A BIBLIOGRAPHY$ 1S

3 2711 00007 9882

973.923 J67r v. 2

Lyndon B. Johnson, a bibliography

D1767067

DISCARD

261-2500   Printed in USA

NOV 7 1988

LYNDON B. JOHNSON: A BIBLIOGRAPHY,
VOLUME TWO

LYNDON B. JOHNSON
A Bibliography, Volume Two

The Career, Times, and Family of the Thirty-Sixth President

Compiled by
Craig H. Roell for the Lyndon Baines Johnson Library

COLUMBIA COLLEGE LIBRARY

 University of Texas Press, Austin

> 973.923 J67r v. 2
>
> Lyndon B. Johnson, a
> bibliography

Copyright © 1988 by the University of Texas Press
All rights reserved
Printed in the United States of America
First Edition, 1988

Requests for permission to reproduce material from this work should be sent to Permissions, University of Texas Press, Box 7819, Austin, Texas 78713-7819.

LIBRARY OF CONGRESS CATALOGING-IN-PUBLICATION DATA
(Revised for vol. 2)

Lyndon B. Johnson, a bibliography.

   Vol. 2 compiled by Craig H. Roell.
   Includes index.
   1. Johnson, Lyndon B. (Lyndon Baines), 1908–1973—
Bibliography.   2. Lyndon Baines Johnson Library.
I. Roell, Craig H.
Z8455.68.L97   1984   016.973923'092'4   83-23264
[E847.J6]   [B]
ISBN 0-292-74017-4

For reasons of economy and speed this volume has been printed from computer-generated tapes furnished by the compiler, who assumes full responsibility for its contents.

Contents

Foreword   ix
Preface   xi
PART 1. Lyndon B. Johnson
I. Lyndon B. Johnson, Writings and Interviews   1
   A. Prepresidential Years, 1908–1963   1
   B. Presidential Years, 1963–1969   3
      1. General   3
      2. Domestic Policy   4
      3. Foreign Policy and the Vietnam War   5
   C. Postpresidential Years, 1969–1973   6
II. Biographical Works   6
III. The Early Years, 1908–1936   9
IV. The Congressional Years, 1937–1948   10
V. The Senatorial Years, 1949–1960   12
   A. General   12
   B. Specific Issues and Legislation   19
   C. Presidential Elections of 1956 and 1960   25
   D. Congressional Colleagues   34
VI. The Vice-Presidential Years, 1961–1963   39
VII. The Presidential Years, 1963–1969   44
   A. The American Presidency   44
   B. The Johnson Presidency   47
      1. General   47
      2. The Johnson White House   59
         a. The Vice President   59
         b. The Cabinet   61
         c. The White House Staff, the Executive Office of the President, and Other Advisers   71
      3. The Media   82
      4. Politics   89
         a. General   89
         b. The Congress   95

        c. The Presidential Election of 1964   102
        d. The Presidential Election of 1968   114
   C. The Johnson Administration   131
     1. America in the 1960s   131
     2. Domestic Policy   144
        a. General   144
        b. The Arts   153
        c. Civil Rights   156
        d. Education   164
        e. The Federal Budget, the Economy, Taxes   170
        f. Health Care and Social Security   183
        g. The Space Program, Science Policy, Defense   185
        h. The Supreme Court, the Federal Courts   193
        i. Urban Development   198
        j. The War on Poverty   202
        k. Miscellaneous Programs   224
     3. Foreign Policy   228
        a. General   228
        b. Asia and India   238
        c. Europe and the Soviet Union   244
        d. Latin America and the Caribbean   249
        e. The Middle East and Africa   255
        f. Other Nations   259
     4. The Vietnam War   259
        a. General   259
        b. The Media   273
        c. Military Policy and Strategy   277
        d. Peace Negotiations   285
        e. Politics and Legal Issues   290
        f. Public Response and Domestic Impact   300
VIII. The Postpresidential Years, 1969–1973   311
   A. General   311
   B. Lyndon B. Johnson Library and LBJ State Park   312
PART 2. Lady Bird Johnson and Family
   I. Lady Bird Johnson, Writings and Interviews   315

II. Biographical Works   316
III. The Prepresidential Years, 1912–1963   317
IV. The Presidential Years, 1963–1969   318
    A. General   318
    B. Politics and Policy   319
        1. Beautification   319
        2. Johnson Family Finances   320
        3. Miscellaneous Politics and Policy   321
V. The Postpresidential Years, 1969–Present   322
    A. General   322
    B. Beautification   324
VI. The Family   325
Appendixes
    1. The Lyndon B. Johnson Presidency: First Administration, 1963–1965   329
    2. Second Administration, 1965–1969   329
    3. Supreme Court Justices   331
    4. Presidential Elections, 1956–1968   331
Sources: Guides and Indexes Consulted   333
Index   335

Foreword

Since the publication of Volume I of the Lyndon B. Johnson Bibliography in 1984, a resurgence of interest in Johnson has created the need for a second volume. We have watched the progress of both works with great interest, knowing that they will provide access to the wealth of material written about the president from Texas. It is again our pleasure to provide funding for this project. Our hope is that this new publication will serve to help students of Lyndon B. Johnson understand him, his life and times.

This project is also a way for us to honor Lady Bird Johnson for whom we have great admiration and affection.

          Joe & Bennie Green
          Rockwell Fund, Inc., Houston, Texas

Preface

This BIBLIOGRAPHY represents a supplemental effort to assemble into an accessible and convenient format the emerging literature addressing the life and times of Lyndon Baines Johnson. The initial project, compiled by the staff of the Lyndon B. Johnson Library and published by the University of Texas Press in 1984 as *Lyndon B. Johnson: A Bibliography,* was intended by its compilers, this bibliographer included, to be foundational, not definitive; supplemental volumes were to capture new works and overlooked titles. This book is the second compilation in what will be a continuing commitment to provide access to the considerable—and ever expanding—literature on Johnson's forty-year career in politics, on Lady Bird Johnson and the family, and on the times in which they lived.

The student of the Johnson years in American history faces a formidable volume of source materials. The various manuscript collections and newspapers accounts alone are overwhelming, and as Lewis L. Gould has shown, immersion in the vast archives of the Lyndon B. Johnson Library is not enough. Scholars must also search the papers of John C. Granbery, Harold Ickes, Pat M. Neff, Hatton Sumners, James V. Allred, Dan Moody, Minnie Fisher Cunningham, Jane Y. McCallum, Ross Sterling, Maury Maverick, W. Lee O'Daniel, and many others "before research on Lyndon Johnson can really be called thorough."[1] This BIBLIOGRAPHY continues the fundamental purpose and scope of its predecessor. As in the first volume, coverage includes books, scholarly articles, signed and select unsigned pieces in the popular press, doctoral dissertations and master's theses, select papers delivered at conferences, and essays. Manuscript

---

[1] Lewis L. Gould, "Robert Caro and George Reedy on Lyndon Johnson: An Essay Review," *Southwestern Historical Quarterly* 87 (July 1983): 62 (57–68).

collections[2] and most foreign publications, newspaper stories, audiovisual materials, juvenile literature, poetry, fiction, and humor again are excluded. In certain cases significant government documents are included, though the plethora of government publications indexed in *American Statistics Index, The Declassified Documents Quarterly Catalog,* and the *Monthly Catalog of United States Government Publications,* as well as the material within *The Congressional Record* remain beyond the scope of the BIBLIOGRAPHY.

This volume is designed for a wide appeal, from students to teachers, scholars, and archivists. It records the work of journalists, historians, economists, political scientists, lawyers, sociologists, and social psychologists. The material has been gathered from more than fifty indexes to periodicals and guides to literature, from dissertation and monograph bibliographies, and from the catalog files of the Lyndon Baines Johnson Library and the University of Texas at Austin libraries, which include the Perry-Castañeda Library, the Lyndon B. Johnson School of Public Affairs Library, the Barker Texas History Center, and the Tarlton Law Library. These sources offer a formidable and wide-ranging access to Johnsonian literature not generally available. Readers should feel comfortable knowing that the guides and indexes listed in the Sources were thoroughly, but selectively, searched for relevant materials that chronicle in the broadest terms the Johnson years. Also, new editions of works previously recorded in volume one are included in the present BIBLIOGRAPHY, as are amended versions of entries that were found to be wrongly categorized or incorrectly cited.

Considerable thought was given to structuring this volume's arrangement to provide maximum usability. Categories are arranged chronologically by subject, each subdivided into as many fields as reasonable to provide clarity and accessibility while minimizing duplication and multiple searching. Nevertheless, there are numerous duplicate or triplicate entries when warranted by their comprehensiveness. An author index keyed to page numbers provides additional reference and ingress. Al-

---

[2] For a convenient guide to the manuscripts and archival collections in the Lyndon B. Johnson Library, see the appendix in Robert A. Divine, ed., *Exploring the Johnson Years* (Austin: University of Texas Press, 1981).

PREFACE xiii

though the BIBLIOGRAPHY again is not annotated, the title and category of each entry offers a sense of its substance and meaning. Bracketed information provides additional explanation when necessary. Accordingly, "General" or "Miscellaneous" categories have been avoided whenever a more specific field could be utilized. Categorization, however, imposes an artificial sorting of information; life is rarely so neat. The diligent researcher will winnow out much related material for any given topic by weaving through several categories. The reader will also notice that coverage is not even. No attempt was made to impose a uniformity of categorization; certain topics have received more attention than others. Indeed, the more meager fields merely signify areas of promising future research.

Every effort has been made to maintain objectivity in the compilation of this BIBLIOGRAPHY. The entries reflect every point of view, from those favorable to those indifferent, adverse, or hostile. Scholarly treatises and journals, the popular press, and recalcitrant or radical periodicals are all valuable for their insight to contemporary perceptions in addition to whatever factual comment they elicit. The BIBLIOGRAPHY contains two types of literature that offer impressions and illuminations of the family and career of the thirty-sixth president. The first is directly devoted to the subject; the other is primarily concerned with other fields, but is *incidentally* relative, providing additional comprehension and yielding the larger and essential perspective. Thus, the BIBLIOGRAPHY will be a useful tool to political and diplomatic historians as well as to social, cultural, economic, military, and business historians, political scientists, sociologists, and students. Similarly, although this book is designed primarily to assist those researching the varied aspects of Lyndon Johnson's life, scholars pursuing such topics as the Eisenhower and Kennedy administrations, the war in Vietnam, American society in the 1960s, the Supreme Court, the U.S. space program, the presidency, the Congress, the media, the political management of domestic and foreign policy, or the various political candidates involved in the presidential elections from 1956 to 1968 will also find the pages invaluable. An appendix has been included that illustrates the cabinets of the first and second Johnson administrations, the Supreme Court and Congressional political majorities during the Johnson years, and information on the presidential elections of 1956–1968.

It is hoped that this considerable catalog of Johnsonian literature, together with the previously published bibliography and future supplements, will provide a path toward probing the complexity and solving the enigma of Lyndon Baines Johnson, to understand how, as Robert A. Divine states in his invitation to scholars, "such a dynamic and gifted political leader failed to transcend his own background—why he tried to solve the problems of the future with the answers of the past. . . . [and] led the nation into strategic disaster."[3]

The research and production of the Lyndon B. Johnson bibliography series, including the present volume, could not have been possible without the generous funding of Mr. and Mrs. Joe M. Green, Jr., and the Rockwell Fund, Inc., of Houston, Texas. The Lyndon Baines Johnson Foundation provided additional financial support. This series is also indebted to the steadfast commitment of Harry J. Middleton, Director of the Lyndon Baines Johnson Library and Museum. Nor would this work have been as comprehensive without the considerable knowledge and input of Tina Lawson Houston, Supervisory Archivist of the Lyndon Baines Johnson Library. Katherine Frankum of the library staff also aided the project. Lewis L. Gould, Eugene C. Barker Centennial Professor in American History, and Robert A. Divine, George W. Littlefield Professor in American History, University of Texas at Austin, contributed valuable insight.

Craig H. Roell
Austin, Texas
March, 1987

---

[3] Robert A. Divine, "The Johnson Literature," in *Exploring the Johnson Years*, p. 21. Divine evaluates the current scholarly assessment of the thirty-sixth president in "The Johnson Revival: A Bibliographical Appraisal," in *The Johnson Years, Volume Two: Vietnam, the Environment, and Science*, edited by Robert A. Divine, pp. 3–20 (Lawrence: University Press of Kansas, 1987).

LYNDON B. JOHNSON: A BIBLIOGRAPHY, VOLUME TWO

PART I

LYNDON B. JOHNSON

I. Lyndon B. Johnson, Writings and Interviews

See also *Congressional Quarterly Weekly Report; Congressional Record; Public Papers of the Presidents of the United States: Lyndon B. Johnson; Weekly Compilation of Presidential Documents*

A. PREPRESIDENTIAL YEARS, 1908–1963

Johnson, Lyndon B. "Cattle Industry Needs Greater Public Understanding." *The Cattleman* 43 (May 1957): 29, 97–98.
———. "East Texas Potential Water Supply Adequate." *East Texas Magazine* 28 (December 1953): 7, 14.
———. "Equality—The Dynamic Ideal of Our Time: Vice President Johnson Addresses Garment Workers' Convention." *Justice* (Internat'l. Ladies Garment Workers Union) 44 (June 1962): 14.
———. "Government Making It Possible for Young Men and Women to Attend College." *Texas Press Messenger* 11 (September 1936): 4.
———. "A Helping Hand for Youth." *Texas Municipalities* 22 (November 1935): 299.
———. "How Lyndon Johnson Sizes Up the State of the Union" (Interview). *U.S. News and World Report* 44 (January 17, 1958): 100–02.
———. "In Memoriam: A Tribute to Sam Rayburn." *New Purpose, New Progress: The Exciting First Year of the New Frontier.* The program for the Inaugural Anniversary Dinner Honoring President John F. Kennedy, January 20, 1962.
———. "Informal Remarks." *Proceedings of the Texas Mid-Continent Oil and Gas Association*, pp. 38–39, 35th Annual Meeting, October 5–6, 1954.

———. "Inter-Basin Canal System Recommended in Bureau Report." *South Texan*, September 1953: 2, 12–13.

———. "Interview with Senator Lyndon B. Johnson: 'Arms Progress Too Slow'." *U.S. News and World Report*, April 11, 1952: 46–60.

———. "Introduction." *After Fifteen Years*, by Leon Jaworski, pp. 1–3. Houston: Gulf Publishing Co., 1961.

———. *Meet the Press: Guest, Senator Lyndon B. Johnson, Democrat, Texas* (Interview). Washington, D.C.: Merkle Press, vol. 4, no. 1, 1960.

———. "New Session of Congress" (Interview). *Newsweek* 47 (January 2, 1956): 13.

———. "Party Leaders Appraise the Record of the Republican 83rd Congress." *Congressional Digest* 33 (October 1954): 239, 241.

———. "President's Broken Promises Push All of Us toward Farm Depression: Democratic Senate Leader Answers Farm Veto Message." *Democratic Digest*, June 1956: 15–16.

———. "Rise of the Cities." *Texas Municipalities* 46 (January 1959): 8–10.

———. "Rising Demand for American Greatness." *Freedom and Union* 13 (July/August 1958): 6–8.

———. "Senator Lyndon B. Johnson Speaks." *First Camper Magazine*, 37th Roll Call, September 18–19, 1953: 1, 5, 12.

———. "Senators Stump for Strong Merchant Marine—Johnson Calls Fleet Essential to Nation's Survival." *Merchant Marine Bulletin* 6 (January/February 1954): 1, 4.

———. "Should the Source of REA's Loan Funds Be Broadened and Its Interest Rate Adjusted to the U.S. Treasury's Borrowing Costs?" *Congressional Digest* 38 (April 1959): 107, 109.

———. "The Space Age and the Engineer." *American Engineer*, August 1958: 11–14.

———. "That Pilot from Arkansas [LBJ's World War 2 Memories]." *Parade*, December 4, 1955: 2.

———. "Vice President Johnson's Views on the Vice Presidency" [Interview]. *Congressional Quarterly Weekly Report* 21 (March 29, 1963): 439–41.

———. "Where U.S. Lags in Defense, What It Must Do to Catch Up" (Interview). *U.S. News and World Report* 44 (January 31, 1958): 56–57.

———. "Will Help All I Can." *Post Office Dispatch* 1 (December 1953): 1.

———, John F. Kennedy, and Stuart Symington. *Meet the Press: Guests, Senators John F. Kennedy, Lyndon B. Johnson, Stuart Symington* (Interview). Washington, D.C.: Merkle Press, vol. 4, no. 28, 1960.

———, Joseph Cogley and John Cogley. *The Negro as an American.* Santa Barbara, Cal.: Center for the Study of Democratic Institutions, Occasional Paper, 1963.

B. PRESIDENTIAL YEARS, 1963 – 1969

1. GENERAL

Johnson, Lyndon B. "The American Way of Life—As Lyndon Johnson Sees It" (Interview). *U.S. News and World Report* 55 (December 9, 1963): 112–14.

———. "I Know the Power of Prayer." Buena Park, Cal.: B. P. Singer Features, No. 1245, n.d.; printed in *I Believe in Prayer.* Minneapolis: T. S. Denison & Co.

———. "Inaugural Address of Lyndon Baines Johnson, President of the United States." *U.S. News and World Report* 58 (February 1, 1965): 102–03.

———. "Johnson Offers Farewell Recommendations." *Congressional Digest* 48 (February 1969): 33.

———. "Johnson: 'Three Goals—Prosperity, Justice, and Peace'." *U.S. News and World Report* 57 (September 21, 1964): 115–16.

———. "LBJ Praises 'the Revolution of the Negro American'." *U.S. News and World Report* 58 (June 14, 1965): 50–52.

———. "My Credo As An American." *Congress Bi-Weekly* 30 (December 16, 1963): 5–6.

———. "Preface." *America, The Beautiful: In the Words of John F. Kennedy,* edited by Robert L. Polley. Elm Grove, Wis.: Country Beautiful Foundation, 1964.

———. "Preface and Comments." *A Visit to the White House: The President Greets Young America and Answers Their Questions.* Philadelphia: Curtis Publishing Co., 1964.

———. "President Johnson Discusses the Presidency and Other Topics." *U.S. Department of State Bulletin* 50 (April 6, 1964): 523–29.

———. "President Johnson Reviews His First One Hundred

Days" (Interview). *Congressional Quarterly Weekly Report* 22 (March 20, 1964): 575–81.

———. "President of All America." *Yale Papers in Political Science* 4 (Fall 1964): 14+.

———. "President Stresses Continuity in Informal First Press Conference." *Congressional Quarterly Weekly Report* 21 (December 13, 1963): 2180–81.

———, and Mrs. Lady Bird Johnson. "Television Interview with the President and Mrs. Johnson." *Weekly Compilation of Presidential Documents* 3 (December 18, 1967): 1687–91.

———, with Bob Considine. "'A President Has Damn Few Friends'—LBJ: Rarely—If Ever—Has an Outgoing President Spoken So Frankly about Himself and the Loneliest Job in the World" (Interview). *This Week Magazine [Washington Sunday Star]*, August 25, 1968: 4–5+.

2. DOMESTIC POLICY

Johnson, Lyndon B. "Beauty for America." *Taming Megalopolis*, edited by Hanford W. Eldredge, vol. 1, pp. 229–32. New York: Praeger, 1967.

———. "Bury the Myth that Business, Consumer Are Opposed—Letter to Consumer Advisory Council." *Advertising Age* 36 (October 18, 1965): 1+.

———. "Discrimination in Employment: Steps Being Taken to Secure Equal Job Opportunities for All." *Yale Papers in Political Science* 3 (August 1963): 10+.

———. "The Great Society." *Saturday Evening Post*, October 31, 1964: 30–31.

———. "An Historic Occasion [Arts Legislation]." *Dance* 39 (November 1965): 34.

———. "President Johnson Outlines His Fiscal Principles." *Congressional Quarterly Weekly Report* 22 (November 27, 1964): 2754–56.

———. "The President Speaks to Educators." *Texas School Board Journal* 11 (September 1964): 3–5.

———, and Barry Goldwater. "Views of the Presidential Candidates on the Future of the U.S. in Space." *Missiles and Rockets* 15 (October 26, 1964): 16–18.

———, and George Meany. "Conversation at the White House: President Johnson and AFL-CIO President George Meany Discuss Social and Economic Conditions in U.S." *AFL-CIO American Federationist* 75 (March 1968) 7–12.

———, et al. "Road for '67: Bumpy But Upward: Reports by Johnson and CEA [Council of Economic Advisers]." *Business Week*, January 28, 1967: 156–58.

3. FOREIGN POLICY AND THE VIETNAM WAR
Johnson, Lyndon B. "The Atlantic Community: Common Hopes and Objectives." *Atlantic Community Quarterly* 2 (Winter 1964/1965): 517–22.
———. "A Bid for Peace ... and a Rebuff." *U.S. News and World Report* 62 (April 3, 1967): 26–27.
———. "The Challenge Ahead." *Social Action* 33 (April 1967): 3–30.
———. "Four Principles of American Foreign Policy." *Congressional Quarterly Weekly Report* 22 (October 16, 1964): 2473–74.
———. "LBJ's Story: 5 Critical Decisions on Vietnam." *U.S. News and World Report* 71 (November 8, 1971): 77–80.
———. "Pattern for Peace in Southeast Asia." *The Puritan Ethic in United States Foreign Policy*, edited by David Lloyd Larson, pp. 207–14. New York: Van Nostrand-Reinhold, 1966.
———. "Peace or War—The Johnson Plan [for Ending the War in Vietnam]." *U.S. News and World Report* 58 (April 19, 1965): 76–78.
———. "President Defines Foreign Policy Principles for a Changing World." *Congressional Quarterly Weekly Report* 22 (April 24, 1964): 793–96.
———. "President Johnson and Secretary McNamara Review the Situation in Viet Nam." *U.S. Department of State Bulletin* 52 (May 17, 1965): 748–57.
———. "President Says Communist China Wants Viet Nam." *Congressional Quarterly Weekly Report* 23 (May 21, 1965): 999-1000.
———. "Southeast Asian Aid." *Current History* 49 (November 1965): 303–04+.
———. "The Transcendent Issues in Today's World." *U.S. Department of State Bulletin* 52 (March 15, 1965): 372–74.
———. "The Vietnam War: The Objectives of the United States." *Vital Speeches* 34 (September 15, 1968): 712–16.
———. "Why We Are in Vietnam." *U.S. News and World Report* 63 (October 16, 1967): 80–82.
———, and The Pan American Union Alliance for Progress Spe-

cial Progress Team. *The Alliance for the People.* Washington, D.C.: Pan American Union Information Series, no. 2, 1963. [341.1-E6676]

———, and The Pan American Union Alliance for Progress Special Progress Team. *Ideological and Political March of the Alliance for Progress.* Washington, D.C.: Pan American Union Information Series, no. 3, 1963. [341.1-E6861]

C. POSTPRESIDENTIAL YEARS, 1969–1973

Johnson, Lyndon B. "Crucial Vietnam Decisions of Johnson Administration Discussed by Former President" (Interview). *Congressional Quarterly Weekly Report* 28 (February 6, 1970): 334–35.

———. "From LBJ: Some Warnings about Today's America." *U.S. News and World Report* 71 (November 29, 1971): 92–93.

———. "Introduction." *Essays on Radicalism in Contemporary America*, edited by Leon Borden Blair. The Walter Prescott Webb Memorial Lectures, no. 6. University of Texas at Arlington, 1971. Distributed by Texas A&M University Press.

———. "LBJ's Story: 5 Critical Decisions on Vietnam." *U.S. News and World Report* 71 (November 8, 1971): 77–80.

———. "Lyndon Johnson Discusses with Walter Cronkite of CBS News, His Decision to Halt the Bombing of North Vietnam and Withdraw from the Presidential Election." *The Listener* 83 (February 12, 1970): 210–12.

———. "Who's No. 1?" (Interview). *Texas Observer*, July 16, 1971: 6.

II. Biographical Works

Bard, Bernard. *LBJ: A Picture Story of Lyndon Baines Johnson.* New York: Lion, 1966.

"Biographical Sketch of Lyndon B. Johnson." *Human Events* 24 (July 11, 1964): 22.

Bremer, Howard F., ed. *Lyndon B. Johnson.* Dobbs Ferry, N.Y.: Oceana, 1971.

Caro, Robert A. "Lyndon Johnson: Dark and Bright." Invitational Address, Fifth Annual Hofstra University Presidential Conference: Lyndon Baines Johnson, A Texan in Washington. Hempstead, New York, April 10–12, 1986.

Carpenter, Liz, ed. *LBJ: Images of a Vibrant Life.* Austin: Friends of the LBJ Library, 1973.

Clarke, Newlon. *LBJ: The Man from Johnson City.* New York: Dodd, Mead, rev. ed., 1966.

Clemons, Cyril. *Mark Twain and Lyndon B. Johnson.* Foreword by Adlai E. Stevenson. Kirkwood, Mo.: Mark Twain Journal, 1967.

Conkin, Paul K. *Big Daddy from the Pedernales: Lyndon Baines Johnson.* Twayne's Twentieth Century American Biography Series. Boston: Twayne Publishers, 1986.

Dugger, Ronnie. *The Politician: The Life and Times of Lyndon Johnson—The Drive for Power, from the Frontier to Master of the Senate.* New York: W. W. Norton, 1982.

———. "Johnsons on the Chisholm Trail." *True West* 29 (February 1955): 44–47.

Exley, Jo Ella Powell, ed. *Texas Tears and Texas Sunshine: Voices of Frontier Women.* College Station: Texas A&M University Press, 1985.

Frantz, Joe B. "Lyndon Baines Johnson." *The Handbook of Texas: A Supplement*, edited by Eldon Stephen Branda, vol. 3, pp. 447–50. Austin: Texas State Historical Association, 1976.

Gould, Lewis L. "Robert Caro and George Reedy on Lyndon Johnson: An Essay Review." *Southwestern Historical Quarterly* 82 (July 1983): 57–68.

"His Mother's Story of LBJ: An Intimate Picture from a Family Manuscript: People and Forces that Shaped LBJ's Character." *U.S. News and World Report* 58 (February 15, 1965): 48–52.

Houk, Rose. *Heart's Home: Lyndon B. Johnson's Hill Country.* Tucson, Arizona: Southwest Parks and Monuments Assn., 1986.

"Johnson Biography, Record in Congress, Leadership, Role as Vice President." *Congressional Quarterly Weekly Report* 21 (November 29, 1963): 2069–88.

"Johnson the Man: Born to Politics—the Story of a Poor Boy Who Came out of the Hills of Texas: How He Got Where He Is." *U.S. News and World Report* 57 (September 7, 1964): 36–40.

Kaye, Tony. *Lyndon Johnson.* World Leaders Past and Present Series. Edgemont, Penn.: Chelsea House, 1988.
"LBJ: He Riz above His Raisin'." *Texas Observer,* April 8, 1977: 18+.
Lynch, Dudley M. *The President from Texas: Lyndon Baines Johnson.* New York: Y. Crowell, 1975.
"Lyndon B. Johnson: United States Senator from Texas." *Texas Edition of Men of Achievement,* edited by Evelyn Miller Crowell, p. 269. Dallas: John Moranz Associates, 1948.
"Lyndon B. Johnson, the New President—The Man and His Record." *U.S. News and World Report* 55 (December 2, 1963): 36–41.
"Lyndon Baines Johnson." *Texas Democracy: A Centennial History of Politics and Personalities of the Democratic Party, 1836–1936,* edited by Frank Carter Adams, vol. III, pp. 167–68. Austin: Democratic Historical Assn., 1937.
McDonald, Archie P., comp. *The Texas Experience.* College Station: Texas A&M University Press, 1986.
MacLean, Don, ed. *Meet LBJ: Lyndon Baines Johnson, President of the United States.* Washington, D.C.: Tatler Magazine, 1964.
"The Man Who Became President." *U.S. News and World Report* 55 (December 9, 1963): 84–86.
Prater, Teresa. "Our Favorite Son [based on an interview with LBJ in November 1972]." *Genesis* [Southwest Texas State University publication] 1 (Spring 1973): 2–5.
"Profile of the Democrats' Second Man: Lyndon B. Johnson—Record Is Mixed, But Leaning to Liberal Side." *Labor* (Railroad Labor Organizations) 42 (July 30, 1960): 3.
"The Public Records of John F. Kennedy and Lyndon B. Johnson: Their Lives, Voting Records, Stands on Issues, Platform." *Congressional Quarterly Weekly Report Special Supplement* 18 (July 22, 1960): 1–29.
"The Public Records of Lyndon B. Johnson and Hubert H. Humphrey: The Lives, Votes and Stands of the 1964 Democratic Candidates." *Congressional Quarterly Weekly Report* 22 (September 11, 1964): 2057–2121.
"Role of Rail Unions Recalled in Lyndon Johnson's Meteoric Career." *Labor* (Railroad Labor Organizations) 45 (December 7, 1963): 3.
Rosenfeld, Paul. "LBJ Country." *Sunday* [*Dallas Times Herald*], November 22, 1970: 6–10.

Sinise, Jerry, with Jakie L. Pruett. *Lyndon Baines Johnson Remembered*. Austin: Eakin Press, 1985.
Taylor, T. V. "Heroines of the Hills." *Frontier Times* 18 (October 1940): 21–22.
Whitney, David C. *The Picture Life of Lyndon Baines Johnson*. New York: New York Review, Vintage Books, 1972.
Wilson, Richard W., and Beulah F. Duholm, comps. *Bunton—Buntin—Bunten—Bunting, Including Family of President Lyndon Baines Johnson: Genealogy*. Lake Mills, Iowa: Graphic Publishing Co., 1967.

III. The Early Years, 1908–1936

Barnett, John. *LBJ Country: A Guide to the Lyndon Baines Johnson National Historic Site* [Birthplace and Boyhood Home], *Johnson City, the Texas White House, LBJ State Park, Hye, Stonewall and Fredericksburg*. Fresno, Cal.: Awani Press, 1970.
Bearss, Edwin C. *Lyndon B. Johnson Birthplace-Cottage: Furnishing Study, 1979, LBJ National Historic Site, Stonewall, Gillespie County, Texas*. Denver: U.S. Dept. of Interior, Denver Service Center, ES/SW Team, National Park Service, 1979.
Bourgeois, Christie Lynne. "Lyndon Johnson's Years with the National Youth Administration." Austin: University of Texas, 1986. M.A. thesis.
Harris, Irving D. "The Psychologies of Presidents." *History of Childhood Quarterly* 3 (Winter 1976): 337–50.
Henderson, Richard B. *Maury Maverick: A Political Biography*. Austin: University of Texas Press, 1970.
Kluckhorn, Frank. "'FDR Was a Second Daddy to Me,' Said LBJ." *Human Events* 24 (July 11, 1964): 5.
Kowert, Bruce. "Lyndon B. Johnson, Boy of Destiny." *The Junior Historian of the Texas State Historical Association* 21 (November 1960): 10–14.
Louchheim, Katie, ed. *The Making of the New Deal: The Insiders Speak*. Cambridge, Mass.: Harvard University Press, 1983.
"Lyndon Baines Johnson Birthplace, Boyhood Home and Ranch."

The Handbook of Texas: A Supplement, edited by Eldon Stephen Branda, vol. 3, pp. 548–49. Austin: Texas State Historical Association, 1976.

McKay, Seth Shepard. *Texas Politics, 1906–1944.* Lubbock: Texas Tech Press, 1952.

Owens, John E. "Extreme Advocacy Leadership in the Pre-Reform House: Wright Patman and the House Banking and Currency Committee." *British Journal of Political Science* 15 (April 1985): 187–205.

Schmelzer, Janet Louise. "The Early Life and Early Congressional Career of Wright Patman, 1894–1941." Fort Worth: Texas Christian University, 1978. Ph.D. dissertation. University Microfilms No. 79–04295.

———. "Wright Patman and the Impeachment of Andrew Mellon." *East Texas Historical Journal* 23 (Spring 1985): 33–46.

Speer, John W. *History of Blanco County.* Austin: Pemberton Press, 1965.

IV. The Congressional Years, 1937–1948

Bearss, Edwin C. *Lyndon B. Johnson and the Hill Country, 1937–1963.* Sante Fe: Southwest Cultural Center Professional Papers No. 3, National Park Service, U.S. Dept. of Interior, 1984. Typewritten.

Burns, Richard Dean, ed. *Harry S. Truman: A Bibliography of His Times and Presidency.* Wilmington, Del.: Scholarly Resources, Inc., 1984.

Caidin, Martin, and Edward Hymoff. *The Mission.* Philadelphia: Lippincott, 1964.

Caro, Robert A. "Lyndon Johnson and the Sad Irons." *Reader's Digest* 124 (February 1984): 129–34.

Cater, Douglass. "The Hard-Won Destiny of Lyndon Johnson." *Reporter* 29 (December 19, 1963): 17–19.

Clayton, James D. *The Years of MacArthur: Triumph and Disaster, 1945–1964.* Boston: Houghton Mifflin, 1985.

Cummings, Milton C., Jr. *Congressmen and the Electorate: Elections for the U.S. House and the President, 1920–1964.* New York: Free Press, 1966.

Felder, Marvin Ray. "The Politics of the Texas Gulf Coast, 1945–1960." Austin: University of Texas, 1960. M.A. thesis.

Fulton, Lewis, Jr. "Johnson Owes Senate Seat to Strange Election in '48." *Human Events* 17 (September 8, 1960): 406.

Green, George Norris. *Establishment in Texas Politics: The Primitive Years, 1938–1957*. Westport, Conn.: Greenwood Press, 1979.

Hine, Darlene C. *Black Victory: The Rise and Fall of the White Primary in Texas*. Millwood, N.Y.: KTO Press, division of Kraus-Thompson, 1979.

———. "The Elusive Ballot: The Black Struggle against the Texas Democratic White Primary, 1932–45." *Southwestern Historical Quarterly* 81 (April 1978): 371–92.

"Johnson Biography, Record in Congress, Leadership Reviewed, Key Votes Cast in House and Senate since 1941." *Congressional Quarterly Weekly Report* 18 (June 24, 1960): 1090–99.

Kahl, Mary. *Ballot Box 13: How Lyndon Johnson Won His 1948 Senate Race by 87 Contested Votes*. Jefferson, N.C.: McFarland, 1983.

Keever, Crawford. *John B. Connally: Portrait in Power*. Austin: Jenkins Publishing Co., 1973.

Ladd, Everett C., Jr., and Charles D. Hadley. *Transformations of the American Party System: Political Coalitions from the New Deal to the 1970s*. 2nd. ed. New York: Norton, 1978.

Lane, Dorothy. "A Sketch of Alice Glass." Course paper for Lewis L. Gould, University of Texas at Austin, May 14, 1986 [c/o LBJ Library].

Leuchtenburg, William E. *In the Shadow of FDR: From Harry Truman to Ronald Reagan*. Ithaca, N.Y.: Cornell University Press, 1983.

Louchheim, Katie, ed. *The Making of the New Deal: The Insiders Speak*. Cambridge, Mass.: Harvard University Press, 1983.

McKay, Seth Shepard. *Texas Politics, 1906–1944*. Lubbock: Texas Tech Press, 1952.

———. "The Texas Senatorial Campaign of 1948." *West Texas Historical Association Year Book* (Abilene) 33 (October 1957): 31–44.

———. *W. Lee O'Daniel and Texas Politics, 1938–1942*. Lubbock: Texas Tech Press, 1944.

———, and Odie B. Faulk. *Texas after Spindletop: The Saga of Texas, 1901–1965*. The Saga of Texas Series, edited by Seymour V. Connor, vol. 6. Austin: Steck-Vaughn Co., 1965.
"The Mystery of Ballot Box 13: the 87 Votes That Sent 'Landslide Lyndon' to the Senate." *Human Events* 24 (June 6, 1964): 8.
"Neck and Neck [1948 Election]." *Time* 52 (September 13, 1948): 23.
Orum, Anthony M. "Taming the River, Part Two: Enter Lyndon Johnson [LBJ in the 1938–40 Congress]." *Texas Observer*, January 11, 1985: 13–19.
"The Story of 87 Votes that Made History [1948 Texas Primary Election that Won Nomination for LBJ to U.S. Senate]." *U.S. News and World Report* 56 (April 6, 1964): 46–50.
Sweeney, Paul. "The Power of LCRA: The Awesome Rise of the Lower Colorado River Authority." *Third Coast* 1 (April 1982): 39–43.
"Texans Who Make Our Laws." *Texas Parade* 1 (May 1937): 8.
United States Congress. *Biographical Directory of the American Congress, 1774–1971*. Washington: U.S. Gov't. Printing Office, 1971.
"Up and at 'em on Box 13: Two Cheers for the FBI." *Texas Observer*, September 23, 1977: 10+.

V. The Senatorial Years, 1949–1960

A. GENERAL

"ACA Says [Senator] Johnson Was 'One of the Most Liberal'." *Human Events* 24 (March 21, 1964): 10.
Adams, Sherman. *Firsthand Report: The Story of the Eisenhower Administration*. New York: Harper and Bros., 1961.
Anderson, Jack, and James Boyd. *Confessions of a Muckraker: The Inside Story of Life in Washington during the Truman, Eisenhower, Kennedy, and Johnson Years*. New York: Random House, 1979.
Bearss, Edwin C. *Lyndon B. Johnson and the Hill Country, 1937–1963*. Sante Fe: Southwest Cultural Center Profes-

sional Papers No. 3, National Park Service, U.S. Dept. of Interior, 1984. Typewritten.
Billington, Monroe L. *The Political South in the 20th Century.* New York: Scribners, 1975.
Branyan, Robert L., and Lawrence H. Larsen. *The Eisenhower Administration, 1953–1961: A Documentary History.* 2 vols. New York: Random House, 1971.
Brendon, Piers. *Ike: His Life and Times.* New York: Harper and Row, 1986.
Brim, Andrea M. "Dubious Ally: Eleanor Roosevelt's Perception of Lyndon Johnson." Course paper, Professor Lewis L. Gould, University of Texas at Austin, May 14, 1986 [c/o LBJ Library].
Broder, David S. "The Politics of Change: Congress Is More Democratic Than Ever, But that May Not Be Helping It at All." *The Washington Post Magazine,* February 2, 1986: 67, 148+.
"Building a 'White House' on Capitol Hill: Senator Lyndon Johnson." *U.S. News and World Report* 46 (February 13, 1959): 64–66.
Burt, Eric. *Eyes on Washington* [covers Johnson, Rayburn, Sam Tallafero]. New York: New Century Publishers, 1955. Pamphlet.
Cater, Douglass. "The Hard-Won Destiny of Lyndon Johnson." *Reporter* 29 (December 19, 1963): 17–19.
"Chains of His Own Forging." *Texas Observer,* April 4, 1956: 3.
"Change and LBJ." *Texas Observer,* March 14, 1959: 4.
Clayton, James D. *The Years of MacArthur: Triumph and Disaster, 1945–1964.* Boston: Houghton Mifflin, 1985.
"Congress: 'Lyndon's Lemmon' Ends." *Human Events* 17 (September 8, 1960): 401.
"Congress: The 'Moderates' Lose Ground." *Human Events* 16 (January 14, 1959): 1–2.
"Congress Opens: Johnson Out Front." *Human Events* 15 (January 13, 1958): 1.
"'Congressional Leader'." *Texas Observer,* June 3, 1960: 4.
Conine, Ernest. "Texans in Congress." *Texas Parade,* 15 (February 1955): 20.
"DAC, Johnson Disagree." *Texas Observer,* March 28, 1956: 5.
Davidson, Roger H., and Walter J. Oleszek. *Congress and Its*

Members. Washington, D.C.: Congressional Quarterly Press, 1981.

Davis, James W., and Delbert Ringquist. *The President and Congress*. Woodbury, N.Y.: Barron's Educational Series, 1975.

"Democrat's Decisive Dozen." *Time* 67 (June 18, 1956): 26.

"Democrats Argue; LBJ Seems Secure." *Texas Observer*, November 14, 1958: 1+.

Dies, Martin. "Morality and Texas Affairs: Recollections of Texas Politics and Politicians." *American Opinion* 7 (September 1964): 35–40.

"Economics of Seven Democrats." *Fortune* 54 (July 1956): 74–77+.

"Era of Senators in Gray Flannel Suits." *Texas Observer*, March 7, 1959: 5.

Fallows, James. "Friendly Persuasion: What LBJ Did Best Was Deal." *Texas Monthly* 4 (July 1976): 24–26+.

Farrow, Stephen B. "Richard Russell and Lyndon Johnson: Principle and Pragmatism in Senatorial Politics, 1949–1952." Knoxville: University of Tennessee, 1979. B.A. senior honors thesis [c/o LBJ Library].

"The Favorite Son Boom." *Texas Observer*, March 14, 1956: 1+.

Felder, Marvin Ray. "The Politics of the Texas Gulf Coast, 1945–1960." Austin: University of Texas, 1960. M.A. thesis.

Fenton, John M. *In Your Opinion . . . The Managing Editor of the Gallup Poll Looks at Polls, Politics and the People from 1945–1960*. Boston: Little, Brown, 1960.

"Four Leaders Who Run Congress." *U.S. News and World Report* 42 (January 11, 1957): 74+.

Frantz, Joe B. "Kennedy and Johnson: The Senatorial Years." *Proceedings of The Philosophical Society of Texas* 31 (December 8, 9, 1967): 22–34.

"Hidden Assumption of Lyndon Johnson." *New Republic* 133 (December 19, 1955): 3.

"A House Divided: New Dedication, The Democratic Party vs. Its Congressional Leaders, 1952–1959." *Texas Observer*, April 15, 1960: 1+.

"How a Senator Makes Up His Mind." *Fortune* 54 (July 1956): 14.

"Ike's 'Texas Yes Men'." *Texas Observer*, June 6, 1958: 3.

"Johnson Biography, Record in Congress, Leadership Reviewed, Key Votes Cast in House and Senate since 1941." *Congressional Quarterly Weekly Report* 18 (June 24, 1960): 1090–99.

"Johnson Boom Gains Ground." *Texas Observer*, September 13, 1957: 5.

"Johnson Compromising Away." *Texas Observer*, March 11, 1960: 5.

"Johnson Gives Political Philosophy." *Texas Observer*, January 2, 1959: 3.

"Johnson-Goldwater Differences Reflected in Senate Voting [1953–1961]." *Congressional Quarterly Weekly Report* 22 (July 31, 1964): 1653.

"The Johnson Juggernaut." *Human Events* 16 (March 4, 1959): 2–3.

"Johnson of Texas: A Summing Up." *Texas Observer*, June 24, 1960: 1+.

"Johnson on Leadership." *Texas Observer*, August 1, 1959: 6.

"Johnson Sidesteps Governor Query." *Texas Observer*, August 22, 1956: 1.

"Johnson Slams Labor—Dixie." *Texas Observer*, October 4, 1957: 8.

"Johnson's Boswell." *Texas Observer*, April 11, 1959: 4.

"Johnson's Effect on Liberalism." *Texas Observer*, May 30, 1959: 5.

"Johnson's Giftie and Others Who Need It." *Texas Observer*, December 19, 1958: 3.

"Johnson's Homecoming, Barbeque in Blanco." *Texas Observer*, August 5, 1960: 1+.

"Johnson's Method." *Texas Observer*, July 1, 1960: 5.

"Johnson's Record." *Texas Observer*, June 3, 1960: 1+.

"Johnson's Record." *Texas Observer*, June 10, 1960: 1+.

"Johnson's Role Assessed." *Texas Observer*, December 26, 1956: 2.

Keever, Crawford. *John B. Connally: Portrait in Power.* Austin: Jenkins Publishing Co., 1973.

Kilpatrick, James Jackson. "Lyndon Johnson: Counterfeit Confederate." *Human Events* 17 (August 25, 1960): 373–76.

"Labor Ranks Texas in D.C." *Texas Observer*, December 20, 1957: 4.

"Last Roundup in Congress—Two Texans in the Saddle:

Speaker Sam Rayburn in the House and Lyndon B. Johnson, Democratic Leader in the Senate." *U.S. News and World Report* 45 (August 22, 1958): 56–58.

Lazarowitz, Arlene. "Years in Exile: The Liberal Democrats, 1950–1959." Los Angeles: University of California, 1982. University Microfilms No. 82–25593.

"LBJ Like Bag with Hole in It." *Texas Observer*, August 22, 1956: 2.

Leuchtenburg, William E. *In the Shadow of FDR: From Harry Truman to Ronald Reagan*. Ithaca, N.Y.: Cornell University Press, 1983.

"Liberalism Admired." *Texas Observer*, October 19, 1955: 2.

"Lyndon Boom Grows." *Texas Observer*, March 21, 1956: 8.

"Lyndon Has the Ball." *Life* 44 (January 20, 1958): 19–21.

"Lyndon Honored; Wants Unity." *Texas Observer*, November 30, 1955: 4.

"Lyndon Johnson: Face of the Democratic Party." *Reader's Digest* 72 (June 1958): 146–48+.

"Lyndon on Highwire." *Texas Observer*, February 19, 1960: 3.

"Lyndon, Price Pledge Fealty." *Texas Observer*, November 6, 1959: 1+.

"Lyndon, Ralph Agree." *Texas Observer*, June 28, 1957: 8.

"Lyndon's Armory Has Many Weapons." *Texas Observer*, November 30, 1955: 3.

"Lyndon's Power and Ralph's Potential." *Texas Observer*, February 7, 1958: 2.

"Lyndon's Regency." *Texas Observer*, January 29, 1960: 4.

"Lyndon's Ten Rules." *Texas Observer*, September 20, 1957: 3.

"Lyndon's Wings Are Clipped." *Texas Observer*, December 5, 1956: 3.

"Lyndon's Work." *Texas Observer*, September 11, 1959: 4.

McKay, Seth Shepard. *Texas and the Fair Deal, 1945–1952*. San Antonio: Naylor Co., 1954.

"Majority Leader's Career, Politics Examined." *Congressional Quarterly Weekly Report* 14 (May 25, 1956): 597–99.

"The Man in the News: Majority Leader Johnson—The Troubles of a 'Moderate'." *U.S. News and World Report* 47 (July 6, 1959): 62–64.

Martin, Glenn R. "Conservatism and Liberalism in the American Congress: A Selected Study of Congressional Voting

Ratings, 1947–1972." Muncie, Ind.: Ball State University, 1973. Ph.D. disseration. University Microfilms No. 74-02941.
"Master Tactician." *Reporter* 18 (January 23, 1958): 19–21.
Mayhew, David R. *Party Loyalty among Congressmen: The Difference between Democrats and Republicans, 1947–1962.* Cambridge, Mass.: Harvard University Press, 1966.
"Minority's Manager." *Time* 61 (January 26, 1953): 21.
Morehead, Richard. *Fifty Years in Texas Politics—from Roosevelt to Reagan—from the Fergusons to Clements.* Burnet, Texas: Eakin Press, 1982.
Morrow, E. Frederick. *Black Man in the White House.* New York: Coward-McCann, 1963.
Natchez, Peter B. "American Politics after Roosevelt: 1948–1964." *Current History* 67 (July 1974): 24–29, 37–38.
"Nation's No. Two Heart Case." *Life* 40 (January 16, 1956): 34–36.
"One Man Show." *Time* 71 (January 20, 1958): 13–14.
Parker, Robert. "Lyndon and Me [Johnson's Driver and Later Maître d' of the Senate Dining Room]." *Washingtonian,* June 1986: 124–27, 190–99.
———, with Richard Rashke. *Capitol Hill in Black and White.* New York: Dodd, Mead & Co., 1986.
"Political Therapy for a Senator." *Life* 39 (August 8, 1955): 38.
Polsby, Nelson W. "Goodbye to the Inner Club." *Congressional Behavior,* edited by Nelson W. Polsby, pp. 105–10. New York: Random House, 1971.
"Pow-Wow on the Pedernales." *Texas Observer,* October 5, 1955: 1+.
"Q & A for LBJ." *Texas Observer,* August 9, 1957: 2.
"Rauh Says Liberalism 'Smothered' by LBJ." *Texas Observer,* June 3, 1960: 3.
"Republican vs. Democrat: What's This about a 'Do-Nothing Congress'?" *U.S. News and World Report* April 13, 1956: 122–24.
"Sen. Humphrey on Sen. Johnson." *Texas Observer,* June 3, 1960: 2.
"Senator Johnson Alters His Tack." *Atlantic Monthly* 199 (March 1957): 14+.

"Senator Johnson Bedazzles 'em." *Texas Observer*, December 12, 1958: 5.

"The Senior Senator's Thinking." *Texas Observer*, November 23, 1955: 1+.

"Solid Leader for the South." *Life* 40 (May 21, 1956): 31–33.

"South Bets on Johnson to Keep Democrats in Line." *U.S. News and World Report* 40 (May 18, 1956): 78+.

Stewart, John G. "Two Strategies of Leadership: Johnson and Mansfield." *Congressional Behavior*, edited by Nelson W. Polsby, pp. 61–92. New York: Random House, 1971.

Sundquist, James L. *The Decline and Resurgence of Congress.* Washington, D.C.: Brookings Institution, 1981.

"Texas and Liberalism in America." *Texas Observer*, April 4, 1956: 3.

"A Texas Brunch for Lyndon B." *Texas Observer*, October 30, 1959: 1.

"Texas Watchdog." *Time* 56 (September 18, 1950): 24.

"They Love Lyndon." *Texas Observer*, December 13, 1957: 2.

Toffler, Al. "The Elusive Record of Lyndon Johnson." *Progressive* 22 (July 1958): 13–16.

———. "LBJ: The Senate's Mr. Energy." *Pageant*, July 1958: 102–09.

"Two Texans [Rayburn and LBJ]." *U.S. News and World Report* November 12, 1954: 14.

"Two Texans Will Call the Signals [Rayburn and LBJ]." *U.S. News and World Report* January 17, 1958: 48–50.

"Under the Dome [Johnson's Tactics]." *Human Events* 16 (January 28, 1959): 2.

United States 83rd Congress, 1st Session, Senate. *Hon. Lyndon B. Johnson, of Texas, Democratic Leader of the Senate of the United States; Tributes by Senate Colleagues, Monday, August 3, 1955.* Washington, D.C.: U. S. Gov't. Printing Office (*Congressional Record*), 1953.

"Upmanship." *Newsweek* 53 (February 2, 1959): 20–21.

"Voice of Opposition." *U.S. News and World Report* 42 (May 24, 1957): 56–58.

Weeks, Oliver Douglas. *Texas Presidential Politics in 1952.* Austin: Institute of Public Affairs, The University of Texas at Austin, 1953.

———. *Texas One-Party Politics in 1956.* Austin: Institute of Public Affairs, The University of Texas at Austin, 1957.

Welch, June Rayfield. *The Texas Senator.* Dallas: G.L.A. Press, 1978.

"Who Runs the Senate?" *Texas Observer,* March 7, 1959: 5.

B. SPECIFIC ISSUES AND LEGISLATION

"Allan, Lyndon Vie for Post." *Texas Observer,* April 11, 1956: 1+.

Andrain, Charles F. "A Scale Analysis of Senators' Attitudes toward Civil Rights [in 1960]." *Western Political Quarterly* 17 (September 1964): 488–503.

"Another Famous Heart Patient Takes Life Easier." *U.S. News and World Report* 40 (March 2, 1956): 22–23.

"Anti-labor Johnson?" *Texas Observer,* February 5, 1957: 3.

"The Battle over 'Civil Rights'." *U.S. News and World Report* August 16, 1957: 16.

Bell, Roger. *Last Among Equals: Hawaiian Statehood and American Politics.* Honolulu: University of Hawaii Press, 1984.

"The Bobby Baker Affair, Chapter Two." *Human Events* 23 (February 8, 1964): 5.

"Bobby Baker and LBJ." *Human Events* 24 (July 11, 1964): 15–16.

Brendlinger, Nancy. "Lyndon Johnson's Involvement in the American Space Program." Paper presented at Fifth Annual Hofstra University Presidential Conference: Lyndon Baines Johnson, A Texan in Washington. Hempstead, New York, April 10–12, 1986.

Chester, Edward W. *U.S. Oil Policy and Diplomacy: A 20th Century Overview.* Westport, Conn.: Greenwood Press, 1983.

"The Cold That Sent a Tremor through the Nation [Reviews President Johnson's Medical History]." *U.S. News and World Report* 58 (February 8, 1965): 33–34.

"Congress: Review—and a Warning." *Human Events* 16 (September 16, 1959): 1.

"The Court: Johnson Torpedoes Reform." *Human Events* 15 (September 1, 1958): 2.

"Curbing the Court." *Human Events* 15 (August 4, 1958): 2.

De Toledano, Ralph. "Lyndon Johnson's Civil Rights Record." *Human Events* 24 (August 15, 1964): 12.

"Democrat Tries for Head in Space Statesmanship." *Business Week*, January 18, 1958: 29–30.
"Democrats: Johnson's Scheme for Spending." *Human Events* 16 (February 4, 1959): 2.
"Democrats Hit Ike Policies: Autumn Elections at Stake." *U.S. News and World Report* 36 (May 21, 1954): 95–97.
"DOT Leader, Lyndon Feud over Health." *Texas Observer*, December 13, 1957: 1+.
"Economy: GOP Returns to Normal (while Liberal Democrats are 'Spenders')." *Human Events* 16 (November 18, 1959): 3.
Engler, Robert. *The Politics of Oil.* New York: Macmillan, 1961.
"Filibuster Begins on Civil Rights Proposals [Provisions of Civil Rights Act of 1960]." *Congressional Quarterly Weekly Report* 18 (March 4, 1960): 331–32.
Fried, Richard M. *Men Against McCarthy.* New York: Columbia University Press, 1976.
"Gas Bill Passage Seen." *Texas Observer*, December 14, 1955: 5.
Gaskin, Thomas M. "Senate Majority Leader Lyndon B. Johnson: The Formosa and Middle East Resolution." Paper presented at Fifth Annual Hofstra University Presidential Conference: Lyndon Baines Johnson, A Texan in Washington. Hempstead, New York, April 10–12, 1986.
———. "Senate Minority Leader Lyndon B. Johnson: U.S. Foreign Policy." Paper presented to American Historical Association, August 16, 1984.
"GOP Rakes Johnson." *Texas Observer*, February 26, 1960: 3.
Greene, John Robert. *The Crusade: The Presidential Election of 1952.* Lanham, Md.: University Press of America, 1985.
Griffith, Robert. *The Politics of Fear: Joseph R. McCarthy and the Senate.* Lexington: University of Kentucky Press, 1970.
"Housing: 'Backdoor' Spending Scored." *Human Events* 16 (February 11, 1959): 3.
"How Lyndon Johnson Sizes Up the State of the Union." *U.S. News and World Report* 44 (January 17, 1958): 100–02.
"Ike vs. Johnson on Congress." *U.S. News and World Report* 47 (October 5, 1959): 111–12.
"Johnson Again Staring at Hospital Walls." *Texas Observer*, July 13, 1955: 1.
"Johnson Cites Racial Point." *Texas Observer*, July 11, 1959: 3.
"Johnson Defends Aid Bill." *Texas Observer*, June 21, 1957: 4.

"Johnson Excoriates the Russian Visitor." *Texas Observer*, September 25, 1959: 8.

"Johnson Flubs on Seniority." *Texas Observer*, January 22, 1957: 3.

"Johnson Gives Views on Civil Rights Plan." *Texas Observer*, May 31, 1957: 5.

"Johnson, Goldwater Records Diverge on Civil Rights." *Congressionaly Quarterly Weekly Report* 22 (August 7, 1964): 1691–98.

"Johnson Makes USIA Cut 'Personal Issue'." *Texas Observer*, May 31, 1957: 3.

"Johnson on Leadership." *Texas Observer*, August 1, 1959: 6.

"Johnson Pledges Oil, Gas Investigations; Is Under Fire." *Texas Observer*, February 29, 1956: 1.

"Johnson Questions Foreign Aid Gifts." *Texas Observer*, April 16, 1957: 6.

"Johnson Rejects New Policy Post." *Texas Observer*, December 19, 1957: 8.

"Johnson Talk Startles Oilmen." *Texas Observer*, November 7, 1958: 2.

"Johnson Talks of Space Ships." *Texas Observer*, December 6, 1957: 8.

"Johnson vs. Eisenhower: Congress Takes the Lead." *U.S. News and World Report* 46 (January 30, 1959): 33–34.

"Johnson's Election Role Is Discussed." *Texas Observer*, May 23, 1958: 5.

"Johnson's Health Fine." *Texas Observer*, June 6, 1956: 8.

Kaufman, Burton I. *Trade and Aid: Eisenhower's Foreign Economic Policy, 1953–1961*. Baltimore: Johns Hopkins University Press, 1982.

"Labor: Knowland Outmaneuvers [Johnson's] Democrats." *Human Events* 15 (May 5, 1958): 1.

Laocoon, Jr. "The First Hurrah: Lyndon Johnson's Program for the New Congress." *Human Events* 16 (January 7, 1959): A1-A4.

"LBJ Deplored Foreign Aid—In 1953." *Human Events* 28 (April 28, 1961): 271.

"LBJ for Vote Bill." *Texas Observer*, August 2, 1957: 8.

"LBJ on Communists, Education, and 1960." *Texas Observer*, April 11, 1959: 3.

"LBJ on LBJ HCL." *Texas Observer*, September 27, 1957: 4.
"LBJ's Civil Rights Play." *Texas Observer*, March 4, 1960: 1+.
"Liberals Support Lyndon for Post." *Texas Observer*, December 12, 1956: 8.
"Lyndon and a Key Senate Post." *Texas Observer*, May 23, 1956: 3.
"Lyndon and Civil Rights." *Texas Observer*, August 16, 1957: 3.
"Lyndon and the Negroes." *Texas Observer*, July 22, 1960: 1.
"Lyndon at the Launching Pad." *Time* 71 (February 17, 1958): 19.
"Lyndon Conducts a Caucus." *Texas Observer*, August 15, 1956: 4.
"Lyndon Eyes Ike's Budget." *Texas Observer*, May 7, 1957: 8.
"Lyndon Eyes 'Sputnik'." *Texas Observer*, October 25, 1957: 7.
"Lyndon Gives [Civil] Rights Views." *Texas Observer*, August 16, 1957: 8.
"Lyndon Hit Coming, Going." *Texas Observer*, July 4, 1959: 5.
"Lyndon Johnson, the 40-Hour Week." *Texas Observer*, December 20, 1957: 3.
"Lyndon Johnson's Gentleman's Agreement." *New Republic* 131 (August 2, 1954): 3–4.
"Lyndon Makes Motion to Preserve Filibuster." *Texas Observer*, January 8, 1957: 8.
"Lyndon Misfires under Pressure." *Texas Observer*, August 22, 1956: 1+.
"Lyndon, Ralph for Billboards." *Texas Observer*, April 11, 1958: 4.
"Lyndon, Sam, and Civil Rights." *Texas Observer*, August 30, 1957: 3.
"Lyndon 'Suppressed' Facts." *Texas Observer*, November 29, 1957: 3.
"Lyndon Talks of Farm Depression." *Texas Observer*, April 25, 1956: 5.
"Lyndon's Court Play Studied as 85th Ends." *Texas Observer*, September 5, 1958: 5.
Martin, John F. *Civil Rights and the Crisis of Liberalism: The Democratic Party, 1945–1975*. Boulder: Westview Press, 1979.
McDougall, Walter A. . . . *The Heavens and the Earth: A Political History of the Space Age*. New York: Basic Books, 1985.

Murray, Charles. *Losing Ground: American Social Policy, 1950–1980.* New York: Basic Books, 1984.

Nash, Gerald D. *United States Oil Policy: Business and Government in Twentieth Century America.* 1968. Reprint. Westport, Conn.: Greenwood Press, 1976.

"New Rights Bill 'South's Victory'." *Texas Observer*, April 22, 1960: 3.

Newberry, Anthony Lake. "Without Urgency or Ardor: The South's Middle-of-the-Road Liberals and Civil Rights, 1945–1960." Athens: Ohio University, 1982. Ph.D. dissertation. University Microfilms No. 8300026.

"No More Butter Till We Get the Guns." *Business Week*, December 1, 1951: 19–20.

Nocera, Joseph. "The Oil Depletion Allowance." *Texas Monthly* 13 (February 1985): 106–07.

Osbourne, Elmo J. "A Senator Looks at Current Power Issues." *Current Magazine* [Austin, Texas], January/February 1955: 3–11.

Oshinsky, David M. *A Conspiracy So Immense: The World of Joe McCarthy.* New York: Free Press, 1983.

Pack, Lindsy Escoe. "The Political Aspects of the Texas Tidelands Controversy." College Station: Texas A&M University, 1979. Ph.D. dissertation. University Microfilms No. 80–11977.

"Pearson Praises Lyndon." *Texas Observer*, August 29, 1958: 3.

"Post, Six Senators Challenge Johnson." *Texas Observer*, November 28, 1956: 5.

Provost, Norma Matlock. "Issues in the Texas Gubernatorial Race of 1954: Shivers versus Yarbrough." Beaumont, Texas: Lamar University, 1981. M.A. thesis. University Microfilms No. 1316804.

"Proxmire Slams Lyndon on Oil and Civil Rights." *Texas Observer*, June 3, 1960: 4.

"Proxmire Stirs Up Debate on Johnson." *Texas Observer*, February 28, 1959: 2.

"Ralph, Lyndon, and Big Oil." *Texas Observer*, August 22, 1958: 3.

"Ralph, Lyndon Split in Public Housing Vote." *Texas Observer*, June 7, 1957: 1+.

"Ralph Recalls 'Faith'; Lyndon Climbs in Flak." *Texas Observer*, December 5, 1958: 8.

"Reaction to Rayburn's Plan." *Texas Observer*, March 14, 1956: 4.
"Rearmament Lags 'Dangerously'—Senators Denounce Fumbling." *Newsweek* 38 (December 3, 1951): 19–22.
Ritchie, Donald A. "Making Fulbright Chairman: Or How the 'Johnson Treatment' Nearly Backfired." *The Society for Historians of American Foreign Relations Newsletter* 15 (No. 3, September 1984): 21–28.
Roubatis, Yiannis P. "The United States Involvement in the Army and Politics of Greece, 1946–1967." Baltimore: Johns Hopkins University, 1981. Ph.D. dissertation. University Microfilms No. 81–16125.
"Sen. Johnson and the Civil Rights Initiative." *Texas Observer*, January 31, 1959: 6.
"Sen. Johnson Maneuvered Jury Decision." *Texas Observer*, August 9, 1957: 3.
"Senate Democratic Boss Lyndon Johnson Goes on the [Anti-Labor] Record [Landrum-Griffin Law]." *United Mine Workers Journal* 71 (January 1, 1960): 8.
"Senate Outlook for 1954: 35 Seats at Stake." *Congressional Quarterly Weekly Report* 11 (October 23, 1953): 1251–62.
"Senator Johnson Trades Again." *Texas Observer*, August 23, 1957: 8.
"Should the Majority Rule? Johnson Says No." *Texas Observer*, January 2, 1959: 5.
"The South and the Court." *Human Events* 15 (September 22, 1958): 2.
"South Sears Sen. Johnson." *Texas Observer*, March 11, 1960: 2.
"The Strange Case of 'Bobby' Baker: Methods Used by a Former Protégé of President Johnson to Pile Up a Fortune." *U.S. News and World Report* 56 (February 10, 1964): 40–43.
"Three Senators and YD's Slice at Johnson." *Texas Observer*, April 11, 1959: 3.
Turner, W. Earl. "How Independent Natural Gas Producers Became Federal Utilities and 'Lyndon Johnson's Finest Hour'." Paper, Energy Media Consultants, Inc., Austin, Texas, February 1984. Typewritten.
"Victory for Lyndon." *Time* 67 (May 14, 1956): 31.
"Watchdog Committee and How It Watches." *Newsweek* 38 (December 3, 1951): 21.

"Watchdog Johnson Follows Truman Path [LBJ Heads Senate National Defense Investigating Committee]." *Business Week,* October 21, 1950: 24–25.

Weeks, Oliver Douglas. *Texas Presidential Politics in 1952.* Austin: University of Texas at Austin, Institute of Public Affairs, 1953.

Wick, James L. "Rating Your Members of Congress by Their Voting on Critical Issues." *Human Events* 16 (December 2, 1959): A1-A8.

"Will Lyndon Control Ralph?" *Texas Observer,* April 9, 1957: 3.

Williams, John. "The Golden Years: History of the LCRA [Lower Colorado River Authority], Part 4." *River Review,* January/February, 1986: 16–19.

———. *The Story of the Lower Colorado River Authority: A 50th Anniversary Retrospective.* Austin: LCRA, 1985.

C. PRESIDENTIAL ELECTIONS OF 1956 AND 1960

"AFL-CIO General Board Backs Kennedy-Johnson for President, Vice President." *Labor* (Railroad Labor Organizations) 42 (September 3, 1960): 1.

Asher, Herbert B. *Presidential Elections and American Politics: Voters, Candidates and Campaigns since 1952.* Homewood, Ill.: Dorsey Press, 1976; 3rd ed., 1984.

"At the Conventions: 'Mr. Speaker' and His Friend." *U.S. News and World Report,* August 10, 1956: 22.

Banks, Jimmy. *Gavels, Grit and Glory: The Billy Clayton Story.* Burnet, Texas: Eakin Press, 1982.

Blanchard, Robert, et al. *Presidential Elections, 1945–1960.* Salt Lake City: University of Utah Press, 1961.

Boyd, William Austin. "Voter Registration and Turnout in the United States, 1952–76." East Lansing: Michigan State University, 1981. Ph.D. dissertation. University Microfilms No. 8117214.

"The Campaign: Political Risks Abound." *Human Events* 17 (August 11, 1960): 337.

Chamberlain, John. "LBJ: Least Popular with U.S.S.R.—He's A New-Fair Dealer, But He Wouldn't Apologize to Khrushchev." *National Review* 8 (July 2, 1960): 421–23+.

"Cities Left Lyndon on Key Test." *Texas Observer,* May 23, 1956: 1+.

Cohen, Dan. *Undefeated: The Life of Hubert H. Humphrey.* Minneapolis: Lerner Publishing Co., 1978.

Cohen, Jeffrey, and David C. Nice. "Party Unity and Presidential Election Performance: 1936–1980." *Presidential Studies Quarterly* 12 (Summer 1982): 317–29.

"Committee of Labor Women for Kennedy and Johnson Now Pushing Drive to Win More Votes for Candidates." *Labor* (Railroad Labor Organizations) 42 (October 29, 1960): 3.

"CQ Chart of Presidential Convention Information, 1948–1968." *Congressional Quarterly Weekly Report* 25 (September 29, 1967): 1.

Cummings, Milton C., Jr. *Congressmen and the Electorate: Elections for the U.S. House and the President, 1920–1964.* New York: Free Press, 1966.

David, Paul, ed. *The Presidential Election and Transition, 1960–1961.* Washington, D.C.: Brookings Institution, 1961.

Davis, John H. *The Kennedys: Dynasty and Disaster, 1848–1983.* New York: McGraw Hill, 1984.

Davis, Kenneth S. *The Politics of Honor: A Biography of Adlai Stevenson.* New York: Putnam, 1967.

Democratic National Committee. National Convention. Chicago, 1956. *Official Report of the Proceedings.* Washington, D.C.: Democratic National Committee/Beacon Press, 1960.

———. National Convention. Los Angeles, 1960. *Official Report of the Proceedings.* Washington, D.C.: National Document Publishers, 1964.

"Democratic Vice Pres. Nominee Lyndon Johnson Directs Criticism of Nixon for His Record on Civil Rights." *AFL-CIO News* 5 (October 22, 1960): 1, 12.

"The Democratic Victory." *Business Week,* November 12, 1960: 43–44.

"Democrats: Doing the Splits." *Human Events* 16 (September 23, 1959): 2–3.

"Democrats: Hubert on the Rise?" *Human Events* 17 (February 18, 1960): 1.

"Democrats: Johnson vs. Reuther." *Human Events* 17 (June 9, 1960): 1.

"Democrats: Kennedy vs. Humphrey." *Human Events* 16 (May 20, 1959): 1.

"Democrats: The Continuing Muddle." *Human Events* 16 (July 1, 1959): 2–3.

"Democrats: Tweedledum or Tweedledee." *Human Events* 16 (September 30, 1959): 4.

"Did LBJ Make John Kennedy President? An Untold Story." *U.S. News and World Report* 62 (January 16, 1967): 42–46+.

Divine, Robert A. *Foreign Policy and U.S. Presidential Elections: 1952–1960.* New York: New Viewpoints, 1974.

"Dixie: With LBJ All the Way." *Human Events* 17 (July 14, 1960): 276.

"DOT Stance on Johnson Is Delayed." *Texas Observer*, May 30, 1959: 1+.

Edwards, Willard. "Lyndon the Great: Johnson of Texas Runs for President." *Human Events* 17 (May 19, 1960): Section II.

———. "Presidential Hopeful Symington: The Democrats Will Take Him—If They Have To." *Human Events* 17 (April 28, 1960): Section III.

"Election Charges Gather Steam." *Texas Observer*, October 17, 1956: 4.

"Goldwater Guess: Johnson-Kennedy Ticket." *Human Events* 17 (June 16, 1960): 1–2.

"GOP: Nixon Toughens as Democrats Divide." *Human Events* 17 (June 2, 1960): 1.

"GOP Rakes Johnson." *Texas Observer*, February 26, 1960: 3.

"GOP Second Place (LBJ Is 'Fictitious Conservative')." *Human Events* 17 (July 21, 1960): 292.

Hadley, Charles D., and Susan E. Howell. "The Southern Split-Ticket Voter, 1952–1976: Republican Conversion or Democratic Decline?" *Party Politics in the South*, ed. by Robert P. Steed, Laurence W. Moreland, and Tod A. Baker, pp. 127–151. New York: Praeger, 1980.

Hajada, Joseph. "Choosing the 1960 Democratic Presidential Candidate: The Case of the Unbossed Delegation." *Kansas Quarterly*, vol. 8, no. 2 (1976): 71–87.

"Hard Campaigning to Bitter End." *Texas Observer*, November 7, 1956: 8.

Henderaker, Ivan, ed. *The 1960 Presidential Election.* New York: Holt, Rinehart & Winston, 1961.

"A House Divided: New Dedication, The Democratic Party vs. Its Congressional Leaders, 1952–1959." *Texas Observer*, April 15, 1960: 1+.

House, James, and William Mason. "Political Alienation in America, 1952–1968." *American Sociological Review* 40 (April 1975): 123–47.

Howell, Michael J. "Theodore H. White as a Speech Critic: An Analysis of His Treatment of Speech-making in Three Presidential Campaigns, 1960–1968." New York: State University of New York, 1972. M.A. thesis. University Microfilms No. M-4273.

Hudson, W. Gail. "The Role of Humor in John F. Kennedy's 1960 Presidential Campaign." Carbondale: Southern Illinois University, 1979. Ph.D. dissertation. University Microfilms No. 7926311.

Hyman, Sidney. "New Focus on the Vice Presidency." *New York Times Magazine*, March 27, 1960: 23.

"Ike: Effectively 'above the Battle'." *Human Events* 17 (August 18, 1960): 353.

"Ike, Johnson Lauded in an LBJ Mail-out." *Texas Observer*, September 16, 1959: 8.

"Issues for '56." *Texas Observer*, November 30, 1955: 4.

"John F. Kennedy Victory Seen as Triumph for Lyndon B. Johnson, Southern Democrats." *Dispatcher* 18 (November 18, 1960): 1, 6.

"Johnson: His Candidacy Goes to Court." *Human Events* 17 (August 11, 1960): 338.

"Johnson Leads South; Little Appeal in East." *Texas Observer*, November 20, 1959: 1+.

"Johnson [Muscles V.P. Spot]." *Human Events* 17 (July 28, 1960): 304.

"Johnson of Texas: A Summing Up." *Texas Observer*, June 24, 1960: 1+.

"Johnson Scored, But Labor Not a Party." *Texas Observer*, May 30, 1959: 3.

"The Johnson Situation." *Texas Observer*, April 18, 1959: 8.

"Johnson's Internecine Warfare." *Texas Observer*, October 24, 1956: 3.

"Johnson's 'Obstacles'." *Texas Observer*, August 14, 1959: 5.

"Johnson's Stance on the Presidency." *Texas Observer*, October 16, 1959: 2.

"Johnson Talks '60." *Texas Observer*, December 25, 1959: 3.

"Kennedy: Campaign Spending Mounts." *Human Events* 17 (April 7, 1960): 2.

"Kennedy: Candidate in Trouble." *Human Events* 16 (December 16, 1959): 1–2.

"Kennedy: Father's Funds, Friends Aid Him." *Human Events* 17 (March 31, 1960): 2.

"Kennedy: Images." *Human Events* 17 (July 14, 1960): 275.

"Kennedy: The Democrats' Rockefeller." *Human Events* 17 (January 21, 1960): 3–4.

"Kennedy: Using the Religious Issue." *Human Events* 17 (May 5, 1960): 2.

"Kennedy and Johnson Open the Campaign: Candidates' Acceptance Speeches." *U.S. News and World Report* 49 (July 25, 1960): 100–04.

"Kennedy-Johnson Battle Shaping Up at Democratic Convention." *AFL-CIO News* 5 (July 9, 1960): 1, 16.

"Kennedy, Johnson Make End Run Around Challenge on Civil Rights." *Human Events* 17 (September 8, 1960): 407.

"Kennedy, LBJ Close for Southern Lead." *Texas Observer*, April 29, 1960: 8.

"Kennedy or Johnson? [Fight for the 1960 Democratic Presidential Nomination]." *U.S. News and World Report* 49 (July 11, 1960): 48–50.

Kennedy, John F., Lyndon B. Johnson, Stuart Symington. *Meet the Press: Guests, Senators John F. Kennedy, Lyndon B. Johnson, Stuart Symington* (Interviews). Washington, D.C.: Merkle Press, vol. 4, no. 28, 1960.

"Labor on LBJ, Taxes." *Texas Observer*, November 20, 1959: 1+.

Ladd, Everett C., Jr., and Charles D. Hadley. *Transformations of the American Party System: Political Coalitions from the New Deal to the 1970s*. 2nd. ed. New York: Norton, 1978.

"LBJ: Oiling Up for L.A." *Human Events* 17 (June 23, 1960): 1–2.

"LBJ: The Campaign's Most Downgraded Man." *Human Events* 17 (October 13, 1960): 482.

"LBJ Barnstorms; Clubs Form." *Texas Observer*, October 30, 1959: 3.

"The LBJ Candidacy." *Texas Observer*, June 24, 1960: 3.

"LBJ Delegates Increasing." *Texas Observer*, January 22, 1960: 2.

"LBJ for President Runs Warm, Cool." *Texas Observer*, June 6, 1959: 8.

"LBJ Forces Try to Stir Sagging Candidacy." *Texas Observer*, June 3, 1960: 3.
"LBJ No. 3 in Poll." *Texas Observer*, June 20, 1959: 6.
"LBJ on Communists, Education, and 1960." *Texas Observer*, April 11, 1959: 3.
"LBJ Strong in Polls." *Texas Observer*, August 28, 1959: 8.
"LBJ Wins in Caucus; Ralph Votes 'No'." *Texas Observer*, January 15, 1960: 2.
"LBJ's Candidacy Watched." *Texas Observer*, January 8, 1960: 2.
"LBJ's Policies on the Texas Stump." *Texas Observer*, November 27, 1959: 6+.
Lewis, Ted. "Johnson Still A Long Shot." *Human Events* 17 (July 14, 1960): 290.
"Liberal ADA Goes All-out Anti-LBJ." *Texas Observer*, July 8, 1960: 5.
"Lyndon: All's Not Well with LBJ and JFK." *Human Events*, 17 (August 25, 1960): 372.
"Lyndon and the Negroes." *Texas Observer*, July 22, 1960: 1.
"Lyndon Introduces Truman at Rally." *Texas Observer*, October 9, 1959: 6.
"Lyndon Johnson and 1960." *Texas Observer*, April 4, 1959: 5.
"Lyndon Slammed Hard by Liberal ADA Group." *Texas Observer*, November 13, 1959: 1+.
"Lyndon's Pitch to 'Middle America'." *Texas Observer*, November 27, 1959: 1+.
"Lyndon's Propaganda." *Human Events* 17 (June 30, 1960): 3.
Malcolm, Donald F. "The Man Who Wants Second Place [JFK]." *New Republic* 135 (July 30, 1956): 13–14.
"Man Out Front [JFK]." *Time* 70 (December 2, 1957): 17–21.
Miller, Warren E., and Teresa E. Levitin. *Leadership and Change: Presidential Elections from 1952–1976*. Lanham, Md.: University Press of America, 1984.
Morehead, Richard. *Fifty Years in Texas Politics—from Roosevelt to Reagan—from the Fergusons to Clements*. Burnet, Texas: Eakin Press, 1982.
Mortensen, Calvin D. "A Comparative Analysis of Political Persuasion on Four Telecast Program Formats in the 1960 and 1964 Presidential Campaigns." Minneapolis: Univierisity of Minnesota, 1967. Ph.D. dissertation. University Microfilms No. 68–07420.

"The Most Talked-about Candidate for 1960 [JFK]." *U.S. News and World Report* 43 (November 8, 1957): 62–64.

"The Next President? Lyndon B. Johnson." *Economist* [Great Britain] 193 (December 26, 1959):1243–44.

"1960: Democratic Frontrunners Fade." *Human Events* 16 (June 3, 1959): 1.

"Nixon: His Needs for '60." *Human Events* 16 (October 14, 1959): 1–2.

"Nixon: His Secret Strategy." *Human Events* 16 (July 29, 1959): 1–2.

"Nixon: In Danger of Defeat?" *Human Events* 17 (March 31, 1960): 1.

"Nixon: Why He Moved Left." *Human Events* 17 (August 4, 1960): 321.

Nixon, Richard M. *The Memoirs of Richard Nixon.* New York: Grosset and Dunlap, 1978.

Ogden, Daniel M., Jr. "The Democratic National Committee in the Campaign of 1960." *Western Political Quarterly* 14 (September 1961): Supplement 27–28.

"The 'Other Campaign' [1960 Vice Presidency]: Johnson vs. Lodge—A Study in Contrasts." *U.S. News and World Report* 49 (October 24, 1960): 78–79.

"Our Poor Lyndon." *Texas Observer*, January 29, 1960: 5.

"The Parties Fight for Texas." *Texas Observer*, October 10, 1956: 7.

"Parties, Platforms, Candidates: Why General Board of AFL-CIO Endorsed Kennedy-Johnson." *AFL-CIO American Federationist* 67 (September 1960): 3–9.

Phillips, Cabell. "How to Be a Presidential Candidate." *New York Times Magazine*, July 13, 1958: 11, 52, 54.

Polsby, Nelson W., and Aaron B. Wildavsky, eds. *Presidential Elections: Strategies of American Electoral Politics.* 3rd ed. New York: Scribners, 1971.

Pomper, Gerald. "From Confusion to Clarity: Issues and American Voters, 1956–1968." *American Political Science Review* 66 (June 1972): 415–28.

Potter, Philip. "How LBJ Got the Nomination [for Vice President in 1960]." *Reporter* 30 (June 18, 1964): 16–20.

"Power Struggle on the Road to the White House." *U.S. News and World Report* 44 (March 28, 1958): 70–72.

"Pres-Elect Kennedy Plans Fast Start on Programs, Meets with

Vice Pres-Elect Johnson on Legislation." *AFL-CIO News* 5 (November 19, 1960): 1, 7.
"Presidential Racing Form." *Texas Observer*, May 16, 1956: 7.
"Proxmire Slams Lyndon on Oil and Civil Rights." *Texas Observer*, June 3, 1960: 4.
"The Public Records of John F. Kennedy and Lyndon B. Johnson: Their Lives, Voting Records, Stands on Issues, Platform." *Congressional Quarterly Weekly Report Special Supplement* 18 (July 22, 1960): 1–29.
"Rauh Says Liberalism 'Smothered' by LBJ." *Texas Observer*, June 3, 1960: 3.
Rayburn, Sam. "The Case for Democrats." *Saturday Evening Post*, October 6, 1956: 32.
"Reuther: Controlling the [Democratic] Candidates." *Human Events* 17 (February 11, 1960): 1.
Riesel, Victor. "How Labor Campaigns for Kennedy in Texas." *Human Events* 17 (October 27, 1960): 521.
Rossman, Jules. "'Meet the Press' and National Elections: The Candidates and the Issues, 1952–1964." East Lansing: Michigan State University, 1968. Ph.D. dissertation. University Microfilms No. 69–11155.
Runyon, John H., Jennefer Verdini, and Sally S. Runyon, eds. *Source Book of American Presidential Campaign and Election Statistics, 1948–1968*. New York: Frederick Ungar, 1971.
Scammon, Richard M., ed. *America at the Polls: A Handbook of American Presidential Election Statistics, 1920–1964*. Pittsburgh: Pittsburgh University Press, 1965.
"Sen. John F. Kennedy, Sen. Lyndon B. Johnson Pledge Fight for 5-Point Program: Health Care for Aged, Minimum Wage, Federal School Aid, Housing, and Mutual Security." *Labor* (Railroad Labor Organizations) 42 (August 6, 1960): 1.
"The Senator at His Precinct." *Texas Observer*, May 9, 1956: 1.
"Setting the Stage for 1960 Campaign?" *U.S. News and World Report* 43 (August 16, 1957): 14.
Sevareid, Eric, ed. *Candidates 1960: Behind the Headlines in the Presidential Race*. New York: Basic Books, 1959.
Shannon, William V. "Lyndon Johnson: Conservative." *Progressive* 24 (January 1960): 9–14.
Smith, James George. "Presidential Elections and Racial Discrimination: Campaign Promises, Presidential Performance

and Democratic Accountability, 1960–1980." Bloomington: Indiana University, 1981. Ph.D. dissertation. University Microfilms No. 82–02984.

Smith, Terry. "How Agencies for J.F., Bob Kennedy Drives Were Picked Is Recalled in *Esquire* Article." *Advertising Age* 36 (March 22, 1965): 14.

"Some Liberals, Stennis Back Lyndon." *Texas Observer*, December 11, 1959: 2.

Sorensen, Theodore C. "Election of 1960." *History of American Presidential Elections*, edited by Arthur M. Schlessinger, Jr., and Fred L. Israel, vol. 9, pp. 3–116. New York: Confucian Press, 1981.

"Sound Dollar: A Slogan for '60." *Human Events* 16 (June 17, 1969): 1.

"Sound Dollar: The Growing Crusade." *Human Events* 16 (June 24, 1959): 1.

"South Considers Lyndon." *Texas Observer*, April 18, 1956: 1.

"A Southern Watchword for '56: 'Moderate'; The Man—Lyndon Johnson; The News—What the South's Up To." *U.S. News and World Report* 39 (December 2, 1955): 67–69.

Stempel, Guido H. III. "The Prestige Press in Two Presidential Elections: 1960 and 1964." *Journalism Quarterly* 42 (Winter 1965): 15–21.

"A Tarheel's View of Senator Johnson." *Texas Observer*, July 15, 1960: 5.

"Texans at Chicago Vote for Johnson . . . Then for Gore and Kennedy for V.P." *Texas Observer*, August 22, 1956: 4+.

Thomas, David Allen. "A Quantitative Content Analysis of Richard Nixon's Treatment of Selected Issues in His Presidential Campaign Oratory in the 1960 and 1968 Elections." East Lansing: Michigan State University, 1973. Ph.D. dissertation. University Microfilms No. 78–12245.

Thomson, Charles A. H., and Francis M. Shattuch. *The 1956 Presidential Campaign*. Washington, D.C.: Brookings Institution, 1960.

"Three Frontrunners for the Democrats [for 1960]: Humphrey, Kennedy, Symington." *U.S. News and World Report* 46 (April 20, 1959): 74–76.

"Toughest Presidency Fight Since '48 Seen . . . Platform Lauded as Most Liberal in Many Years." *Labor* (Railroad Labor Organizations) 42 (July 23, 1960): 1, 3.

Trent, Judith. "Richard Nixon's Methods of Identification in the Presidential Campaigns of 1960 and 1968: A Content Analysis." *Today's Speech* 19 (Fall 1971): 23–30.

"Twenty Questions about Dick Nixon." *Human Events* 17 (September 22, 1960): 441–44.

"Twenty Questions about Jack Kennedy." *Human Events* 17 (September 29, 1960): 461–62.

"Union Leaders Size Up Kennedy and Johnson." *U.S. News and World Report* 49 (July 11, 1960): 96–99.

Weeks, Oliver Douglas. *Texas in the 1960 Presidential Election.* Austin: University of Texas at Austin, Institute of Public Affairs, 1961.

———. *Texas One-Party Politics in 1956.* Austin: University of Texas at Austin, Institute of Public Affairs, 1957.

"Why AFL-CIO General Board Endorsed Kennedy and Johnson over Nixon and Lodge." *United Paper* (United Papermakers and Paperworkers) 4 (September 12, 1960): 7.

Wick, James L. "The Kennedy Revolution: Part I." *Human Events* 17 (June 28, 1960): 311–12.

———. "The Kennedy Revolution: Part II: The Past Is Prologue, You Ain't Seen Nuthin' Yet." *Human Events* 17 (August 4, 1960): 329–32.

"With the Candidates: Humphrey, Brown, Johnson, Kennedy." *Human Events* 17 (March 3, 1960): 1–2.

"With the Candidates: Kennedy, Johnson, Symington." *Human Events* 17 (February 25, 1960): 2.

Zikmund, Joseph II "Suburban Voting in Presidential Elections, 1948–1964." *Midwest Journal of Political Science* 12 (May 1968): 239–58.

Zwikl, Kurt D. "The Candidates and the Issues: An Examination of the 1960 Presidential Election in Lehigh County, Pennsylvania." Bethlehem, Penn.: Lehigh University, 1982. M.A. thesis.

D. CONGRESSIONAL COLLEAGUES

Anderson, Clinton P., with Milton Viorst. *Outsider in the Senate: Senator Clinton Anderson's Memoirs.* New York: World, 1970.

Anderson, Jack, and Fred Blumenthal. *The Kefauver Story.* New York: Dial Press, 1956.

Andrain, Charles F. "A Scale Analysis of Senators' Attitudes toward Civil Rights [in 1960]." *Western Political Quarterly* 17 (September 1964): 488–503.

Brown, D. Clayton. "Sam Rayburn and the Development of Public Power in the Southwest." *Southwestern Historical Quarterly* 78 (October 1974): 140–54.

Burt, Eric. *Eyes on Washington* [covers Johnson, Rayburn, Sam Tallafero]. New York: New Century Publishers, 1955. Pamphlet.

Champagne, Anthony. *Congressman Sam Rayburn.* New Brunswick, N.J.: Rutgers University Press, 1984.

Chodorov, Frank. "Senator Kennedy's 'Right to Loaf' Bill." *Human Events* 16 (November 25, 1959): A1-A4.

Cohen, Dan. *Undefeated: The Life of Hubert Horatio Humphrey.* Minneapolis: Lerner Publications, 1978.

"Congress: Mr. Sam's House Rules." *Time,* January 12, 1959: 20–21.

"Congress: The 'Moderates' Lose Ground." *Human Events* 16 (January 14, 1959): 1–2.

"Congress: What Mr. Sam Wants." *Time,* March 24, 1958: 24.

Cook, Fred J. *The Nightmare Decade: The Life and Times of Senator Joe McCarthy.* New York: Random House, 1971.

Davidson, Roger H., and Walter J. Oleszek. *Congress and Its Members.* Washington, D.C.: Congressional Quarterly Press, 1981.

Davis, Kenneth S. *The Politics of Honor: A Biography of Adlai Stevenson.* New York: Putnam, 1967.

"Democrat's Decisive Dozen." *Time* 67 (June 18, 1956): 26.

"'Don't Spare Ike', Rayburn Advises." *Texas Observer,* August 29, 1956: 5.

Dulaney, H. G., and Edward Hake Phillips, comps. and eds. *"Speak, Mr. Speaker"* [Sam Rayburn]. Bonham, Texas: Sam Rayburn Foundation, 1978.

"Economics of Seven Democrats." *Fortune* 54 (July 1956): 74–77+.

Emswiler, Marilyn. "Mr. Speaker: Sam Rayburn." *Texas Historian* 33 (March 1973): 20–25.

"Era of Senators in Gray Flannel Suits." *Texas Observer,* March 7, 1959: 5.

Ewing, Floyd F. "Samuel Taliaferro Rayburn." *The Handbook*

of Texas: A Supplement, edited by Eldon Stephen Branda, vol. 3, p. 781. Austin: Texas State Historical Association, 1976.

Fairlie, Henry. *The Kennedy Promise: The Politics of Expectation.* Garden City, N.Y.: Doubleday, 1973.

Farrow, Stephen B. "Richard Russell and Lyndon Johnson: Principle and Pragmatism in Senatorial Politics, 1949–1952." Knoxville: University of Tennessee, 1979. B.A. senior honors thesis [c/o LBJ Library].

"Four Leaders Who Run Congress." *U.S. News and World Report* 42 (January 11, 1957): 74+.

Frantz, Joe B. "Kennedy and Johnson: The Senatorial Years." *Proceedings of The Philosophical Society of Texas* 31 (December 8, 9, 1967): 22–34.

Goldston, Robert. *The American Nightmare: Senator Joseph R. McCarthy and the Politics of Hate.* Indianapolis: Bobbs-Merrill, 1973.

Hardeman, D. B. "Unseen Side of the Man They Called Mr. Speaker." *Life,* December 1, 1961: 21.

Healy, Paul F. "They're Just Crazy about Sam." *Saturday Evening Post,* November 24, 1951: 22.

Hildenbrand, William F., and Kathryn Allamong Jacob, eds. *Guide to Research Collections of Former U.S. Senators, 1789–1982.* Washington, D.C.: U.S. Senate, Bicentennial Publication no. 1, 1983.

Hinga, Don. "Sam Rayburn: Texas Squire." *Southwest Review* 29 (Summer 1944): 471–80.

"A House Divided: New Dedication, The Democratic Party vs. Its Congressional Leaders, 1952–1959." *Texas Observer,* April 15, 1960: 1+.

"The Hubert Humphrey Record." *U.S. News and World Report* 65 (July 1, 1968): 36–41.

"It Is Still the House that 'Mr. Sam' the Speaker Runs." *Newsweek,* February 13, 1961: 26–28.

"Jack [Kennedy] Visits LBJ Ranch." *Texas Observer,* November 18, 1960: 1+.

"Johnson, Kennedy, Symington Votes Compared." *Congressional Quarterly Weekly Report* 18 (July 8, 1960): 1195–96.

Kennon, Donald R. "Sam Rayburn." *The Speakers of the U.S. House of Representatives: A Bibliography, 1789–1984,* edited by Donald R. Kennon, pp. 288–60. Baltimore: Johns Hopkins University Press, 1985.

"Labor: Knowland Outmaneuvers [Johnson's] Democrats." *Human Events* 15 (May 5, 1958): 1.
"Last Roundup in Congress—Two Texans in the Saddle: Speaker Sam Rayburn in the House and Lyndon B. Johnson, Democratic Leader in the Senate." *U.S. News and World Report* 45 (August 22, 1958): 56–58.
Lazarowitz, Arlene. "Years in Exile: The Liberal Democrats, 1950–1959." Los Angeles: University of California, 1982. University Microfilms No. 82–25593.
"Liberal Record of Hubert Humphrey." *Human Events* 24 (September 26, 1964): 1–2.
"Lyndon, Sam, and Civil Rights." *Texas Observer*, August 30, 1957: 3.
"Lyndon's Power and Ralph's Potential." *Texas Observer*, February 7, 1958: 2.
McKay, Seth Shepard. *Texas and the Fair Deal, 1945–1952*. San Antonio: Naylor Co., 1954.
"Mister Speaker [Sam Rayburn]." *Time*, September 27, 1943: 19–22.
"'Mr. Democrat' [Sam Rayburn] Sets a Record for Serving." *U.S. News and World Report* March 16, 1959: 26.
"Mr. Speaker Sam." *Newsweek*, January 10, 1955: 18–20.
Newberry, Anthony Lake. "Without Urgency or Ardor: The South's Middle-of-the-Road Liberals and Civil Rights, 1945–1960." Athens: Ohio University, 1982. Ph.D. dissertation. University Microfilms No. 8300026.
Nixon, Richard M. *The Memoirs of Richard Nixon*. New York: Grosset and Dunlap, 1978.
Oshinsky, David M. *A Conspiracy So Immense: The World of Joe McCarthy*. New York: Free Press, 1983.
Phillips, Edward. "Sam Rayburn." *Texas Almanac and State Industrial Guide, 1986–1987*, edited by Mike Kingston, pp. 154–55. Dallas: Dallas Morning News, Sesquicentennial Edition, 1985
Potenziani, David D. "Look to the Past: Richard B. Russell and the Defense of Southern White Supremacy." Athens: University of Georgia, 1981. Ph.D. dissertation. University Microfilms No. 82–01574.
"Proxmire Stirs Up Debate on Johnson." *Texas Observer*, February 28, 1959: 2.
"Ralph, Lyndon, and Big Oil." *Texas Observer*, August 22, 1958: 3.

"Ralph, Lyndon Split in Public Housing Vote." *Texas Observer,* June 7, 1957: 1+.

"Ralph Recalls 'Faith'; Lyndon Climbs in Flak." *Texas Observer,* December 5, 1958: 8.

"Rayburn OK's FCC White Wash." *Texas Observer,* January 24, 1958: 3.

"Rayburn's Strategy: Help Ike If It Helps Democrats." *U.S. News and World Report* January 8, 1954: 51–53.

"Reaction to Rayburn's Plan." *Texas Observer,* March 14, 1956: 4.

Reinhard, David W. *The Republican Right since 1945.* Lexington: University Press of Kentucky, 1983.

"The Rise of the Brothers Kennedy." *Look* 21 (August 6, 1957): 18–24, 27.

"Sam Rayburn: Using 42 Years of Savvy to Help Democrats." *Business Week,* December 4, 1954: 166–70.

Schapsmeier, Edward L., and Frederick H. Schapsmeier. *Dirksen of Illinois: Senatorial Statesman.* Urbana: University of Illinois Press, 1984.

"Senate: Behind Proxmire's Rebellion." *Human Events* 16 (March 18, 1959): 1–2.

Smallwood, James. "Sam Rayburn and the Rules Committee Change of 1961." *East Texas Historical Journal* 11 (Spring 1973): 51–54.

Solberg, Carl. *Hubert Humphrey: A Political Biography.* New York: Norton, 1984.

Steely, Jim. "Mr. Democrat . . . Mr. Speaker . . . Mr. Sam [Rayburn Library]." *Texas Highways* 24 (March 1977): 24–29.

"Strauss: Political Crucifixion." *Human Events* 16 (June 24, 1959): 1–2.

Swados, Harvey. *Standing Up for the People: The Life and Work of Estes Kefauver.* New York: E. P. Dutton, 1972.

Tananbaum, Duane A. "The Bricker Amendment Controversy: Its Origins and Eisenhower's Role." *Diplomatic History* 9 (Winter 1985): 73–93.

"Three Senators and YD's Slice at Johnson." *Texas Observer,* April 11, 1959: 3.

Turner, Russell. "Senator Kennedy, the Perfect Politician." *American Mercury* 84 (March 1957): 33–40.

"Two Texans Will Call the Signals [Rayburn and LBJ]." *U.S. News and World Report* January 17, 1958: 48–50.

United States Congress. *Biographical Directory of the Ameri-*

can Congress, 1774–1971. Washington: U.S. Gov't. Printing Office, 1971.

United States 83rd Congress, 1st Session, Senate. *Hon. Lyndon B. Johnson, of Texas, Democratic Leader of the Senate of the United States; Tributes by Senate Colleagues, Monday, August 3, 1955.* Washington, D.C.: U.S. Gov't. Printing Office (*Congressional Record*), 1953.

Voorhis, Jerry. "Rayburn of Texas." *New Republic*, July 10, 1944: 44–46.

Wick, James L. "Rating Your Members of Congress by Their Voting on Critical Issues." *Human Events* 16 (December 2, 1959): A1-A8.

VI. The Vice-Presidential Years, 1961–1963

Acheson, Dean G. "Dean Acheson's Version of Robert Kennedy's Version of the Cuban Missile Affair." *Esquire* 71 (February 1969): 76–77.

Anderson, Jack, and James Boyd. *Confessions of a Muckraker: The Inside Story of Life in Washington during the Truman, Eisenhower, Kennedy, and Johnson Years.* New York: Random House, 1979.

"Bad Year for LBJ." *Human Events* 19 (August 11, 1962): 597.

"Barry." *Human Events* 19 (December 29, 1962): 993.

Bearss, Edwin C. *Lyndon B. Johnson and the Hill Country, 1937–1963.* Sante Fe: Southwest Cultural Center Professional Papers No. 3, National Park Service, U.S. Dept. of Interior, 1984. Typewritten.

"Billie Sol Whitewash." *Human Events* 19 (June 16, 1962): 435.

Bowles, Nigel P. "The Organization of the Office of Congressional Relations under Presidents Kennedy and Johnson." Paper presented at the Annual Conference of the American Politics Group of the Political Studies Assn., 1981, Gregynog, Powys, Wales.

Brands, Henry William, Jr. "The Eisenhower Administration and the Cold War." Austin: University of Texas, 1985. Ph.D. dissertation.

"Bundy of the White House." *Saturday Evening Post* 235 (March 10, 1962): 82–85.

Burner, David, and Thomas R. West. *The Torch Is Passed: The*

Kennedy Brothers and American Liberalism. New York: Atheneum, 1985.

Cater, Douglass. "The Hard-Won Destiny of Lyndon Johnson." *Reporter* 29 (December 19, 1963): 17–19.

Collier, Peter, and David Horowitz. *The Kennedys: An American Drama.* New York: Summit, 1984; paper, Warner Books, 1985.

Davis, John H. *The Kennedys: Dynasty and Disaster, 1848–1983.* New York: McGraw Hill, 1984.

De Toledano, Ralph. "Lyndon Johnson's Civil Rights Record." *Human Events* 24 (August 15, 1964): 12.

"Deep in the Heart of Senegal with the L.B.J.s." *Life,* April 14, 1961: 135–37.

Enthoven, Alain C., and K. Wayne Smith. *How Much Is Enough? Shaping the Defense Program, 1961–1968.* New York: Harper and Row, 1971.

Fairlie, Henry. *The Kennedy Promise: The Politics of Expectation.* Garden City, N.Y.: Doubleday, 1973.

Feerick, John D. *The Vice Presidents of the U.S.* 3rd ed. New York: Watts, 1977.

"Foreign Aid: LBJ's Dual Mission." *Human Events* 18 (June 23, 1961): 389.

Fulton, Lewis, Jr. "LBJ and Bobby Baker." *Human Events* 24 (April 4, 1964): 11.

"Goldberg to Replace Lyndon on '64 Ticket?" *Human Events* 22 (October 19, 1963): 10.

Goldstein, Joel K. "The American Vice-Presidency, 1953–1978." London: Oxford University, 1978. Ph.D. dissertation.

Harvey, Paul. "LBJ Hard-Selling the Moon." *Human Events* 22 (November 16, 1963): 6.

Hilsman, Roger. *To Move a Nation: The Politics of Foreign Policy in the Administration of John F. Kennedy.* New York: Doubleday, 1967.

Hoppe, Art. "Whatever Happened to LBJ?" *Human Events* 19 (August 25, 1962): 647.

"How LBJ Spreads Goodwill." *Human Events* 19 (September 29, 1962): 735.

Hurley, Robert Michael. "President John F. Kennedy and Vietnam, 1961–1963." Honolulu: University of Hawaii, 1970. Ph.D. dissertation. University Microfilms No. 71-21563.

"Johnson Biography, Record in Congress, Leadership, Role as

Vice President." *Congressional Quarterly Weekly Report* 21 (November 29, 1963): 2069–88.
"Johnson's Expensive Promises." *Human Events* 19 (December 15, 1962): 965.
Keever, Crawford. *John B. Connally: Portrait in Power.* Austin: Jenkins Publishing Co., 1973.
Kennedy, Robert F. *Thirteen Days: A Memoir of the Cuban Missile Crisis.* New York: Norton, 1969.
Knaggs, John R. *Two-Party Texas: The John Tower Era, 1961–1984.* Austin: Eakin Press, 1986.
Knapp, Daniel, and Kenneth Polk. *Scouting the War on Poverty: Social Reform Politics in the Kennedy Administration.* Lexington, Mass.: D. C. Heath, 1971.
Kozar, Paul Michael. "The Politics of Deterrence: A Comparative Assessment of American and Soviet Defense Policy, 1960–1964." Washington, D.C.: Georgetown University, 1984. Ph.D. dissertation.
Lasky, Victor. "What Happened to LBJ?" *Human Events* 21 (April 20, 1963): 46.
"LBJ, Back in the Headlines: Foreign Travel Is Just One of the Aspects of the Vice-Presidential Job as He Interprets It." *U.S. News and World Report.* 53 (August 20, 1962): 37–41.
"LBJ Foresees." *Texas Observer*, May 26, 1962: 2.
"LBJ Swings TFX Deal?" *Human Events* 20 (March 23, 1963): 222.
Lester, Robert Leon. "Developments in Presidential-Congressional Relations: FDR–JFK." Charlottesville: University of Virginia, 1969. Ph.D. dissertation. University Microfilm No. 70–4808.
Lewis, Fulton, Jr. "Lyndon Pulled the Strings [Urban Renewal]." *Human Events* 18 (August 11, 1961): 514.
Light, Paul C. "The Institutional Vice Presidency." *Presidential Studies Quarterly* 13 (Spring 1983): 198–211.
"Lyndon Johnson—A New Kind of Vice President." *U.S. News and World Report* 50 (January 23, 1961): 50–51.
"Lyndon Johnson: What the Future Holds." *U.S. News and World Report* 52 (March 5, 1962): 49–52.
Martin, Ralph G. *A Hero for Our Time.* New York: Macmillan, 1983.
Matusow, Allen J. "John F. Kennedy and the Intellectuals." *The Wilson Quarterly* 7 (Autumn 1983): 140–53.

McDougall, Walter A. . . . *The Heavens and the Earth: A Political History of the Space Age.* New York: Basic Books, 1985.

Natoli, Marie D. "Vice Presidential Selection: The Political Considerations." *Presidential Studies Quarterly* 10 (Spring 1980): 163–70.

Oates, Stephen B. "NASA's Manned Spacecraft Center at Houston, Texas." *Southwestern Historical Quarterly* 67 (January 1964): 350–75.

"Odyssey of Camel Man from Pakistan [Goodwill Ambassador Bashir Ahmed Visits Vice President Johnson's Ranch]." *Life,* October 27, 1961: 75–77.

Parmet, Herbert S. *Jack: The Struggle of John F. Kennedy.* New York: Dial Press, 1980.

Paterson, Thomas G., and William J. Brophy. "October Missiles and November Elections: The Cuban Missile Crisis and American Politics, 1962." *Journal of American History* 73 (June 1986): 87–119.

"Ralph, Lyndon, and the Filibuster." *Texas Observer,* February 21, 1963: 9+.

"Retail Clerks' President [James A. Suffridge] Accompanies Vice President Johnson on Diplomatic and Fact-Finding Mission to Far and Near East." *Retail Clerks Advocate* 64 (June 1961): 1.

Rice, Gerard T. *The Bold Experiment: JFK's Peace Corps.* Notre Dame, Ind.: University of Notre Dame Press, 1985.

Riesel, Victor. "Bobby Eager to Run for Massachusetts Governor in '66 [LBJ's Presidential Strategy]." *Human Events* 20 (February 2, 1963): 87.

———. "JFK Starts '64 Campaign." *Human Events* 21 (May 18, 1963): 106.

Ruth, Robert W. "What Lyndon Johnson Found Next Door to Russia [Scandinavian Tour, September 1963]." *U.S. News and World Report* 55 (September 23, 1963): 73–74.

"Senate: Who Leads the Democrats?" *Human Events* 18 (January 13, 1961): 18.

"Some Tough Talk from Lyndon Johnson about Where We Stand in World Affairs." *United Mine Workers Journal* 72 (October 15, 1961): 9.

Sorenson, Theodore C. *Decision-Making in the White House.* New York: Columbia University Press, 1963.

Suffridge, James A. "Asia's Labor Movement and Battle for Free

World [Report of Vice President Johnson's Labor Advisor after Six-Nation Tour]." *Retail Clerks Advocate* 64 (July 1961): 16–20.

Tanzer, Lester, ed. *The Kennedy Circle.* Washington, D.C.: Luce, 1961.

"Texas: Blakley's Ties to LBJ." *Human Events* 18 (April 21, 1961): 243.

"Texas: Will GOP Win LBJ's Seat?" *Human Events* 18 (March 17, 1961): 163.

"Thirty Questions about the Kennedy Administration." *Human Events* 17 (November 17, 1960): 569–74.

"Three Men on War and Peace." *Texas Observer,* December 27, 1962: 10+.

Trohan, Walter. "Washington's Inflo of Gold: President and Vice President Multimillionaires." *Human Events* 18 (February 17, 1961): 107.

United Press International and American Heritage Magazine, comp. *Four Days: The Historical Record of the Death of President Kennedy.* New York: American Heritage Publishing Co., dist. by Simon and Schuster, 1983.

"Vice President Honored by Administration and Congressional Leaders on 25th Anniversary of First Election to Congress." *Labor* (Railroad Labor Organizations) 43 (April 21, 1962): 2.

"Vice President Johnson Carves Out a New Career [His Influence in the Kennedy Administration]." *U.S. News and World Report* 51 (August 21, 1961): 56–58.

"Vice President Johnson Chief Speaker at AFL-CIO Economic and Legislative Conference." *AFL-CIO News* 7 (January 20, 1962): 3.

"Waiting for Proof on Johnson." *Business Week,* July 23, 1960: 70–71.

Walton, Richard J. *Cold War and Counter Revolution.* New York: Viking, 1972.

Washington, D.C. Inaugural Committee. *Official Program, Inaugural Ceremonies of John F. Kennedy, Thirty-fifth President of the United States and Lyndon B. Johnson, Thirty-seventh Vice President of the United States. Washington, D.C., January 20, 1961.* Washington, D.C.: Presidential Inaugural Committee, 1961.

"What Is an LBJ?" *Texas Observer,* October 18, 1963: 8.

"White House Opens Series of Regional Meetings; Vice President Johnson Principle Speaker [White House Conference on Domestic Affairs, Chicago]." *Federation News* 73 (November 4, 1961): 1.

Zeiger, Henry A. *Robert F. Kennedy: A Biography.* New York: Meredith, 1968.

VII. The Presidential Years, 1963–1969

A. THE AMERICAN PRESIDENCY

Berger, Raoul. *Executive Privilege.* New York: Bantam Books, 1975.

———. "Presidential Monopoly of Foreign Relations." *Michigan Law Review* 71 (November 1972): 1–58.

Berman, Larry, Fred I. Greenstein, and Alvin S. Felzenberg, with Doris Lidtke. *Evolution of the Modern Presidency: A Bibliographical Survey.* Washington, D.C.: American Enterprise Institution for Public Policy Research, Studies in Political and Social Processes, 1977.

Bickel, Alexander M. "Congress, the President and the Power to Wage War." *Chicago-Kent Law Review* 48 (Fall-Winter 1971): 131–47.

Bratton, Daniel L. "The Rating of Presidents." *Presidential Studies Quarterly* 13 (Summer 1983): 400–404.

Brennan, Paul Edward. "The War-Making Powers of the American President as Commander-in-Chief of the Armed Forces." Fullerton: California State College, 1968. M.A. thesis. University Microfilms No. M-1537.

Bundy, McGeorge, and William P. Bundy. "How Foreign Policy Is Made—Logic and Experience." *University of Pittsburgh Law Review* 30 (Spring 1969): 437–57.

Carbone, Donald J. "The Executive Office of the President as a Management Tool." *Perspectives in Defense Management,* February 1967: 27–38.

Clark, Keith C., and Lawrence J. Legere, eds. *The President and the Management of National Security: A Report by the Institute for Defense Analysis.* New York: Praeger, 1969.

Cohen, Jeffrey A. "Passing the President's Program: Presidential-Congressional Relations, 1789–1974." Ann Arbor: University of Michigan, 1979. Ph.D. dissertation. University Microfilms No. 79-25127.

Corwin, Edward S. *The President: Office and Powers.* 5th ed. New York: New York University Press, 1984

Covington, Cary R. "Congressional Support for the President: The View from the White House." Paper prepared for the annual meeting of the American Political Science Assn., Washington, D.C., August 30–September 2, 1984.

Cronin, Thomas E., and Sanford D. Greenberg, eds. *The Presidential Advisory System.* New York: Harper and Row, 1969.

Davis, Vincent, ed. *The Post-Imperial Presidency.* New Brunswick, N.J.: Transaction Books, 1980.

DeGregorio, William A. *The Complete Book of U.S. Presidents.* New York: Dembner Books, dist. by Norton, 1984.

Destler, Irving McArthur. "Presidents and Bureaucrats: Organizing the Government for Foreign Policy." Princeton, N.J.: Princeton University, 1971. Ph.D. dissertation. University Microfilms No. 72-13739.

Edwards, George C. III. *The Public Presidency: The Pursuit of Popular Support.* New York: St. Martin's Press, 1983.

———, and Stephen J. Wayne, eds. *Studying the Presidency.* Knoxville: University of Tennessee Press, 1983.

Fishel, Jeff. *Presidents and Promises: From Campaign Pledge to Presidential Performance.* Washington, D.C.: Congressional Quarterly Service, 1985.

Fisher, Louis. *Constitutional Conflicts between Congress and the President.* Princeton, N.J.: Princeton University Press, 1985.

———. *Presidential Spending Power.* Princeton, N.J.: Princeton University Press, 1975.

———. *White House-Congress Relationships: Information Exchange and Lobbying.* Washington, D.C.: Congressional Research Service, 1978.

Flash, Edward S., Jr. *Economic Advice and Presidential Leadership: The Council of Economic Advisers.* New York: Columbia University Press, 1965.

Gawthrop, Louis. *Bureaucratic Behavior in the Executive Branch.* New York: Free Press, 1969.

Goldsmith, William M. *The Growth of Presidential Power.* Vol. 3. *Triumph and Reappraisal.* New York: Chelsea, 1974.

Greenstein, Fred I., et al. *Evolution of the Modern Presidency: A Bibliographical Survey.* Washington, D.C.: American Enterprise Institute for Public Policy Research, 1977.

Halperin, Morton H. "The President and the Military [FDR to Nixon]." *Foreign Affairs* 50 (January 1972): 310–24.

Jamieson, Kathleen Hall. *Packaging the Presidency: A History and Criticism of Presidential Campaign Advertising.* New York: Oxford University Press, 1984.

Kelly, O. "The Secret Files of J. Edgar Hoover." *U.S. News and World Report,* December 19, 1983: 45–50.

Kernell, Samuel Houston. "Presidential Popularity and Electoral Preference: A Model of Short-Term Political Change." Berkeley: University of California, 1975. Ph.D. dissertation. University Microfilms No. 76–15256.

Krukones, Michael G. *Promises and Performance: Presidential Campaigns as Policy Predictors.* Lanham, Md.: University Press of America, 1984.

Lee, Jong R. "Presidential Vetoes from Washington to Nixon." *Journal of Politics* 37 (May 1975): 522–46.

Martin, Janet M. "The President's Cabinet—An Examination of Recruitment and Background Characteristics." Paper delivered at annual meeting of Midwest Political Assn., Chicago, April 20–23, 1983.

Merriam, Robert E. "The Bureau of the Budget as Part of the President's Staff." *Annals of the American Academy of Political and Social Sciences* 307 (September 1956): 15–23.

Moe, Ronald C., ed. *Congress and the President.* Pacific Palisades, Cal.: Goodyear Publishing Co., 1971.

Monroe, Kristen R. "Economic Influences on Presidential Popularity." *Public Opinion Quarterly* 42 (Fall 1978): 360–69.

Nelson, Michael, ed. *The Presidency and the Political System.* Washington, D.C.: Congressional Quarterly, 1984.

Parker, Glenn R. *Political Beliefs about the Structure of Government: Congress and the Presidency.* Beverly Hills, Cal.: Sage Publications, 1974.

Reedy, George E. *The Twilight of the Presidency.* New York: World Press, 1970.

Ripley, Randall B., and Grace A. Franklin, eds. *Policy-Making in the Federal Executive Branch.* New York: Free Press, 1975.

Robinson, Donald A. "Presidents and Party Leadership." Paper presented at the American Political Science Assn., Chicago, August 29-September 2, 1974.

Rourke, Francis E. "Executive Fallability: Presidential Management Styles." *Administration and Society*, vol. 6, no. 2 (1974): 171–77.

Schaffler, Dorothy, and Dorothy M. Mathews. *The Powers of the President as Commander in Chief of the Army and Navy of the United States.* New York: Da Capo Press, 1974.

Schlesinger, Arthur M., Jr. "On Presidential Succession." *Political Science Quarterly* 89 (Fall 1974): 475–506.

Sigelman, Lee. "Presidential Popularity and Presidential Elections." *Public Opinion Quarterly* 43 (Winter 1979): 532–34.

Tatalovich, Raymond, and Byron W. Daynes. *Presidential Power in the United States.* Monterey, Cal.: Brooks/Cole, 1984.

Thompson, Kenneth W., ed. *The American Presidency: Principles and Problems Series.* 3 vols. Lanham, Md.: University Press of America; and Charlottesville: White Burkett Miller Center, University of Virginia, 1982–84.

———, ed. *The Virginia Papers on the Presidency: The White Burkett Miller Center Forums.* 22 vols. Lanham, Md.: University Press of America; and Charlottesville: White Burkett Miller Center, University of Virginia, 1981–87.

Watson, H. Lee. "Congress Steps Out: A Look at Congressional Control of the Executive." *California Law Review* 63 (July 1975): 983-1094.

White, Daniel Ernest. "Access to the President: Time Management in the White House." Riverside: University of California, 1973. Ph.D. dissertation. University Microfilms No. 73-23840.

B. THE JOHNSON PRESIDENCY

1. GENERAL

Adams, Joey. *LBJ's Texas Laughs.* New York: F. Fell, 1964.

"After 15 Months—What Businessmen Think of LBJ." *U.S. News and World Report* 58 (February 22, 1965): 98–102.

Alexander, Holmes. "Did LBJ Put Prosperity above Preparedness?" *Human Events* 25 (December 11, 1965): 10.
―――. "LBJ's First Mistake?" *Human Events* 22 (December 21, 1963): 1, 3.
Anderson, Jack, and James Boyd. *Confessions of a Muckraker: The Inside Story of Life in Washington during the Truman, Eisenhower, Kennedy, and Johnson Years.* New York: Random House, 1979.
Anderson, James E. "Presidential Management of the Bureaucracy and the Johnson Presidency: A Preliminary Exploration." *Congress and the Presidency* 11 (Autumn 1984): 137–64.
"Answers to Vital Questions about the Coming Johnson Revolution." *Human Events* 24 (November 14, 1964): 1.
"As Johnson Really Takes Over: Kennedy Administration Fading into History—Result: New Faces, New Ways of Doing Business." *U.S. News and World Report* 56 (April 6, 1964): 31–33.
"As LBJ Takes Over." *Human Events* 22 (December 7, 1963): 4.
"At Home on the Range." *Business Week*, January 4, 1964: 19–20.
Bailey, Charles W. II. "LBJ . . . Man in Charge." *Look* 28 (March 10, 1964): 24–25.
Beebe, Lucius. "Lyndon Johnson: Evolution of an Instant Statesman." *Human Events* 23 (January 25, 1964): 6A.
Benningfeld, Damond. "Shapers of Austin, 1966–1976." *Austin* 28 (February 1986): 85.
"A Better Day for LBJ: An Appraisal of His Foreign and Domestic Policies." *Economist* (Great Britain) 246 (January 27, 1973): 12–13.
Brauer, Carl M. *Presidential Transitions: Eisenhower through Reagan.* New York: Oxford University Press, 1986.
Briggs, C. M. "From Credibility Gap to Futility Fugue." *NASPA Journal* 5 (April 1968): 311–13.
Bundy, McGeorge. *Strength of Government.* Cambridge, Mass.: Harvard University Press, 1968.
Burlage, Robb K. *Johnson with Eyes Open.* New York: Students for a Democratic Society Political Education Project, 196?. Pamphlet.
"Challenge to an Operation Man: Views and Methods of President Johnson." *Economist* (Great Britain) 210 (January 11, 1964): 107–08.

"The Changes LBJ Has Brought in 6 Months." *U.S. News and World Report* 56 (May 18, 1964): 46–50+.

Cohen, Wilbur J., ed. *The New Deal: 50 Years After—A Historical Assessment.* Austin: University of Texas, LBJ School of Public Affairs, LBJ Library, 1984.

"The Cold That Sent a Tremor through the Nation [Reviews President Johnson's Medical History]." *U. S. News and World Report* 58 (February 8, 1965): 33–34.

Condray, Suzanne Elizabeth. "Speechwriting in Rhetorical Criticism: An Extension of Theory As Applied to the Johnson Administration." Baton Rouge: Louisiana State University and Agricultural and Mechanical College, 1980. Ph.D. dissertation. University Microfilms No. 81-03632.

Congressional Quarterly Service. *CQ Guide to Current American Government* [the Presidency, Congress, Key Issues 1965, Supreme Court, Politics 1964–66]. Washington, D.C.: Congressional Quarterly Service, Fall 1965.

"Congressmen Size Up LBJ and His First Six Months." *U.S. News and World Report* 56 (June 8, 1964): 57–59.

Dallek, Robert. "Caro vs. Johnson." *Reviews in American History* 12 (March 1984): 148–53.

"A Day in the Life of the President: From Dawn until Midnight with Lyndon Johnson." *U.S. News and World Report* 56 (March 2, 1964): 36–45.

Divine, Robert A. *The Johnson Years, Volume One: Foreign Policy, the Great Society, and the White House.* Lawrence: University Press of Kansas, 1987 [Paper edition of *Exploring the Johnson Years* (University of Texas Press, 1981)].

———, ed. *The Johnson Years, Volume Two: Vietnam, the Environment, and Science.* Lawrence: University Press of Kansas, 1987.

Dixler, E. "Back to the 1960s [Hofstra University Conference on the Johnson Presidency]." *Nation* 242 (April 26, 1986): 573–74.

Driscoll, Tom. "LBJ—Our Top Helicopter Commuter: Rotors Are Familiar Sight over the White House." *Rotor & Wing,* December 1967: 10–17.

Dunlap, Carol. "LBJ and Dorris Kearns." *Parade* [*Houston Post*], November 14, 1971: 4–7.

Edwards, George C. *The Public Presidency: The Pursuit of Popular Support.* New York: St. Martin's Press, 1983.

"An End—a Beginning: President Johnson's First Week—Special Issue." *Newsweek*, December 9, 1963: 19–48.

"The Fabled Past: Painter of Presidents [Elizabeth Shounatoff]." *The North Shore Journal* [Locust Valley, New York Leader Supplement] 16 (August 29, 1985): all.

Fallows, James. "Friendly Persuasion: What LBJ Did Best Was Deal." *Texas Monthly* 4 (July 1976): 24–26+.

"Fashion Czar in the White House: President Johnson Sets Style of His Own." *Business Week*, March 21, 1964: 94+.

Fenyvesi, Charles. "Lyndon Johnson, Greatness and Tragedy." *National Jewish Monthly* 87 (February 1973): 22.

Fishel, Jeff. *Presidents and Promises: From Campaign Pledge to Presidential Performance*. Washington, D.C.: Congressional Quarterly Service, 1985.

"The Flying White House [Air Force One]." *Look* 28 (June 2, 1964): 86–96.

Freeman, O. "The Public Philosophy of the Kennedy/Johnson Presidencies." *The Virginia Papers on the Presidency: The White Burkett Miller Center Forums, Vol. 16, Part I*, edited by Kenneth W. Thompson, pp. 101–26. Lanham, Md.: University Press of America, 1984.

Goldman, Eric. *Meet the Press: Guest, Eric Goldman, Author of "The Tragedy of Lyndon Johnson"* (Interview). Washington, D.C.: Merkle Press, vol. 13, no. 6, 1969.

Goldsmith, William M. *The Growth of Presidential Power*. Vol. 3. *Triumph and Reappraisal*. New York: Chelsea, 1974.

Greenfield, Meg. "The Fine Art of President-Baiting [Reviews Anti-Johnsonian Literature]." *Reporter* 31 (September 24, 1964): 29–33.

Grogan, F. L. "Candidate Promises and Presidential Performance, 1964–1972." Paper presented at the Midwest Political Science Assn. meeting, April 21, 1977 (place unknown).

Halberstam, David. "Lyndon." *Esquire* 77 (August 1972): 73–78.

Hall, Chester Gordon, Jr. "The United States Civil Service Commission: Arm of the President or of Congress?" Washington, D.C.: American University, 1965. Ph.D. dissertation. University Microfilms No. 65-9930.

Hamby, Alonzo L. *Liberalism and Its Challengers: F.D.R. to Reagan*. New York: Oxford University Press, 1985.

Hardesty, Robert L. *The LBJ the Nation Seldom Saw.* San Marcos: Southwest Texas State University and Southwest Texas Development Foundation, August 27, 1983.
Harris, Irving D. "The Psychologies of Presidents." *History of Childhood Quarterly* 3 (Winter 1976): 337–50.
Hart, Roderick. *Verbal Style and the Presidency.* Human Communication Research Series. New York: Academic Press, Harcourt, Brace Jovanovich, 1984.
Harvey, Paul. "Billy Graham and LBJ." *Human Events* 27 (September 30, 1967): 11.
"Him and Her: *Life* Visits with the White House Beagles." *Life,* June 19, 1964: 68A–70, 73.
"Honorary Degree." *The Alcalde* (University of Texas) 53 (September 1964): 12–15.
"How Congressmen Rate the New President." *U.S. News and World Report* 55 (December 9, 1963): 78–83.
"How LBJ is Doing His Job." *U.S. News and World Report,* August 3, 1964, pp. 34–37.
"How the President Feels about His Troubles: War in Vietnam, Crisis in the Cities, Budget Troubles, Rebellious Congress, Loss of Popularity." *U.S. News and World Report* 63 (September 18, 1967): 50–51.
"How Things Are Changing for LBJ: An Administration That Was Riding High Has Started to Encounter Obstacles, Frustrations, and Reversals." *U.S. News and World Report* 60 (June 6, 1966): 40–43.
"'I Am More Liberal than Eleanor Roosevelt'—Johnson." *Human Events* 23 (July 11, 1964): 10.
"Inside the White House." *Newsweek,* March 1, 1967: 27–29.
Jetton, Walter, with Arthur Whitman. "The LBJ Barbeque Cook Book: The Favorite Tastes of Our Leading Citizen." *This Week Magazine* [*Washington Sunday Star*], June 6, 1965: 8–10.
"Johnson Dresses Down: Inauguration." *Business Week,* December 19, 1964: 30.
"'Johnson Era' about to Begin." *Human Events* 24 (December 26, 1964): 15.
"Johnson Sets His Course: The New President Quickly Laid Down Guidelines for 1964." *U.S. News and World Report* 55 (December 6, 1963): 35–36.

"The Johnson Years: A Look at the Record." *U.S. News and World Report* 64 (April 15, 1968): 46–47.

"The Johnsons in the White House." *Look* 28 (March 10, 1964): 15–23.

Jordan, Barbara. "LBJ: An Atypical Texan in Washington." Keynote Address, Fifth Annual Hofstra University Presidential Conference: Lyndon Baines Johnson, A Texan in Washington. Hempstead, New York, April 10–12, 1986.

Kaye, Tony. *Lyndon Johnson.* World Leaders Past and Present Series. Edgemont, Penn.: Chelsea House, 1988.

Kellerman, Barbara. *The Political Presidency: Practice of Leadership from Kennedy to Reagan.* New York: Oxford University Press, 1984.

Kenen, Isaiah L. "Analysis: Lyndon Baines Johnson." *Near East Report* 17 (January 31, 1973): 18–19.

Kettl, Donald F. *Leadership at the FED.* New Haven, Conn.: Yale University Press, 1986.

———. *The Regulation of American Federalism.* Baton Rouge: Louisiana State University Press, 1984.

Kilpatrick, James Jackson. "LBJ Must Be Happy to See Old Year Out." *Human Events* 27 (January 7, 1967): 14.

Kluckhorn, Frank. "'FDR Was a Second Daddy to Me,' Said LBJ" *Human Events* 24 (July 11, 1964): 5.

Knoll, Erwin. "The Legacy of LBJ." *Progressive* 33 (January 1969): 17–20.

Koontz, Hilda E. "Transition [in the History of National City Christian Church] and the Presidential Years." *National City Promise,* Summer 1985: 14.

Kress, Paul F. "LBJ—A Review Essay." *Southern Humanities Review* 18 (Summer 1984): 245–55.

Krock, Arthur. "Impressions of Johnson, the Kennedys, and Today's Government" (Interview). *U.S. News and World Report* 61 (December 19, 1966): 44–49.

Kurland, Gerald. *Lyndon Baines Johnson: President Caught in an Ordeal of Power.* Outstanding Personality Series, no. 24. Charlotteville, N.Y.: Smaller Press, 1972.

"The Last 100 Days." *Newsweek* 76 (August 24, 1970): 68.

"LBJ: Behind the Smile and Handshakes." *Human Events and Special Edition* 24 (July 11, 1964): all.

"LBJ: 'One-Term' President?" *Human Events* 26 (February 26, 1966): 5.

"LBJ: The Operator." *Human Events* 24 (October 3, 1964): 13.
"LBJ: Rides a Horse Named 'Lady B'." *Life*, July 31, 1964: 24B.
"LBJ as President: 'I Believe It Will Be Said That We Tried'." *U.S. News and World Report* 74 (February 5, 1973): 72–75.
"LBJ Glimpses the Millennium." *Human Events* 24 (May 9, 1964): 1.
"LBJ's Economy Image." *Human Events* 22 (December 28, 1963): 4.
"LBJ's Many Ways of Free-Wheeling." *Human Events* 24 (April 25, 1964): 11.
"LBJ's Mood in Time of Trouble: Associates, Personal Friends, and Impartial Observers Provide a Composite Closeup of LBJ Today." *U.S. News and World Report* 64 (April 8, 1968): 68–70.
"LBJ's '100 Days'—A Record Piling Up." *U.S. News and World Report* 58 (April 26, 1965): 41–44.
"LBJ's *The Vantage Point*: A Review Symposium; Three Views. *Social Science Quarterly* 53 (September 1972): 396–416.
"LBJ's Way of Operating: What Makes It Different." *U.S. News and World Report* 56 (January 13, 1964): 35–37.
Lemann, Nicholas. "Mah 'fellummurrukuns.'" *Texas Monthly* 14 (January 1986): 178.
Leuchtenburg, William E. *In the Shadow of FDR: From Harry Truman to Ronald Reagan*. Ithaca, N.Y.: Cornell University Press, 1983.
Lewis, Ted. "The Thousand Days of LBJ: An Appraisal." *Human Events* 26 (September 17, 1966): 12.
Lichtenstein, Nelson, ed., Eleanora W. Schoenebaum, and Michael L. Levine, assoc. eds. *Political Profiles: The Johnson Years*. New York: Facts on File, Inc., 1976.
"Light Bulb Lyndon: A Phony Economizer." *Human Events* 24 (July 11, 1964): 21.
"Lyndon B. Johnson: A Presidency Tempered in Congress." *Congressional Quarterly Weekly Report* 31 (January 27, 1973): 124–29.
"Lyndon Johnson: The Ringmaster." *Human Events* 25 (April 17, 1965): 2.
"The Lyndon Johnson Touch: A New Personal Impress." *Round Table* (Great Britain), June 1964: 255–61.
"The Man Who is Chief: President Johnson is Little Understood, Shines as a Bargainer and Decision-Maker, Looks on

Himself as a Doer More than a Thinker." *Business Week*, November 30, 1963: 25–26.

Martin, Ralph G. *A Hero for Our Time*. New York: Macmillan, 1983.

Matusow, Allen J. *The Unraveling of America: A History of Liberalism in the 1960s*. The New American Nation Series. New York: Harper and Row, 1984.

McCarthy, Dennis V. N., with Philip W. Smith. *Protecting the President: The Insider Story of a Secret Service Agent*. New York: Morrow, 1985.

McDonald, Archie P., comp. *The Texas Experience*. College Station: Texas A&M University Press, 1986.

McQuaid, Kim. *Big Business and Presidential Power: From FDR to Reagan*. New York: William Morrow, 1982.

McReynolds, David. "Johnson: Liberal at Home, Conservative Abroad." *Saturday Night* (Canada) 80 (June 1965): 19–21.

McWilliams, Carey. "The Bitter Legacy of LBJ." *Nation*, September 9, 1968: 198–201.

Miller, Arthur. "Political Issues and Trust in Government: 1964–1970." *American Political Science Review* 68 (September 1974): 951–72.

"Mixed Praises for LBJ's Hundred Days." *Life* 56 (February 28, 1964): 4.

Moley, Raymond. "The Great Prestidigitator: LBJ Finds 'Problems,' Invents 'Solutions'." *Human Events* 27 (October 21, 1967): 12.

Moyers, Bill D. "Second Thoughts." Banquet address, Fifth Annual Hofstra University Presidential Conference: Lyndon Baines Johnson, A Texan in Washington. Hempstead, New York, April 10–12, 1986.

Neustadt, Richard E. "How LBJ is Doing His Job." *U.S. News and World Report* 57 (August 3, 1964): 34–37.

———, and Ernest R. May. *Thinking in Time: The Uses of History for Decision-Makers*. New York: Free Press, 1986.

"The New Era in Washington: Its Meaning—The Goals Johnson Will Set for the Country." *U.S. News and World Report* 55 (December 9, 1963): 35–37.

"New Frontier Policies to be Continued by Johnson." *Public Utilities Fortnightly* 72 (December 19, 1963): 50–51.

"New Surgery for the President—Facts about LBJ's Health."

U.S. News and World Report 61 (November 14, 1966): 48–49.

"New Twists to the 'Johnson Revolution'." *Human Events* 26 (January 22, 1966): 1, 10.

"Next for LBJ—'Agonizing Reappraisal': Problems Come Home to Roost—War, Racial Strife, Deficit, Troubles with Congress, Allies, and the Dollar." *U.S. News and World Report* 63 (August 14, 1967): 32–34.

"Now the Trumpet Summons Again: The Whole World Changed When Clocks Showed 12:30 P.M. in Dallas." *Business Week*, November 30, 1963: 21–24.

Polsby, Nelson W. *Congress and the Presidency*. 3rd ed. Englewood Cliffs, N.J.: Prentice-Hall, 1976.

"The President Is Sworn In." *Texas Observer*, November 29, 1963: 7.

"President Johnson: Man on the Spot." *This Is Why*, No. 113, August 1967.

"President Johnson at War with Himself." *Human Events* 24 (June 27, 1964): 1.

"President Johnson's Book [*My Hope for America*] Is U.S. Literary First." *Publisher's Weekly* 186 (September 21, 1964): 37.

"President Johnson's Frontiers." *Texas Observer*, November 29, 1963: 8+.

"President's Club: The New Elite." *Human Events* 25 (June 19, 1965): 14.

"A President's Health: It's Meaning to the Nation." *U.S. News and World Report* 59 (October 18, 1965): 33–36.

"President's State of Adversity: Political, Social and Economic Pressures on the Johnson Administration." *Economist* (Great Britain) 226 (January 20, 1968): 20+.

"Ready—In His Own Right: Preaching Prudence and Reasonableness, President Johnson Starts His First Full Term." *Business Week*, December 26, 1964: 11–13.

Reedy, George E. "Lyndon Baines Johnson: Politician and Communicator." *Virginia Papers on the Presidency: The White Burkett Miller Center Forums, Vol. 12, Part 1*, edited by Kenneth W. Thompson, pp. 29–48. Lanham, Md.: University Press of America, 1983.

———. *The Twilight of the Presidency*. New York: World Press, 1970.

Riccards, Michael P. "Failure of Nerve: How the Liberals Killed

Liberalism." Paper presented at Fifth Annual Hofstra University Presidential Conference: Lyndon Baines Johnson, A Texan in Washington. Hempstead, New York, April 10–12, 1986.

Riesel, Victor. "Reuther Closer to LBJ Than He Was to JFK." *Human Events* 24 (March 14, 1964): 8.

Schlesinger, Arthur M., Jr. "What Kind of President Will Johnson Make?" *U.S. News and World Report* 57 (November 16, 1964): 53–55.

———, and Robert Burns, eds. *Congress Investigates: A Documentary History, 1792–1974.* 5 vols. New York: Chelsea House, 1983.

Schott, Richard L., and Dagmar S. Hamilton. *People, Positions, and Power: The Political Appointments of Lyndon Johnson.* Chicago: University of Chicago Press, 1983.

Schuyler, Michael. "The Bitter Harvest: Lyndon B. Johnson and the Assassination of John F. Kennedy." *Journal of American Culture* 8 (Fall 1985): 101–09.

Sclanders, Ian. "Year One of the Johnson Era." *MacLean's* (Canada) 78 (March 20, 1965): 13–16+.

Shannon, William V. "LBJ: The First Six Months." *Hadassah Magazine* 46 (June 1965): 3+.

Shinn, Roger L. "The Hate-Johnson Syndrome." *Christianity and Crisis* 27 (July 10, 1967): 157–58.

Shogan, Robert. *None of the Above: Why Presidents Fail—And What Can Be Done about It.* New York: New American Library, 1982.

Sidey, Hugh, and Yoichi Okamato. "The President's Private Reserve—An Intimate Portfolio: Johnson in the White House." *Life* (Special Issue: The Presidency) 65 (July 5, 1968): 32–50.

Siegel, Frederick F. *Troubled Journey: From Pearl Harbor to Ronald Reagan.* New York: Hill and Wang, 1984.

Soloveytchik, George. "President Johnson's Problems." *Contemporary Review* 209 (September 1966): 120–26.

"Some Like LBJ, Some Don't." *Human Events* 24 (October 7, 1964): 11.

"Some Texans on LBJ." *Texas Observer*, November 13, 1964: 8.

Steele, John L. "The Texan Sits Tall in the Saddle: Johnson on the Job." *Life* 55 (December 13, 1965): 26–35.

Stern, Laurence M. "Lyndon Johnson Today." *Progressive* 29 (September 1965): 13–15.

Stewart, Malcolm. "Domestic and International Policy as the Johnson Administration Goes into High Gear." *Magazine of Wall Street* 113 (December 14, 1963): 298–301+.
Stone, I. F. *I. F. Stone's Weekly, 1953–1971.* Millwood, N.Y.: Krause Reprint and Periodicals.
"The Story of Johnson's Health: Report from Medical Authorities." *U.S. News and World Report* 56 (January 27, 1964): 40–42.
Strout, Richard L. "T.R.B. from Washington: The Johnson Style." *New Republic,* December 7, 1963: 2+.
———. *TRB: Views and Perspectives on the Presidency.* New York: Macmillan, 1979.
"Surgery Renews Interest in Disability Question [President Johnson's Past and Present Health Record]." *Congressional Quarterly Weekly Report* 23 (October 8, 1965): 2049–52.
Sweeney, Paul. "LBJ's Other Legacy." *Third Coast* 4 (June 1985): 41.
Tatalovich, Raymond, and Byron W. Daynes. *Presidential Power in the United States.* Monterey, Cal.: Brooks/Cole, 1984.
Texas Monthly Magazine. *Texas Our Texas: 150 Moments That Made Us the Way We Are.* Austin: Texas Monthly Press, 1986.
Thompson, Kenneth W., ed. *The American Presidency: Principles and Problems Series.* 3 vols. Lanham, Md.: University Press of America; and Charlottesville: White Burkett Miller Center, University of Virginia, 1982–84.
———, ed. *The Johnson Presidency: Twenty Intimate Perspectives of Lyndon B. Johnson.* Portraits of American Presidents Series, vol. 5. Lanham, Md.: University Press of America, 1986. Charlottesville: White Burkett Miller Center, University of Virginia, co-publisher.
———, ed. *The Virginia Papers on the Presidency: The White Burkett Miller Center Forums.* 22 vols. Lanham, Md.: University Press of America; and Charlottesville: White Burkett Miller Center, University of Virginia, 1981–87.
"Three Weeks of Lyndon." *Human Events* 22 (December 21, 1963): 4.
Trohan, Walter. "The New Status Symbol: "Skinny-Dippin' with LBJ." *Human Events* 23 (February 15, 1964): 6.
Tyerman, D. "New Deal on the New Frontier: Kennedy-John-

son Washington Atmosphere Compared." *Economist* (Great Britain) 217 (November 6, 1965): 583–84.

Tyler, Gus, Roger Kingsbury, and George F. Gilder. "Johnson's Moment in History." *New Leader* 51 (April 8, 1968): 3–9.

"Unions Voice Grief, Rally to President Johnson." *AFL-CIO News* 8 (December 7, 1963): 2.

United Press International and American Heritage Magazine, comp. *Four Days: The Historical Record of the Death of President Kennedy.* New York: American Heritage Publishing Co., dist. by Simon and Schuster, 1983.

"Was There a Plot to Assassinate LBJ?" *U.S. News and World Report* 56 (April 27, 1964): 48–49.

Washington, D.C. Inaugural Committee. *Inauguration 1965 Guide Book.* Washington, D.C.: Presidential Inaugural Committee, 1965.

———. *Threshold of Tomorrow: The Great Society—The Inauguration of Lyndon Baines Johnson, 36th President of the United States and Hubert Horatio Humphrey, 38th Vice President of the United States, January 20, 1965.* Washington, D.C.: Presidential Inaugural Committee, 1965.

Ways, Max. "Intellectuals and the Presidency: Many Attacks on LBJ Are Really Aimed at a Bigger, More Permanent Target—The Nation's 'Power Structure'." *Fortune* 75 (April 1967): 146–49+.

———. "The Two Lyndon Johnsons and the U.S. of 1964." *Fortune* 69 (January 1964): 80–83+.

"What Kind of President Will Johnson Make Now?" *U.S. News and World Report,* November 16, 1964: 53–55.

"What Will LBJ Be Like as President?" *Human Events* 22 (December 7, 1963): 1–2.

"What's Right with LBJ." *Texas Observer,* February 16, 1968: 1+.

"Where's LBJ's 'Economy Government'?" *Human Events* 26 (April 23, 1966): 3.

Williams, John. "Needed: More Trust in Government." *Human Events* 26 (January 29, 1966): 8–9.

Woodward, C. Vann. *Responses of the President to Charges of Misconduct.* New York: Delacorte Press, 1974.

Wright, Lawrence. "Lyndon's Lincoln: It Isn't Just a Big White Car. It's a Symbol of the Texas Braggadocio." *Texas Monthly* 11 (February 1983): 106–07.

2. THE JOHNSON WHITE HOUSE

A. THE VICE PRESIDENT

Bowen, William. "What's New about the New Hubert Humphrey." *Fortune* 72 (August 1965): 142–45+.

Cohen, Dan. *Undefeated: The Life of Hubert Horatio Humphrey.* Minneapolis: Lerner Publications, 1978.

Cousins, Norman. "Journeys with Humphrey: Memoir of a Mission that Failed." *Saturday Review* 61 (March 4, 1978): 10–18.

Feerick, John D. *The Vice Presidents of the U.S.* 3rd ed. New York: Watts, 1977.

Fleming, Thomas J. "Selling the Product Named Hubert Humphrey." *New York Times Magazine,* October 13, 1966: 45–47, 139–51.

Goldstein, Joel K. "The American Vice-Presidency, 1953–1978." London: Oxford University, 1978. Ph.D. dissertation.

"HEW—Humphrey Feuding Moves into the White House." *Oil, Paint, and Drug Reporter* 185 (January 13, 1964): 3+.

"How Will Industry Fare under the Next Vice President?" *Steel* 155 (September 7, 1964): 27–28.

"Humphrey: A Strong No. 2—A Leader in His Own Right." *Business Week,* November 13, 1965: 175–76+.

"Humphrey Gets a Summons to Stand In: He Will Be Acting President While Johnson Undergoes Surgery." *Business Week,* October 9, 1965: 28–29.

Humphrey, Hubert H. "Five Guidelines for the Future: Policy Statement by the Vice President of the United States." *Common Market* 7 (May 1967): 103–08.

———. "Humphrey Looks at His Future: An Interview with the Vice President." *U.S. News and World Report* 64 (May 27, 1968): 54–60.

———. *Meet the Press: Guest, Hubert H. Humphrey, the Vice President of the United States* (Interview). Washington, D.C.: Merkle Press, vol. 10, no. 11, 1966.

———. *Meet the Press: Guest, Hubert H. Humphrey, the Vice President of the United States* (Interview). Washington, D.C.: Merkle Press, vol. 11, no. 48, 1967.

———. *Meet the Press: Guest, The Honorable Hubert H. Humphrey, the Vice President of the United States* (Interview). Washington, D.C.: Merkle Press, vol. 10, no. 44, 1966.

———. "A Small Revolution [in Federal, State, Local Government Relationships]." *American County Government* 31 (September 1966): 20–21+.

———. *The Vice Presidency: A Conversation with Hubert H. Humphrey* (Interview). New York: National Education Television Transcript, April 1965.

———. "What I Expect of Congress." *Nation's Business* 52 (December 1964): 33+.

Meryman, Richard. "Hubert Humphrey Talks His Self-Portrait." *Life*, September 27, 1968: 22B-31.

Nixon, Richard M. "We Need a Vice Presidency Now." *Saturday Evening Post* 237 (January 18, 1964): 6.

Oberdorfer, Don. "The Job [House Speaker] John McCormack Dreads." *Saturday Evening Post*, March 21, 1964: 66–68.

Ryskind, Allan H. *Hubert, An Unauthorized Biography of the Vice President*. New Rochelle: Arlington House, 1968.

"Size-Up of New 'Vice President' [House Speaker McCormack]." *U.S. News and World Report*, December 30, 1963: 26–27.

Solberg, Carl. *Hubert Humphrey: A Political Biography*. New York: Norton, 1984.

"The Succession: A Heartbeat Away [House Speaker McCormack]." *Newsweek*, December 16, 1963: 23–24.

"Unrest and Revolt—Humphrey's Views." *U.S. News and World Report* 61 (August 14, 1967): 10.

Wechsler, James A. "Humphrey at War with Himself." *Progressive* 30 (July 1966): 10–13.

"What Sort of President Would [House Speaker] McCormack Make?" *Esquire* 62 (July 1964): 90–93.

"What the New No. 2 Man Is Really Like." *U.S. News and World Report* 58 (January 25, 1965): 41–43.

"Why Humphrey Didn't Go [Why LBJ Didn't Send Humphrey to Represent U.S. at Funeral of Sir Winston Churchill]." *U.S. News and World Report* 58 (February 15, 1965): 53–54.

B. THE CABINET

Agnew, B. "Key Men of the New Department of Transportation." *Fleet Owner* 62 (May 1967): 69–75.

Alexander, Holmes. "John Connor, New Commerce Head." *Human Events* 25 (January 30, 1965): 14.

"Anti-Trust Gets New Gospel: Donald F. Turner is Division's New Chief." *Business Week,* August 14, 1965: 27.

Ball, George W. *The Discipline of Power.* Boston: Atlantic-Little, Brown, 1968.

———. *Meet the Press: Guest, George W. Ball, the Under-Secretary of State* (Interview). Washington, D.C.: Merkle Press, vol. 8, no. 7, 1964.

———. *The Past Has Another Pattern: Memoirs.* New York: Norton, 1982.

"Banking's Spotlight on Dixon Donnelley: Assistant to the Secretary of Treasury." *Banking* 58 (January 1966): 58+.

"Banking's Spotlight on Donald Frank Turner: Assistant Attorney General in Charge of Anti-Trust Division." *Banking* 58 (August 1965): 56+.

"Banking's Spotlight on Franklin Robert Saul: New Assistant to the Secretary of Treasury." *Banking* 58 (October 1965): 48.

"Banking's Spotlight on Frederick Lewis Deming—New Treasury Under Secretary for Monetary Affairs." *Banking* 57 (February 1965): 45.

"Banking's Spotlight on Henry Hamill Fowler—Secretary of Treasury." *Banking* 57 (May 1965): 49.

"Banking's Spotlight on John Thomas Connor: Secretary of Commerce." *Banking* 58 (December 1965): 43–44.

"Banking's Spotlight on Joseph M. Bowman—Treasury's Congressional Liaison." *Banking* 56 (June 1964): 50.

"Banking's Spotlight on Peter D. Sternlight: Deputy Under-Secretary of the Treasury for Monetary Affairs." *Banking* 58 (March 1966): 60.

Banks, Louis. "Economy under New Management: Secretary of the Treasury H. H. Fowler." *Fortune* 71 (May 1965): 96–99+.

Barclay, H. W. "McNamara at Work." *Automotive Industries* 135 (December 1, 1966): 19–21.

Best, James J. "Presidential Cabinet Appointments:

1953–1976." *Presidential Studies Quarterly* 11 (Winter 1981): 62–66.

Borklund, Carl W. *Men of the Pentagon: From Forrestal to McNamara.* New York: Praeger, 1966.

Boyd, Alan S. "The Proposed Department of Transportation." *Traffic Quarterly* 20 (July 1966): 311–21.

Brown, Harold. *Meet the Press: Guest, Dr. Harold Brown, Secretary of the Air Force* (Interview). Washington, D.C.: Merkle Press, vol. 10, no. 21, 1966.

Bundy, William P. *Meet the Press: Guest, William P. Bundy, Assistant Secretary of State for East Asian and Pacific Affairs* (Interview). Washington, D.C.: Merkle Press, vol. 11, no. 35, 1967.

"Cabinet-Level Trips to Moscow Part of 'Bridge-Building' Plans." *Human Events* 27 (March 18, 1967): 13.

"Changes to Watch for in the Cabinet." *U.S. News and World Report* 55 (December 2, 1963): 42.

Clark, Ramsey. *Meet the Press: Guest, Ramsey Clark, Attorney General of the United States* (Interview). Washington, D.C.: Merkle Press, vol. 12, no. 8, 1968.

Cohen, S. E. "Commerce Department Moves to Play More Active Role in Aiding Business." *Advertising Age* 38 (January 23, 1967): 4+.

———. "Connor Is Key Influence in Making Regulation of Business More Flexible." *Advertising Age* 37 (May 2, 1966): 4+.

———. "LBJ's Cabinet Merger Proposal Stirs Reappraisal of Commerce Department's Role." *Advertising Age* 38 (January 23, 1967): 4+.

"Commerce Post Goes to Connor." *Business Week*, December 19, 1964: 30.

Connolly, R. "McNamara's Fading Magic." *Electronic News* 12 (January 9, 1967): 21.

"Connor: How He Works for Business." *Nation's Business*, 53 (November 1965): 36–37+.

Connor, John Thomas. "Evolution of a Business and Government Partnership." *Iron Age* 196 (August 26, 1965): 60–63.

Day, J. Edward. "When in Washington, Hang Up While You're Talking: Former Cabinet Member Offers Some Slightly Irreverent Views in His Orientation for Innocents." *Nation's Business* 53 (July 1965): 38–39+.

De Toledano, Ralph. "LBJ's 'Little List' of Cabinet Changes." *Human Events* 27 (December 23, 1967): 8.

"TFX: Scandal That Won't Die [McNamara]." *Human Events* 27 (August 26, 1967): 7.

"Did the 'Whiz Kids' Flunk Their Arms Test?" *U.S. News and World Report* 60 (April 25, 1966): 40–42.

"An Educator Takes on Problem Pupil—HEW: John W. Gardner Shoulders the Mammoth Catch-All Health, Education and Welfare Department." *Business Week*, August 14, 1965: 32+.

Elson, Robert R. "An 'In' Man for the Cabinet: John W. Gardner Is Secretary of Health, Education and Welfare." *Fortune* 72 (October 1965): 154–57.

"Fight All the Way: Plan to Establish a Department of Transportation." *Forbes Magazine* 98 (August 15, 1966): 41–42+.

Finnegan, G. B. "Budgeting à la McNamara: Defense Department System to be Model for All Federal Agencies." *Journal of Accountancy* 121 (February 1966): 14+.

"First Secretary of HUD, R. C. Weaver." *Engineering News-Record* 176 (March 3, 1966): 13.

"Focus on 1964: Cold War Strategists Predict New Moves." *Nation's Business* 51 (December 1963): 60–68.

"For McNamara, a Rougher Round [regarding Vietnam]." *Business Week*, February 19, 1966: 162–64+.

"Four Get New Posts from LBJ: Donald F. Turner to Head Justice Department's Anti-Trust Division." *Business Week*, May 1, 1965: 26–27.

Fowler, Henry H. *Meet the Press: Guest, Henry H. Fowler, Secretary of the Treasury* (Interview). Washington, D.C.: Merkle Press, vol. 9, no. 15, 1965.

Frankel, Max. "The President's 'Just-A-Minute Man'—Dean Rusk." *New York Times Magazine*, September 12, 1965: 48–49, 148–156.

Freeburg, Russell. "Fowler: A Surprise Choice for the Post [Secretary of Treasury]." *Finance* 83 (April 1965): 27–28+.

Gardner, John W. "'Integrating' America—The Problems: Interview with John W. Gardner, Secretary of Health, Education and Welfare." *U.S. News and World Report* 62 (May 8, 1967): 64–69.

———. *Meet the Press: Guest, John W. Gardner, Secretary of*

Health, Education and Welfare (Interview). Washington, D.C.: Merkle Press, vol. 11, no. 52, 1967.

"The 'Get Rusk' Movement—Is It Aimed at LBJ?" *U.S. News and World Report* 63 (November 20, 1967): 51–52.

"Good Hard Look for Department of Justice Head: Harvard Professor Is Named Top Anti-Truster: Donald F. Turner." *National Petroleum News* 57 (June 1965): 86.

"The Great Society's Advance Man: Robert Weaver, First Negro Member of Cabinet, Will Head New Housing and Urban Development Department." *Business Week*, January 22, 1966: 51–52.

Green, Harry A. "Bureaucracy and Functional Representation: A Critique of the [Department of] Urban Affairs Controversy." *Research Reports in Social Science* 8 (February 1965): 1–18.

Halberstam, David. "The Programming of Robert McNamara." *Harper's Magazine* 242 (February 1971): 37–71.

Henry, John B. II. "February, 1968 [Tet Offensive]." *Foreign Policy*, no. 4, Fall 1971: 3–33.

Holton, R., and S. E. Cohen. "Consumer Unit Doesn't Belong in Cabinet." *Advertising Age* 37 (December 12, 1966): 128.

"House Votes Transportation Department Bill." *Congressional Quarterly Weekly Report* 24 (September 2, 1966): 1881–84.

"How the White House Is Changing: Kennedy Team Adjusts to Johnson Style." *U.S. News and World Report* 55 (December 23, 1963): 34–36.

"How to Prevent a Nuclear War: Warning to America by Joint Chiefs of Staff Challenging McNamara over whether U.S. Should Build a Defense against Nuclear Attack." *U.S. News and World Report* 62 (May 15, 1967): 31–33.

"How Will Clark Tip the Scales? New Top Man at Justice Department, Attorney General Ramsey Clark." *Business Week*, March 11, 1967: 160+.

Hoxie, R. Gordon. "The Cabinet in the American Presidency, 1789–1984." *Presidential Studies Quarterly* 14 (Spring 1984): 209–30.

Jefferis, Frank, and Bruce Byron. "Case History Surrounding the Legislative Bill to Establish a Department of Transportation." Course paper, Professor Richard Schott, LBJ School of Public Affairs, February 12, 1975 [c/o LBJ Library].

"Job for a New Department: Safer Cars, Fewer Traffic Jams,

Faster Planes, Better Ships [LBJ's Proposed Transportation Department]." *U.S. News and World Report* 60 (March 14, 1966): 39–40.

"Johnson Gets a Fence Mender: C.R. Smith, Secretary of Commerce." *Business Week*, February 24, 1968: 46.

Katzenbach, Nicholas DeB., et al. *Meet the Press—Special Edition: Guests, Nicholas DeB. Katzenbach, Chairman, President's Commission on Law Enforcement and Administration of Justice* [and Five other Members of the Commission] (Interviews). Washington, D.C.: Merkle Press, February 19, 1967.

Kennedy, Ross A. "Dissent and Decision-Making: A Study of George Ball's and John McNaughton's Opposition to the Vietnam War." *Fletcher Forum* 9 (Winter 1985): 69–104.

"Key Men in Defense." *U.S. News and World Report* 64 (January 1, 1968): 26–28.

Kiker, Douglas. "The Education of Robert McNamara." *Atlantic Monthly* 219 (March 1967): 49–55.

King, James D., and James W. Riddlesperger, Jr. "Presidential Appointments to the Cabinet, Executive Office, and White House Staff." *Presidential Studies Quarterly* 16 (Fall 1986): 691–99.

Kraft, Joseph. "Washington Insight: The Enigma of Dean Rusk." *Harper's Magazine* 231 (July 1965): 100–03.

Lalli, F. "Weaver's Frustrating Year: Errors, Politics Mar HUD Start." *House and Home* 29 (October 1966): 12 +.

"LBJ Hails a New Era for U.S. Transportation." *Railway Age*. 162 (April 10, 1967): 26–27.

"LBJ Joins Narcotics, Abuse Bureaus under Justice Department." *American Druggist* 157 (February 26, 1968): 17–18.

"LBJ's Department of Transportation and Highway Safety Proposals." *Fleet Owner* 61 (April 1966): 86–93.

"LBJ's Farm Secretary Blamed for Income Drop." *Human Events* 24 (July 11, 1964): 23.

Lewis, Ted. "McNamara Case Puts Johnson in Deep Water: Secrecy Fetish Backfires [World Bank Appointment]." *Human Events* 27 (December 9, 1967): 1.

Lowi, Theodore J. "Why Merge Commerce and Labor?" *Challenge* 15 (July/August 1967): 12–15.

"Mac the Knifed [Defense Secretary McNamara]." *Human Events* 27 (December 9, 1967): 4.

Mann, Dean E., with Jameson W. Doig. *Assistant Secretaries: Problems and Processes of Appointment.* Washington, D.C.: Brookings Institute, 1965.

Marrow, A. J. "Managerial Revolution in the State Department." *Personnel* 43 (November 1966): 8–18.

Martin, Janet Marie. "Cabinet Secretaries from Truman to Johnson: An Examination of Theoretical Frameworks for Cabinet Studies." Columbus: Ohio State University, 1985. Ph.D. dissertation. University Microfilms No. 8526212.

"McNamara—From Sword to Ploughshare." *Economist* (Great Britain) 225 (December 2, 1967): 955–56.

"McNamara Scales Down His Buying." *Business Week,* July 16, 1966: 34.

"McNamara's Impact on Defense Policies." *Congressional Quarterly Weekly Report* 25 (December 1, 1967): 2437–45.

Meyers, Harold B. "Professor Turner's Turn at Anti-Trust [Assistant Attorney General]." *Fortune* 72 (September 1965): 168–71+.

Moley, Raymond. "Who Has the President's Ear? White House Staff vs. Cabinet." *Human Events* 27 (March 4, 1967): 6.

Moynihan, Daniel Patrick, ed. *The Defenses of Freedom: The Public Papers of Arthur J. Goldberg.* New York: Harper and Row, 1966.

"New Double Yoke for Labor and Commerce." *Business Week,* January 14, 1967: 140.

"New Look Coming in Commerce Department: J. T. Connor, New Secretary." *Steel* 156 (January 18, 1965): 29.

"New Secretary of Commerce." *Fortune* 71 (February 1965): 47.

"New Voice on Economic Policy: President's Bid to Merge Commerce and Labor Departments." *Business Week,* February 18, 1967: 157–58+.

Norton, Hugh S. "The Department of Transportation: A Study of Organizational Futility." *Public Utilities Fortnightly* 78 (December 22, 1966): 19–25.

O'Brien, Lawrence F. "From White House to Capitol: How Things Get Done—Interview with the Newest Member of the Cabinet [Special Assistant to the President for Congressional Affairs, Lawrence F. O'Brien]." *U.S. News and World Report* 59 (September 20, 1965): 68–73.

———. "Larry O'Brien Discusses White House Contacts with Capitol Hill" (Interview). *Congressional Quarterly Weekly Report* 23 (July 23, 1965): 1434–36.

Pfiffner, James W. "White House Staff Versus the Cabinet: Centripetal and Centrifugal Roles." *Presidential Studies Quarterly* 16 (Fall 1986): 666–90.

Powers, Richard Gid. *Secrecy and Power: The Life of J. Edgar Hoover.* New York: Free Press, 1986.

"Pres. Johnson Orders Transfer of U.S. Community Relations Service from Commerce Dept. to Justice Dept." *AFL-CIO News* 11 (February 19, 1966): 4.

"President Signs Transportation Department Bill: Provisions." *Congressional Quarterly Weekly Report* 24 (October 21, 1966): 2573+.

"Prime Movers of the Great Society: Secretary of Health, Education, and Welfare J. W. Gardner." *Business Week*, May 21, 1966: 130–32+.

"Program of Department of Commerce for Business Concerns under the President's Balance-of-Payments Program." *Federal Reserve New York Monthly Review* 47 (April 1965): 93–95.

"Pros and Cons of Proposed Merger of Commerce, Labor Departments." *Steel* 160 (January 23, 1967): 56–57.

Raines, Edgar F., Jr., and Maj. David R. Campbell. *The Army and the Joint Chiefs of Staff: Evolution of Army Ideas on the Command, Control, and Coordination of the U.S. Armed Forces, 1942–1985.* Washington, D.C.: Analysis Branch, U.S. Army Center of Military History, 1985.

Reilly, Richard L. "Alan S. Boyd: A Profile of the Head of the Important New Department of Transportation." *Highway User*, December 1966: 20–22.

Riesel, Victor. "Johnson's Unknown Ace Trouble-Shooter Is New Secretary of Labor in 'Shadow Cabinet'." *Human Events* 24 (October 17, 1964): 3.

———. "Secret Treasury Task Force Works on Labor-Commerce Merger: Department of Economic Resources." *Human Events* 27 (February 11, 1967): 10.

"Road Looks Open for Johnson Plan for Department of Transportation." *Business Week*, March 12, 1966: 105.

Roherty, James M. *Decisions of Robert S. McNamara: A Study of the Role of the Secretary of Defense.* Coral Gables, Fla.: University of Miami Press, 1970.

Rosen, Gerald R. "Can (Acting Secretary) Alexander Trowbridge Change Commerce?" *Dun's Review and Modern Industry* 90 (August 1967): 33–34+.

Rusk, Dean. *Meet the Press: Guest, Dean Rusk, Secretary of State* (Interview). Washington, D.C.: Merkle Press, vol. 8, no. 31, 1964; vol. 9, no. 20, 1965.
———. *Meet the Press: Guest, The Honorable Dean Rusk, Secretary of State* (Interview). Washington, D.C.: Merkle Press, vol. 10, no. 4, 1966.
———. *Meet the Press: Guest, Honorable Dean Rusk, Secretary of State* (Interview). Washington, D.C.: Merkle Press, vol. 11, no. 16, 1967.
Ryskind, Allan H. "LBJ's Defense Trademark: 'Made by Melman'?" *Human Events* 24 (February 29, 1964): 7.
"Sec. of HEW John W. Gardner Says Industry Has Done Little to Fight Air Pollution." *Oil, Chemical and Atomic Union News* 22 (December 1966): 9.
"Sec. of Interior Stewart L. Udall Well Qualified for Facing Conservation Problem." *Retail Clerks Advocate* (Retail Clerks Internat'l. Assn.) 69 (August 1966): 11.
"Secretary Dillon and the Treasury: Some Achievements." *Banking* 57 (March 1965): 43+.
Seligman, Daniel. "McNamara's Management Revolution." *Fortune* 72 (July 1965): 116–20.
"Senate's Bombing Inquiry Finds McNamara at Fault." *U.S. News and World Report* 63 (September 11, 1967): 102–03.
Shapley, Deborah. *Robert McNamara: Soldier of the American Century.* New York: Morrow, 1986.
Skolnikoff, Eugene B. "Scientific Advice in the State Department." *Science,* November 25, 1966: 980–85.
Stanley, David T. *Changing Administrations: The 1961 and 1964 Transitions in Six Departments.* Washington, D.C.: Brookings Institution, 1965.
"State Department in Trouble? Bureaucratic Problems." *U.S. News and World Report* 63 (July 3, 1967): 45–47.
"State Department Personnel Transferred to Office of Economic Opportunity." *Human Events* 28 (February 24, 1968): 11.
Stern, Sol. "The Defense [Department] Intellectuals." *Ramparts* 5 (February 1967): 30–37.
"The Story of Robert McNamara: Report on Washington's Most Controversial Figure." *U.S. News and World Report* 61 (July 25, 1966): 32–38+.
"Strategic Problems Detailed by McNamara." *Aviation Week and Space Technology* 82 (March 1, 1965): 62–66.

Stupak, Donald J. "Dean Rusk on International Relations: An Analysis of His Philosophical Perspectives." *Australian Outlook* (Australia) 25 (April 1971): 13–28.

Sypher, Alden H. "They're Not Jobs for Little Men: The U.S. Cabinet." *Nation's Business* 55 (September 1967): 33–34.

Taft, Walter J. "How Alan Boyd Views His New Job: Department of Transportation Effectiveness Will Depend on Public's Support." *Railway Age* 161 (November 21, 1966): 34–35.

Taylor, Henry J. "Should Defense Secretary McNamara Resign?" *Human Events* 25 (July 25, 1965): 1.

"They All Want to Call the Shots: Transportation Industry Groups Trying to Limit the Powers of the Proposed Department of Transportation." *Business Week*, May 28, 1966: 78+.

"Transportation Cabinet Post Requested." *Public Utilities Fortnightly* 77 (March 31, 1966): 40–41.

Trask, Roger R. *The Secretaries of Defense: A Brief History, 1947–1985.* Washington, D.C.: DOD, Office of the Sec. of Defense, Historical Office, 1985.

"Treasury Gets Its Man [Henry H. Fowler]: President Picked a Man Respected by Bankers, Businessmen, Politicians." *Business Week*, March 27, 1965: 152–54.

Trewhitt, Henry L. *McNamara: His Ordeal in the Pentagon.* New York: Harper and Row, 1971.

"Trowbridge Steps Up at Commerce: President Johnson's Appointment of Alexander Trowbridge as Secretary Is Strong Indication the Idea of Merging Commerce and Labor Has Been Put Off." *Business Week*, May 27, 1967: 31.

Turner, Donald R. "Is Bigness Badness? Views of Anti-Trust Chief." *Steel* 156 (June 21, 1965): 28.

Udall, Stewart L. "We Must Save the Beauty of Our Land." *The Carpenter* (United Brotherhood of Carpenters and Joiners) 84 (April 1964): 2–5.

"Untangling the Nation's Lifeline: Alan S. Boyd, the First Secretary of Transportation." *Business Week*, November 26, 1966: 111–12+.

"Urban Cabinet Post Created by Congress: HHFA Becomes Voice of Metropolitan Centers through HUD." *National Civic Review* 54 (October 1965): 482.

Vance, Cyrus R. *Meet the Press: Guest, Cyrus R. Vance,*

Deputy Secretary of Defense (Interview). Washington, D.C.: Merkle Press, vol. 11, no. 22, 1967.

Viorst, Milton. "Incidentally, Who Is Dean Rusk?" *Esquire* 69 (April 1968): 98–101+.

"Voice for Business in U.S. Policy: Commerce Secretary John T. Connor." *Business Week*, March 13, 1965: 96–98+.

Weaver, Robert C. "The First Twenty Years of HUD." *APA Journal* [American Planning Association], Autumn 1985, pp. 463–74.

"What New Urban Department [HUD] Will Do." *U.S. News and World Report* 59 (August 30, 1965): 63.

"What the President Is Proposing: New Transportation Department." *Business Week*, January 22, 1966: 158+.

"What Went Wrong in the Pentegon: LBJ's Decision to Let Robert S. McNamara End His Seven-Year Rule over the Military." *U.S. News and World Report* 63 (December 11, 1967): 41–43.

Wheeler, Earle G. *Meet the Press: Guest, Gen. Earle G. Wheeler, Chairman, Joint Chiefs of Staff* (Interview). Washington, D.C.: Merkle Press, vol. 11, no. 9, 1967.

"The White House: New Traffic Center? The Proposed Department of Transportation." *Dun's Review and Modern Industry* 87 (May 1966): 110–12+.

"The Whiz Kid Steps Aside: Defense Secretary McNamara Leaves to Take on Job of President of World Bank." *Business*, December 2, 1967: 31–33.

"Who's to Be Who in the New Johnson Term [the Cabinet]." *U.S. News and World Report* 57 (December 21, 1964): 27–29.

Willmann, John B. *The Department of Housing and Urban Development*. New York: Praeger, 1967.

"Wirtz Emerges from 'Second Fiddle' Job: Labor Secretary Is Expected to Rise in Importance under the Johnson Administration." *Business Week*, December 21, 1963: 78–80.

"A Woman in the Cabinet?" *Human Events* 24 (December 5, 1964): 2.

Zuckert, Eugene M. "The Service Secretary: Has He a Useful Role? [The Centralization of Three Armed Services under Defense Secretary McNamara]." *Foreign Affairs* 44 (April 1966): 458–79.

C. THE WHITE HOUSE STAFF, THE EXECUTIVE OFFICE OF THE PRESIDENT, AND OTHER ADVISERS

Abelson, Philip H. "The President's Science Advisers." *Minerva* 3 (Winter 1965): 149–58.

Ackley, Gardner. "Where Business Is Heading: An Interview with the President's Top Economic Adviser" (Interview). *U.S. News and World Report* 60 (April 11, 1966): 46–52.

"Advisers to Four Presidents Explain: Where 'New Economics' Went Wrong." *U.S. News and World Report* 64 (January 15, 1968): 36–39.

Allison, David. "The Science Brains Trust." *International Science and Technology* 4 (January 1965): 61–68.

Alsop, Stewart. "Johnson Takes Over: How the New President Won His Key Fight to Keep the Kennedy Team Together." *Saturday Evening Post*, February 15, 1964: 17–23.

"The Texas Mafia Moves In [Johnson Staff]." *Saturday Evening Post*, March 21, 1964: 14.

Anderson, James E. "Presidential Management of the Bureaucracy and the Johnson Presidency: A Preliminary Exploration." *Congress and the Presidency* 11 (Autumn 1984): 137–64.

———, and Jared E. Hazleton. *Managing Macroeconomic Policy: The Johnson Presidency.* Administrative History of the Johnson Presidency Series. Austin: University of Texas Press, 1986.

Arnold, Peri E. *Making the Managerial Presidency: Comprehensive Reorganization Planning, 1905–1980.* Princeton, N.J.: Princeton University Press, 1986.

"Banking's Spotlight on James S. Duesenberry, Council of Economic Advisers." *Banking* 58 (April 1966): 62.

"Banking's Spotlight on the Council of Economic Advisers." *Banking* 57 (January 1965): 43–44.

Bedworth, David A. "An Analysis of Selected Presidential Advisory Commissions on Health-Related Problems, 1948–1973." Urbana: University of Illinois, 1976. Ph.D. dissertation. University Microfilms No. 76–16091.

Benze, James G. "Presidential Management: The View from the Bureaucracy." *Presidential Studies Quarterly* 15 (Fall 1985): 768–81.

Berman, Larry. "Johnson and the White House Staff." *Exploring the Johnson Years*, edited by Robert A. Divine, pp. 187–213. Austin: University of Texas Press, 1981. Republished in paperback as *The Johnson Years, Volume One: Foreign Policy, the Great Society, and the White House*. Lawrence: University Press of Kansas, 1987.

———. "The Evolution of a Presidential Staff Agency: Variations in How the Bureau of the Budget-Office of Management and Budget Has Responded to Presidential Needs." Princeton, N.J.: Princeton University, 1977. Ph.D. dissertation. University Microfilms No. 77–21436.

———. *The Office of Management and Budget and the Presidency, 1921–1979*. Princeton, N.J.: Princeton University Press, 1979.

———. "The Office of Management and Budget that Almost Wasn't." *Political Science Quarterly* 92 (Summer 1977): 281–303.

Bock, Joseph G. "The National Security Assistant and the White House Staff, 1947–1984: Foreign Policy Implications." Washington, D.C.: American University, 1985. Ph.D. dissertation. University Microfilms No. 85–13644.

———, and Duncan L. Clarke. "The National Security Assistant and the White House Staff: National Security Policy Decisionmaking and Domestic Political Considerations, 1947–1984." *Presidential Studies Quarterly* 16 (Spring 1986): 258–79.

Bowles, Nigel P. "Congressional Liaison in the Johnson Administration: Some Perspectives." Paper presented at the Annual Meeting of the Western Political Science Assn., 1979, Portland, Oregon.

———. "The Organization of the Office of Congressional Relations under Presidents Kennedy and Johnson." Paper presented at the Annual Conference of the American Politics Group of the Political Studies Assn., 1981, Gregynog, Powys, Wales.

———. *The White House and Capitol Hill: The Politics of Presidential Persuasion*. New York: Oxford University Press, 1987.

———. "White House Congressional Liaison on Domestic Policy under Lyndon Baines Johnson with Special Reference to the Office of Congressional Relations." Oxford, England:

Nuffield College, Oxford University, 1983. Ph.D. dissertation.
Brandon, Henry. "State of Affairs: Bundy and Beyond." *Saturday Review* 49 (January 22, 1966): 18.
Bundy, McGeorge. "Adviser to Two Presidents Looks at Trends in Europe." *U.S. News and World Report* 61 (July 4, 1966): 80–83.
———. *Meet the Press: Guest, McGeorge Bundy, Special Assistant to the President for National Security Affairs* (Interview). Washington, D.C.: Merkle Press, vol. 9, no. 12, 1965.
———. *Meet the Press: Guest, McGeorge Bundy, Special Assistant to the President* (Interview). Washington, D.C: Merkle Press, vol. 10, no. 8, 1966.
Burke, John P. "Responsibilities of Presidents and Advisers: A Theory and Case Study of Vietnam Decision Making." *Journal of Politics* 46 (August 1984): 818–45.
Callaway, Rhonda. "Bill Moyers: The Prodigal Son." Paper prepared for Undergraduate History Seminar, Professor Lewis L. Gould, University of Texas at Austin, May 14, 1986 [c/o LBJ Library].
Campbell, Alex. "Walt Whitman Rostow." *New Republic* 157 (November 4, 1967): 15–17.
Carey, William D. "Presidential Staffing in the Sixties and Seventies." *Public Administration Review* 29 (September/October 1969): 450–58.
Cavanagh, Jerome P., et al. *Meet the Press: Guest, Mayor Jerome Cavanagh, Detroit* [and Five Other Mayors Assess the President's Advisory Commission on Civil Disorders] (Interview). Washington, D.C.: Merkle Press, vol. 12, no. 9, 1968.
Chamberlain, John. "President Johnson Ignored Good Advice While Listening to Kennedy Holdovers." *Human Events* 31 (July 17, 1971): 14.
"Change-Over of Science Advisers." *Nature*, December 14, 1968: 1067–68.
Christian, George. *Meet the Press: Guest, George Christian, Special Assistant and Press Secretary to President Lyndon B. Johnson* (Interview). Washington, D.C.: Merkle Press, vol. 13, no. 3, 1969.
———. *The President Steps Down: A Personal Memoir of the Transfer of Power.* New York: Macmillan, 1970.

"Civil Disorder Panel [President's Advisory Commission on Civil Disorders] Blames 'White Racism' for Riots." *Congressional Quarterly Weekly Report* 26 (March 8, 1968): 469–73.

Clifford, Craig Edward. "[J. J. 'Jake'] Pickle on the Potomac." *Third Coast* 1 (April 1982): 24–31.

Cochrane, James L. "Economists and Presidential Decision Making: The Johnson Years." *Presidential Studies Quarterly* 8 (Winter 1978): 32–35.

"Congress Is Cool on Riot Study: President's Panel [Advisory Commission on Civil Disorders]." *Business Week*, March 9, 1968: 31–32.

"The Council of Economic Advisers [1965 Members]." *Banking* 57 (January 1965): 43–44.

Cronin, Thomas E. "White House—Department Relations." *The Institutionalized Presidency*, edited by Norman Thomas and Hans Baade, pp. 147–99. Dobbs Ferry, N.Y.: Oceana, 1970.

———, and N. C. Thomas. "Educational Policy Advisors and the Great Society." *Public Policy* 19 (Fall 1970): 659–86.

———, and Sanford D. Greenberg, eds. *The Presidential Advisory System*. New York: Harper and Row, 1969.

Davis, Eric Lyle. "Congressional Liaison: The People and the Institutions." *Both Ends of the Avenue: The Presidency, the Executive Branch, and Congress*, edited by Anthony King, pp. 59–95. Washington, D.C.: American Enterprise Institute for Public Policy Research, 1983.

De Toledano, Ralph. "'Ten Pillars of Economic Wisdom': Council of Economic Advisors." *Human Events* 25 (April 3, 1965): 6.

Elzy, Martin I. "Another Celebration of Our Heritage: The Johnson White House and the Nation's Bicentennial." *Proceedings and Papers of the Georgia Association of Historians, 1983*, pp. 70–77.

"False Prophets: A Note on the President's Council of Economic Advisers." *Barron's* 46 (December 26, 1966): 1.

Flash, Edward S., Jr. *Economic Advice and Presidential Leadership: The Council of Economic Advisers*. New York: Columbia University Press, 1965.

"Fortas: LBJ's 'Mr. Fixit'." *Human Events* 28 (July 6, 1968): 3.

Frankel, Max. "The Importance of Being Bundy." *New York Times Magazine*, March 28, 1965: 32–33.

"George Reedy Explains That He Holds a View-Point." *Editor and Publisher* 97 (April 25, 1964): 19.

Goldstein, Walter. "The Science Establishment and Its Political Control." *American Government and Political Change*, edited by William R. Nelson, pp. 248–58. New York: Oxford University Press, 1967.

Halberstam, David. "The Very Expensive Education of McGeorge Bundy." *Harper's Magazine* 239 (July 1969): 21–41.

Harris, Gayle T. "Advisory Bodies Created by the President and by Congress, 1955 through March, 1968." Washington, D.C.: Library of Congress Legislative Reference Service, April 17, 1968. Typewritten.

———. "Committees, Commissions, Boards, Councils and Task Forces Created to Advise the President, The Congress or Executive Agencies since 1965." Washington, D.C.: Library of Congress Legislative Reference Service, August 20, 1968. Typewritten.

Hazlitt, Henry. "Is Poverty the Cause of Riots [President's Advisory Commission on Civil Disorders]?" *Human Events* 27 (August 12, 1967): 1.

Heinlein, Jay Clarke. "The Johnson Staff and National Security Policy." *Essays on Modern Politics and History*, edited by Han-Kyo Kim. Athens: Ohio University Press, 1970.

Heller, Walter W. *Meet the Press: Guest, Dr. Walter W. Heller, Former Chairman, Council of Economic Advisers* (Interview). Washington, D.C.: Merkle Press, vol. 9, no. 39, 1965.

Herken, Gregg F. *Counsels of War* [Atomic Diplomacy and Soviet-American Relations from Truman to Reagan]. New York: Knopf, 1984.

"High-Level Help on Economic Guideposts: President's Advisory Committee on Labor-Management Policy." *Business Week*, May 14, 1966: 42–43.

Hollomon, J. Herbert. "Government and Science: How Science Policy Is Developed." *Science* 143 (January 1964): 427–29.

"Hornig Asks Study of a Science Department." *Scientific Research*, September 30, 1968: 9–10.

Hornig, Donald F. "The Evolving Federal Role." *Science and the University*, edited by Boyd Keenan, pp. 40–58. New York: Columbia University Press, 1966.

———. "The President's Special Assistant for Science and Technology Addresses the American Physical Society." *Physics Today* 17 (July 1964): 34–38.

"How LBJ Picks His Men." *Nation's Business* 53 (July 1965): 36–37+.

"How the Style Shifts at CEA [Council of Economic Advisers]." *Business Week*, January 30, 1965: 73–74+.

"How Washington Makes Its Forecast." *Business Week*, December 30, 1967: 80–82+.

Howard, Anthony. "At the White House, Intellectual-in-Residence [John P. Roche]." *New York Times Magazine*, March 12, 1967: 34+.

Humphrey, David C. "Tuesday Lunch at the Johnson White House: A Preliminary Assessment." *Diplomatic History* 8 (Winter 1984): 81–101.

"In Science Policy, Who Holds the Power?" *Science News*, April 8, 1967: 326.

Isaacson, Walter, and Evan Thomas. *The Wise Men: Six Friends and the World They Made*. New York: Simon and Schuster, 1986.

Jacob, Bernard E. "Supreme Court Justices: Presidential Advising and Other Non-judicial Roles." Paper presented at Fifth Annual Hofstra University Presidential Conference: Lyndon Baines Johnson, A Texan in Washington. Hempstead, New York, April 10–12, 1986.

"The Johnson Staff: New Faces, New Ways at the White House." *U.S. News and World Report* 55 (December 2, 1963): 44.

"Johnson Taps His Financial Team." *Business Week*, April 24, 1965: 26–27.

"Johnson's Men: Valuable Hunks of Humanity." *New York Times Magazine*, May 3, 1964: 11+.

"Johnson's 'Professor of Budgeting'." *Human Events* 24 (February 29, 1964): 8.

Kamath, P. M. *Executive Privilege versus Democratic Accountability: The Special Assistant to the President for National Security Affairs, 1961–1969*. New Delhi, India: Radiant Publishers, 1981.

Kaufman, Felice Ann. "A Follow-Up Study of the 1964–1968 Presidential Scholars." Athens: University of Georgia, 1979. Ph.D. dissertation. University Microfilms No. 80–10601.

Kettl, Donald F. "The Econmic Education of Lyndon Johnson: Guns, Butter, and Taxes." *The Johnson Years, Volume Two:*

Vietnam, the Environment, and Science, edited by Robert A. Divine, pp. 54–78. Lawrence: University Press of Kansas, 1987.

King, James D., and James W. Riddlesperger, Jr. "Presidential Appointments to the Cabinet, Executive Office, and White House Staff." *Presidential Studies Quarterly* 16 (Fall 1986): 691–99.

Lacy, A. B. "The Development of the White House Office, 1939–1967." Paper presented at the Annual Meeting of the American Political Science Assn., Chicago, 1967.

Lambright, W. Henry. *Presidential Management of Science and Technology: The Johnson Presidency.* Administrative History of the Johnson Presidency Series. Austin: University of Texas Press, 1985.

Lane, Thomas A., Gen. "LBJ Can't Win Viet War with Present Advisers." *Human Events* 27 (December 30, 1967): 11.

Lasky, Victor. "Civil Rights Hints on Viet Rile Presidential Advisors." *Human Events* 25 (May 15, 1965): 9.

"LBJ's Brand Goes on the Economy." *Business Week,* January 25, 1964: 71–74+.

"LBJ's Inflation Watcher: Arthur M. Ross, Commissioner of Labor Statistics." *Forbes* 97 (May 15, 1966): 36.

"LBJ's 'Outside Man': Donald C. Cook (Economic Adviser)." *Business Week,* February 13, 1965: 27.

Leib, Charles. "Who the President Listens To." *Nation's Business* 13 (April 1965): 32.

Lewis, Ted. "How the White House Claque Polishes the Johnson Image." *Human Events* 25 (September 18, 1965): 8.

———. "Only Three JFK Aides Remain." *Human Events* 24 (April 25, 1964): 2.

"A Look at the Inner Workings in the White House." *U.S. News and World Report* 60 (June 13, 1966): 78–85.

Lyons, Gene. "The President and His Experts." *Annals of the American Academy of Political and Social Sciences* 394 (1971): 36–45.

Macy, John W. "Presidential Advisors, Personnel and the Johnson Presidency." *Virginia Papers on the Presidency: The White Burkett Miller Center Forums, Vol. 16, Part 1,* edited by Kenneth W. Thompson, pp. 43–64. Lanham, Md.: University Press of America, 1984.

———, Bruce Adams, and J. Jackson Walter. *America's*

Unelected Government: Appointing the President's Team. Cambridge, Mass.: Ballinger Publishing Co., 1983.

"The Men Johnson Will Lean On." *Business Week,* November 30, 1963: 27–28.

"The Men Who Are Close to Johnson: Coming—Broad But Gradual Changes." *U.S. News and World Report* 55 (December 9, 1963): 43–45.

Moley, Raymond. "Who Has the President's Ear? White House Staff vs. Cabinet." *Human Events* 27 (March 4, 1967): 6.

Morgan, Thomas B. "The Most Happy Fella in the White House [Walt Rostow]." *Life* 63 (December 1, 1967): 80–80B+.

Morgenthau, Hans J. "Bundy's Doctrine of War without End." *New Republic* 159 (November 2, 1968): 18–20.

Moskin, J. Robert. "The Dangerous World of Walt Rostow." *Look* 31 (December 12, 1967): 27–31.

Mowery, David C., Mark S. Kamlet, and John P. Crecine. "Presidential Management of Budgetary and Fiscal Policymaking." *Political Science Quarterly* 95 (Fall 1980): 395–425.

"Moyers Will Become Newsday's Publisher." *Editor and Publisher* 99 (December 17, 1966): 12+.

Munroe, Pat. "Reedy in the White House; Salinger to the Capitol?" *Editor and Publisher* 97 (March 28, 1964): 14–15+.

Nash, Bradley D., et al. *Organizing and Staffing the Presidency.* New York: Center for the Study of the Presidency, 1980.

Naveh, David. "The Political Role of Academic Advisers: The Case of the U.S. President's Council of Economic Advisers, 1946–1976." *Presidential Studies Quarterly* 11 (Fall 1981): 492–510.

"New Economists Leave Their Last Testament: Kennedy-Johnson Economic Advisers Close Up Shop." *Business Week,* January 18, 1969: 102+.

"New Role for CEA: President's Top Economists Are Now Trouble Shooters for Wage and Price Policies." *Business Week,* April 2, 1966: 30–31.

Newman, Frank J. "The Era of Expertise: The Growth, the Spread and Ultimately the Decline of the National Commitment to the Concept of the Highly Trained Expert: 1945–1970." Stanford, Cal.: Stanford University, 1981. Ph.D. dissertation. University Microfilms No. 82–02023.

"No More Depressions? Interview with Walter W. Heller,

Chairman of President's Council of Economic Advisers." *U.S. News and World Report,* June 29, 1964: 58–63.

Norton, Hugh S. *The Employment Act and the Council of Economic Advisers, 1946–1976.* Columbia: University of South Carolina Press, 1977.

O'Donnell, Barbara. "The President's Pilot." *New Hampshire Profiles* 24 (April 1975): 33+.

"Out of the Catalyst into the Fire: Princeton's Donald F. Hornig to be President Johnson's Science Adviser." *Business Week,* December 14, 1963: 72+.

"Panel Puts Its Stamp on New Postal Setup: Kappel [President's] Commission [on Postal Organization] Recommends the Post Office Be Run by a Government-Owned Corporation." *Business Week,* March 9, 1968: 127–28+.

Pickens, Donald K. "LBJ, The Council of Economic Advisers, and the Burden of New Deal Liberalism." Paper presented at Fifth Annual Hofstra University Presidential Conference: Lyndon Baines Johnson, A Texan in Washington. Hempstead, New York, April 10–12, 1986.

Pika, Joseph A. "White House Boundary Roles: Marginal Men Amidst the Palace Guard [Office of Congressional Relations]." *Presidential Studies Quarterly* 16 (Fall 1986): 700–15.

Pipe, G. Russell. "Congressional Liaison: The Executive Branch Consolidates Its Relations with Congress." *Public Administration Review* 26 (March 1966): 14–24.

"Planning to Keep the Ball Rolling: Johnson's Council of Economic Advisers." *Business Week,* November 14, 1964: 23–25.

"President Howard Coughlin Attends White House Meeting of Labor Advisory Council to President's Committee on Equal Employment Opportunity." *White Collar* (Office and Professional Employees Internat'l. Union), no. 221, April 1964: 1, 3.

"President's Advisors Want Radical World Changes." *Human Events* 24 (October 3, 1964): 3.

"The President's Right-Hand Man." *U.S. News and World Report* 60 (May 30, 1966): 16.

President's Science Advisory Board, Panel on Education Innovation. *Educational Opportunity Bank* (Zacharias Report). Washington, D.C.: U.S. Gov't Printing Office, 1967.

Redford, Emmette S., and Richard T. McCulley. *White House Operations: The Johnson Presidency.* Administrative History of the Johnson Presidency Series. Austin: University of Texas Press, 1986.

Riddlesperger, James W., Jr., and James D. King. "Presidential Appointments to the Cabinet, Executive Office, and White House Staff." *Presidential Studies Quarterly* 16 (Fall 1986): 691–99.

Riesel, Victor. "LBJ Has 3 Brain Trusts Working on Anti-Strike Formula." *Human Events* 26 (December 24, 1966): 6.

Roche, John P. "Taming the NSC: The Imperial LBJ." *National Review*, March 27, 1987: 40–42.

Rosen, Gerald R. "Talk with Gardner Ackley: President Johnson's Top Economic Adviser Assesses the Boom, the Steel Impasse and Inflation." *Dun's Review and Modern Industry* 86 (July 1965): 36–38.

Samuelson, Paul A. "What the Future Holds for Business: Interview with LBJ's Task Force Head [Paul A. Samuelson]." *U.S. News and World Report* 57 (December 14, 1964): 64–68+.

"Scholar Who's No. 2 at the White House: Presidential Aide Walt Rostow." *Business Week*, March 25, 1967: 122–23+.

Schott, Richard L., and Dagmar S. Hamilton. *People, Positions, and Power: The Political Appointments of Lyndon Johnson.* Chicago: University of Chicago Press, 1983.

"Science Adviser Hornig Discusses His Job." *Chemical and Engineering News* 45 (November 27, 1967): 28–29.

Sidey, Hugh. "The White House Staff vs. the Cabinet: An Interview with Bill Moyers." *Inside the System: A Washington Monthly Reader*, edited by Charles Peters and Timothy J. Adams, pp. 23–42. New York: Praeger, 1970.

Sloan, John W. "President Johnson, the Council of Economic Advisers, and the Failure to Raise Taxes in 1966 and 1967." *Presidential Studies Quarterly* 15 (Winter 1985): 89–98.

Small, William E. "Horning and the OST [Office of Science and Technology]: The First 1,162 Days." *Scientific Research*, April 1967: 63–67.

Smith, Nancy Kegan. "Presidential Task Force Operation during the Johnson Administration." *Presidential Studies Quarterly* 15 (Spring 1985): 320–29.

Stieber, Jack. "The President's [Advisory] Committee on Labor-Management Policy." *Industrial Relations* 5 (February 1966): 1–19.

Taylor, Henry J. "Adlai Stevenson Rates High on List of LBJ Confidants." *Human Events* 24 (July 25, 1964): 4.

"They Twist Arms without Hurting: Never Have Liaison Men Worked More Effectively between White House and Capitol Hill than under the Johnson Administration." *Business Week*, April 24, 1965: 82+.

"To Russia with Love: Rostow." *Human Events* 27 (March 11, 1967): 3.

Tobin, James. *The Intellectual Revolution in U.S. Economic Policy Making* [Kennedy and Johnson Council of Economic Advisers]. London: Longmans, Green & Co., 1966.

Trohan, Walter. "Kennedy Aides Unhappy with LBJ." *Human Events* 23 (February 22, 1964): 6.

Tugwell, Rexford G. "The President and His Helpers: A Review Article." *Political Science Quarterly* 82 (June 1967): 253–67.

Valenti, Jack. "Confessions of a Presidential Assistant Who Deeply Misses the Joy of Power." *The Washington Post Magazine*, March 4, 1984: 12–14.

"Voice for Consumer [Johnson Creates New Post of Special Assistant to President for Consumer Affairs]." *AFL-CIO American Federationist* 71 (March 1964): 13–18.

"Washington's New Set of White House VIPs: The President Relies More Heavily on Advisers for His Ideas than His Predecessor." *Business Week*, March 14, 1964: 32+.

"The Way U.S. Leaders Size Up the World Now: First-Hand Reports on How the President's Most Intimate Advisers Are Measuring the World's Key Areas." *U.S. News and World Report* 59 (November 15, 1965): 42–44.

"What the Future Holds for America: As the President's 'Idea Men' See It." *U.S. News and World Report* 56 (June 22, 1964): 40–44+.

"White House Advisers Urge Stepped-up War on Pollution [President's Science Advisory Committee]." *AFL-CIO News* 10 (November 13, 1965): 4.

"The White House at Work: A Mystery Explained [Functions of President Johnson's Appointments Secretary, W. Marvin Watson]." *U.S. News and World Report* 60 (February 7, 1966): 36–37.

"White House Scouts for Top Aides." *Business Week*, December 12, 1964: 31.

"White House Staff Turnover Continues High." *Congressional Quarterly Weekly Report* 25 (March 3, 1967): 307–09.
"White House Superstructure for Science." *Chemical and Engineering News* 42 (October 19, 1964): 78–92.
"Who Runs the Whole U.S. Show in the World? Johnson's Reliance on Civilian Staff for Formation of Military Strategy." *U.S. News and World Report* 62 (June 5, 1967): 37–39.
"Who's Writing LBJ's Speeches." *U.S. News and World Report* 58 (June 28, 1965): 57.
Wolanin, Thomas E. *Presidential Commissions, Truman to Nixon.* Madison: University of Wisconsin Press, 1975.
Wright, Deil S. "The Advisory Commission on Intergovernmental Relations." *Public Administration Review* 25 (September 1965): 193–202.
"Young Bill Moyers Is Emerging as LBJ's Chief Staff Assistant." *Human Events* 24 (May 23, 1964): 3.

3. THE MEDIA

"Ad Men Say Johnson's a Cinch." *Printers' Ink* 288 (September 18, 1964): 7.
Alexander, Herbert E. "The High Cost of TV Campaigns." *Television Quarterly* 5 (Winter 1966): 47–65.
Alexander, Holmes. "Johnson Administration Spokesman Issues New Instructions: What to Print." *Human Events* 25 (October 23, 1965): 10.
Altschuler, Bruce E. *Keeping a Finger on the Public Pulse: Private Polling and Presidential Elections.* Westport, Conn.: Greenwood Press, 1982.
———. "Lyndon Johnson and the Public Polls." *Public Opinion Quarterly* 50 (Fall 1986): 285–99.
Baughman, James Lewis. "Warriors in the Wasteland: The Federal Communications Commission and American TV, 1958–1967." New York: Columbia University, 1981. Ph.D. dissertation. University Microfilms No. 8125241.
"Behind LBJ's TV 'Chat' [of December 20, 1967]." *Human Events* 28 (January 6, 1968): 3.
"Burch Hindsight: TV Badly Used—GOP Ex-Chairman Says Politicians Laid Egg in Tube Last Year." *Broadcasting* 68 (March 22, 1965): 88.
Cahalan, Joseph M. "Congress, Mass Communications and

Public Policy—The Public Broadcast Act of 1967." New York: New York University, 1971. Ph.D. dissertation. University Microfilms No. 72-3955.

Chester, Edward W. *Radio, Television and American Politics.* New York: Sheed and Ward, 1969.

Christian, George. *Meet the Press: Guest, George Christian, Special Assistant and Press Secretary to President Lyndon B. Johnson* (Interview). Washington, D.C.: Merkle Press, vol. 13, no. 3, 1969.

"Color First on Capitol Hill: Technical Challenges Make LBJ's State of Union Address More Complex, Costly." *Broadcasting* 70 (January 17, 1966): 69–70.

Cormier, Frank, James Deakin, and Helen Thomas. *The White House Press on the Presidency: News Management and Co-Option.* Lanham, Md.: University Press of America, 1983.

Cornwell, Elmer E., Jr. "Presidential News: The Expanding Public Image." *The American Presidency: Vital Center*, edited by Elmer E. Cornwell, Jr., pp. 28–29. Fairlawn, N.J.: Scott, Foresman, 1966.

"The Credibility Gap." *Nation* 204 (April 17, 1967): 484.

Diamond, Edwin, and Stephen Bates. *The Spot: The Rise of Political Advertising on Television.* Cambridge, Mass.: M.I.T. Press, 1984.

Dickinson, William B., Jr. "Politician and the Press [the press as a 1964 political target]." *Editorial Research Reports*, September 2, 1964: 643–60.

Donovan, Hedley. *Roosevelt to Reagan: A Reporter's Encounter with Nine Presidents.* New York: Harper and Row, 1985.

"Eastern Found Jet Power in TV: High-Quality, Dignified Image Results from Inauguration Sponsorship." *Broadcasting* 68 (June 21, 1965): 33–34.

Edwards, Jack. "The Honesty Gap in Washington." *Human Events* 25 (December 4, 1965): 15.

"Equal Time: President's News Conferences Subject to Law." *Printers' Ink* 289 (October 9, 1964): 6.

"Equal Time Applicable to LBJ News Sessions: That's the FCC Vote." *Broadcasting* 67 (October 5, 1964): 45–46.

"FCC Puts Presidential Press Conference under Demands of Equal Time Law." *Sponsor* 18 (October 5, 1964): 3.

Findley, Paul. *They Dare to Speak Out: People and Institutions Confront Israel's Lobby.* Westport, Conn.: Lawrence Hill & Co., 1984.

Fleming, R. "Inside Look at LBJ's Talks." *Broadcasting* 70 (April 25, 1966): 72.

Fowler, George. "President Johnson Finally Holds a Formal News Conference." *Human Events* 26 (July 30, 1966): 8–9.

French, Blaire Atherton. *The Presidential Press Conference: Its History and Role in the American Political System.* Lanham, Md.: University Press of America, 1982.

Funkhouser, G. R. "Trends in Media Coverage of the Issues of the '60s." *Journalism Quarterly* 50 (Autumn 1973): 553–38.

Gitlin, Todd A. "'The Whole World Is Watching': Mass Media and the New Left, 1965–1970." Berkeley: University of California, 1977. Ph.D. dissertation. University Microfilms No. 78-12574.

Goggin, M. L. "The Ideological Content of Presidential Communications: The Message—Tailoring Hypothesis Revisited [Presidents Johnson and Reagan Compared]." *American Politics Quarterly* 12 (July 1984): 361–84.

Gutin, Myra Greenberg. "The President's Partner: The First Lady as Public Communicator, 1920–1976." Ann Arbor: University of Michigan, 1983. Ph.D. dissertation. University Microfilms No. 8324192.

Haight, Timothy, and Richard Brody. "The Mass Media and Presidential Popularity." *Communication Research* 4 (January 1977): 41–60.

Hart, Roderick. *Verbal Style and the Presidency.* Human Communication Research Series. New York: Academic Press, Harcourt, Brace Jovanovich, 1984.

"He's Back in the Saddle Again—President Johnson Holds First White House News Conference in a Year." *Broadcasting* 71 (July 25, 1966): 42.

"The 'Image' Johnson Is Trying to Create." *U.S. News and World Report* 56 (February 3, 1964): 32–33.

"Informed News Conference with the President Is Better than a TV Extravaganza." *Editor and Publisher* 99 (January 22, 1966): 15.

"International Problems Dominate February [1964] Press

Conference." *Congressional Quarterly Weekly Report* 22 (March 6, 1964): 475–78.

"Johnson and the Press—What the Grumbling Is About." *U.S. News and World Report* 58 (March 22, 1965): 49–51.

"Johnson Calls Rowan Home to Run USIA [U.S. Information Agency]." *Editor and Publisher* 97 (January 25, 1964): 12.

Johnson, Karen S. "The Portrayal of Lame-duck Presidents by the National Print Media." *Presidential Studies Quarterly* 16 (Winter 1986): 50–65.

Johnson, Miles Beardsley. *The Government Secrecy Controversy: A Dispute Involving the Government and the Press in the Eisenhower, Kennedy, and Johnson Administrations.* New York: Vantage Press, 1967.

Johnson, Paul. "The Media and the Presidency." *Encounter* 64 (November 1984): 8–14.

"Johnson's Inauguration—Broadcasters' Field Day." *Broadcasting* 68 (January 25, 1965): 72–73.

Kirk, Russell. "Many Reporters Growing Cool toward Johnson." *Human Events* 25 (February 27, 1965): 8.

Kraft, Joseph. "The Politics of the Washington Press Corps." *Harper's Magazine* 230 (June 1965): 100–05.

"LBJ Bombs Press with Blockbuster Headline." *Editor and Publisher* 101 (April 6, 1968): 9+.

"LBJ Gets Earful from Publishers." *Editor and Publisher* 99 (August 13, 1966): 9+.

"The LBJ Image: What's Happening." *U.S. News and World Report* 59 (July 19, 1965): 35–37.

"LBJ Meets the Press and Likes It." *Editor and Publisher* 97 (March 7, 1964): 57.

"LBJ Plans Series of Radio-TV Reports to the Nation." *Human Events* 27 (August 26, 1967): 12.

"LBJ Prefers Small Meetings with the Press." *Editor and Publisher* 99 (October 1, 19660: 15.

"LBJ Prefers to Meet the Press Informally." *Editor and Publisher* 99 (March 12, 1966): 11.

"LBJ Sets Minimum in Press Relations." *Editor and Publisher* 98 (March 27, 1965): 13.

"LBJ's Five Years with Reporters." *Editor and Publisher* 102 (January 4, 1969): 15.

"LBJ's Press Parley Pattern Wins Favor." *Editor and Publisher* 97 (April 25, 1965): 19.

"LBJ's Press Relations Snarled in Velvet Rope." *Editor and Publisher* 100 (May 6, 1967): 14.
"LBJ's Reckless Driving Was Covered Up by Press." *Human Events* 23 (February 18, 1964): 12.
"LBJ's U.S. Information Agency." *Human Events* 26 (October 29, 1966): 4.
Lee, Richard W., ed. *Politics and the Press.* Washington, D.C.: Acropolis, 1970.
Lewis, Ted. "LBJ Wants More Managed News." *Human Events* 26 (January 29, 1966): 14.
"'Lights! Cameras! Action!' The LBJ News Conference—A Smoothly Staged Production [with Prearranged Questions]." *U.S. News and World Report* 59 (September 20, 1965): 66–67.
Locander, Robert. "Modern Presidential In-Office Communications: The National, Direct, Local, and Latent Strategies." *Presidential Studies Quarterly* 13 (Spring 1983): 242–54.
Manheim, Jarol B. "The News Conference and Presidential Leadership of Public Opinion: Does the Tail Wag the Dog?" *Presidential Studies Quarterly* 11 (Spring 1981): 177–88.
"Manipulating the News LBJ Style." *Human Events* 24 (July 11, 1964): 16.
McNeil, Neil V. "The Washington Correspondents: Why Do Some 'Drop Out'?" *Journalism Quarterly* 43 (Summer 1966): 257–63.
"Meanwhile at the LBJ Ranch: News Made on Spur of the Moment." *Editor and Publisher* 97 (January 4, 1964): 9–10.
Mendelsohn, Harold, and Irving Crespi. *Polls, Television, and the New Politics.* San Francisco: Chandler, 1970.
Mortensen, C. David. "The Influence of Television on Policy Discussion." *Quarterly Journal of Speech* 54 (October 1968): 277–81.
"New LBJ News Secretary, George Christian, Knows Texas Politics." *Broadcasting* 71 (December 19, 1966): 66.
"News Show Draws Darts: TV Newsmen Complain about Staged Rehash of LBJ Conference." *Broadcasting* 70 (June 27, 1966): 60.
Paletz, David L., and Robert M. Entman. "Presidents, Power, and the Press." *Presidential Studies Quarterly* 10 (Summer 1980): 416–26.

Phillips, Glen D. "The Use of Radio and Television by Presidents of the United States." Ann Arbor: University of Michigan, 1968. Ph.D. dissertation. University Microfilms No. 69-12206.

"President and Press Corps—What to Expect." *U.S. News and World Report* 56 (April 20, 1964): 15.

Pryor, Richard ("Cactus"). *Inside Texas*. Bryan, Texas: Shoal Creek Publishers, 1982.

Ragsdale, Lyn. "Presidents and Publics: The Dialogue of Presidential Leadership, 1949–1979." Madison: University of Wisconsin, 1982. Ph.D. dissertation. University Microfilms No. 83-04284.

Ragsdale, Warner. "President's Operation: Calm Press Gets Full Facilities." *Editor and Publisher* 98 (October 16, 1965): 59.

Reedy, George E. "Tension between the White House and the Press Is Not Catastrophic." *Editor and Publisher* 99 (July 2, 1966): 10+.

"Reporters Restless with LBJ Sessions." *Editor and Publisher* 97 (February 8, 1964): 54.

Rinn, Fauneil. "The Presidential Press Conference." *The Presidency*, edited by Aaron Wildavsky, pp. 327–36. Boston: Little, Brown, 1969.

Robinson, John P. "Perceived Media Bias and the 1968 Vote: Can the Media Affect Behavior after All?" *Journalism Quarterly* 49 (Summer 1972): 239–46.

———. "The Press as King-Maker: What Surveys Show from the Last Five Campaigns." *Journalism Quarterly* 51 (Winter 1974): 587–94.

Scott, Paul. "LBJ Plans Fireside Chats in Fall." *Human Events* 28 (August 24, 1968): 1.

Singer, Benjamin D. "Violence, Protest, and War in Television News: The U.S. and Canada Compared." *Public Opinion Quarterly* 34 (Winter 1970–1971): 611–16.

Small, William J. *Political Power and the Press*. New York: Norton, 1972.

Smith, Craig Allen. "The Audience of the 'Rhetorical Presidency': An Analysis of Presidential-Constituent Interactions, 1963–1981." *Presidential Studies Quarterly* 13 (Fall 1983): 613–22.

———, and Kathy B. Smith. "Presidential Values and Public

Priorities: Recurrent Patterns in Addresses to the Nation, 1963–1984." *Presidential Studies Quarterly* 15 (Fall 1985): 743–53.
Smith, Merriman. "Fair Game in LBJ's Press Calls." *Editor and Publisher* 98 (December 18, 1965): 13.
Spragens, William C. *From Spokesman to Press Secretary: White House Media Operations.* Lanham, Md.: University Press of America, 1980.
Stuart, Anthony. "Is Television Becoming a Political Tool?" *Human Events* 25 (January 9, 1965): 11.
"TASS Newsman Is Guest at LBJ Ranch." *Human Events* 27 (January 14, 1967): 16.
Tebbel, John, and Sarah Miles Watts. *The Press and the Presidency from George Washington to Ronald Reagan.* New York: Oxford University Press, 1985.
Thompson, Kenneth W. *Ten Presidents and the Press.* Lanham, Md.: University Press of America, 1983.
"Tight Pace for LBJ News Talk." *Editor and Publisher* 97 (April 25, 1964): 19.
"Trail Herder Moyers Assesses Press Cooling toward LBJ." *Human Events* 24 (February 29, 1964): 1.
"The Truth about LBJ's Credibility." *Look* 31 (May 2, 1967): 70–72.
Turner, Kathleen J. *Lyndon Johnson's Dual War: Vietnam and the Press.* Chicago: University of Chicago Press, 1985.
"TV Is Major Source for LBJ Speech: Both Radio and Television Are Far Ahead of Newspapers." *Broadcasting* 69 (August 2, 1965): 68.
Wallace, Mike, and Gary Paul Gates. *Close Encounters: Mike Wallace's Own Story.* New York: Morrow, 1984.
"White House TV Studio Gets First Live Use." *Broadcasting* 68 (February 8, 1965): 65.
Wicker, Tom. "Television in the Political Campaign." *Television Quarterly* 5 (Winter 1966): 13–26.
Wilson, Bob. "LBJ's PR Empire." *Human Events* 27 (May 6, 1967): 15.
"World's Biggest TV Studio Ready to Give Record-Breaking Coverage to Inauguration of President Johnson." *Broadcasting* 68 (January 18, 1965): 78–79.
"You're Not Bad Guys at Night (LBJ Quips) [Johnson and the Press]." *Editor and Publisher* 97 (April 11, 1964): 15.

4. Politics

A. GENERAL

Agranoff, Robert. *The Management of Election Campaigns.* Boston: Holbrook Press, 1976.
"Baker Case: A Glimpse of 'Inside' Politics." *U.S. News and World Report* 62 (February 6, 1967): 42–43.
"Billie Sol Estes: Old Friend of Lyndon's." *Human Events* 24 (July 11, 1964): 14.
Billington, Monroe L. *The Political South in the 20th Century.* New York: Scribners, 1975.
"Bobby Baker and LBJ." *Human Events* 24 (July 11, 1964): 15–16.
"The Bobby Baker Affair, Chapter Two." *Human Events* 23 (February 8, 1964): 5.
Brown, Roger O. "Party and Bureaucracy: From Kennedy to Reagan." *Political Science Quarterly* 97 (Summer 1982): 279–94.
Burner, David, and Thomas R. West. *The Torch Is Passed: The Kennedy Brothers and American Liberalism.* New York: Atheneum, 1985.
Cary, William L. *Politics and the Regulatory Agencies.* New York: McGraw-Hill, 1967.
Catchpole, Terry. "Dear Billie . . . . With Best Wishes, Lyndon." *Human Events* 24 (February 29, 1964): 6.
———. "The League of Women Voters: Its Partisan Slip Is Showing." *Human Events* 25 (July 3, 1965): 7.
Chamberlain, John. "Is the 'LBJ' Label Becoming a Handicap?" *Human Events* 26 (August 20, 1966): 1.
Collier, Peter, and David Horowitz. *The Kennedys: An American Drama.* New York: Summit, 1984; paper, Warner Books, 1985.
Congressional Quarterly Service. *CQ Guide to Current American Government* [the Presidency, Congress, Key Issues 1965, Supreme Court, Politics 1964–66]. Washington, D.C.: Congressional Quarterly Service, Fall 1965.
Cooper, Joseph, and Gary Bombardier. "Presidential Leadership and Party Success." *Journal of Politics* 30 (November 1968): 1012–27.
Cotter, Cornelius P., et al. *Party Organization in American Politics.* New York: Praeger, 1984.

Crawford, Ann Fears, and Jack Keever. *John B. Connally: Portrait in Power*. Austin: Jenkins Publishing Co., 1973.

Danigelis, Nicholas L. "Race and Political Activity in the United States, 1948–1968: A Trend Analysis." Bloomington: Indiana University, 1973. Ph.D. dissertation. University Microfilms No. 74-09417.

Davidson, Roger H. *Coalition-Building for Depressed Areas Bills: 1955–1965*. Indianapolis: Bobbs-Merrill, College Division, Inter-University Case Program no. 3, 1967.

Davis, John H. *The Kennedys: Dynasty and Disaster, 1848–1983*. New York: McGraw Hill, 1984.

De Toledano, Ralph. "How to Win Elections: LBJ's $300 Million Boondoggle in Maine." *Human Events* 25 (October 30, 1965): 9.

———. "Nixon Hits 'Radicals of the Left'." *Human Events* 25 (October 16, 1965): 14.

———. "Will LBJ Swing Left or Right?" *Human Events* 26 (June 18, 1966): 13.

Derthick, Martha, and Paul J. Quirk. *The Politics of Deregulation*. Washington, D.C.: Brookings Institution, 1985.

Duffey, Joseph. "The Liberals' Plight." *Christianity and Crisis* 27 (October 16, 1967): 231–33.

Eller, J. N. "GOP Salutes President for 89th's Record." *America* 113 (November 6, 1965): 520.

Evans, M. Stanton. "Is There a Conservative Majority?" *Human Events* 27 (September 30, 1967): 12, 14.

Fallaci, Oriana. "Robert Kennedy Answers Some Blunt Questions." *Look*, March 9, 1965: 60–63.

Ford, Gerald R. "What Can Save the GOP." *Fortune* 71 (January 1965): 140–41+.

Fulton, Lewis, Jr. "LBJ and Bobby Baker." *Human Events* 24 (April 4, 1964): 11.

Goldwater, Barry. "How the Johnson Administration Encourages Left-Wing Extremism." *Human Events* 25 (November 27, 1965): 3.

"Goodwin Strives to Enlist Radical Students for LBJ." *Human Events* 25 (October 23, 1965): 1.

"Growing Rift of LBJ and Kennedys." *U.S. News and World Report* 62 (January 2, 1967): 22–27.

Gruberg, Martin. *Women in American Politics*. Oshkosh, Wis.: Academic Press, 1968.

Halberstam, David. *The Unfinished Odyssey of Robert Kennedy.* New York: Random House, 1968.
Heuvel, William V., and Milton Gwirtzman. *On His Own: Robert F. Kennedy 1964–1968.* Garden City, N.Y.: Doubleday, 1970.
House, James, and William Mason. "Political Alienation in America, 1952–1968." *American Sociological Review* 40 (April 1975): 123–47.
Huckshorn, Robert J. "Presidential Politics, 1963: Prelude to Uncertainty [Kennedy, Johnson, Presidential Transition, and the Republican Dilemma]." *American Government Annual, 1964–65,* pp. 23–43. New York: Holt, 1964.
"Johnson Gives Labor the Word: Union Chiefs Got More Than Dinner at the White House." *Business Week,* May 9, 1964: 23–24.
Kellerman, Barbara. "Campaigning since Kennedy: The Family as Surrogate." *Presidential Studies Quarterly* 10 (Spring 1980): 244–53.
Kimball, Penn. *Bobby Kennedy and the New Politics.* Englewood Cliffs, N.J.: Prentice Hall, 1968.
Knaggs, John R. *Two-Party Texas: The John Tower Era, 1961–1984.* Austin: Eakin Press, 1986.
Kohlmeier, Louis. "President Johnson's Hometown Coterie Wheels and Deals in Land, Broadcasting, Buy into Austin Banks." *Wall Street Journal,* August 11, 1964: 1.
Kolkey, Jonathan Martin. *The New Right, 1960–1968: With Epilogue, 1969–1980.* Lanham, Md.: University Press of America, 1983.
Ladd, Everett C., Jr., and Charles D. Hadley. *Transformations of the American Party System: Political Coalitions from the New Deal to the 1970s.* 2nd ed. New York: Norton, 1978.
Laird, Melvin R. "Laird Outlines GOP Alternative to 'Great Society'." *Congressional Quarterly Weekly Report* 23 (March 5, 1965): 354–59.
"LBJ and RFK." *Human Events* 22 (December 21, 1963): 5.
"LBJ in Action—What Those 'Nonpolitical' Trips Are Like: Lyndon B. Johnson Is Back on the Campaign Trail." *U.S. News and World Report* 61 (September 12, 1966): 38–39.
"LBJ Muzzles Democratic Orators." *Human Events* 24 (September 12, 1964): 11.
Lewis, Ted. "Bobby's New Book to Point Up Differences with LBJ." *Human Events* 27 (November 11, 1967): 13.

———. "LBJ Problems: Bobby Baker and TFX." *Human Events* 22 (December 21, 1963): 2.

"Liberalism's Little-Known Sugar Daddy [National Committee for an Effective Congress]." *Human Events* 27 (July 1, 1967): 8.

Lisagor, Peter. "Will Success Spoil LBJ's Carnival of Compatibility with Big Business, Big Labor, and Big Government?" *Nation's Business* 52 (December 1964): 21–22.

"Louisiana Rebuffs Lyndon." *Human Events* 23 (January 25, 1964): 1A.

Lubell, Samuel. "The Negro and the Democratic Coalition." *Commentary* 138 (August 1964): 19–27.

"Lyndon and the Baker Affair." *Human Events* 22 (December 28, 1963): 5.

"Lyndon's Pals: His Hometown Coterie Wheels and Deals in Land and Broadcasting." *Wall Street Journal*, August 11, 1964: 1.

Martin, John F. *Civil Rights and the Crisis of Liberalism: The Democratic Party, 1945–1975.* Boulder: Westview Press, 1979.

Matusow, Allen J. *The Unraveling of America: A History of Liberalism in the 1960s.* The New American Nation Series. New York: Harper and Row, 1984.

McMenamin, Michael, and Walter McNamara. *Milking the Public: Political Scandals of the Dairy Lobby from L.B.J. to Jimmy Carter.* Chicago: Nelson-Hall, 1980.

Milkis, Sidney M. "Party Leadership, Policy Reform and the Development of the Modern Presidency: The Impact of the Roosevelt and Johnson Presidencies on the American Party System." Paper prepared for delivery at the 1984 Annual Meeting of the American Political Science Assn., The Washington Hilton, August 30-September 2, 1984.

Miller, Arthur. "Political Issues and Trust in Government: 1964–1970." *American Political Science Review* 68 (September 1974): 951–72.

Morehead, Richard. *Fifty Years in Texas Politics—from Roosevelt to Reagan—from the Fergusons to Clements.* Burnet, Texas: Eakin Press, 1982.

Morley, Felix. "Sloppy Elections Do Not a Great Society Make." *Nation's Business* 54 (January 1966): 25–26.

Natchez, Peter B. "American Politics after Roosevelt: 1948–1964." *Current History* 67 (July 1974): 24–29, 37–38.

Newfield, Jack. "The Bobby Phenomenon." *Nation* 203 (November 14, 1966): 505–07.
Nixon, Richard M. "Johnson's 'Budget Brinkmanship'—Inflation: The Major Domestic Issue of the '66 Elections." *Human Events* 26 (March 19, 1966): 12.
O'Brien, David M. *Storm Center: The Supreme Court in American Politics.* New York: Norton, 1986.
Peirce, Neal R., ed. *Politics in America, 1945–1966.* 2nd ed. Washington, D.C.: Congressional Quarterly, Inc., 1967.
"Pentagon in Politics an LBJ Switch." *Human Events* 24 (September 5, 1964): 3.
Plimpton, George, and Jean Stein, eds. *American Journey: The Times of Robert Kennedy.* New York: Harcourt, Brace, Jovanovich, 1970.
"Politically the Tide Begins to Turn." *Business Week*, March 5, 1966: 52–53.
"The Poverty Warriors' Strategy: Consolidate Poor into Voting Bloc." *Human Events* 25 (August 14, 1965): 2.
Pyle, Christopher H. "Military Surveillance of Civilian Politics, 1967–1970." New York: Columbia University, 1974. Ph.D. dissertation.
Reinhard, David W. "The Republican Right: Leadership, Policies, and Intra-Party Politics, 1945–1965." University Park: Pennsylvania State University, 1981. Ph.D. dissertation. University Microfilms No., 81-20460.
———. *The Republican Right since 1945.* Lexington: University Press of Kentucky, 1983.
"Republicans Offer Their Own Report on the 'State of the Union.'" *Congressional Quarterly Weekly Report* 24 (January 21, 1966): 252–54.
"Republicans Report on the State of the Union." *U.S. News and World Report* 67 (February 5, 1968): 78–84.
"RFK versus LBJ." *Statist* 191 (March 17, 1967): 518.
Riesel, Victor. "Labor Chiefs Work to Prevent Anti-LBJ Vote." *Human Events* 26 (July 26, 1966): 11.
Ross, Douglas. *Robert F. Kennedy: Apostle of Change.* New York: Trident Press, 1968.
Ryskind, Allan H. "The Politics Behind Civil Rights in Selma." *Human Events* 25 (February 27, 1965): 12.
Sabato, Larry J. *The Rise of Political Consultants: New Ways of Winning Elections.* New York: Basic Books, 1981.

Scheer, Robert "A Political Portrait of Bobby Kennedy." *Ramparts* 5 (February 1967): 11–17.
Schott, Richard L., and Dagmar S. Hamilton. *People, Positions, and Power: The Political Appointments of Lyndon Johnson.* Chicago: University of Chicago Press, 1983.
Schulz, Bill. "Polls Provide Optimistic Note for Conservatives—Many LBJ Programs Unpopular Even in Districts He Carried in '64." *Human Events* 26 (August 20, 1966): 14.
Shannon, William V. *The Heir Apparent: Robert Kennedy and the Struggle for Power.* New York: Macmillan Co., 1967.
"Some Like LBJ, Some Don't." *Human Events* 24 (October 7, 1964): 11.
Stuart, Anthony. "Is Television Becoming a Political Tool?" *Human Events* 25 (January 9, 1965): 11.
Taylor, Henry J. "Does CORE's Collective Bargaining Restrain Trade?" *Human Events* 24 (September 5, 1964): 13.
Thimmesch, Nick, and William Johnson. *Robert Kennedy at 40.* New York: Norton, 1965.
Thompson, Kenneth. "Big Scramble in Texas Politics: Bad News for LBJ." *Human Events* 27 (November 25, 1967): 8.
———. "Close Race: John Tower vs Waggoner Carr." *Human Events* 26 (October 22, 1966): 12.
Trohan, Walter. "Politics Still Dominate Selection of U.S. Justices." *Human Events* 27 (July 1, 1967): 13.
Von Hippel, Frank, and Joel Primack. *The Politics of Technology.* Stanford, Cal.: Stanford University Press, 1970.
Ware, Alan. *The Breakdown of Democratic Party Organization, 1940–80.* New York: Oxford University Press, 1985.
Wechsler, James A. "The Two-Front War: Johnson vs. Kennedy—The Political Rivalry between LBJ and RFK." *Progressive* 31 (May 1967): 21–24.
"What's Happening to the Democrats? Splinters in the Party." *U.S. News and World Report* 63 (December 18, 1967): 31–33.
"Why 'Liberals' Grumble about LBJ: The Johnson Administration Is Going Too Far Abroad and Not Far Enough at Home." *U.S. News and World Report* 59 (July 5, 1965): 40–42.
Wildavsky, Aaron. *The Politics of the Budgetary Process.* 2nd ed. Boston: Little, Brown, 1974.
Zeiger, Henry A. *Robert F. Kennedy: A Biography.* New York: Meredith, 1968.

B. THE CONGRESS

"Anger on the Hill: A Rebellious Congress Reflects the Decline in President's Popularity." *Business Week*, October 14, 1967: 33–35.

"Back of the 'Conservative Coalition' [of Republicans and Southern Democrats]." *Congressional Quarterly Weekly Report* 23 (November 12, 1965): 2295–2306.

"The Balky 90th Congress: The Record Shows a Long Life with Little Legislation." *U.S. News and World Report* 65 (August 5, 1968): 32–33.

Borst, Philip W. "President Johnson and the 89th Congress: A Functional Analysis of a System under Stress." Claremont, Cal.: Claremont Graduate School, 1968. Ph.D. dissertation. University Microfilms No. 6818257.

Bowles, Nigel P. *The White House and Capitol Hill: The Politics of Presidential Persuasion.* New York: Oxford University Press, 1987.

"Breaking Down the Old Order: Johnson Congress." *Business Week*, September 18, 1965: 25–26.

"The Changing Mood of [the 89th] Congress." *U.S. News and World Report* 60 (May 2, 1966): 28–30.

Cohen, Jeffrey A. "Passing the President's Program: Presidential-Congressional Relations, 1789–1974." Ann Arbor: University of Michigan, 1979. Ph.D. dissertation. University Microfilms No. 79-25127.

"Congress Backs Johnson on 93% of Roll Call Votes [in 1965]." *Congressional Quarterly Weekly Report* 23 (November 26, 1965): 2387–97.

"Congress Begins to Rebel [against Johnson]." *Economist* (Great Britain) 215 (June 19, 1965): 1393–94.

"Congress Ends 'Honeymoon' with LBJ." *Human Events* 23 (January 4, 1964): 4.

"Congress Grants 47.6% of Johnson's Specific Requests." *Congressional Quarterly Weekly Report* 26 (January 12, 1968): 43–60.

"Congress Grants 55.8% of Johnson's Specific Requests: CQ's Johnson Boxscore for 1966." *Congressional Quarterly Weekly Report* 24 (December 2, 1966): 2911–26.

"Congress Grants 57.6% of Johnson's Specific Requests." *Congressional Quarterly Weekly Report* 22 (October 23, 1964): 2561–69.

"Congress Moves Slowly on Johnson's Requests: CQ's Johnson Boxscore for 1967." *Congressional Quarterly Weekly Report* 25 (March 31, 1967): 467–80.
"Congress Races the Johnson Deadline." *Business Week*, June 27, 1964: 32–33.
"Congress Sinking McNamara's 'Floating Arsenal' Plan." *Congressional Quarterly Weekly Report* 25 (April 21, 1967): 637–41.
"Congress Unusually Cooperative with President's Program [Item-by-Item Breakdown]." *Congressional Quarterly Weekly Report* 23 (November 19, 1965): 2341–55.
"Congress 1964—The Year in Review." *Congressional Quarterly Weekly Report* 22 (October 9, 1964): 2373–86.
"Congress 1965—The Year in Review: What the 89th Congress Did and Did Not Do." *Congressional Quarterly Weekly Report* 23 (October 29, 1965): 2155–90.
"Congress 1966: The Year in Review—Economy, War Dominate." *Congressional Quarterly Weekly Report* 24 (October 21, 1966): 2543–60.
"Congress 1967—The Year in Review." *Congressional Quarterly Weekly Report* 25 (December 15, 1967): 2515–45.
"[Congressional] Support of President Drops in 1966 Votes: LBJ Wins 79% Compared with 93% in 1965." *Congressional Quarterly Weekly Report* 24 (December 23, 1966): 3048–59.
"'Conservative Coalition' [in 1964 Congress]." *Congressional Quarterly Weekly Report* 22 (November 27, 1964): 2741–50.
"'Conservative Coalition' Shows New Life." *Congressional Quarterly Weekly Report* 24 (December 30, 1966): 3078–90.
"CQ's Johnson Boxscore for 1965." *Congressional Quarterly Weekly Report* 23 (April 23, 1965): 762–72.
"CQ's Johnson Boxscore for 1966." *Congressional Quarterly Weekly Report* 24 (April 15, 1966): 783–94.
"CQ's Johnson Boxscore for 1968." *Congressional Quarterly Weekly Report* 26 (April 19, 1968): 847–60+.
Davidson, Roger H., and Walter J. Oleszek. *Congress and Its Members*. Washington, D.C.: Congressional Quarterly Press, 1981.
Democratic National Committee. "Democratic Gains in 89th

Congress Boon to President's Program Goals." *The Democrat* 4 (November 21, 1964): 1–4.
"Democrats from North and South Split on 24% of Votes [in 1964 Congress]." *Congressional Quarterly Weekly Report* 22 (December 25, 1964): 2835–40.
"Democrats in Congress Divided on 29% of Vote [in 1966]." *Congressional Quarterly Weekly Report* 25 (February 3, 1967): 176–79.
"Democrats' Regional Divisions Remain Great in 1965 [in both House and Senate: North and South Split]." *Congressional Quarterly Weekly Report* 23 (November 26, 1965): 2399–2402.
Dierenfield, Bruce Jonathan. "Congressman Howard W. Smith: A Political Biography." Charlottesville: University of Virginia, 1981. Ph.D. dissertation. University Microfilms No. 82-19058.
"Election Year Had Little Effect on Voting Participation [in 1964 Congress]." *Congressional Quarterly Weekly Report* 22 (October 30, 1964): 2598–2601.
Emmert, J. Richard. "Freshman Congressmen: Variations in Support for Presidential Legislation, 1953–1968." Providence, R.I.: Brown University, 1970. Ph.D. dissertation. University Microfilms No. 7113861.
"End of the Honeymoon." *Newsweek*, February 15, 1965: 62.
Evans, Rowland, and Robert Novak. "Can Johnson Get Congress Moving?" *Saturday Evening Post* 237 (April 4, 1964): 34, 38–39.
"Final Boxscore on 90th Congress, 1st Session." *Human Events* 27 (December 30, 1967): 15.
"First Session of Great Society Congress." *Public Utilities Fortnightly* 76 (November 11, 1965): 44–45.
Glass, Andrew J. "Mike Mansfield: Majority Leader." *Congress in Change: Evolution and Reform*, edited by Norman J. Ornstein. New York: Praeger, 1975.
Goehlert, Robert U., and John R. Sayre. *The United States Congress: A Bibliography.* New York: Free Press, 1982.
Hartley, Robert E. *Charles H. Percy: A Political Perspective.* Chicago: Rand McNally, 1975.
Haveles, Harry P., Jr. "The Power to Persuade: Presidential Leadership in Congress—Lyndon Johnson and the 89th and 90th Congresses." Cambridge, Mass.: Harvard University, 1976. Honors thesis in Government.

Healy, Paul F. "Speaker of the House [John W. McCormack]." *Columbia* 44 (March 1964): 9.
Hildenbrand, William F., and Kathryn Allamong Jacob, eds. *Guide to Research Collections of Former U.S. Senators, 1789–1982*. Washington, D.C.: U.S. Senate, Bicentennial Publication no. 1, 1983.
"Home Rule: LBJ's First Defeat." *Human Events* 25 (October 16, 1965): 3.
"The House Will Be Its Own Master: Congressmen Head Back to Work Feeling They Have a Mandate Not to Go All the Way with LBJ." *Business Week*, January 7, 1967: 36–39.
"How Johnson Fared with an Unhappy Congress." *U.S. News and World Report* 63 (December 25, 1967): 18–20.
"In Tune with the Leader: Democratic Majorities in Congress Are Ready and Willing to Give Johnson What He Wishes." *Business Week*, January 2, 1965: 16–17.
James, Peggy A., and Kathleen Pritchard. "Presidential Influence on Congress: The Use and Impact of Favors." Paper presented at American Political Science Assn., Washington, D.C., August 28–31, 1986.
"Johnson Won 88% of 1964 Roll Calls." *Congressional Quarterly Weekly Report* 22 (October 30, 1964): 2593–97.
"Johnson's New Consensus." *Business Week*, April 9, 1966: 25–26.
Kennon, Donald R. "John William McCormack." *The Speakers of the U.S. House of Representatives: A Bibliography, 1789–1984*, edited by Donald R. Kennon, pp. 266–72. Baltimore: Johns Hopkins University Press, 1985.
"LBJ and Congress: The Next 100 Days—All Signs Point to a Showdown in Congress." *U.S. News and World Report* 56 (March 30, 1964): 31–32.
"LBJ and Congress—Why the Magic Is Gone [Key Members of Congress Respond]." *U.S. News and World Report* 60 (March 21, 1966): 53–55.
"LBJ Gets Some Lumps: 'No Confidence'." *Human Events* 27 (January 7, 1967): 4.
"LBJ Plans to Pack Ways and Means Committee with Pro-Medicare Majority." *Human Events* 24 (December 19, 1964): 3.
"LBJ Torpedoes Dirksen." *Human Events* 26 (April 30, 1966): 4.
"LBJ vs. Congress: Collision Course." *U.S. News and World Report* 62 (April 3, 1967): 23–24.

Lewis, Ted. "Gloom in Democratic Ranks: Election Returns Shatter Johnson 'Consensus'." *Human Events* 26 (November 1966): 15.

Light, Paul C. "Passing Nonincremental Policy: Presidential Influence in Congress, Kennedy to Carter." *Congress and the Presidency* 9 (Winter 1981–82): 61–82.

"A Look at the Government's Top-Ranking Democrat [House Speaker McCormack]." *U.S. News and World Report*, September 8, 1969: 14–16.

Mansfield, Mike. "Dirksen and LBJ—Strange Allies: What the 'Ev and Lyndon' Friendship Means" (Interview). *U.S. News and World Report* 63 (December 11, 1967): 72–75.

Martin, Glenn R. "Conservatism and Liberalism in the American Congress: A Selected Study of Congressional Voting Ratings, 1947–1972." Muncie, Ind.: Ball State University, 1973. Ph.D. dissertation. University Microfilms No. 74-02941.

Matsunaga, Spark, and Ping Chen. *Rulemakers of the House.* Urbana: University of Illinois Press, 1978.

"McCormack's Power—Next to Speaker Cannon's." *U.S. News and World Report*, January 18, 1965: 20.

"Members Roll-Call Vote Record—79%: Lowest in Years [89th Congress, 1966]." *Congressional Quarterly Weekly Report* 24 (November 4, 1966): 2749–53.

"Much 1964 Congressional Action Was Aimed at Blocking Administrative Moves." *Advertising Age* 35 (October 5, 1964): 78.

"New Congress Starts to Rock LBJ's Boat." *Business Week*, January 14, 1967: 28–29.

"90th Congress: The Men: A Strong GOP Voice." *Business Week*, November 12, 1966: 41–44.

"Now Congress Is Starting to Roll: A Change in President Johnson's Strategy and Tactics." *U.S. News and World Report* 56 (February 17, 1964): 37.

"Ominous Signs for LBJ [Democrats Withdrawing Support]." *Human Events* 27 (May 27, 1967): 3.

"On Johnson Boxscore: Congress Acts Favorably on Johnson Requests [in 1968]." *Congressional Quarterly Weekly Report* 26 (November 1968): 3131–48+.

"Party Majorities Again Split on 'Great Society' Items." *Congressional Quarterly Weekly Report* 24 (December 9, 1966): 2989–93.

Peabody, Robert L. "Party Leadership Change in the United States House of Representatives, 1955–66." *American Political Science Review* 61 (September 1967): 675–93.
"Political Chief [Clark Clifford] at the Pentagon: Congress Is Heating Up Its Opposition to the Administration on Defense." *Business Week*, January 27, 1968: 96–98 +.
Polsby, Nelson W. *Congress and the Presidency.* 3rd ed. Englewood Cliffs, N.J.: Prentice-Hall, 1976.
———. "A Vote on the President's Modest Proposal [to Amend the Constitution and Extend Terms of House of Representatives to Four Years]." *Public Administration Review* 26 (September 1966): 156–59.
"President Johnson Won 79% of Roll-Call Votes in 1967." *Congressional Quarterly Weekly Report* 26 (January 5, 1968): 1–12.
"Presidential Treatment [Johnson's Relations with Congress]." *Economist* (Great Britain) 212 (July 11, 1964): 149–50.
"President's Club Comes under Sharp GOP Criticism." *Congressional Quarterly Weekly Report* 24 (September 9, 1966): 1967–85.
"Putting Congress through Hoops Demonstrates Johnson's Savvy." *Business Week*, April 3, 1965: 32.
"The Real Story of Revolt [against the Administration] in Congress: As Told by Members Themselves." *U.S. News and World Report* 63 (November 13, 1967): 36–39.
Renka, Russell D. "Comparing Presidents Kennedy and Johnson as Legislative Leaders." *Presidential Studies Quarterly* 15 (Fall 1985): 806–25.
———. "Legislative Leadership in the Kennedy and Johnson Presidencies." Paper presented at annual meeting of the Southwestern Political Science Assn., Houston, Texas, April 1978.
Schaffer, William R. *Party and Ideology in the United States Congress.* Lanham, Md.: University Press of America, 1980.
Schapsmeier, Edward L., and Frederick H. Schapsmeier. *Dirksen of Illinois: Senatorial Statesman.* Urbana: University of Illinois Press, 1984.
Silver, Howard J. "Presidential Performance with Congress, 1954–1973." Columbus: The Ohio State University, 1974. Ph. D. dissertation. University Microfilms No. 763554.
Steele, John L. "The Lethargic 88th vs. LBJ." *Life* 55 (December 13, 1963): 3.

Stewart, John G. "Two Strategies of Leadership: Johnson and Mansfield." *Congressional Behavior*, edited by Nelson W. Polsby, pp. 61–92. New York: Random House, 1971.
"Strange Story of a Senate Committee: A Maverick Chairman—At Odds with LBJ—Holds the Gavel of the Once-Powerful Senate Foreign Relations Committee [Senator James W. Fulbright]." *U.S. News and World Report* 60 (April 4, 1966): 32+.
"Strongest LBJ Supporters and Opponents Listed: Survey of House and Senate." *Human Events* 27 (January 7, 1967): 12.
Sullivan, Terry. "Position-taking and Conversion: The Correlates of Presidential Support during Lyndon Johnson's 90th Congress." Paper prepared for the annual American Political Science Association convention, Chicago, September 1–4, 1983.
Sundquist, James L. *The Decline and Resurgence of Congress.* Washington, D.C.: Brookings Institution, 1981.
"Support of President Drops in 1966 Votes: [LBJ] Wins 79%, Compared with 93% in 1965." *Congressional Quarterly Weekly Report* 24 (December 23, 1966): 3048–59.
"They Twist Arms without Hurting: Never Have Liaison Men Worked More Effectively between White House and Capitol Hill than under the Johnson Administration." *Business Week,* April 24, 1965: 82+.
Trohan, Walter. "Is the Honeymoon Over?" *Human Events* 26 (February 26, 1966): 7.
Turesky, Stanley Fred. "A Time to Talk and a Time to Listen: A Study of the Relationship between the Chairman of the Senate Foreign Relations Committee and the President of the United States." Providence, R.I.: Brown University, 1973. Ph.D. dissertation. University Microfilms No. 743086.
United States Congress. *Biographical Directory of the American Congress, 1774–1971.* Washington, D.C.: U.S. Gov't. Printing Office, 1971.
"Votes against LBJ." *Economist* (Great Britain) 225 (November 18, 1967): 734.
"What Congress Did and Did Not Do [1964 Session]." *U.S. News and World Report* 57 (October 12, 1964): 35–37.
"What's Happening in Congress Now: An Urge to Say 'No' to Anything Proposed by LBJ—'Great Society' Is Stalled." *U.S. News and World Report* 63 (October 30, 1967): 29–31.

Wolfinger, Raymond E. "Filibusters: Majority Rule, Presidential Leadership, and Senate Norms." *Congressional Behavior*, edited by Nelson W. Polsby, pp. 111–27. New York: Random House, 1971.

Zeidenstein, Harvey G. "Presidential Popularity and Presidential Support in Congress: Eisenhower to Carter." *Presidential Studies Quarterly* 10 (Spring 1980): 224–33.

C. THE PRESIDENTIAL ELECTION OF 1964

"The Abnormal Election: The American Presidential Election of 1964." *Parliamentary Affairs* (Great Britain) 18 (Spring 1965): 186–95; (Summer 1965): 306–17; (Autumn 1965): 368–79; and 19 (Winter 1965/1966): 37–47; (Spring 1966): 175–90; (Summer 1966): 324–31; (Autumn 1966): 505–15; and 20 (Winter 1966/1967): 49–58; (Summer 1967): 258–73.

"Ad Men Say Johnson's a Cinch." *Printer's Ink* 288 (September 18, 1964): 7.

"Agencies Map Varied Motifs for Barry, LBJ." *Advertising Age* 35 (August 31, 1964): 1+.

Alexander, Herbert E. "The High Cost of TV Campaigns." *Television Quarterly* 5 (Winter 1966): 47–65.

Alexander, Holmes. "Barry Moving—Again." *Human Events* 23 (January 11, 1964): 10.

———. "Goldwater vs. Johnson." *Human Events* 22 (December 28, 1963): 3.

Annunziata, Frank. "The Revolt against the Welfare State: Goldwater Conservatism and the Election of 1964." *Presidential Studies Quarterly* 10 (Spring 1980): 254–65.

"As Democrats See It [the 1964 Race]." *U.S. News and World Report* 57 (September 7, 1964): 29–31.

Asher, Herbert B. *Presidential Elections and American Politics: Voters, Candidates and Campaigns since 1952.* Homewood, Ill.: Dorsey Press, 1976; 3rd ed., 1984.

Babu, R. Ramesh. "The Centre Versus the Fringe: The 1964 American Presidential Election." *International Studies* (India) 6 (April 1965): 367–420.

Bailey, F. Lee, Jr. "Johnson Versus Goldwater: A Surprise Package for Farmers?" *Banking* 57 (October 1964): 88+.

"Baker Case: Potential Election Issues—G.O.P. Criticizes Insurance Man's KTBC Time Purchase." *Broadcasting* 66 (February 3, 1964): 72.

"Barry Flays Columnists: Goldwater Comments on His Defeat." *Editor and Publisher* 97 (November 7, 1964): 11.

"Barry Ready to Meet LBJ in TV Debates." *Broadcasting* 67 (July 20, 1964): 36.

"Barry vs. LBJ—The Fireworks Start." *U.S. News and World Report* 57 (September 14, 1964): 31–32.

"Barry's Ad Men: How Erwin Wasey Will Push Goldwater." *Printers' Ink* 288 (August 21, 1964): 7.

"Barry's Chances against LBJ: Issues Abound." *U.S. News and World Report* 56 (June 22, 1964): 31–33.

Baum, William, et al. "The Myth of Republican 'Establishment' and the Goldwater Nomination in 1964." *Dalhousie Review* (Canada) 45 (Winter 1965/66): 479–91.

"Boardwalk Goes All Out for Democratic Convention." *Business Week*, August 15, 1964: 28–29.

"Bob Kennedy Spent $1,206,000 in Ads in Political Campaign." *Advertising Age* 35 (December 14, 1964): 62.

"Bobby Kennedy on LBJ's '64 Ticket? A Look Behind the 'Kennedy for Vice President' Push." *U.S. News and World Report* 56 (March 23, 1964): 42–44.

Boller, Paul F., Jr. *Presidential Campaigns.* New York: Oxford University Press, 1984.

Boyd, William Austin. "Voter Registration and Turnout in the United States, 1952–76." East Lansing: Michigan State University, 1981. Ph.D. dissertation. University Microfilms No. 8117214.

"Brief Bedfellows: Political Candidates Select Agencies." *Printers' Ink* 288 (September 11, 1964): 7–8.

Brown, R. L. "Goldwater's Agency: New York-Based Ad Agency—Erwin Wasey, Ruthrauff & Ryan." *Sales Management* 93 (September 18, 1964): 36–38+.

"Burch Hindsight: TV Badly Used—GOP Ex-Chairman Says Politicians Laid Egg in Tube Last Year." *Broadcasting* 68 (March 22, 1965): 88.

Burnham, Walter Dean. "American Voting Behavior and the 1964 Election." *Midwest Journal of Political Science* 12 (February 1968): 1–40.

"Businessman's Vote: It's Going to Be a Tough Decision." *Business Week*, September 5, 1964: 23–25.

Carney, Francis M., and Frank H. Way, Jr. *Politics, 1964.* Belmont, Cal.: Wadsworth Publishing Co., 1964.
Chamberlain, Henry. "Rallying Call for American Conservatives [The Goldwater Campaign]." *Modern Age* 8 (Fall 1964): 343–49.
Chamberlain, John. "1964: The Year of the Non-Candidates." *Human Events* 24 (May 2, 1964): 11.
"Civil Rights: A Key But 'Submerged' Issue in 1964." *Congressional Quarterly Weekly Report* 22 (October 2, 1964): 2322–26.
Cohen, Jeffrey, and David C. Nice. "Party Unity and Presidential Election Performance: 1936–1980." *Presidential Studies Quarterly* 12 (Summer 1982): 317–29.
Communist Party of the United States of America. *Passage to Progress: The 1964 Election Mandate and the Road Ahead.* New York: New Century Publishers, 1964. Pamphlet.
"Comparisons: German Reaction to the Republican Nomination of Barry Goldwater." *Economist* (Great Britain) 212 (July 25, 1964): 344.
"Complete Text of the 1964 Democratic Platform." *U.S. News and World Report* 57 (September 7, 1964): 94–99.
"Convention Book Ads Raise Funds for Democrats." *Advertising Age* 35 (August 31, 1964): 4.
Cormier, Frank. "Johnson in the Driver's Seat for the Campaign." *Editor and Publisher* 97 (October 31, 1964): 13+.
Cosman, Bernard. *Five States for Goldwater.* University: University of Alabama Press, 1966.
"CQ Chart of Presidential Convention Information, 1948–1968." *Congressional Quarterly Weekly Report* 25 (September 29, 1967): 1.
Crosby, R. W. "Both Parties Woo Business." *Iron Age* 194 (September 3, 1964): 25–26.
Cummings, Milton C., Jr. *Congressmen and the Electorate: Elections for the U.S. House and the President, 1920–1964.* New York: Free Press, 1966.
De Toledano, Ralph. "Behind the 'Mississippi Controversy' at the Democratic Convention." *Human Events* 24 (September 12, 1964): 8.
———. "Is It Certain President Johnson Will Win?" *Human Events* 24 (June 13, 1964): 6.
———. "LBJ Puts the Pentagon in the Political Campaign." *Human Events* 24 (September 5, 1964): 3.

Dell, George W. "Republicans Nominee: Barry M. Goldwater." *Quarterly Journal of Speech* 50 (December 1964): 399–404.
Democratic National Committee. "500,000 Get-Out-the-Vote Workers to Aid in Bid Drive for Record Vote." *The Democrat* 4 (October 19, 1964): 1–8.
———. "A Johnson Landslide." *The Democrat* 4 (November 6, 1964): 1–4.
———. "LBJ Carries Campaign into 11 States as First Lady Whistle-Stops in South." *The Democrat* 4 (October 12, 1964): 1–8.
———. "1964 Democratic National Convention." *The Democrat* (Souvenir Edition) 4 (August 24, 1964): 1–27.
———. "President Pleas for National Unity; Scores Goldwater on Nuclear Sanity." *The Democrat* 4 (September 14, 1964): 1–8.
———. "President to Campaign in 30 States; Scores Any Talk of Overconfidence." *The Democrat* 4 (September 28, 1964): 1–8.
———. "'64 Campaign Begins." *The Democrat* 4 (September 7, 1964): 1–8.
———. "Voter Drive in High Gear." *The Democrat* 4 (October 26, 1964): 1–8.
———. "Voter Drive Record." *The Democrat* 4 (September 28, 1964): 1–8.
———. "What Goldwater Said, 1953–1964." *Democratic National Committee Report* [Washington, D.C.] July 12, 1964.
"The Democratic Party in Atlantic City." *Texas Observer*, September 4, 1964: 3+.
"Democratic Plank Vows Continued Consumer Aid." *Advertising Age* 35 (August 31, 1964): 2.
"Democrats Point LBJ as Hero; Call GOP Warmongering Party." *Human Events* 24 (October 17, 1964): 15.
Dickinson, William B., Jr. "Negro Voting [in 1964]." *Editorial Research Reports*, October 14, 1964: 743–60.
———. "Politician and the Press [The Press as a 1964 Political Target]." *Editorial Research Reports*, September 2, 1964: 643–60.
Donovan, Frank R. *The Americanism of Barry Goldwater*. New York: Macfadden-Bartell Corp., 1964.
Duke, Paul. "Southern Politics and the Negroes in 1964." *Reporter* 31 (December 17, 1964): 18–21.

"Education: The GOP Flunks Out [1964 Democratic and Republican Party Platforms]." *AFL-CIO American Federationist* 71 (October 1964): 21–24.
Field, John O., and Ronald E. Anderson. "Ideology in the Public's Conceptualization of the 1964 Election." *Public Opinion Quarterly* 33 (Fall 1969): 380–98.
"Financial Planks in the Party Platforms." *Banking* 57 (October 1964): 57+.
"Focus on 1964: Political Parties Plan New Strategies." *Nation's Business* 51 (December 1963): 40–41+.
Forbes, Malcolm S. "GOP Convention." *Forbes Magazine* 94 (August 1, 1964): 10.
———. "Is It Senator Humphrey?" *Forbes Magazine* 94 (August 1, 1964): 9.
———. "No Time for Throttle-Bottoms [The Importance of the Democratic Vice-Presidential Candidate]." *Forbes Magazine* 93 (May 1, 1964): 11.
"440 for LBJ; 359 for Barry." *Editor and Publisher* 97 (October 31, 1964): 9–13.
Frommer, Arthur, ed. *Goldwater from A—Z: A Critical Handbook.* New York: Frommer Pasmantier Publishing Corp., 1964.
"Getting Across to Voters: Goldwater Scores with the Crowds and Democrats Plug Away." *Business Week,* September 19, 1964: 32–33.
"Goldwater and the Alliance." *Economist* (Great Britain) 212 (July 18, 1964): 229–30.
"Goldwater Champing at the Bit; LBJ Holds the Reins." *Broadcasting* 67 (August 3, 1964): 66.
"Goldwater, Miller Campaign on 'Moral Leadership' Issue [Republican Attack on President Johnson in 1964]." *Congressional Quarterly Weekly Report* 22 (October 16, 1964): 2455–57.
"Goldwater Portrait Edition." *Human Events* 23 (January 25, 1964): 1–16.
"Goldwater Swings at News Commentators." *Broadcasting* 67 (November 9, 1964): 24+.
"Goldwater vs. LBJ—'64 Choice? 'Stop Goldwater' Strategy Is in Complete Disarray." *U.S. News and World Report* 56 (June 15, 1964): 35–37.
Goldwater, Barry M. *Where I Stand.* New York: McGraw-Hill, 1964.

———. "Where I Stand on the Issues." *Human Events* 24 (October 24, 1964): 11.
"Goldwater's Economics." *Business Week*, September 26, 1964: 176–78+.
"Goldwater's Hour—Sweeps Nomination with Ease." *Business Week*, July 18, 1964: 23–25.
"GOP Campaign: Special Report." *Business Week*, August 1, 1964: 16–20.
"GOP Candidates' Position Papers." *Saturday Review* 47 (September 9, 1964): 41–42.
"GOP Claims ABC Failed to Clear Good Time Slots—Complaint by Erwin Wasey, Ruthrauff & Ryan." *Advertising Age* 35 (November 2, 1964): 2.
"GOP Group Charges Neglect of Defense." *Aviation Week and Space Technology* 81 (October 26, 1964): 34.
Haber, Robert Alan. *Taking Johnson Seriously*. New York: Students for a Democratic Society, 1964? Pamphlet.
Hadley, Charles D., and Susan E. Howell. "The Southern Split-Ticket Voter, 1952–1976: Republican Conversion or Democratic Decline?" *Party Politics in the South*, ed. by Robert P. Steed, Laurence W. Moreland, and Tod A. Baker, pp. 127–151. New York: Praeger, 1980.
Heady, R. "Inauguration to Be Showcase for New Marketing Face of Eastern Air Lines." *Advertising Age* 36 (January 18, 1965): 3+.
Hess, Karl. *In a Cause That Will Triumph: The Goldwater Campaign and the Future of Conservatism*. Garden City, N.Y.: Doubleday, 1967.
"His Own Kind of Campaign—Barry Goldwater." *Business Week*, July 25, 1964. 122–24+.
Hofstadter, Richard. "The Goldwater Debacle." *Encounter* 24 (January 1965): 66–70.
Horton, Frank. "LBJ Campaigns with Tax-Paid Posters." *Human Events* 24 (March 14, 1964): 15.
"How Democrats Expect to Win [in 1964]." *Nation's Business* 52 (June 1964): 76+.
"How Democrats Plan Victory: South No Longer a Sure Thing in a Presidential Year." *U.S. News and World Report* 57 (August 31, 1964): 25–30.
"How Oil Marketers Will Vote." *National Petroleum News* 56 (October 1964): 61–64.

"How Republicans Expect to Win." *Nation's Business* 52 (June 1964): 77–78+.

"How to Win against Prosperity: Goldwater Will Push Basic Theme of Cutting Government Power—Targets: McNamara and Reds." *Business Week*, August 1, 1964: 16–19.

"How Union Leaders Feel about Johnson Now: Will the Johnson Administration Be 'Liberal' Enough to Suit Them?" *U.S. News and World Report* 56 (March 2, 1964): 86–88.

Howell, Michael J. "Theodore H. White as a Speech Critic: An Analysis of His Treatment of Speech-making in Three Presidential Campaigns, 1960–1968." New York: State University of New York, 1972. M.A. thesis. University Microfilms No. M-4273.

"Humphrey Comes Up Strong for the Number Two Spot." *Business Week*, August 8, 1964: 17–18.

Humphrey, Hubert H. "Humphrey's Acceptance Speech [August 27, 1964]." *Congressional Quarterly Weekly Report* 22 (August 28, 1964): 2014–15.

———. *Meet the Press: Guest, Senator Hubert H. Humphrey, Democratic Vice-Presidential Candidate* (Interview). Washington, D.C.: Merkle Press, vol. 8, no. 34, 1964.

"If Lyndon Johnson Wins Big: Big Plans Afoot for a New Johnson Administration." *U.S. News and World Report* 57 (October 12, 1964): 48–50+.

"In the Home Stretch—Can Goldwater Still Make It?" *U.S. News and World Report* 57 (October 19, 1964): 35–38.

Inter-University Consortium for Political and Social Research. *Codebook for the 1964 American National Election Survey*. Ann Arbor: Inter-University Consortium for Political and Social Research, 1964.

"Is It to Be the Kennedy Brothers vs. LBJ?" *U.S. News and World Report* 59 (July 12, 1964): 50–52.

Jamieson, Kathleen Hall. *Packaging the Presidency: A History and Criticism of Presidential Campaign Advertising*. New York: Oxford University Press, 1984.

"Johnson and Humphrey—A Political Saga." *U.S. News and World Report* 57 (November 16, 1964): 56–58.

"Johnson Broadcast Holding Hit by G.O.P." *Broadcasting* 66 (March 30, 1964): 131.

"The Johnson Sweep: What Johnson Plans Now." *U.S. News and World Report* 57 (November 16, 1964): 33–37.

Johnson, Walter. "Have Faith in the Twentieth Century [Evaluation of the 1964 Presidential Election Campaign]." *Bulletin of the Atomic Scientists* 21 (January 1965): 10–15.

Katona, George. "How Right Are the Polls? It's Now Lyndon Johnson over Barry Goldwater by a Wide Margin." *U.S. News and World Report* 57 (September 21, 1964): 33–36.

Kluckhorn, Frank. "ADA Runs the Johnson Show." *Human Events* 24 (October 3, 1964): 1.

Kornberg, Allan, et al. "The [1964] National Elections and Comparative Positions of Negroes and Whites on [Foreign and Domestic] Policy." *South Atlantic Quarterly* 57 (Summer 1968): 405–18.

Kramer, Gerald H. "Short-Term Fluctuations in U.S. Voting Behavior, 1896–1964." *American Political Science Review* 65 (March 1971): 131–43.

Kraus, Sidney. "Presidential Debates in 1964." *Quarterly Journal of Speech* 50 (February 1964): 19–23.

Krukones, Michael G. *Promises and Performance: Presidential Campaigns as Policy Predictors.* Lanham, Md.: University Press of America, 1984.

———. "Presidential Campaigns as Predictors of Performance in Office: 1912–1972." Oxford, Ohio: Miami University, 1979. Ph.D. dissertation. University Microfilms No. 7920291.

"Labor Drive for LBJ Hits Own Backlash." *Business Week*, September 12, 1964: 49–50+.

Lachman, Seymour P. "Barry Goldwater and the 1964 Religious Issue." *Journal of Church and State* 10 (Autumn 1968): 389–404.

Lambert, D. E. "Petroleum and the Party Platforms." *World Oil.* 159 (October 1964): 11–12.

"LBJ vs. BMG." *Human Events* 23 (February 1, 1964): 13.

"LBJ vs. Goldwater—A Study in Contrasts." *U.S. News and World Report.* 57 (September 7, 1964): 32–35.

"LBJ Warned He May Lose Ethnic Vote." *Human Events* 24 (August 15, 1964): 3.

Leuthold, David. "Voter Attitudes in 1964." *University of Missouri Business and Government Review* 6 (January/February 1965): 21–27.

"Liberal Record of Hubert Humphrey." *Human Events* 24 (September 26, 1964): 1–2.

Lisagor, Peter. "Presidential Race Is Never A Sure Thing." *Nation's Business* 52 (August 1964): 21–22.

"Listing of the 1964 Republican Presidential Campaign Staff." *Congressional Quarterly Weekly Report* 22 (September 25, 1964): 2222–29.

Lokos, Lionel. *Hysteria 1964: The Fear Campaign against Barry Goldwater.* New Rochelle, N.Y.: Arlington House, 1967.

Lubell, Samuel. "The Changing U.S. Electorate: Long Range Democratic Problems and Republican Opportunities." *Fortune* 70 (July 1964): 132–35 +.

"Lyndon Plays It Cool: Democrats Prepare for Atlantic City." *Business Week*, August 15, 1964: 27.

Martin, John Bartlow. "Election of 1964." *History of American Presidential Elections*, edited by Arthur M. Schlesinger, Jr. and Fred L. Israel, vol. IX, pp. 119–243. New York: Confucian Press, 1981.

Maynard, P. J. "Candidates and the Platforms." *Magazine of Wall Street* 115 (September 19, 1964): 8–10 +.

McKenna, William J. "The 1964 Presidential Election—The Issues and the Campaign." *Economics and Business Bulletin of the School of Business Administration, Temple University* 17 (September 1964): 32–38.

Meyers, David S. "Editorials and Foreign Affairs in the 1964 Presidential Campaign." *Journalism Quarterly* 45 (Summer 1968): 211–18.

Miller, Warren E., and Teresa E. Levitin. *Leadership and Change: Presidential Elections from 1952–1976.* Lanham, Md.: University Press of America, 1984.

Morley, Felix. "Election Winner Will Face Historic Problems." *Nation's Business* 52 (March 1964): 27–28.

Mortensen, Calvin D. "A Comparative Analysis of Political Persuasion on Four Telecast Program Formats in the 1960 and 1964 Presidential Campaigns." Minneapolis: University of Minnesota, 1967. Ph.D. dissertation. University Microfilms No. 68-07420.

Mullen, James J. "Newspaper Advertising in the Johnson-Goldwater Campaign." *Journalism Quarterly* 45 (Summer 1968): 219–25.

Nelson Frederick. "Of Course the GOP Candidate Must Be Conservative." *Human Events* 22 (December 28, 1963): 1, 2.

"New Mandate: President Johnson's Devastating Victory." *Business Week*, November 7, 1964: 33–34.

"1964 Campaigns Generated Heavy Political Ad Lineage." *Editor and Publisher* 97 (December 12, 1964): 9–11+.

"1964 Democratic Convention—Proceedings [Highlights, Credentials Fight, Quotes, Chronology; LBJ-HHH: Nominations, Acceptance Speeches; Platform: Analysis, Hearings, Text.]" *Congressional Quarterly Weekly Report* 22 (August 28, 1964): 1957–65+.

"The 1964 Election: A Review of the Johnson-Goldwater Race for the Presidency." *Congressional Quarterly Weekly Report* 25 (September 29, 1967): 1931–37.

Novak, Robert D. *The Agony of the G.O.P. 1964*. New York: Macmillan, 1965.

"Nowhere to Go But to Johnson: Labor's Political Outlook." *Business Week*, July 25, 1964: 47–48.

"Nuclear 'Responsibility' Dominates Defense Issues [in 1964 Election]." *Congressional Quarterly Weekly Report* 22 (October 2, 1964): 2311–21.

"Opening the Big Campaign: The Republican Primary in New Hampshire." *Business Week*, February 29, 1964: 28–29.

Payne, Bruce. "American Political Structure—The Meaning of the Election [1964]." *Yale Papers in Political Science* 4 (Fall 1964): 22+.

Perlo, Victor. "Financial Forces in the 1964 U.S. Elections. *New Times* (Moscow), August 19, 1964: 6–9.

"Platforms Differ on Defense and Space." *Aviation Week and Space Technology* 81 (August 31, 1964): 20–21.

"Political Ad Wheels Start to Turn." *Advertising Age* 35 (September 7, 1964): 1+.

"Political Mood of U.S. Now—What a Nationwide Survey Shows." *U.S. News and World Report* 57 (August 24, 1964): 54–63.

Polsby, Nelson W., and Aaron B. Wildavsky, eds. *Presidential Elections: Strategies of American Electoral Politics*. 3rd ed. New York: Scribners, 1971.

Pomper, Gerald. "From Confusion to Clarity: Issues and American Voters, 1956–1968." *American Political Science Review* 66 (June 1972): 415–28.

"Power Issue in 1964 Presidential Platforms." *Public Utilities Fortnightly* 74 (September 24, 1964): 43–44.

"Professionals Emerge as a Political Force: Scientists and Engineers for Johnson." *Aviation Week and Space Technology* 81 (October 12, 1964): 26.

"The Public Records of Lyndon B. Johnson and Hubert H. Humphrey: The Lives, Votes and Stands of the 1964 Democratic Candidates." *Congressional Quarterly Weekly Report* 22 (September 11, 1964): 2057–2121.

"The Real Story the '64 Elections Tell: Massive Study Shows Republicans Have a Lot to Worry About." *U.S. News and World Report* 58 (June 7, 1965): 50–52.

"Republicans Hit Kennedy-Johnson Record." *Engineering News-Record* 173 (July 16, 1964): 21.

Riesel, Victor. "Humphrey for Veep?" *Human Events* 22 (December 28, 1963): 10.

———. "Union Chiefs Preparing Massive Anti-Goldwater Drive." *Human Events* 24 (June 20, 1964): 10.

Rogers, Donald I. "LBJ's Patsy: Business." *Human Events* 24 (June 6, 1964): 12.

Rossman, Jules. "'Meet the Press' and National Elections: The Candidates and the Issues, 1952–1964." East Lansing: Michigan State University, 1968. Ph.D. dissertation. University Microfilms No. 69-11155.

Runyon, John H., Jennefer Verdini, and Sally S. Runyon, eds. *Source Book of American Presidential Campaign and Election Statistics, 1948–1968.* New York: Frederick Ungar, 1971.

Ryskind, Morris. "Liberals Are Now Chanting: 'All the Way with LBJ!'" *Human Events* 23 (February 22, 1964): 11.

Scammon, Richard M., ed. *America at the Polls: A Handbook of American Presidential Election Statistics, 1920–1964.* Pittsburgh: Pittsburgh University Press, 1965.

"School Aid: What LBJ and Goldwater Believe." *U.S. News and World Report* 56 (September 28, 1964): 15.

Schwartz, Tony. *The Responsive Chord.* New York: Anchor Books, 1974.

Segal, David R. "Partisan Realignment in the U.S.: The Lessons of the 1964 Election." *Public Opinion Quarterly* 32 (Fall 1968): 441–44.

Shadegg, Stephen. *What Happened to Goldwater.* New York: Holt, Rinehart & Winston, 1965.

Shannon, William V. *The Heir Apparent: Robert Kennedy and the Struggle for Power.* New York: Macmillan Co., 1967.

Shaw, Malcolm. "The Abnormal Election [1964]." *Parliamen-*

tary Affairs (Great Britain) 18 (Spring 1965): 186–95; 18 (Summer 1965): 306–17; 18 (Autumn 1965): 368–79; 19 (Winter 1965/66): 37–47; 19 (Spring 1966): 175–90; 19 (Summer 1966): 324–31.

Shinn, Roger L. "Election Issues: 1964." *Social Action* 31 (1964): 4+.

"Six vs. LBJ: Latest on the Republican Scramble [for Presidential Nomination]." *U.S. News and World Report* 56 (January 13, 1964): 57–58.

Smith, James George. "Presidential Elections and Racial Discrimination: Campaign Promises, Presidential Performance and Democratic Accountability, 1960–1980." Bloomington: Indiana University, 1981. Ph.D. dissertation. University Microfilms No. 82-02984.

Smith, Terry. "Bobby's Image." *Esquire* 63 (April 1965): 62–63, 132–40.

———. "How Agencies for J.F., Bob Kennedy Drives Were Picked Is Recalled in Esquire Article." *Advertising Age* 36 (March 22, 1965): 14.

Stempel, Guido H. III. "The Prestige Press in Two Presidential Elections: 1960 and 1964." *Journalism Quarterly* 42 (Winter 1965): 15–21.

"'Stop Goldwater' Move Collapses at Cleveland." *Congressional Quarterly Weekly Report* 22 (June 12, 1964): 1183–86.

Taylor, Henry J. "The Catholic Issue and LBJ." *Human Events* 24 (March 28, 1964): 10.

———. "LBJ—RFK Feud." *Human Events* 24 (July 18, 1964): 12.

"Third-Party Presidential Candidates in the 1964 Campaign." *Congressional Quarterly Weekly Report* 22 (October 16, 1964): 2465–66.

"'Third Party' Taking Shape: Angry South Finds Leader in George Wallace of Alabama." *U.S. News and World Report* 61 (October 3, 1966): 44–45.

"310 Papers Support LBJ, 272 for Barry." *Editor and Publisher* 97 (October 17, 1964): 14.

"Truly Pivotal Election [1964]." *AFL-CIO American Federationist* 71 (October 1964): 1–3.

Tyler, Gus. "Goldwater: Front Man for Counter Revolution." *AFL-CIO American Federationist* 71 (October 1964): 3–7.

United States Department of Commerce. Bureau of the Census.

"Voter Participation in the National Election: November 1964." *Current Population Reports*, Series p-20, no. 143, October 25, 1965.

Van den Bosch, Govert W., ed. *Political Issues and Business in 1964*. Ann Arbor, Mich.: Foundation for Research and Human Behavior, 1964.

"Views of the Presidential Candidates on the Future of the U.S. in Space." *Missiles and Rockets* 15 (October 26, 1964): 16–18.

Wallace, George C. "Why Wallace Withdrew—in the Governor's Own Words." *U.S. News and World Report* 57 (August 3, 1964): 565–68.

"What Unions Did to Help the Democrats [in 1964]." *U.S. News and World Report* 57 (November 9, 1964): 19–27.

"When Politics Rip Apart Old Loyalties: Businessmen Widely Split on Presidential Race." *Business Week*, October 24, 1964: 38+.

"White House, Democratic Committee Work Together: Campaign Organization behind President Lyndon B. Johnson and Sen. Hubert Humphrey." *Congressional Quarterly Weekly Report* 22 (October 16, 1964): 2447–54.

White, Theodore H. "Memo to a Future Historian: Landslide 1964." *Life* 57 (November 13, 1964): 32–45.

"Why Labor Endorses Johnson and Humphrey." *AFL-CIO American Federationist* 71 (September 1964): 1–6.

Wiener, Leonard. "Stock Market and Presidential Elections—Natural Allies." *U.S. News and World Report*, January 16, 1984: 60–61.

Zikmund, Joseph II "Suburban Voting in Presidential Elections, 1948–1964." *Midwest Journal of Political Science* 12 (May 1968): 239–58.

D. THE PRESIDENTIAL ELECTION OF 1968

"ADA Splinters [over LBJ]." *Human Events* 28 (February 24, 1968): 5.

Adamany, David. *The Presidential Nominating Conventions of 1968*. Washington, D.C.: Center for Information on America, 1968.

"AFL-CIO Gets Wooed for 1968 to Win Labor's Political Support." *Business Week*, December 16, 1967: 76+.

"AFL-CIO Puts Chips on Humphrey." *Business Week*, April 13, 1968: 103.
Aiken, George D. "The Triumph of Media over Matter: Vietnam and the '68 Elections." *War/Peace Report* 89 (March 1968): 14–16.
Allen, Robert S. "Humphrey to Take on McCarthy in Wisconsin." *Human Events* 28 (January 13, 1968): 7.
———. "Humphrey Will Soon Announce His Candidacy." *Human Events* 28 (April 20, 1968): 7.
———. "Kennedy Forces Budget $5 Million for Nomination Push." *Human Events* 28 (April 6, 1968): 7.
Altschuler, Bruce E. *Keeping a Finger on the Public Pulse: Private Polling and Presidential Elections*. Westport, Conn.: Greenwood Press, 1982.
———. "Kennedy Decides to Run: 1968." *Presidential Studies Quarterly* 10 (Summer 1980): 348–52.
"Amidst the Wreckage, Hubert." *Texas Observer*, September 6, 1968: 1+.
"Arabs Hail Johnson 'Defeat'; Israelis Sorry but Cautious." *Jewish Observer—Middle East Review* 17 (April 5, 1968): 5.
Arrendell, Odes Charles. "Coverage of the 1968 Democratic and Republican Presidential Campaigns by Texas Daily Newspapers: An Evaluation Related to Social Responsibility Theory." Austin: University of Texas, 1969. Ph.D. dissertation. University Microfilms No. 70-10745.
Asher, Herbert B. *Presidential Elections and American Politics: Voters, Candidates and Campaigns since 1952*. Homewood, Ill.: Dorsey Press, 1976; 3rd ed., 1984.
"Bobby-for-President Forces Want 'Open' 1968 Convention." *Human Events* 27 (July 29, 1967): 7.
"Bobby Kennedy's Strategy Now: On the '68 Ticket with LBJ?" *U.S. News and World Report* 63 (October 23, 1967): 34–35.
Boyd, William Austin. "Voter Registration and Turnout in the United States, 1952–76." East Lansing: Michigan State University, 1981. Ph.D. dissertation. University Microfilms No. 8117214.
Brock, Bernard L. "1968 Democratic Campaign: A Political Upheaval." *Quarterly Journal of Speech* 55 (February 1969): 26–55.
Broder, David S. "Election of 1968." *History of American Presidential Elections*, edited by Arthur M. Schlesinger, Jr. and

Fred L. Israel, vol. 9, pp. 249–365. New York: Confucian Press, 1981.

———. "LBJ's Re-Election Problems." *Human Events* 27 (January 7, 1967): 13.

Burnham, Walter Dean. "Election 1968: The Abortive Landslide." *Transaction* 6 (December 1968): 18–24.

"Campaign '68 Yields Record Buys." *Broadcasting* 76 (January 6, 1969): 60–61.

"Can Humphrey Stop RFK?" *Newsweek*, April 29, 1968: 23–31.

"Can LBJ Be Beaten?" *Human Events* 27 (August 19, 1967): 2.

Carney, Francis M., and Frank H. Way, Jr. *Politics, 1968*. Belmont, Cal.: Wadsworth Publishing Co., 1967.

Catchpole, Terry. "COPE Bigwigs Growing Desperate about '68 Prospects." *Human Events* 27 (November 4, 1967): 12, 14.

———. "How Labor Almost Elected Humphrey." *Human Events* 28 (November 16, 1968): 10.

Chamberlain, John. "Can Nixon Really End the War?" *Human Events* 28 (April 6, 1968): 1.

———. "Why the 1968 Election Is Still a Toss-Up." *Human Events* 27 (August 12, 1967): 5.

"Chicago: Law and Disorder." *Business Week*, August 31, 1968: 16.

"Chicago Sweats It Out." *Business Week*, July 13, 1968: 36–37.

"Chicago Trying Hard to Keep the Lid On." *Business Week*, August 17, 1968: 24–25.

Christian, George. *The President Steps Down: A Personal Memoir of the Transfer of Power*. New York: Macmillan, 1970.

"Close Call in Chicago." *Broadcasting* 75 (September 2, 1968): 26–27.

"A Close Look at Wallace's Words and Actions." *Human Events* 28 (October 19, 1968): 8–10.

Cohen, Jeffrey, and David C. Nice. "Party Unity and Presidential Election Performance: 1936–1980." *Presidential Studies Quarterly* 12 (Summer 1982): 317–29.

"The Collapse of Liberalism." *Human Events* 28 (October 26, 1968): 6.

Collier, Peter, and David Horowitz. *The Kennedys: An American Drama*. New York: Summit, 1984; paper, Warner Books, 1985.

"Concern about McCarthy." *Economist* (Great Britain) 225 (December 23, 1967): 1227–28.

Congressional Quarterly Service. *The Presidential Nominating Conventions 1968*. Washington, D.C.: Congressional Quarterly Service, 1968.

"Conservative Battle Is Hardly Over, but Nixon Victory Provides Great Opportunity." *Human Events* 28 (November 10, 1968): 1, 4.

"CQ Chart of Presidential Convention Information, 1948–1968." *Congressional Quarterly Weekly Report* 25 (September 29, 1967): 1.

Crespi, Irving. "Structural Sources of the George Wallace Constituency." *Social Science Quarterly* 52 (June 1971): 115–32.

Davis, John H. *The Kennedys: Dynasty and Disaster, 1848–1983*. New York: McGraw Hill, 1984.

De Toledano, Ralph. "Is Bobby's Bandwagon Already Slowing Down?" *Human Events* 28 (May 4, 1968): 7.

———. *RFK: The Man Who Would Be President*. New York: Putnam, 1967.

———. "Rockefeller Off and Running for '68." *Human Events* 27 (December 30, 1967): 1.

———. "Which Advisers Will Nixon Listen to This Year? Will He Take Advantage of Liberal Disarray?" *Human Events* 28 (February 3, 1968): 7.

"Democratic Runners: McCarthy—Man of Conscience." *Economist* (Great Britain) 227 (April 27, 1968): 45.

"Democrats for Peaceful Action: Americans for Democratic Action and the 'Dump Johnson' Movement." *Economist* (Great Britain) 224 (September 30, 1967): 1191–92.

"Democrats Nail Down a Platform." *Engineering News-Record* 181 (August 29, 1968): 29–30.

"Democrats Shift to L & N Reflects Party's Problems." *Advertising Age* 39 (September 23, 1968): 1+.

Duncan, Donald. *Support Our Soldiers: Reject Humphrey-Nixon-Wallace*. New York: National Mobilization Committee to End the War in Vietnam, 1968. Pamphlet.

Edwards, Willard. "Five Senators LBJ Most Wants to Defeat in '68." *Human Events* 25 (October 2, 1965): 8.

"Election '68: Civil Rights and the Next President." *Economist* (Great Britain) 227 (April 20, 1968): 23–24.

"Election '68: Democrats Up in the Air—Mr. Johnson's Withdrawl." *Economist* (Great Britain) 227 (April 6, 1968): 31–32.
"Election '68: Fence Sitters for Humphrey." *Economist* (Great Britain) 227 (April 20, 1968): 20.
"Election '68: Here Comes Bobby." *Economist* (Great Britain) 226 (March 30, 1968): 42+.
"Election '68: Hoosier Puzzle." *Economist* (Great Britain) 227 (April 27, 1968): 41.
"Election '68: Vietnam Goes to Chicago." *Economist* (Great Britain) 228 (August 24, 1968): 25+.
"Election '68 Democratic Runners: Humphrey to Unite Democrats?" *Economist* (Great Britain) 227 (April 20, 1968): 19–20.
"Era of Democrats Ending? A Shattered Strategy." *U.S. News and World Report* 65 (September 16, 1968): 29–31.
Evans, M. Stanton. "Races to Watch in '68." *National Review*, October 19, 1968: 29–33.
———. "The Meaning of Miami [the Republican National Convention]." *Human Events* 28 (August 24, 1968): 8.
———. "Why the GOP Must Move Right." *Human Events* 28 (November 23, 1968): 1, 6.
Faber, Harold, ed. *The New York Times Election Handbook, 1968*. New York: New American Library, Inc., 1968.
"The Fight to Dump LBJ." *Newsweek*, March 25, 1968: 21–22.
"For '68: Rising Talk of a Rockefeller-Reagan Ticket." *U.S. News and World Report* 63 (July 3, 1967): 50–51.
"Fortune Exchange with the Candidates on the U.S. Economy." *Fortune* 78 (October 1968): 230–34.
Frady, Marshall. *Wallace*. New York: World Publishing Co., 1968.
Germond, Jack, W. "The Strange Case of Nelson Rockefeller." *Progressive* 32 (June 1968): 16–20.
Glick, Edward M., ed. *The 1968 Campaign: Anatomy of a Crucial Election*. Washington, D.C.: American Institute for Political Communication, 1970.
Gold, Victor. "The Rise and Stand of George Corley Wallace." *Human Events* 28 (January 27, 1968): 7–9.
Goldwater, Barry. "LBJ's 'Help Hubert' Campaign." *Human Events* 26 (February 5, 1966): 2.

———. "LBJ/Wallace Hard to Beat." *Human Events* 27 (December 2, 1967): 11.
Goodwin, Richard N. "The Night McCarthy Turned to Kennedy." *Look*, October 15, 1968: 102.
"GOP Votes for Unity: Nixon's Nomination." *Business Week*, August 10, 1968: 21–24.
"Governor William Scranton Starts 1968 Campaign: Proposes 'Great Society' Jr. for Pennsylvania." *Human Events* 25 (June 5, 1965): 3.
Grant, Donald. "May Lawrence—Is She Hubert's Secret Weapon?" *Advertising Age* 39 (October 14, 1968): 1+.
———. "Nixon Intensifies Ad Efforts; Fund Lack Hurts HHH." *Advertising Age* 39 (October 21, 1968): 2.
Greene, Jerry. "McCarthy Now Threatens to Go to Paris Talks." *Human Events* 28 (July 6, 1968): 6.
Halberstam, David. "McCarthy and the Divided Left." *Harper's Magazine* 236 (March 1968): 32–44.
———. "The Man Who Ran against Lyndon Johnson." *Harper's Magazine* 237 (December 1968): 47–66.
———. "Travels with Bobby Kennedy." *Harper's Magazine* 237 (July 1968): 51–66.
———. *The Unfinished Odyssey of Robert Kennedy*. New York: Random House, 1968.
Hansen, Donald C., and Theodore Lippman, Jr. *Muskie*. New York: Norton, 1971.
Harris, Louis. "Part Way with RFK—The Price He Paid." *Newsweek*, May 20, 1968: 35.
Heren, Louis. "Peace and U.S. Politics." *Atlas*, May 1968: 14–16.
Herzog, Arthur. *McCarthy for President*. New York: Viking, 1969.
Heuvel, William V., and Milton Gwirtzman. *On His Own: Robert F. Kennedy 1964–1968*. Garden City, N.Y.: Doubleday, 1970.
"HHH: Fitting Close to Chicago Fiasco [Democratic National Convention]." *Human Events* 28 (September 7, 1968): 1.
Higdon, Hal. "Indiana: A Test for Bobby Kennedy." *New York Times Magazine*, May 5, 1968: 32–33.
Hoopes, Townsend. "LBJ's Account of March, 1968." *New Republic* 163 (March 14, 1970): 17–19.

"How Democrats Plan to Win." *U.S. News and World Report* 65 (September 2, 1968): 26–29.
"How Hubert Humphrey, Richard Nixon, George Wallace Stand on Business Issues." *Nation's Business* 56 (September 1968): 44–55.
"How McCarthy Scored." *Business Week*, April 6, 1968: 26.
Howell, Michael J. "Theodore H. White as a Speech Critic: An Analysis of His Treatment of Speech-making in Three Presidential Campaigns, 1960–1968." New York: State University of New York, 1972. M.A. thesis. University Microfilms No. M-4273.
"Hubert and John." *Texas Observer*, September 6, 1968: 6+.
"Hubert H. Humphrey: Why Organized Labor Is Behind Him All the Way." *American Labor* 1 (July 1968): 22–29.
"The Hubert Humphrey Record." *U.S. News and World Report* 65 (July 1, 1968): 36–41.
"Humphrey Hammers against the Odds." *Business Week*, October 19, 1968: 34–36.
"Humphrey Steps Out on His Own." *Business Week*, April 20, 1968: 40–41.
"Humphrey vs. Nixon: Pre-Campaign Size-Up." *U.S. News and World Report* 65 (August 26, 1968): 21–23.
"Humphrey Wins Battered Prize." *Business Week*, August 31, 1968: 11–12.
Humphrey, Hubert H. "Humphrey Looks at His Future: An Interview with the Vice President." *U.S. News and World Report* 64 (May 27, 1968): 54–60.
———. "Humphrey Statement [Announcing His Candidacy for the Democratic Nomination]." *Congressional Quarterly Weekly Report* 26 (May 3, 1968): 1011–13.
———. *Meet the Press: Guest, Vice President Hubert H. Humphrey, Democratic Presidential Candidate* (Interview). Washington, D.C.: Merkle Press, vol. 12, no. 42, 1968.
"Independent to Be Reckoned With: George Wallace." *Economist* (Great Britain) 226 (March 2, 1968): 31–32.
"The Inside Story of the Latest Bobby-LBJ Break." *U.S. News and World Report* 64 (April 1, 1968): 30–32.
Inter-University Consortium for Political and Social Research. *Codebook for the 1968 American National Election Survey.* Ann Arbor: Inter-University Consortium for Political and Social Research, 1968.

"Is Robert Kennedy Trying to Upset LBJ in '68?" *U.S. News and World Report* 63 (October 2, 1967): 39–40.

Joyner, Conrad. "Eugene McCarthy and Vision of American Politics." *Polity*, vol. 3, no. 4 (1971): 550–56.

Kempton, Murray. "The Decline and Fall of the Democratic Party." *Saturday Evening Post*, November 2, 1968: 19–21.

"Kennedy Enters the Democratic Presidential Race." *Congressional Quarterly Weekly Report* 26 (March 22, 1968): 609–13.

"Kennedy vs. Humphrey: Getting Set for '68 or '72." *U.S. News and World Report* 60 (March 28, 1966): 54–55.

"Kennedy—Factors in His Decision to Seek the Democratic Nomination for President." *Congressional Quarterly Weekly Report* 26 (March 15, 1968): 549–50.

Kennedy, Robert F. *Meet the Press: Guest, Senator Robert F. Kennedy* (Interview). Washington, D.C.: Merkle Press, vol. 12, no. 11, 1968.

Kensworthy, E. W. "Eugene McCarthy Hits the Road." *New Republic*, November 25, 1967: 11–13.

Kimball, Penn. *Bobby Kennedy and the New Politics*. Englewood Cliffs, N.J.: Prentice-Hall, 1968.

Kingsbury, Roger. "Hubert Humphrey's Problems." *New Leader* 51 (July 8, 1968): 6–8.

———. "Humphrey's Strategy of Optimism." *New Leader* 51 (May 6, 1968): 3–5.

Kirkpatrick, Samuel A., and Melvin E. Jones. "Vote Direction and Issue Cleavage in 1968." *Social Science Quarterly* 51 (December 1970): 689–705.

Knoll, Erwin. "A Fourth Party?" *Progressive* 32 (November 1968): 13–15.

Kopkind, Andrew. "The McCarthy Campaign." *Ramparts* 6 (March 1968): 50–55.

Kovenock, David M., and James W. Prothro. *Explaining the Vote: Presidential Choices in the Nation and States, 1968*. Chapel Hill, N.C.: Institute for Research in Social Science, 1973.

Lalli, F. "Candidate Humphrey Promises Housing More of the Same." *House and Home* 34 (October 1968): 6.

Langguth, A. J. "1964: Exhilaration, 1968: Frustration, 1970: Hopelessness." *New York Times Magazine*, October 4, 1970, pp. 26–27+.

Larner, Jeremy. *Nobody Knows: Reflections on the McCarthy Campaign of 1968.* New York: Macmillan, 1970.
"LBJ: 'One-Term' President?" *Human Events* 26 (February 26, 1966): 5.
"LBJ vs. HHH on Vietnam: Where They Differ." *U.S. News and World Report* 65 (September 23, 1968): 42–43.
"LBJ Weighs His Mistakes: Few Things Are Working Out as LBJ Had Planned." *U.S. News and World Report.* 64 (January 15, 1968): 40–41.
"LBJ's Mood in Time of Trouble: Associates, Personal Friends, and Impartial Observers Provide a Composite Closeup of LBJ Today." *U.S. News and World Report* 64 (April 8, 1968): 68–70.
"LBJ's Plans for Winning in '68." *U.S. News and World Report* 62 (June 12, 1967): 46–48.
Lee, Ronald Emery. "The Rhetoric of the 'New Politics': A Case Study of Robert F. Kennedy's 1968 Presidential Primary Campaign." Iowa City: University of Iowa, 1981. Ph.D. dissertation. University Microfilms No. 8128428.
Lewis, Joseph. *What Makes Reagan Run.* New York: McGraw-Hill, 1968.
Lewis, Ted. "Barring Miracle, LBJ Will Lose in '68: Prediction after Month-Long Tour." *Human Events* 27 (September 9, 1967): 1.
———. "LBJ in 1968? You Can Get an Argument." *Human Events* 26 (December 24, 1966): 5.
"Liberals Crank Up for '68." *Human Events* 27 (July 15, 1967): 3.
Lowenstein, Allard K. *Meet the Press: Guest, Allard K. Lowenstein, Co-Chariman, National Conference of Concerned Democrats* [The 'Dump Johnson' Movement] (Interview). Washington, D.C.: Merkel Press, vol. 11, no. 49, 1968.
Lurie, Leonard. *The Running of Richard Nixon.* New York: New American Library, 1968.
Macalusco, Theodore F. "Parameters of 'Rational' Voting: Vote Switching in the 1968 Election." *Journal of Politics* 37 (February 1975): 202–34.
Mailer, Norman. *Miami and the Siege of Chicago: An Informal History of the Republican and Democratic Conventions of 1968.* Chicago: World, 1968.

"The Making of Gene McCarthy." *Newsweek*, March 25, 1968: 22–24.

Marsh, Robert. *Agnew: The Unexamined Man.* New York: Evans, 1971.

Martin, Harold H. "George Wallace, The Angry Man's Candidate." *Saturday Evening Post*, June 15, 1968: 23–25.

McCarry, Charles. "Win with Rockefeller." *Saturday Evening Post*, February 24, 1968: 80–83.

"McCarthy Campaign Just Won't Fade Away." *Business Week*, July 6, 1968: 20–21.

McCarthy, Eugene Joseph. "Liberal Reform Undermines Positive Results of '68 Campaign." *Politicks and Other Human Interests* 1 (April 25, 1978): 19–20.

———. *The Year of the People.* Garden City, N.Y.: Doubleday, 1969.

Meryman, Richard. "Hubert Humphrey Talks His Self-Portrait." *Life*, September 27, 1968: 22B-31.

Miles, Michael. "Reagan and the Respectable Right." *New Republic*, April 20, 1968: 25–28.

Miller, Arthur. "The Battle of Chicago: From the Delegates' Side." *New York Times Magazine*, September 15, 1968: 29–31.

Miller, Warren E., and Teresa E. Levitin. *Leadership and Change: Presidential Elections from 1952–1976.* Lanham, Md.: University Press of America, 1984.

"Minorities Come Through for HHH." *Texas Observer*, November 15, 1968: 10.

Murray, David. "The Rise of Ronald Reagan." *Progressive* 32 (February 1968): 18–22.

Myers, David S. "Editorials and Foreign Affairs in the 1968 Presidential Campaign." *Journalism Quarterly* 47 (Spring 1970): 57–64.

Nevin, David. *Muskie of Maine.* New York: Random House, 1972.

Newfield, Jack. "Kennedy Lays Out a 'Gut' Campaign." *Life*, March 29, 1968: 28–29.

———. "Kennedy's Search for a New Target." *Life*, April 12, 1968: 35.

Nicholas, H. G. "The 1968 Presidential Elections." *Journal of American Studies* 3 (July 1969): 1–15.

"Nixon-Agnew: A Winning Ticket?" *Human Events* 28 (August 17, 1968): 1, 4.
"Nixon Comes on Strong." *Business Week*, March 30, 1968: 31–33.
"Nixon-Humphrey Debate: Economic Views." *Business Week*, September 28, 1968: 130–32.
"Nixon Looks to November: Here's His Strategy." *U.S. News and World Report* 65 (June 29, 1968): 28–29.
"Nixon vs. Humphrey vs. Wallace: If They Run—The Outlook." *U.S. News and World Report* 64 (June 10, 1968): 41–43.
"Nixon vs. LBJ—'68 Choice?" *U.S. News and World Report* 62 (April 17, 1967): 42–45.
Nixon, Richard M. *The Memoirs of Richard Nixon*. New York: Grosset and Dunlap, 1978.
———. "Nixon Tells How '68 Race Stands: Exclusive Interview with Former Vice President." *U.S. News and World Report* 63 (November 20, 1967): 74–80.
"Nixon's Views in a Nutshell." *U.S. News and World Report* 64 (March 11, 1968): 43–44.
O'Mara, Richard. "Discovering Spiro Agnew." *Nation*, September 2, 1968: 175–77.
"Off to an Early Start: Republican Contenders for Nomination." *Business Week*, May 13, 1967: 33–35.
Plimpton, George, and Jean Stein, eds. *American Journey: The Times of Robert Kennedy*. New York: Harcourt, Brace, Jovanovich, 1970.
"The 'Police Riot'." *Texas Observer*, September 6, 1968: 14+.
"Political Troubles Ahead for LBJ: War, Taxes, Riots, Crime, Inflation, Federal Budget." *U.S. News and World Report* 63 (September 25, 1967): 46–50.
"Politics '68: [*Christian Science Monitor*] Poll Boosts Nixon." *Human Events* 28 (September 21, 1968): 5.
"Politics '68: COPE, LBJ and Labor." *Human Events* 27 (November 18, 1967): 5.
"Politics '68: COPE, Texas." *Human Events* 27 (November 23, 1967): 5.
"Politics '68: HHH Moves Left." *Human Events* 28 (July 6, 1968): 5.
"Politics '68: Humphrey, Wisconsin, Indiana." *Human Events* 28 (April 13, 1968): 5.

"Politics '68: Kennedy, McCarthy." *Human Events* 28 (March 30, 1968): 5.
"Politics '68: Labor Backs LBJ." *Human Events* 27 (December 16, 1967): 5.
"Politics '68: LBJ." *Human Events* 27 (December 9, 1967): 5.
"Politics '68: LBJ and Labor, McCarthy." *Human Events* 27 (November 25, 1967): 5.
"Politics '68: LBJ Defeat?" *Human Events* 27 (December 2, 1967): 5.
"Politics '68: McCarthy." *Human Events* 28 (January 20, 1968): 5.
"Politics '68: New Hampshire, McCarthy." *Human Events* 28 (March 23, 1968): 5.
"Politics '68: Nixon." *Human Events* 28 (February 3, 1968): 5.
"Politics '68: Nixon, Rockefeller, Reagan, McCarthy." *Human Events* 28 (March 16, 1968): 5.
"Politics '68: Nixon's Significant Lead." *Human Events* 28 (August 31, 1968): 5.
"Politics '68: NY Times on 'ABJ' ['Anybody But Johnson']." *Human Events* 28 (March 9, 1968): 5.
"Politics '68: Wallace, Kennedy, COPE, Reagan." *Human Events* 28 (April 20, 1968): 5.
"Politics 1968: The Big Show." *Newsweek*, January 8, 1968: 17–22.
Polsby, Nelson W. *Citizen's Choice: Humphrey or Nixon.* Washington, D.C.: Public Affairs Press, 1968.
———, and Aaron B. Wildavsky, eds. *Presidential Elections: Strategies of American Electoral Politics.* 3rd ed. New York: Scribners, 1971.
Pomper, Gerald. "From Confusion to Clarity: Issues and American Voters, 1956–1968." *American Political Science Review* 66 (June 1972): 415–28.
"Preparations at Fort Chicago." *Texas Observer*, August 23, 1968: 4+.
"Presidential Candidates 1968: Nixon vs Humphrey, The Men and the Issues." *Human Events Special Edition* 28 (September 28, 1968): all.
"Presidential Hopefuls' Stands Compared on Major Issues." *Congressional Quarterly Weekly Report* 26 (May 3, 1968): 981–90+.
"Presidential Possibles—Where They Stand." *Nation's Business* 56 (January 1968): 36–58.

Quirk, John J. "McCarthy Fights for an Open Convention." *Commonweal*, August 9, 1968: 516–18.
"Race for the White House: The Story of New Hampshire." *U.S. News and World Report* 64 (March 25, 1968): 40–41.
Rand, Ayn. "The Presidential Candidates, 1968." *Objectivist* 7 (June 1968): 1–6.
Raveling, Gordon R. "Hubert Humphrey's Rebuttal of Criticism on the Vietnam Issue in the 1968 Presidential Campaign." College Park: University of Maryland, 1969. M.A. thesis.
"Ready for the Challengers: President Johnson." *Economist* (Great Britain) 225 (November 25, 1967): 851–52.
Reagan, Ronald. "Governor Reagan Talks of the Issues and His Plans" (Interview). *U.S. News and World Report* 64 (March 25, 1968): 56–62.
Reddy, John. "Can Humphrey Hold His Party Together?" *Readers Digest*, July 1968: 105–10.
Reichley, A. James. "How Nixon Plans to Bring It Off." *Fortune* 76 (December 1967): 124–27+.
Republican National Convention. *Official Report of the Proceedings of the Twenty-ninth Republican National Convention, 1968*. Baltimore: Dulany-Vernay, 1968.
"Review of Presidential Candidates' Organizations." *Congressional Quarterly Weekly Report* 26 (June 21, 1968): 1533–39.
Riesel, Victor. "Big Labor Plans to Spend $25 Million to Re-Elect LBJ." *Human Events* 27 (December 30, 1967): 9.
———. "Big Labor Plays a Political Waiting Game." *Human Events* 28 (April 13, 1968): 10.
———. "Bobby Silent as Aides Organize 'Dump-LBJ' Movement." *Human Events* 27 (October 7, 1967): 11.
———. "Goldberg to Woo Liberals to RFK Camp: Why the Ambassador Resigned." *Human Events* 28 (May 11, 1968): 6.
———. "Labor Scoffs at Reports LBJ Won't Run: Powerful Machinery Already Set Up for Re-Electing Johnson-Humphrey." *Human Events* 27 (January 7, 1967): 7.
———. "Labor Strategists Fear Rank-and-File Revolt against LBJ in '68." *Human Events* 27 (September 30, 1967): 7.
———. "Labor Union Chieftains Rush to Aid LBJ's Stop-Bobby Drive." *Human Events* 28 (April 6, 1968): 6.
———. "More Trouble for LBJ in '68? Reuther Bolts AFL-

CIO Political Machine." *Human Events* 27 (October 21, 1967): 6.

———. "Rocky Launches Long-Range Drive for GOP Presidential Nomination." *Human Events* 25 (February 13, 1965): 1.

Roberts, Steven V. "Edmund Sixtus Muskie Takes the Low-Key Road." *New York Times Magazine*, October 20, 1968: 33.

———. "McCarthy Campaign Enters New Phase." *Commonweal*, April 26, 1968: 165–67.

———. "Tapping the Resentment Vote: The Appeal of George C. Wallace." *New Leader* 51 (March 11, 1968): 9–10.

"Rockefeller: Rebublican 'Dark Horse'?" *U.S. News and World Report* 62 (May 8, 1967): 47–50.

Rockefeller, Nelson. "Rockefeller Talks on the Issues: Interview with New York's Governor." *U.S. News and World Report* 64 (June 24, 1968): 44–46 +.

Rogers, Warren. "Bobby's Decision." *Look*, April 16, 1968: 73.

"Romney's Chances to Head [GOP] Ticket." *U.S. News and World Report* 61 (December 1966): 29–30.

Ross, Douglas. *Robert F. Kennedy: Apostle of Change.* New York: Trident Press, 1968.

Rostow, Walt W. *The Diffusion of Power: An Essay in Recent History.* New York: Macmillan, 1972.

Runyon, John H., Jennefer Verdini, and Sally S. Runyon, eds. *Source Book of American Presidential Campaign and Election Statistics, 1948–1968.* New York: Frederick Ungar, 1971.

Rustin, Bayard. "The Liberal Coalition and the 1968 Elections." *AFL-CIO American Federationist* 74 (November 1967): 12–15.

Ryskind, Allan H. "Is Humphrey A Moderate?" *Human Events* 28 (May 11, 1968): 5.

Ryskind, Morris. "The Democrats Secret Weapon." *National Review*, August 13, 1968: 801–02.

Schecter, William. *Countdown '68: Profiles for the Presidency.* New York: Fleet Press, 1967.

Schlesinger, Arthur M., Jr. "Vietnam and the 1968 Elections." *New Leader* 50 (November 6, 1967): 5–12.

Schneier, Edward. "The Scar of Wallace." *Nation*, November 4, 1968: 454–57.

Scott, Paul. "Big Labor to Spend $20 Million on HHH Race." *Human Events* 28 (September 14, 1968): 1.

———. "Humphrey Considers Flight to Paris: Dramatic 'Peace' Move." *Human Events* 28 (October 5, 1968): 1.

———. "Kennedy and King Form Political Alliance: Senator to Support D.C. March." *Human Events* 28 (March 30, 1968): 1.

———. "LBJ to Hit 'Unholy Alliance' in '68 Campaign: Target—GOP and Southern Democrats." *Human Events* 27 (December 9, 1967): 14.

Sewer, Arnold. "Gene McCarthy's Winning of Wisconsin." *Progressive* 32 (June 1968): 24–26.

Shelly, Walter Lumley. "Political Profiles of the Nixon, Humphrey, and Wallace Voters in the Texas Panhandle, 1968: A Study in Voting Behavior." Lubbock: Texas Tech University, 1972. Ph.D. dissertation. University Microfilms No. 73-4074.

"A Shock of Violence Hits the Campaign: The Shooting of Robert F. Kennedy." *Business Week*, June 8, 1968: 38–42.

"Showdown in Chicago." *Texas Observer*, August 23, 1968: 3.

"Six Months to Go: Johnson's Plan Now." *U.S. News and World Report* 65 (August 5, 1968): 34–35.

"'68 Election as LBJ Sees It." *U.S. News and World Report* 64 (February 5, 1968): 36–37.

Smith, James George. "Presidential Elections and Racial Discrimination: Campaign Promises, Presidential Performance and Democratic Accountability, 1960–1980." Bloomington: Indiana University, 1981. Ph.D. dissertation. University Microfilms No. 82-02984.

"The Split in Both [Democratic and Republican] Parties." *U.S. News and World Report* 64 (April 1, 1968): 34–35.

St. John, Jeffrey. *Countdown to Chaos: Chicago, August 1968, Turning Point in American Politics*. Los Angeles: Nash, 1969.

"The State of the Union—A Republican Appraisal." *Congressional Quarterly Weekly Report* 26 (February 2, 1968): 173–75.

Taylor, Henry J. "Bobby's Opportunism on McCarthy Candidacy." *Human Events* 28 (January 20, 1968): 11.

———. "Senators Say Johnson May Yet Run Again." *Human Events* 28 (August 17, 1968): 14.

Thomas, David Allen. "A Quantitative Content Analysis of

Richard Nixon's Treatment of Selected Issues in His Presidential Campaign Oratory in the 1960 and 1968 Elections." East Lansing: Michigan State University, 1973. Ph.D. dissertation. University Microfilms No. 78-12245.

"Top Republicans Talk about Their Choices for '68." *U.S. News and World Report* 62 (February 6, 1967): 40–41.

Trent, Judith. "Richard Nixon's Methods of Identification in the Presidential Campaigns of 1960 and 1968: A Content Analysis." *Today's Speech* 19 (Fall 1971): 23–30.

"Two Democratic Splinters Seen Certain for '68: Wallace and the Leftists." *Human Events* 27 (August 12, 1967): 11.

Tyler, Gus. "The Case for Hubert Humphrey." *Progressive* 32 (August 1968): 16–19.

United States Department of Commerce. Bureau of the Census. "Voting and Registration in the Election of November 1968." *Current Population Reports*, Series p-20, no. 192, December 2, 1969.

"The Vietnam Plank." *Texas Observer*, September 6, 1968: 3+.

Wainstock, Dennis Dean. "The 1968 Presidential Campaign and Election." Morgantown: West Virginia University, 1984. Ph.D. dissertation. University Microfilms No. 84-29880.

Wallace, George C. *Meet the Press: Guest, George C. Wallace, Former Governor of Alabama* (Interview). Washington, D.C.: Merkle Press, vol. 11, no. 17, 1967.

———. "Wallace Sets Fire to the '68 Campaign" (Interview). *U.S. News and World Report* 65 (September 30, 1968): 32–36.

Wechsler, James A. "Reagan, Romney, and Republicanism." *Progressive* 30 (August 1966): 23–25.

———. "What Makes McCarthy Run?" *Progressive* 32 (January 1968): 23–26.

"Where Labor Stands: The Platforms and the Candidates." *AFL-CIO American Federationist* 75 (October 1968): 3–11.

"Where They Stand: Humphrey and Nixon Answer MW's Questions." *Merchandising Week* 100 (October 14, 1968): 22–25.

"Who Has the Best Chance against President Johnson in 1968? George Romney." *Sales Management* 97 (October 1, 1966): 44–45.

"Why It Will Be a Johnson-Humphrey Ticket Again in '68." *U.S. News and World Report* 62 (February 13, 1967): 40–43.

"Why Johnson Withdrew: The Real Story from Insiders." *U.S. News and World Report* 64 (April 15, 1968): 39–41, 46–47.

"Why LBJ Is Quitting: The Real Reasons." *U.S. News and World Report* 65 (July 22, 1968): 25–27.

Widener, Alice. "Will 1968 Be A Repeat of 1948?" *Human Events* 27 (March 18, 1967): 1.

Widick, B. J. "Why They Like Wallace." *Nation*, October 14, 1968: 358–59.

"Will Kennedy Challenge LBJ?" *U.S. News and World Report* 64 (February 12, 1968): 42–43.

"Will LBJ Get Four Years More? What Polls and Election Trends Show." *U.S. News and World Report* 63 (November 27, 1967): 38–41.

Wilson, Richard. "This Is Humphrey." *Look*, July 9, 1968: 41–46.

"The Winner: How and What He Won." *Newsweek* 9 (September 1968): 30–37.

Wise, David. "How Bobby Plans to Win It." *Saturday Evening Post*, June 1, 1968: 23–27.

Witcover, Jules. *85 Days: The Last Campaign of Robert Kennedy*. New York: Putnam, 1969.

———. "Is There Really a New Nixon?" *Progressive* 32 (March 1968): 14–26.

———. *The Resurrection of Richard Nixon*. New York: G. P. Putnam, 1969.

———. "Robert F. Kennedy: The Making of an Electorate." *The Progressive* 31 (January 1967): 17–20.

———. *White Knight: The Rise of Spiro Agnew*. New York: Random House, 1972.

"Withdrawal Announcement LBJ's Greatest Mistake?" *Human Events* 28 (April 13, 1968): 4.

"'Yippies' Will Help Taunt Democrats in Chicago: Massive Leftist Demonstrations Planned." *Human Events* 28 (April 6, 1968): 12–13.

Zeiger, Henry A. *Robert F. Kennedy: A Biography*. New York: Meredith, 1968.

C. THE JOHNSON ADMINISTRATION

1. AMERICA IN THE 1960S

"Affluence in the U.S.—The Other Side of the 'Poverty' Story." *U.S. News and World Report* 57 (December 7, 1964): 76–77.

"Aftermath of Riots [following King Assassination]: What Next?" *U.S. News and World Report* 64 (April 22, 1968): 27–37.

Albert, Judith C., and Stewart E. Albert, eds. *The Sixties Papers: Documents of a Rebellious Decade*. New York: Praeger, 1984.

Allen, Robert L. *Black Awakening in Capitalistic America: An Analytical History*. Garden City, N.Y.: Doubleday, 1969.

American Civil Liberties Union. *Day of Protest, Night of Violence: The Century City Peace March: A Report*. [June 23, 1967]. Los Angeles: Sawyer, 1967.

American Council on Education. *The Campus and the Racial Crisis*. Washington, D.C.: American Council on Education, 1969.

Anderson, Jervis. *A. Philip Randolph: A Biographical Portrait*. New York: Harcourt Brace Jovanovich, 1973.

"As Rioting Spread—Race Troubles: Record of 109 Cities." *U.S. News and World Report* 63 (August 14, 1967): 32–40, 44–46.

"Assessing the Sixties." *Texas Today* 1 (February 1970): 4, 23.

Batchelder, Alan. "Poverty: The Special Case of the Negro." *American Economic Review* 55 (May 1965): 530–40, 545–48.

Belknap, Michael R. *Federal Law and Southern Order: Racial Violence and Constitutional Conflict in the Post-Brown South*. Athens: University of Georgia Press, 1987.

———. "The Vindication of Burke Marshall: The Southern Legal System and the Anti-Civil Rights Violence of the 1960's." *Emory Law Journal* 33 (Winter 1984): 93–133.

Bell, Daniel, and Irving Kristol, eds. *Confrontation: The Student Rebellion and the Universities*. New York: Basic Books, 1969.

Bell, Inge Powell. *CORE and the Strategy of Nonviolence*. New York: Random House, 1968.

Berube, Maurice R., et al. *The Urban School Crisis: An Anthology of Essays.* New York: League for Industrial Democracy, 1966.
Bowen, David. *The Struggle Within: Race Relations in the United States.* New York: W. W. Norton, 1965.
Branden, Anne. "The Southern Freedom Movement in Perspective." *Monthly Review* 17 (July/August 1965): all.
Brink, William, and Louis Harris. *Black and White: A Study of U.S. Racial Relations Today.* New York: Simon and Schuster, 1967.
Brown, H. Rap. "The Black Hand on the Big Trigger" (Interview). *Maclean's* (Canada) 80 (November 1967): 32–33.
Button, James Wickham. *Black Violence: Political Impact of the 1960's Riots.* Princeton, N.J.: Princeton University Press, 1978.
Butwin, Miriam, and Patricia Pirmantgen. *Protest II: Civil Rights and Black Liberation, the Anti-War Movement.* Minneapolis: Lerner, 1972.
Carson, Clayborne. *In Struggle: SNCC and the Black Awakening of the 1960's.* Cambridge, Mass.: Harvard University Press, 1981.
———. "Mass Struggle, Racial Consciousness, and Black Nationalist Leadership in the 1960's." Paper presented at annual meeting of the Organization of American Historians, San Francisco, April 1980.
"Civil Disorder Panel [President's Advisory Commission on Civil Disorders] Blames 'White Racism' for Riots." *Congressional Quarterly Weekly Report* 26 (March 8, 1968): 469–73.
Claque, Ewan. "Unemployment—What Do the Figures Mean?" *Michigan Business Review* 17 (November 1965): 25–29.
Clark, Wayne A. "An Analysis of the Relationship between Anti-Communism and Segregationist Thought in the Deep South, 1948–1964." Chapel Hill: University of North Carolina, 1976. Ph.D. dissertation. University Microfilms No. 77-02025.
"Climax Near in Negro Revolt." *U.S. News and World Report* 58 (March 29, 1965): 27–29.
Cloward, Richard A., and Frances Fox Piven. *The Politics of Turmoil: Essays on Poverty, Race, and the Urban Crisis.* New York: Pantheon Books, 1974.

Cohen, Jerome. "Social Work and the Culture of Poverty." *Social Work* 9 (January 1964): 3–11.
Cohen, Mitchell, and Dennis Hale, eds. *The New Student Left: An Anthology.* Boston: Beacon Press, 1966.
Colby, Vineta, ed. *American Culture in the Sixties.* New York: H. W. Wilson, 1964.
"The Collapse of Liberalism." *Human Events* 28 (October 26, 1968): 6.
"County Official's Guide to the Kerner Report [President's Advisory Commission on Civil Disorders]." *American County Government* 33 (June 1968): 12–24+.
"The Courts, HEW, and Southern School Desegregation." *Yale Law Journal* 77 (December 1967): 321–65.
Coyle, David Cushman. *Breakthrough to the Great Society.* Dobbs Ferry, N.Y.: Oceana, 1965.
"Crisis in Race Relations: It's in the North." *U.S. News and World Report* 57 (August 10, 1964): 23–25.
Danigelis, Nicholas L. "Race and Political Activity in the United States, 1948–1968: A Trend Analysis." Bloomington: Indiana University, 1973. Ph.D. dissertation. University Microfilms No. 74-09417.
Davidson, Arthur T. "The Role of the Historic Black Colleges in the Training of Black Professionals." Address presented at the Alumnae Banquet at Johnson C. Smith University, Charlotte, North Carolina, March 15, 1982.
De Toledano, Ralph. "'Long Hot Summer' Begins in Washington." *Human Events* 27 (June 10, 1967): 12.
"Defense Cuts Bring New Kind of Job Crisis: Professional Specialists—Engineers, Scientists, Technicians—Losing Jobs and Arms Contracts Are Cancelled." *U.S. News and World Report* 56 (May 18, 1964): 80–83.
Delli Carpini, Michael X. *Stability and Change in American Politics: The Coming of Age of the Generation of the 1960's.* New York: New York University Press, 1986.
Dickstein, Morris. *Gates of Eden: American Culture in the Sixties.* New York: Basic Books, 1977.
"Dispute between [J. Edgar] Hoover and [Martin Luther] King: The FBI's Answer to Criticisms." *U.S. News and World Report* 57 (December 7, 1964): 46+.
Dorman, Michael. *We Shall Overcome.* New York: Dial Press, 1964.

Dorsen, Norman. "Poverty, Civil Liberties, and Civil Rights: A Symposium." *New York Law Review* 41 (April 1966): 328–52.

Draper, Hal. *Berkeley: The New Student Revolt.* New York: Grove Press, 1965.

Dunne, George H., ed. *Poverty in Plenty.* Foreword by Sargent Shriver. Conference on Poverty-in-Plenty: The Poor in Our Affluent Society, Washington, D.C., January 23, 1964. New York: P. J. Kenedy and Sons, 1964.

Eisenhower, Dwight David. "The Choice Americans Must Make." *Nation's Business* 53 (October 1965): 34–37+.

Emspak, Frank. "The Days of Protest." *New World Review* 33 (December 1965): 8–10.

Eszterhas, Joe, and M. D. Roberts. *Thirteen Seconds: Confrontation at Kent State.* New York: Dodd, Mead, 1970.

Evans, Kenneth James, Jr. "The Era of Student Unrest: Student Personnel Professional Associations' Perceptions of Major Campus Changes Occurring between 1964 and 1970." Pittsburgh: University of Pittsburgh, 1980. Ph.D. dissertation. University Microfilms No. 8112671.

"Explosion in the Cities: Ghetto Unrest Flares into Hot Summer of Racial Violence across U.S." *Business Week*, July 29, 1967: 21–27.

Fact-Finding Commission on Columbia Disturbances. *Crisis at Columbia: Report of the Fact-Finding Commission Appointed to Investigate Disturbances at Columbia University in April and May 1968.* New York: Vintage, 1968.

Fager, Charles E. *Selma 1965: The March that Changed the South.* New York: Scribner's, 1974; reprinted, Boston: Beacon Press, 1985.

Farmer, James. *Freedom—When?* [C.O.R.E.] New York: Random House, 1965.

———. *Lay Bare the Heart: An Autobiography of the Civil Rights Movement.* New York: Arbor House, 1985.

Featherman, David, and Robert Hauser. "Changes in the Socioeconomic Stratification of the Races, 1962–1973." *American Journal of Sociology* 82 (November 1976): 621–51.

Fernandez, Benedict J. *In Opposition: Images of American Dissent in the Sixties.* New York: Da Capo, 1968.

Fisher, Randall M. *Rhetoric and American Democracy: Black*

Protest through Vietnam Dissent. Lanham, Md.: University Press of America, 1985.

Flacks, Robert. "The Liberated Generation: An Exploration of the Roots of Student Protest." *Journal of Social Issues* 23 (July 1967): 52–75.

Fogelson, Robert M. "From Resentment to Confrontation: The Police, the Negroes, and the Outbreak of 1960s Riots." *Political Science Quarterly* 83 (June 1968): 217–47.

Frantz, T. T. "Protest Prone Students and Institutions." *NASPA Journal* 6 (October 1968): 91–93.

Freedman, Alex S., ed. "Symposium: Views on American Poverty." *Journal of Human Relations*, volume 15, Second Quarter (1967): 146–68.

Gallagher, B. G. *Campus in Crisis.* New York: Harper, 1974.

Gallaway, Lowell E. "The Negro and Poverty." *Journal of Business* 40 (January 1967): 27–35.

Gallup, George. "The Mood of America at This Time" (Interview). *U.S. News and World Report* 61 (September 19, 1966): 50–54.

Garrow, David J. *Bearing the Cross: Martin Luther King, Jr. and the Southern Christian Leadership Conference.* New York: Morrow, 1986.

———. *The FBI and Martin Luther King, Jr.: From "Solo" to Memphis.* New York: Norton, 1981.

———. "Martin Luther King, Jr.: An Honorable Man." *Focus* 12 (January 1984): 3, 5, 7.

Geschwender, James A. "Social Structure and the Negro Revolt." *Social Forces* 43 (December 1964): 248–56.

"Good Times—But People Are Unhappy: Findings of a Nationwide Survey." *U.S. News and World Report* 62 (May 22, 1967): 50–55.

Granberg, Donald, and John Seidel. "Social Judgements of the Urban and Vietnam Issues in 1968 and 1972." *Social Forces* 55 (September 1976): 1–15.

"Great Society Setback [Race Riots]." *Human Events* 27 (August 5, 1967): 3.

Gruen, Victor. *The Heart of Our Cities: The Urban Crisis, Diagnosis and Cure.* New York: Simon and Schuster, 1964.

Gwartney, James. "Changes in the Nonwhite/White Income Ratio—1939–1967 [Emphasis on Education]." *American Economic Review* 60 (December 1970): 872–83.

Hamby, Alonzo L. *Liberalism and Its Challengers: F.D.R. to Reagan.* New York: Oxford University Press, 1985.

Handlin, Oscar. *Fire-Bell in the Night: The Crisis in Civil Rights.* New York: Beacon Press, 1964.

Harrington, Michael. "The Cost of Poverty." *Liberation* 9 (October 1964): 7–11.

———. *The Other America: Poverty in the United States.* New York: Macmillan, 1962.

Harris, Janet. *Students in Revolt.* New York: McGraw-Hill, 1970.

Harrison, Cynthia Ellen. "Prelude to Feminism: Women's Organizations, the Federal Government and the Rise of the Women's Movement, 1942 to 1968." New York: Columbia University, 1982. Ph.D. dissertation. University Microfilms No. 8222402.

Hazlitt, Henry. "Is Poverty the Cause of Riots [President's Advisory Commission on Civil Disorders]?" *Human Events* 27 (August 12, 1967): 1.

———. "The Life and Death of the Welfare State." *Human Events* 29 (January 4, 1969): 5–12.

Hodgson, Godfrey. *America in Our Time: From World War II to Nixon—What Happened and Why.* Garden City, N.Y.: Doubleday, 1976.

Holland, Susan S. "Long-Term Unemployment in the 1960s." *Monthly Labor Review* 88 (September 1965): 1069–76.

Humphrey, Hubert H. "The Technology Gap and the Brain Drain." *Defense, Science, and Public Policy,* edited by Edwin Mansfield, pp. 175–79. New York: Norton, 1968.

"Is the U.S. Drifting toward Anarchy? Riots, Crime, Demonstrations, Campus Revolts, 'Hippies,' Defiance of Draft . . ." *U.S. News and World Report* 63 (December 4, 1967): 50–52.

"It Looks Like a 'Hot Summer'—with Selma the Beginning." *U.S. News and World Report* 58 (March 22, 1965): 32–33.

Jacobs, Paul, and Saul Landau. *Then New Radicals: A Report with Documents.* New York: Random House, 1966.

Jones, Jenkin Lloyd. "Can We Reunite the Country? Aftermath of the [King Assassination] Riots." *Human Events* 28 (April 20, 1968): 1.

Katz, Milton S. "Peace, Politics, and Protest: SANE and the American Peace Movement, 1957–1972." St. Louis: St.

Louis University, 1973. Ph.D. dissertation. University Microfilms No. 74-04531.
Kehde, Ned, ed., comp. *The American Left, 1955–1970: A National Union Catalog of Pamphlets Published in the U.S. and Canada.* Westport, Conn.: Greenwood Press, 1976.
Kelman, Steven J. "SDS: Troubled Voice of the New Left." *New Leader* 48 (September 27, 1965): 8–13.
King, Martin Luther, Jr. "Behind the Selma March." *Saturday Review* 48 (April 3, 1965): 16–18.
———. *Meet the Press: Guest, Dr. Martin Luther King, Jr., President, Southern Christian Leadership Conference* (Interview). Washington, D.C.: Merkle Press, vol. 11, no. 33, 1967.
———. *Meet the Press: Special Edition Guest, Dr. Martin Luther King, Jr., President, Southern Christian Leadership Conference* (Interview). Washington, D.C.: Merkle Press, August 21, 1966.
———. "Selma—The Shame and the Promise: The Negroes' Fight for Voting Rights and Human Dignity." *I.U.D. Agenda* (Industrial Union Department) 1 (March 1965): 18–21.
———. *Where Do We Go from Here: Chaos or Community?* New York: Harper and Row, 1967.
———. "Why We Can't Wait." *Life*, May 15, 1964: 98.
Kirk, B. A. "Identity Crisis—1965." *Journal of College Student Personnel* 6 (June 1965): 194–99.
Kirk, John G., ed. *America Now.* New York: Atheneum, 1968.
Kolkey, Jonathan Martin. "The New Radical Right, 1960–1968." Los Angeles: University of California, 1979. Ph.D. dissertation. University Microfilms No. 7921429.
———. *The New Right, 1960–1968: With Epilogue, 1969–1980.* Lanham, Md.: University Press of America, 1983.
Kolko, Gabriel. *Anatomy of a War: Vietnam, the United States, and the Modern Historical Experience.* New York: Pantheon, 1986.
Krosney, Herbert. *Beyond Welfare: Poverty in the Supercity.* New York: Holt, Rinehart, and Winston, 1966.
Kunen, James Simon. "Campus Unrest—The Leaflet Wars." *Esquire* 99 (June 1983): 281–82.
Lampman, Robert. "One-fifth of a Nation: the Problem of Poverty." *Challenge* 12 (April 1964): 11–13.

Lasch, Christopher. *The Agony of the American Left.* New York: Alfred A. Knopf, 1969.
Leuchtenburg, William E. *A Troubled Feast: American Society since 1945.* Boston: Little, Brown, 1979.
Levitas, Mitchell. *America in Crisis.* New York: Holt, Rinehard, and Winston, 1969.
Lewis, Fulton, Jr. "'Peace' Groups Plan March on Washington." *Human Events* 25 (April 17, 1965): 3.
"A Little Richer and Better Educated: Census Bureau Reports a Rise in the Economic Status of Negroes." *Business Week,* November 6, 1965: 136+.
Lowi, Theodore J. *The End of Liberalism.* New York: Norton, 1969.
"Loyalty Day Marked across U.S." *Human Events* 27 (May 13, 1967): 7.
Lubove, Roy, ed. *Poverty and Social Welfare in the United States.* Melbourne, Fla.: Krieger, 1972.
Luce, Phillip Abbott. *The New Left.* New York: David McKay Co., 1966.
Mailer, Norman. *Armies of the Night* [Pentagon Protest March of October 21, 1967]. Cleveland: World, 1968.
"Martin Luther King [Assassination Commentary]." *Human Events* 28 (April 13, 1968): 3.
Martin, Howard H. "The Rhetoric of Academic Protest." *Central State Speech Journal* 17 (November 1966): 244–50.
Matusow, Allen J. "From Civil Rights to Black Power: The Case of SNCC, 1960–1966." *Twentieth-Century America: Recent Interpretations,* edited by Barton J. Berstein and Allen J. Matusow, pp. 531–56. New York: Harcourt, Brace and World, 1969.
———. *The Unraveling of America: A History of Liberalism in the 1960s.* The New American Nation Series. New York: Harper and Row, 1984.
McCord, William. *Mississippi: The Long, Hot Summer.* New York: Norton, 1965.
McKissick, Floyd B. "Long, Hot Summer of Race Trouble Ahead? Interview with Floyd B. McKissick, Director of CORE." *U.S. News and World Report* 60 (May 23, 1966): 34–38, 40–42.
Meier, August. "New Currents in the Civil Rights Movement." *New Politics* 2 (Summer 1963): 7–32.

"Middle-Class Revolt Brewing: Social, Economic, Political Dissatisfaction." *U.S. News and World Report* 64 (June 3, 1968): 52–54.

Middleton, Neil, ed. *The I. F. Stone's Weekly Reader.* New York: Random House, 1973.

Miller, Arthur. "Political Issues and Trust in Government: 1964–1970." *American Political Science Review* 68 (September 1974): 951–72.

Miller, Michael V., and Susan Gilmore, eds. *Revolution at Berkeley.* New York: Dial Press, 1965.

"The Mood of America in Election Year: What a National Survey Shows—Business, Taxes, Civil Rights, Foreign Affairs, War Scares, Farm Problems, Corruption in Government." *U.S. News and World Report* 56 (March 30, 1964): 68–73.

"More Violence and Race War? Effects of Dr. King's Tragedy." *U.S. News and World Report* 64 (April 15, 1968): 31–34.

Morris, Charles. *A Time of Passion: America 1960–1980.* New York: Harper and Row, 1984.

Moynihan, Daniel Patrick. *Meet the Press: Guest, Daniel P. Moynihan* [Regarding status of American blacks] (Interview). Washington, D.C.: Merkle Press, vol. 9, no. 44, 1965.

———, et al. "Poverty in Our Midst." *Social Action* 30 (April 1964): 4–35.

Murray, N. "The Silent Majority Myth." *NASPA Journal* 9 (July 1971): 32–36.

Muste, A. J. "The Civil Rights Movement and the American Establishment." *Liberation* 9 (February 1965): 7–11.

"Negro Leaders Dividing—Unity on Civil Rights Issue Fractured by a Catch Phrase—'Black Power'." *U.S. News and World Report* 61 (July 18, 1966): 31–32+.

"New Element Is Introduced in Civil Rights Movement: CQ Special Report on 'Black Power'." *Congressional Quarterly Weekly Report* 24 (July 8, 1966): 1431.

Newman, Dorothy K. "The Negro's Journey to the City: Hope for Better Jobs and More Education Have Led to a Migration Unparalleled in American History." *Monthly Labor Review* 88 (May 1965): 502–07; (June 1965): 644–49.

O'Brien, James Putnam. "The Development of a New Left in the United States, 1960–1965." Madison: University of Wisconsin, 1971. Ph.D. dissertation. University Microfilms No. 71-25738.

O'Reilly, Kenneth. *Hoover and the Un-Americans: The FBI, HUAC, and the Red Menace.* Philadelphia: Temple University Press, 1983.
Oates, Stephen B. *Let the Trumpets Sound: The Life of Martin Luther King, Jr.* New York: Harper and Row, 1982.
Orshansky, Mollie. "Counting the Poor: Another Look at the Poverty Profile." *Social Security Bulletin* 28 (January 1965): 3–29 [excerpts printed in *Monthly Labor Review* 88 (March 1965): 300–09].
———. "More about the Poor in 1964." *Social Security Bulletin* 29 (May 1966): 3–38.
———. "Recounting the Poor—A Five Year Review [1959–64]." *Social Security Bulletin* 29 (April 1966): 20–37.
———. "The Shape of Poverty in 1966." *Social Security Bulletin* 31 (March 1968): 3–32.
———. "Who's Who among the Poor?" *Social Security Bulletin* 28 (July 1965): 3+.
Parker, Thomas F. *Day by Day: The Sixties.* New York: Facts on File, 1983.
Parrish, John B. "Poverty in America: The Myth and the Reality." *Human Events* 28 (July 13, 1968): 8–10.
Peterson, Richard E. "Organized Student Protest in 1964–1965." *Journal of NAWDAC* 30 (Winter 1967): 50–56.
———. *The Scope of Organized Student Protest in 1964–1965.* Princeton, N.J.: Education Testing Service, 1966.
Phillips, Donald E. *Student Protest, 1960–1970: An Analysis of the Issues and Speeches—Revised Edition with a Comprehensive Bibliography.* Lanham, Md.: University Press of America, 1985.
Podwal, Mark H. *The Decline and Fall of the American Empire.* New York: Darien House, 1971.
"Political Mood of U.S. Now—What a Nationwide Survey Shows." *U.S. News and World Report* 57 (August 24, 1964): 54–63.
"The 'Poor People's March': Its Demands, the Prospects." *U.S. News and World Report* 64 (May 13, 1968): 44–45.
"Poverty in America: Report of the Council of Economic Advisers." *Monthly Labor Review* 87 (March 1964): 285–91.
"Poverty in Appalachia: A Report after Five Years of Aid." *U.S. News and World Report* 65 (June 29, 1968): 50–53.
"Poverty U.S.A." *Newsweek*, February 17, 1964: 36.

Powers, Richard Gid. *Secrecy and Power: The Life of J. Edgar Hoover.* New York: Free Press, 1986.
President's Commission on Campus Unrest. *The Report of the President's Commission on Campus Unrest.* New York: Arno, 1970.
"Prosperity Wears an Uneasy Smile." *Business Week,* March 26, 1966: 43–45.
"Report on the 'Soaring Sixties': Measuring U.S. Growth." *U.S. News and World Report* 55 (November 11, 1963): 42–45.
Reuther, Walter P. *Reuther on First Things First* [UAW chief on problems of changing U.S. social, economic, political conditions]. Santa Barbara, Cal.: Center for the Study of Democratic Institutions, 1964.
Riesel, Victor. "LBJ Warned about Plans for New Summer Riots." *Human Events* 28 (January 13, 1968): 9.
"Riot Season—1967." *U.S. News and World Report* 62 (June 26, 1967): 23–24.
Rockefeller Panel Report. *The Performing Arts: Problems and Prospects.* New York: McGraw-Hill, 1965.
Rossi, Peter, and Zahava Blum. *Class, Status, and Poverty.* Baltimore: Johns Hopkins University Press, 1968.
———. *Social Stratification and Poverty.* Brookline, Mass.: American Academy of Arts and Sciences, 1967.
Rothschild, Mary Aickin. *A Case of Black and White: Northern Volunteers and the Southern Freedom Summers, 1964–1965.* Contributions in Afro-American and African Studies, No. 69. Westport, Conn.: Greenwood Press, 1982.
Rowow, I. "Aged, Family and Friends." *Social Security Bulletin* 28 (November 1965): 18–20.
Rustin, Bayard. "From Protest to Politics: The Future of the Civil Rights Movement." *Commentary* 39 (February 1965): 25–31.
Sampson, Edward E. "Student Activism and the Decade of Protest." *Journal of Social Issues* 23 (July 1967): 1–33.
Sarratt, Reed. *The Ordeal of Desegregation: The First Decade.* New York: Harper and Row, 1966.
Sayres, Sohnya, Anders Stephanson, Stanley Aronowitz, Frederic Jameson, eds. *The Sixties, Without Apology.* Minneapolis: University of Minnesota Press, 1984.
Schulke, Flip, ed. *Martin Luther King, Jr.: A Documentary . . . Montgomery to Memphis.* New York: Norton, 1976.
Schuyler, George. "A Cool Appraisal of Martin Luther King:

He Reaped the Whirlwind." *Human Events* 28 (April 20, 1968): 8.

———. "A Long, Hard Look at the Long, Hot Summer." *Human Events* 27 (August 12, 1967): 8.

———. "Martin Luther King's Ominous Warning: 'Hotter Summer' Ahead: Negro Leader Plans to Combine Civil Rights Drive with Viet Nam Peace Campaign." *Human Events* 27 (April 15, 1967): 10.

Scott, Paul. "Kennedy and King Form Political Alliance: Senator to Support D.C. March." *Human Events* 28 (March 30, 1968): 1.

———. "King and Carmichael Map Summer Strategy: Massive Attacks on Big Cities." *Human Events* 28 (March 2, 1968): 9.

"Senior Citizens Organize." *America* 113 (November 6, 1965): 519.

Shachtman, Tom. *Decade of Shocks: Dallas to Watergate, 1963–1974.* New York: Poseidon, 1983.

Shaffer, Helen B. "The Persistence of Poverty." *Editorial Research Reports,* February 5, 1964: 83–89.

Sheppard, Harold L., and Herbert C. Striner. *Civil Rights, Employment, and the Social Status of American Negroes: Based on a Report for the U.S. Commission on Civil Rights.* Washington, D.C.: Upjohn Institute for Employment Research, Studies in Employment and Unemployment, June 1966.

Sherrard, Thomas D., ed. *Social Welfare and Urban Problems: Papers Presented before the National Conference on Social Welfare.* New York: Columbia University Press, 1968.

"Shifting Patterns in Race Problem: What Negro Leaders Want Now." *U.S. News and World Report* 59 (August 23, 1965): 32–34.

Silberman, Charles E. "What Hit the Teenagers: A Massive Case of Youth Unemployment." *Fortune* 71 (April 1965): 130–33+.

Skidmore, Max J. "The Tumultuous Decade: The American of the 1960s." *Indian Journal of American Studies* (India), vol. 9, no. 2, 1979: 38–50.

Skolnick, Jerome H. "Student Protest." *AAUP Bulletin* 55 (September 1969): 309–26.

Smith, Tom W. "America's Most Important Problem: A Trend

Analysis, 1946–1976." *Public Opinion Quarterly* 44 (Summer 1980): 164–80.
Sommers, Albert T. "The Economic Environment of the Middle Sixties." *Conference Board Record* 1 (September 1964): 1–56.
"Spotlight on 'Hippies': A First Hand Report." *U.S. News and World Report* 62 (May 8, 1967): 61–63.
Stafford, Walter W. "Dilemmas of Civil Rights Groups in Developing Urban Strategies and Changes in American Federalism, 1933–1970." *Phylon* 37 (March 1976): 59–72.
Stone, I. F. *I. F. Stone's Weekly, 1953–1971*. Millwood, N.Y.: Krause Reprint and Periodicals.
Taylor, George. "United States' Water Crisis [Remarks of AFL-CIO Dept. of Research Economist]." *AFL-CIO American Federationist* 73 (March 1966): 8–14.
Tyler, Gus. "The Liberal Crisis—Now: Perils of Polarization." *New Leader* 51 (October 7, 1968): 3–7.
United States Commission on Civil Rights. *A Time to Listen—A Time to Act: Voices from the Ghettos of the Nation's Cities*. Washington, D.C.: U.S. Gov't. Printing Office, November 1967.
United States Conference of Mayors. "City Problems of 1965." *Annual Proceedings of the U.S. Conference of Mayors, 1965*. Washington, D.C.: U.S. Conference of Mayors, 1965.
———. "City Problems of 1966." *Annual Proceedings of the U.S. Conference of Mayors, 1966*. Washington, D.C.: U.S. Conference of Mayors, 1966.
United States Office of Economic Opportunity. *Dimensions of Poverty*. Washington, D.C.: U.S. Gov't. Printing Office, 1965.
United States. National Advisory Commission on Civil Disorders. *Report*. Washington, D.C.: U.S. Gov't. Printing Office, 1966.
University of Texas, School of Architecture. *Texas Conference on Our Environmental Crisis* (November 21–23, 1965). Austin: University of Texas Press, 1966.
Velvel, Lawrence R. *Undeclared War and Civil Disobedience: The American System in Crisis*. New York: Dunellen, 1970.
Waskow, Arthur. *From Race Riot to Sit-In*. Garden City, N.Y.: Doubleday, 1966.
Ways, Max. "On the Campus: A Troubled Reflection of the

144   THE PRESIDENTIAL YEARS

U.S." *Fortune* 72 (September 1965): 130–35 + ; (October 1965): 140–47 + .
Weaver, Robert C. *Dilemmas of Urban America.* Cambridge, Mass.: Harvard University Press, 1965.
Weisbrod, Burton A., ed. *The Economics of Poverty: An American Paradox.* Englewood Cliffs, N.J.: Prentice-Hall, 1965.
Westin, Alan F., ed. *Freedom Now!* New York: Basic Books, 1964.
Westly, David L., and Richard G. Braungart. "Class and Politics in the Family Backgrounds of Student Political Activists." *American Sociological Review* 31 (October 1966): 690–92.
"When Will the Violence End? RFK Assassination." *Human Events* 28 (June 15, 1968): 1, 4.
"Where the [King Assassination] Riots Hit Hardest." *Human Events* 28 (April 20, 1968): 6.
Widener, Alice. "New Youth Technique: Violent Non-Violence." *Human Events* 25 (February 27, 1965): 3.
Wiegand, G. C. "Changes in Political, Social, and Economic Philosophy during the Period 1940–1964." *Commercial and Financial Chronicle* 200 (September 24, 1964): 10 + .
Wilkins, Roy. "The Riots of 1964: The Causes of Racial Violence." *Notre Dame Lawyer,* vol. 40, no. 5 (1965): 552–57.
———. "The Way to Racial Peace in America" (Interview). *U.S. News and World Report* 63 (September 25, 1967): 80–86.
"Winds of Discontent Buffet U.S.: Although Prosperity Never Has Been Greater, Vietnam, Civil Rights, and Inflation Make for an Unhappy Mood." *Business Week,* February 3, 1968: 22–24.
Wolfenstein, Eugene Victor. *The Victims of Democracy: Malcolm X and the Black Revolution.* Berkeley and Los Angeles: University of California Press, 1979.
"'Yippies' Will Help Taunt Democrats in Chicago: Massive Leftist Demonstrations Planned." *Human Events* 28 (April 6, 1968): 12–13.

2. DOMESTIC POLICY

A. GENERAL

Alexander, Holmes. "Skepticism Needed When Evaluating Claims of LBJ's 'Great Society'." *Human Events* 25 (January 2, 1965): 15.

DOMESTIC POLICY—GENERAL

"At the Center of Our Concerns: Johnson's State of the Union Message." *Business Week,* January 15, 1966: 25–26.

Benson, George. "Thoughts about the 'Great Society'." *Human Events* 24 (October 3, 1964): 6.

Berens, John F. "The FBI and Civil Liberties from Franklin Roosevelt to Jimmy Carter: An Historical Overview." *Michigan Academician* 13 (Fall 1980): 131–44.

Biemiller, Andrew J. "The 88th Congress—A Record of Achievement." *AFL-CIO American Federationist* 71 (November 1964): 7–11.

"Bigger Slice Goes to Poorer Areas: Great Society Programs Speed Up." *Business Week,* November 27, 1965: 54+.

Black, Eugene R. "The Domestic Dividends of Foreign Aid." *Columbia Journal of World Business* 1 (Fall 1965): 21–27.

Blissett, Marlan. "Untangling the Mess [The Great Society Reevaluated]." Paper presented at Fifth Annual Hofstra University Presidential Conference: Lyndon Baines Johnson, A Texan in Washington. Hempstead, New York, April 10–12, 1986.

Blum, John Morton. "The Great Society: Continuities." Paper delivered at LBJ Library, March 14, 1986, sponsored by the History Dept. and the Law School, University of Texas at Austin, and the LBJ Library.

Bowles, Nigel P. *The White House and Capitol Hill: The Politics of Presidential Persuasion.* New York: Oxford University Press, 1987.

———. "White House Congressional Liaison on Domestic Policy under Lyndon Baines Johnson with Special Reference to the Office of Congressional Relations." Oxford, England: Nuffield College, Oxford University, 1983. Ph.D. dissertation.

Bowman, LeRoy. "A Humanist Response to the Great Society." *Humanist* 25 (March/April 1965): 41–43.

Brandon, Henry. "Prospectus for the Great Society." *Saturday Review* 48 (January 30, 1965): 14–15.

Brinton, Howard J. "Reshaping of the Great Society: The New 90th Congress." *Magazine of Wall Street* 119 (November 26, 1966): 242–45+.

Brinton, John J. "As Congress Yields to Johnson's Power of Persuasion and Opens the Flood-Gets of Spending." *Magazine of Wall Street* 116 (May 1, 1964): 160–63+.

Burns, James MacGregor, ed. *To Heal and to Build: The Pro-*

grams of Lyndon B. Johnson. New York: McGraw-Hill, 1968.
"Business and LBJ." *Human Events* 22 (December 14, 1963): 5.
Califano, Joseph A., Jr. "How Great Was the Great Society?" Address at The Great Society: A Twenty Year Critique, Lyndon B. Johnson Library, Austin, April 19, 1985.
Capp, Glenn R., comp. *The Great Society: A Sourcebook of Speeches.* Belmont, Cal.: Dickenson, 1967.
Chamberlain, John. "Where 'Great Society' Comes From." *Human Events* 25 (January 30, 1965): 15.
"Congress Backs Away from Larger Federal Role in 1966." *Congressional Quarterly Weekly Report* 25 (February 10, 1967): 211–17.
Coyle, David Cushman. *Breakthrough to the Great Society.* Dobbs Ferry, N.Y.: Oceana, 1965.
Crosby, R. W. "State of Union Message Creates Confusion." *Iron Age* 197 (January 20, 1966): 26–27.
De Toledano, Ralph. "The 'Great Society'—How Costly?" *Human Events* 25 (January 23, 1965): 7.
———. "LBJ to Propose Executive Branch Takeover of Independent Agencies." *Human Events* 24 (December 19, 1964): 1.
Democratic National Committee. "Blueprint for Progress: President Sets Objectives." *The Democrat* 4 (November 21, 1964): 4.
———. " *The Johnson Administration: First Session of the 89th Congress, January 4–October 23, 1965.* Washington, D.C.: Democratic National Committee, Research Division Factbook, November 1965. Typewritten.
Duesenberry, James S. "Domestic Policy Objectives and the Balance of Payments." *Journal of Finance* 21 (May 1966): 345–53, 360–68.
Elkins, Dov Peretz. "Johnson's Great Society and the Jewish Tradition." *Jewish Digest* 11 (December 1965): 1–5.
Eller, J. N. "GOP Salutes President for 89th's Record." *America* 113 (November 6, 1965): 520.
———. "Laws-by-Pound No Measure for Congress." *America* 116 (April 29, 1965): 185.
Etzioni, Amitai. "Consensus and Reforms in the Great Society." *Sociological Inquiry,* vol. 40, no. 1 (1970): 113+.
"First Session of Great Society Congress." *Public Utilities Fortnightly* 76 (November 11, 1965): 44–45.

Flacks, Richard. "Is the Great Society Just a Barbecue?" *New Republic* 154 (January 29, 1966): 18–23.
"Formulating [Johnson's '68] Presidential Program Is Long Process." *Congressional Quarterly Weekly Report* 26 (January 26, 1968): 111–14.
Fulbright, J. William. "The Great Society is a Sick Society." *New York Times Magazine*, August 20, 1967: 30 +.
"Getting A Call from the Great Society." *Chemical Week* 96 (January 16, 1965): 27.
"The Great Risk of the Great Society." *Nation's Business* 53 (March 1965): 27–28.
"'The Great Society: A 20-Year Critique.' Reports on a Symposium Held April 18–19 in the LBJ Auditorium on U.T. Campus." *On Campus* (University of Texas) 12 (April 20–May 5, 1985): 5–13.
"The 'Great Society' and Its Future: A Progress Report." *U.S. News and World Report* 61 (December 19, 1966): 32–35.
"'Great Society' Faces the Future—Changes Congress Is Making." *U.S. News and World Report* 63 (July 10, 1967): 32–33.
"[Great Society] Planners Say $500 Billion Needed for New 'Facilities'." *Human Events* 27 (March 11, 1967): 6.
Hale, J. Russell. "Dream and Reality: The Great Society." *Dial* 4 (Summer 1965): 222–23.
Hanrahan, Jack, and Phil Hahn. *The Great Society Fun and Games Book*. New York: Grosset and Dunlap, 1965.
Hazlitt, Henry. "The Life and Death of the Welfare State." *Human Events* 29 (January 4, 1969): 5–12.
Henderson, W. L., and D. L. Smith. "Parsimonious Fiscal Policy of the Great Society." *Taxes* 43 (November 1965): 705–14.
Hirsch, R. G. "Poverty and the Great Society: The Jewish Approach." *Jewish Heritage* 9 (Winter 1966/67): 57–63.
"House and Senate Key Votes for 1964." *Congressional Quarterly Weekly Report* 22 (October 9, 1964): 2387–94.
"How LBJ Hopes to Improve America." *U.S. News and World Report* 64 (January 29, 1968): 27–29.
"How Much Will Johnson Do for the Unions?" *Business Week*, March 6, 1965: 128 +.
Humphrey, Hubert H. *The Cause Is Mankind: A Liberal Program for Modern America*. New York: Praeger, 1964.
Hutchison, Bruce. *Toward a Great Society: The U.S. Role in a*

Troubled World. Winnipeg, Manitoba: Winnipeg Free Press, 1965. Pamphlet.

"Impact of LBJ's Brand on Business." *Steel* 154 (January 6, 1964): 43–44.

"Job, School, Welfare and Housing Proposals [of Johnson Administration] Reviewed." *Congressional Quarterly Weekly Report* 26 (March 15, 1968): 539–45.

"Johnson and the New Congress: Chances for 'Great Society' Look Good." *U.S. News and World Report* 57 (November 23, 1964): 31–32.

"Johnson Congress: What It Will Do." *Nation's Business* 52 (December 1964): 32–33+.

"Johnson Puts 'Great Society' in Moth Balls." *United Mine Workers Journal* 78 (January 15, 1967): 3–4, 10–11.

"Johnson Shows a Different Style: Foreign and Domestic Policies." *Business Week*, November 4, 1967: 27–29.

"Johnson Takes the Slow Road: No Radical Change in Either Domestic or Foreign Policy." *Business Week*, November 19, 1966: 37–38.

"Johnson Wants Wall St. Barbeque." *Human Events* 24 (October 31, 1964): 6.

"Johnson's Grand Design." *Business Week*, January 9, 1965: 19–21.

"Johnson's Great Society: Economy Version." *Statist* (Emergency Edition), January 10, 1967: 10.

"Johnson's New Year—Meanwhile, Back at the Capitol." *Statist* 191 (January 6, 1967): 21–22.

"Johnson's Program and Its Prospects: Tax Cut, Poverty, Civil Rights—Stress on Domestic Problems and Issues, Less on Foreign Affairs." *U.S. News and World Report* 56 (January 20, 1964): 29–31.

Jones, Jenkin Lloyd. "'Great Society' Has Proved to Be Unworkable." *Human Events* 27 (December 2, 1967): 12.

———. "The New Materialism of the 'Great Society'." *Human Events* 25 (October 30, 1965): 6.

Jordan, Barbara C., and Elspeth D. Rostow. *The Great Society: A Twenty Year Critique.* Austin: Lyndon B. Johnson Library and Lyndon B. Johnson School of Public Affairs, 1986.

Kaufman, K. A. "LBJ's Speech Stresses Domestic Strife." *Iron Age* 201 (January 25, 1968): 62–63.

Keyserling, Leon H. "Pseudo-Liberal Phrases vs. Johnson's

DOMESTIC POLICY—GENERAL 149

Progressive Deeds." *AFL-CIO Free Trade Union News* 23 (March 1968): 4–5.
Kilpatrick, James Jackson. "Is LBJ's 'Great Society' Unconstitutional?" *Human Events* 25 (February 6, 1965): 6.
———. "Will the Aluminum Dumping End LBJ's Honeymoon with Industry?" *Human Events* 25 (November 20, 1965): 6.
Kluger, Pearl. "Progressive Presidents and Black Americans." New York: Columbia University, 1974. Ph.D. dissertation. University Microfilms No. 75–29298.
"LBJ and Businessmen—Climate Gets Cooler." *U.S. News and World Report.* 59 (November 29, 1965): 39–41.
"LBJ Outlines Ambitious Program." *Engineering News-Record.* 174 (January 14, 1964): 34–36.
"LBJ Pushes Spending Programs." *Human Events* 27 (September 2, 1967): 3.
"LBJ to Press for Remainder of Kennedy Program." *Public Utilities Fortnightly.* 74 (December 3, 1964): 41–42.
"LBJ's Domestic Plans Face a Cool Congress." *Business Week,* January 22, 1966: 28–30.
"LBJ's 'Great Society'—What Will It Be?" *U.S. News and World Report* 57 (November 23, 1964): 33–37.
"LBJ's Myth of Job Reduction." *Human Events* 24 (February 29, 1964): 13.
"LBJ's Obliging Congress Leaves a Record to Build Upon." *Engineering News-Record* 177 (October 17, 1966): 16–17.
"LBJ's '100 Days'—A Record Piling Up." *U.S. News and World Report* 58 (April 26, 1965): 41–44.
Lisagor, Peter. "Pause Would Be Refreshing: The Creation of the Great Society." *Nation's Business* 53 (September 1965): 23–24.
Martire, D. "Evaluating the State of the Union Message." *Magazine of Wall Street* 117 (January 22, 1966): 420–23.
McKaig, J. E. "State of Union: Texas Style—An Inspirational Message from a Doer." *Magazine of Wall Street* 115 (January 23, 1965): 416–19.
"Measured Reaction to Johnson's State of the Union Message in the Electronics Industry." *Electronic News* 12 (January 16, 1967): 1+.
Mermelstein, David. "Political Economy of the Great Society." *Journal of Human Relations*, vol. 18, no. 2 (1970): 840–48.
Merriam, Ida C. "Social Welfare Expenditures, 1964–65." *Social Security Bulletin* 28 (October 1965): 3–16.

Montoya, Joseph M. "The Federal Role in Building the Great Society." *New Mexico Business* 18 (December 1965): 1–4.
"More 'Social'—Less 'Security'." *Human Events* 26 (November 5, 1966): 13.
Murray, Charles. *Losing Ground: American Social Policy, 1950–1980.* New York: Basic Books, 1984.
Myers, H. B. "LBJ's Romance with Business." *Fortune* 70 (September 1964): 130–33 +.
"Now It's the Unions That Are Worrying LBJ." *U.S. News and World Report* 60 (February 28, 1966): 86–88.
"Party Majorities Again Split on 'Great Society' Items." *Congressional Quarterly Weekly Report* 24 (December 9, 1966): 2989–93.
"Paying on the Great Society." *Chemical Week* 99 (July 30, 1966): 15.
Phillips, Charles F. "Three Wars: Poverty, Civil Rights, and the Cold War." *Vital Speeches* 30 (October 1, 1964): 757–59.
Picque, Nicholas D. "Building the Great Society, LBJ Style." *Christianity and Crisis* 24 (January 11, 1965): 272–74.
———. "Lyndon Johnson and the 89th Congress." *Christianity and Crisis* 25 (September 20, 1965): 184–187.
Powers, S. P. "Cooperative Federalism: No Cut Seen in Domestic Programs [because of Vietnam]." *Public Management* 48 (February 1966): 40–42.
"President Johnson and His Program." *Texas Observer*, September 4, 1964: 5 +.
"President Johnson Hints Extra [Congressional] Session to Spur Bills." *AFL-CIO News* 9 (May 9, 1964): 1, 10.
"President Johnson Tells Labor: Public Works Seen If Job Lag Persists." *AFL-CIO News* 9 (May 9, 1964): 1, 10.
"President Optimistic, Emphasizes Domestic Goals [State of Union Message, January 4, 1965]." *Congressional Quarterly Weekly Report* 23 (January 8, 1965): 37–38.
Reopel, Michael R., and Lance W. Bardsley. "Strategies for Governance: Domestic Policymaking in the Johnson Administration." Paper presented at Fifth Annual Hofstra University Presidential Conference: Lyndon Baines Johnson, A Texan in Washington. Hempstead, New York, April 10–12, 1986.
Reston, James. "The Great Society: Are We Ready for It?" *Johns Hopkins Magazine* 16 (March 1965): 8–11.

Rogers, Donald I. "What Is 'Work and Sacrifice' in the 'Great Society'?" *Human Events* 25 (March 13, 1965): 10.

Rosenberg, Benjamin B. "Jewish Community Faces the Great Society: Implications for the Philosophy and Program of Jewish Communal Services." *Journal of Jewish Communal Service* 43 (Fall 1966): 14–21.

Rothman, Rozann. *The Great Society at the Grass Roots: Local Adaptation to Federal Initiatives of the 1960's: Champaign-Urbana.* Lanham, Md.: University Press of America, 1984.

Ryskind, Morris. "Is the 'Great Society' Just Alice's Wonderland?" *Human Events* 25 (October 2, 1965): 6.

Schulz, Bill. "Polls Provide Optimistic Note for Conservatives—Many LBJ Programs Unpopular Even in Districts He Carried in '64." *Human Events* 26 (August 20, 1966): 14.

Schwarz, John E. *America's Hidden Success: a Reassessment of Twenty Years of Public Policy.* New York: Norton, 1983.

"75 Million Jobs Key Goal, President Johnson Tells U.S. Labor: Labor Asked to Help Spur Passage of Major Administration Bills." *AFL-CIO News* 8 (December 7, 1963): 1, 8.

Shaffer, Samuel. "LBJ and the Fabulous 89th Go Home." *Newsweek* 66 (November 1, 1965): 21–23.

"Shake-Up in Congress Signals a Slower Pace of Great Society Programs." *Engineering News-Record* 177 (November 17, 1966): 62–63.

Simms, J. Carroll. "College Students' Impressions of the Great Society." *Southern Journal of Business* 2 (October 1967): 49–56.

Smith, Nancy Kegan. "Presidential Task Force Operation during the Johnson Administration." *Presidential Studies Quarterly* 15 (Spring 1985): 320–29.

Stark, John R. "Great Society—Concept and Cost." *University of Missouri Business and Government Review* 7 (September/October 1966): 5–13.

———. "The Economic Case for the Great Society." *Challenge* 15 (January/February 1967): 22–25.

Stolley, Richard B. "Will Congress Nail Together the Great Society?" *Life* 58 (January 15, 1965): 36–37.

Stringfellow, William. "The Great Society as Myth." *Dial* 5 (Autumn 1966): 252–57.

Taylor, Henry J. "Does CORE's Collective Bargaining Restrain Trade?" *Human Events* 24 (September 5, 1964): 13.

"There's More on the Way: President is Pressing for Action on Whole List of Bills." *Business Week*, August 7, 1965: 28–29.

"Time for Action: President Johnson Calls in AFL-CIO Executive Council to Ask Labor's Help in Getting Needed Legislation Enacted." *Advance* (Clothing Workers of America) 49 (December 15, 1963): 8.

"Time of Testing: Johnson's State of the Union Message." *Business Week*, January 14, 1967: 25–26.

Trohan, Walter. "'Socialism' Is the Quickest Way to Spell 'Great Society'." *Human Events* 25 (April 24, 1965): 9.

"Union at War [Comment on LBJ's State of Union Message, 1966]." *Economist* (Great Britain) 218 (January 15, 1966): 175–76.

United States Department of Labor. *1966 Manpower Report to the President of the United States.* Washington, D.C.: U.S. Gov't. Printing Office, 1967.

———. *1967 Manpower Report to the President of the United States.* Washington, D.C.: U.S. Gov't. Printing Office, 1968.

Warner, Robert M. "The Anatomy of a Speech: Lyndon Johnson's Great Society Address." *Michigan Historical Collections Bulletin* 28 (December 1978): 1–15.

Washington, D.C. Inaugural Committee. *Threshold of Tomorrow: The Great Society; The Inauguration of Lyndon Baines Johnson, 36th President of the United States and Hubert Horatio Humphrey, 38th Vice President of the United States, January 20, 1965.* Washington, D.C.: Presidential Inaugural Committee, 1965.

"What LBJ Didn't Say: State of the Union Message." *Human Events* 28 (January 27, 1968): 1, 4.

"What Now? (How the New President Will Handle Issues of Importance to Business)." *Chemical Week* 93 (November 30, 1963): 19–20.

"What the 'Great Society' Is Going to Cost." *U.S. News and World Report* 59 (October 18, 1965): 50–52.

"When Everybody Is on Welfare [Summarizes Report Entitled, 'Social Development, Key to the Great Society']." *U.S. News and World Report* 61 (August 1, 1966): 72.

"Who'll Be Helped, Hurt by LBJ's Plans [Commentary on 1967 State of Union Message]." *U.S. News and World Report* 62 (January 23, 1967): 27–30.

"Why Abba Schwartz Was Eased Out of His Job." *Human Events* 26 (March 26, 1966): 11.
Wicker, Tom. "Requiem for the Great Society." *Saturday Evening Post* 242 (January 25, 1969): 30+.
Wilkinson, Kenneth P., Michael J. Camasso, and Albert C. Luloff. "Nonmetropolitan Participation in Programs of the Great Society." *Social Science Quarterly* 65 (December 1984): 1092–1103.
Williams, John. "What Is the 'Great Society'?" *Human Events* 26 (June 4, 1966): 6.
Williams, Whiting. *America's Mainspring and the Great Society: A Pick-and-Shovel Outlook.* New York: Frederick Fell, Inc., 1967.
Witkin, Gordon. "The Great Society: How Great Has it Been?" *U.S. News and World Report,* July 2, 1984: 31.
Yarmolinsky, Adam. "The 'Great Society'—Another American Dream?" *World Today* 24 (May 1968): 203–08.

B. THE ARTS

Alexander, Holmes. "Arts and the Federal Subsidy." *Human Events* 25 (May 15, 1965): 10.
Berman, Ronald. *Culture and Politics* [Reviews the National Endowment for the Humanities]. Lanham, Md.: University Press of America, 1983.
Biddle, Livingston. "President Lyndon B. Johnson: The Arts, Humanities, and Cultural Values." Paper prepared for the 20th Anniversary of the Great Society, Lyndon B. Johnson Library, Austin, Texas, March 1985.
Bloom, Kathryn. "A New Federal Education Program in the Arts and Humanities." *Music Educators Journal* 51 (January 1965): 37–38, 117.
Brademas, John. "Government, the Arts, and the Public Happiness." *Music Educators Journal* 52 (April/May 1966): 41–45.
"Federal Arts and Humanities Foundation Gains Support." *Congressional Quarterly Weekly Report* 23 (April 30, 1965): 837–39.
"Federal Subsidy a Reality: Congress Passes Arts Bill." *International Musician* (American Federation of Musicians) 64 (November 1965): 3.

Getlein, Frank. "Government in Art." *New Republic* 150 (February 15, 1964): 36–37.
"Government Aid Seen Vital to Survival of Arts [Remarks of Herman Kenin, Amer. Fed. of Musicians President]." *AFL-CIO News* 9 (May 23, 1964): 11.
Greenfield, Meg. "The Politics of Art." *Reporter* 35 (September 22, 1966): 25–30.
Hanks, Nancy. "Government and the Arts." *Saturday Review* 53 (February 28, 1970): 32.
Harris, Mark. "Government as Patron of the Arts." *New York Times Magazine*, September 13, 1964: 35, 139–40.
Heckscher, August. "Arts and the National Government." *American Culture in the Sixties*, edited by Vineta Colby, pp. 92–106. New York: H. W. Wilson, 1964.
———. "Arts and the National Government: A Report to the President." *Taming Megalopolis, Volume I, What Is and What Could Be*, edited by H. W. Eldredge, pp. 549–76. New York: Praeger, 1967.
"Hecksher Urges President to Carry Out Kennedy's Program for Advisory Arts Panel." *Architectural Record* 135 (April 1964): 10.
Hess, Thomas B. "Arts in the Great Society." *Art News* 64 (September 1965): 21.
"Johnson Inherits Cultural Leadership." *Architectural Forum* 120 (January 1964): 5.
Kaderlan, Norman. *Bibliography on the Administration of the Arts, 1958–69*. Madison: University of Wisconsin Arts Council, 1969.
Keppel, Francis. "Encouraging Legislation in the Arts." *Higher Education* [HEW] 20 (March 1964): 3–4, 20–21.
Kilpatrick, James Jackson. "Arts and Humanities Act Creates Bureaucratic Chaos." *Human Events* 25 (September 4, 1965): 2.
———. "President's Bill on Arts and Humanities." *Human Events* 25 (April 3, 1965): 3.
Kirk, Elise K. *Music at the White House: A History of the American Spirit*. Urbana: University of Illinois Press, 1986.
"Labor Guides Set for Grants under Arts and Humanities Act." *AFL-CIO News* 12 (April 1, 1967): 8.
Lloyd, Norman. "Status of the Arts in America." *Music Educators Journal* 52 (November/December 1965): 47–48, 131–35.

McDonald, William F. *Federal Relief Administration and the Arts: The Origins and Administrative History of the Arts Projects of the Works Progress Administration.* Columbus: Ohio State University Press, 1969.

"National Arts Council." *Congress and the Nation, 1945–1964,* pp. 1321–22. Washington, D.C.: Congressional Quarterly Service, 1965.

"New Patron [of the Arts]." *Nation* 200 (January 18, 1965): 42.

"Pres. Johnson Offers Broad Program of Federal Aid to Arts and Humanities." *AFL-CIO News* 10 (March 20, 1965): 4.

"President Signs Arts, Humanities Bill into Law." *Congressional Quarterly Weekly Report* 23 (October 1, 1965): 1969–71.

Rosenberg, Harold. *Discovering the Present: Three Decades of Art, Culture, and Politics.* Chicago: University of Chicago Press, 1973.

Stevens, Roger L. "The State of the Arts—a 1966 Balance Sheet." *Saturday Review,* March 12, 1966: 24–25.

Straight, Michael. "Arts Go Begging." *New Republic* 160 (March 22, 1969): 13–15.

———. "Something for the Arts." *New Republic* 152 (March 13, 1965): 11–15.

———. *Twigs for an Eagle's Nest: Government and the Arts, 1965–1978.* Berkeley, Cal.: Devon Press, 1979.

Sung, Kayser, et al. "America and Asia: Annual Survey." *Far Eastern Economic Review* (Hong Kong) 57 (July 13, 1967): 63–115; 61 (July 4, 1968): 21–77.

Taylor, Harold. "Arts in America." *Dance* 39 (November 1965): 70–74.

Thompson, Frank, Jr. "Arts in Congress." *Music Journal* 22 (September 1964): 27, 77–79.

———. "Report on a Year of Progress [Congressional Progress of Bill to Establish Foundation on Arts and Humanities]." *International Musician* (American Federation of Musicians) 64 (July 1965): 7.

Ustinov, Peter. "Politics and the Arts." *Atlantic* 218 (July 1966): 44–48.

Von Eckardt, Wolf. "Sour Note." *AIA Journal* [American Institute of Architects] 41 (February 1964): 12, 14.

———. "Stalling on the Arts." *New Republic* 150 (March 21, 1964): 8.

C. CIVIL RIGHTS

Abraham, Henry J. *Freedom and the Court: Civil Rights and Civil Liberties in the United States.* New York: Oxford University Press, 1967.

Alexander, Holmes. "Nub of Civil Rights Bill: Centralized Government Control." *Human Events* 24 (May 16, 1964): 14.

Allen, Robert S. "Filibuster Threat All But Kills Civil Rights Bill This Session." *Human Events* 27 (November 25, 1967): 13.

Belknap, Michael. *Federal Law and Southern Order: Racial Violence and Constitutional Conflict in the Post-Brown South.* Athens: University of Georgia Press, 1987.

Benakraitis, NiJole, and Joe R. Feagin. *Affirmative Action and Equal Opportunity: Action, Inaction, Reaction.* Boulder, Col.: Western Press, 1978.

Benetar, David L., et al. "Implications for Business of the Civil Rights Act of 1964." *Record of the Association of the Bar of the City of New York* 20 (March 1965): 128–47.

Bickel, Alexander M. "The Civil Rights Act of 1964." *Commentary* 38 (August 1964): 33–39.

Blumberg, Rhoda Lois. *Civil Rights: The 1960's Freedom Struggle.* Boston: Twayne, 1984.

Booker, Simon. "Twenty Years Later: The Untold Civil Rights Legacy of Lyndon B. Johnson." *Jet* 68 (May 13, 1985): 12–16.

Bullock, Charles S. III, and Charles M. Lamb. *Implementation of Civil Rights Policy.* Monterey, Cal.: Brooks and Cole, 1984.

Bureau of National Affairs. *The Civil Rights Act of 1964: What It Means to Employers, Businessmen, Unions, Employees, Minority Groups.* Washington, D.C.: Bureau of National Affairs, 1964.

Byrd, Harry F. "The Other Side of the Voting Rights Bill." *U.S. News and World Report* 58 (April 12, 1965): 86–88.

"Civil Rights Bill Foes Come Up with New Weapon: Will Use LBJ's Call for Local 'Disorder' Control." *Human Events* 28 (February 3, 1968): 10.

"The Civil Rights Law Goes into Action." *U.S. News and World Report* 57 (July 20, 1964): 44–45.

"Cloture on Civil Rights Breaks 26-Year Precedent [First time in its history the Senate voted to close off the debate on a civil rights filibuster]." *Congressional Quarterly Weekly Report* 22 (June 12, 1964): 1169–72.

"Congress Is Cautious on Integrated Housing Policy in 1965 and 1966." *Congressional Quarterly Weekly Report* 24 (October 14, 1966): 2485–86.

"Controversy in Congress over 'Open Housing': Pro and Con." *Congressional Digest* 45 (November 1966): 257–85.

"Controversy over the 'Equal Employment Opportunity' Provisions of the Civil Rights Bill: Pro and Con." *Congressional Digest* 43 (March 1964): 67–93.

Davidson, Arthur T. "Medical History: The Role of the Historic Black Colleges in the Training of Black Professionals." *Journal of the National Medical Association* 75 (October 1983): 1019–1022.

De Toledano, Ralph. "Lyndon Johnson's Civil Rights Record." *Human Events* 24 (August 15, 1964): 12.

"Drive Pledged [by AFL-CIO Executive Council] to Win Pres. Johnson's Civil Rights Plan." *AFL-CIO News* 12 (March 4, 1967): 1, 5.

Dye, Thomas R. *The Politics of Equality.* Indianapolis: Bobbs-Merrill, 1971.

Emerson, Thomas I., et al. *Political and Civil Rights in the United States: A Collection of Legal and Related Materials in Two Volumes.* 2 vols., 3rd ed. Boston: Little, Brown and Co., 1967.

"Enforcing Civil Rights Laws: A Prohibitive Job?" *U.S. News and World Report* 59 (December 6, 1965): 55–57.

"Equal Pay for Women: Its Effect." *U.S. News and World Report* 56 (June 15, 1964): 91–92.

"Equal Pay Law Seen Opening New Opportunities for Women [Remarks of Asst. Sec. of Labor Esther Peterson]." *AFL-CIO News* 9 (August 29, 1964): 7.

"Equal Rights for Women Gaining at Rapid Pace [Report of Advisory Council on the Status of Women]." *AFL-CIO News* 11 (June 11, 1966): 5.

"Fairer Wages for the Fair Sex." *Business Week*, June 6, 1964: 74.

Findlay, James. "Religion and Politics in the Sixties: The Churches and the Civil Rights Act of 1964." Paper pre-

sented at Fifth Annual Hofstra University Presidential Conference: Lyndon Baines Johnson, A Texan in Washington. Hempstead, New York, April 10–12, 1986.
Fisher, Linda L. "Presidential Implementation: Johnson, the War on Poverty, and Civil Rights." Paper presented to the annual meeting of the Midwest Political Science Assn., Cincinnati, Ohio, April 16–18, 1981.
———. "The Presidency and Civil Rights: a Case Study of the Johnson Administration." Washington, D.C.: George Washington University, 1982. Ph.D. dissertation.
Gardner, John W. "'Integrating' America—The Problems: Interview with John W. Gardner, Secretary of Health, Education and Welfare." *U.S. News and World Report* 62 (May 8, 1967): 64–69.
Garrow, David J. *The FBI and Martin Luther King, Jr.: From "Solo" to Memphis.* New York: Norton, 1981.
Gittell, Marilyn. "The Illusion of Affirmative Action." *Change,* October 1975: 39–43.
Glazer, Nathan. *Ethnic Dilemmas—1964–1982.* Cambridge, Mass.: Harvard University Press, 1983.
"Government's Plan to Desegregate the Suburbs." *U.S. News and World Report* 61 (October 10, 1966): 76–78.
"Great Society Setback [Race Riots]." *Human Events* 27 (August 5, 1967): 3.
Greenawalt, Kenneth W., and William S. Greenawalt. "Legal Aspects of Civil Rights in the United States and the Civil Rights Act of 1964." *Journal of the International Commission of Jurists* 5 (Winter 1964): 247–74; 6 (Summer 1965): 4–53.
Gropman, Alan L. *The Air Force Integrates, 1945–1964.* Washington, D.C.: Air Force, Office of Air Force History, 1978.
Gross, H. R. "Important Questions about LBJ's 'Voting Rights' Bill." *Human Events* 25 (April 10, 1965): 3.
Hamilton, Charles V. "Social Policy and the Welfare of Black Americans: From Rights to Resources." *Political Science Quarterly,* vol. 101, no. 2 (1986): 239–55.
Hamilton, Harry. "The Senate Lets L.B.J. Down." *America* 115 (July 16, 1966): 56.
Hecht, Neil. "From Seisin to Sit-in: Evolving Property Concepts [Sit-in Demonstrations at 'White Only' Restaurants]." *Boston University Law Review* 44 (Fall 1964): 435–66.

Hindell, Keith. "Civil Rights Breaks the Cloture Barrier [Breaking the Senate Filibuster]." *Political Quarterly* 36 (April/June 1965): 142–53.

"House Passes [1966] Civil Rights Bill, Retains Housing Section." *Congressional Quarterly Weekly Report* 24 (August 12, 1966): 1719–23.

Humphrey, Hubert H. "Civil Rights Responsibilities of the Federal Government: Outline." *Congressional Quarterly Weekly Report* 23 (April 9, 1965): 618.

———. "Humphrey Opens Civil Rights Debate with Detailed Defense." *Congressional Quarterly Weekly Report* 22 (April 3, 1964): 655–57.

"In the North, Also: School Integration." *Social Action Special Issue* 32 (September 1965): 3–46.

Jenkins, Timothy Lionel. "Study of Federal Effort to End Job Bias: A History, a Status Report, and a Prognosis." *Howard Law Journal* 14 (Summer 1968): 259–329.

"Johnson's Hypocrisy on Civil Rights." *Human Events* 24 (July 11, 1964): 20.

Jones, Augustus Joseph, Jr. "Bureaucracy and the Politics of Enforcement: A Comparative Agency Study on the Implementation of Title VI of the Civil Rights Act of 1964." St. Louis: Washington University, 1980. Ph.D. dissertation. University Microfilms No. 8103685.

———. *Law, Bureaucracy, and Politics: The Implementation of Title VI of the Civil Rights Act of 1964.* Lanham, Md.: University Press of America, 1982.

Kahn, Tom, and August Meier. "Recent Trends in the Civil Rights Movement." *New Politics* 3 (Spring 1964): 34–53.

Katzenbach, Nicholas DeB. *Meet the Press: Guest, Nicholas DeB. Katzenbach, Attorney General of the United States* [Interview on Johnson Administration's Voting Rights Bill]. Washington, D.C.: Merkle Press, vol. 9, no. 13, 1965.

Kilpatrick, James Jackson. "Senate Considers Votings Rights Bill of 1965." *Human Events* 25 (May 22, 1965): 3.

Kilson, Martin. "Whither Integration?" *American Scholar*, vol. 45, no. 3 (1976): 368–76.

King, Martin Luther, Jr. "Civil Rights No. 1—The Right to Vote." *New York Times Magazine* 14 (March 14, 1965): 21–27.

Kommers, Donald P. "The Right to Vote and Its Implementation." *Notre Dame Lawyer* 34 (June 1964): 365–410.

"Labor Drive Backs Civil Rights Law." *AFL-CIO News* 9 (September 5, 1964): 1, 6.
"Labor Strongly Backs New Civil Rights Bill." *AFL-CIO News* 11 (May 28, 1966): 1, 10.
Lawson, Steven F. *In Pursuit of Power: Southern Blacks and Electoral Politics, 1965–1982*. New York: Columbia University Press, 1985.
"LBJ and Civil Rights." *Human Events* 24 (March 28, 1964): 13.
"LBJ and Joe Rauh Capitalizing on Signing of Poll-Tax Amendment." *Human Events* 23 (February 22, 1964): 9.
"LBJ Woos Southern Leaders while Pushing Civil Rights." *Human Events* 23 (February 18, 1964): 11.
"LBJ's New Batch of 'Civil Rights'." *Human Events* 26 (May 14, 1966): 9.
"LBJ's New 'Rights' Law." *Human Events* 27 (February 25, 1967): 3–4.
"LBJ's Proposed Tax Hike." *Human Events* 27 (August 12, 1967): 3.
"LBJ's Voting Rights Speech." *Human Events* 25 (March 27, 1965): 1, 2.
Librach, Clifford. "LBJ as a Legislative Leader: The Voting Rights Act of 1965." Washington, D.C.: Georgetown University, 1973. M.A. thesis.
Lichtman, Allan J. "The Federal Assault against Voting Discrimination in the Deep South, 1957–1967." *Journal of Negro History* 54 (October 1969): 346–67.
Lockard, Duane. "The Politics of Antidiscrimination Legislation." *Harvard Journal of Legislation* 3 (December 1965): 3–61.
Martin, John F. *Civil Rights and the Crisis of Liberalism: The Democratic Party, 1945–1975*. Boulder: Westview Press, 1979.
Mashayekhi, Gholam-Hossein. "The Effect of the Equal Opportunity Provisions of the Civil Rights Act of 1964 on the Economic Situation of Non-White Males." Clemson, S.C.: Clemson University, 1976. Ph.D. dissertation. University Microfilms No. 77–13616.
McCord, John A., ed. *With All Deliberate Speed: Civil Rights Theory and Reality*. Urbana: University of Illinois Press, 1969.
Montgomery, Roosevelt. "The Presidency, the Bureaucracy, and Affirmative Action: A Case Study of the Johnson

Administration, 1963–1969." Lincoln: University of Nebraska, 1985. Ph.D. dissertation. University Microfilms No. 8521467.

Murphy, Thomas E. "Female Wage Discrimination: A Study of the Equal Pay Act, 1963–1970." *University of Cincinnati Law Review* 39 (Fall 1970): 615–49.

Murray, Pauli, and Mary Eastwood. "Jane Crow and the Law: Sex Discrimination and Title VII." *George Washington Law Review* 34 (December 1965): 232–56.

"Negro Leaders Meet LBJ." *U.S. News and World Report* 55 (December 16, 1963): 48–49.

"New Civil Rights Law—Now to Get It Enforced." *U.S. News and World Report* 57 (July 13, 1964): 33–34.

"New Crackdown on Local Schools: A Showdown Nears in South, Pressure Builds in North, as Washington Steps Up Attack on Segregated Schools." *U.S. News and World Report* 60 (May 2, 1966): 25–27.

"New Drive to Fulfill These Rights: White House Conference on Civil Rights." *Business Week*, May 28, 1966: 38–40.

"1964 Rights Act Stirs Widespread Federal Activity [Provisions]." *Congressional Quarterly Weekly Report* 23 (April 9, 1965): 617+.

"Now under Fire: Guidelines for Integration [of Schools and Hospitals]." *U.S. News and World Report* 61 (October 17, 1966): 74–76.

"On Equal Pay for Women." *U.S. News and World Report* 23 (March 1964): 115–17.

"On Its Way into Law: Civil Rights Bill." *Business Week*, June 13, 1964: 25–28.

Parker, Robert, with Richard Rashke. *Capitol Hill in Black and White.* New York: Dodd, Mead & Co., 1986.

Parker, Robert. "Lyndon and Me [Johnson's Driver and Later Maître d' of the Senate Dining Room]." *Washingtonian*, June 1986: 124–27, 190–99.

Payne, Thomas. "The Civil Rights Act of 1964." *Montana Business Quarterly* 2 (Fall 1964): 16–26. Also printed in *Harvard Law Review* 78 (January 1965): 684–96.

Piven, Frances Fox, and Richard A. Cloward. "The Case against Urban Desegregation: In Some Areas It Is against the Interests of Urban Negro Poor in Housing and Education." *Social Work* 12 (January 1967): 12–21.

Potenziani, David D. "Look to the Past: Richard B. Russell and

the Defense of Southern White Supremacy." Athens: University of Georgia, 1981. Ph.D. dissertation. University Microfilms No. 82-01574.
"Pres. Johnson Issues Order to Protect Women against Discrimination in Both Federal Employment and Private Firms which Have Federal Contracts." *AFL-CIO News* 12 (October 28, 1967): 11.
"Pres. Johnson Pledges No Turnback on Rights [White House Conference on Civil Rights]." *AFL-CIO News* 11 (June 4, 1966): 1, 12.
"President Johnson Hails Labor Role in Bias Fight [1964 Civil Rights Act]." *AFL-CIO News* 9 (March 21, 1964): 1, 4.
"President Johnson Sees Landmark in New Equal Pay Law." *AFL-CIO News* 9 (June 20, 1964): 9.
"President Lyndon B. Johnson: A Special Issue Devoted to a National Symposium on Civil Rights." *Texas Times* [University of Texas at Austin] 4 (February 1973): 1–16.
Pycior, Julie Leininger. "Lyndon, La Raza and the Paradox of Texas History." Paper presented at Fifth Annual Hofstra University Presidential Conference: Lyndon Baines Johnson, A Texan in Washington. Hempstead, New York, April 10–12, 1986.
Pyle, Christopher H., and Richard Morgan. "Johnson Civil Rights Shake-Up: Streamlining or Side Tracking?" *New Leader* 48 (October 11, 1965): 3–6.
Rachlin, Carl. "The 1964 Civil Rights Law: A Hard Look." *Law in Transition Quarterly* 2 (Spring 1965): 67–86.
Raskin, A. H. "Civil Rights: The Law and the Unions." *Reporter* 31 (September 10, 1964): 23–28.
Ringer, James A., Jr. "The 1968 Civil Rights Bill: Realization of President Johnson's Commitment." Princeton, N.J.: Princeton University, 1985. B.A. senior thesis.
Rodgers, Harrell R., and Charles S. Bullock III. *Law and Social Change: Civil Rights Laws and Their Consequences.* New York: McGraw-Hill, 1972.
Ryskind, Allan H. "The Politics Behind Civil Rights in Selma." *Human Events* 25 (February 27, 1965): 12.
"School Desegregation and the Office of Education Guidelines." *Georgetown Law Journal* 55 (November 1966): 325–51.
"School Integration Report." *Congressional Quarterly Weekly Report* 24 (February 18, 1966): 413.

Schwartz, Bernard, ed. *Statutory History of the United States: Civil Rights.* Vol. 2. New York: Chelsea House, 1970.

"Senate Passes Voting Rights Bill, 77–19." *Congressional Quarterly Weekly Report* 23 (May 28, 1965): 1007–09.

Shaffer, Helen B. "Negro Revolution: Next Steps [Johnson Administration]." *Editorial Research Reports,* July 21, 1965: 523–42.

Sherry, John H. "The New Federal Civil Rights Act: What It Is and What It Means to the Nation's Hosts." *Cornell Hotel and Restaurant Administration Quarterly* 6 (May 1965): 10–11+; 6 (August 1965): 3–6.

Sigelman, Lee, and Dixie Mercer McNeil. "White House Decision-Making under Stress: A Case Analysis [of the Tet Offensive]." *American Journal of Political Science* 24 (November 1980): 652–73.

Simchak, Morag. "The Equal Pay Act of 1963: Its Implementation and Enforcement." *AAUW Journal* 61 (March 1968): 117–19.

Slaiman, Donald. "Civil Rights: The Facts and the Challenge—What the Law Does and Does Not Do and Labor's Special Responsibilities." *AFL-CIO American Federationist* 71 (September 1964): 7–12.

Stewart, John G. "The Testing of Lyndon B. Johnson: Civil Rights in the Senate." *Christianity and Crisis* 24 (March 2, 1964): 23–26.

Sultan, Allen. "Property Rights vs. Human Rights [Civil Rights Act of 1964]." *Challenge* 13 (October 1964): 34–37.

"Sweeping Voting Rights Bill Introduced in Congress [in Wake of Civil Rights Demonstrations in Selma, Alabama]." *Congressional Quarterly Weekly Report* 23 (March 19, 1965): 427–28+.

"Threat to Cut Off Aid: Biggest Push Yet for School Integration." *U.S. News and World Report* 58 (March 1, 1965): 50–51.

"Tipping the Balance on Civil Rights: Senate Minority Leader [Everett M.] Dirksen." *Business Week,* May 30, 1964: 20–21.

United States Commission on Civil Rights. *Equal Opportunity in Farm Programs: An Appraisal of Services Rendered by Agencies of the United States Department of Agriculture; a Report.* Washington, D.C.: U.S. Gov't. Printing Office, 1965.

"Voting Rights." *Congressional Quarterly Weekly Report* 23 (June 4, 1965): 1052–57.
"Voting Rights Bill Criticized on Varied Grounds." *Congressional Quarterly Weekly Report* 23 (April 2, 1965): 585–88.
Warren, Earl. "Lyndon B. Johnson and Civil Rights." *Texas Law Review* 51 (January 1973): 196–206.
Waters, G. E. "Sex, State Protective Laws and the Civil Rights Act of 1964." *Labor Law Journal* 18 (June 1967): 344–52.
Watters, Pat. "The South Learns to Live with the Civil Rights Law." *Reporter* 31 (August 13, 1964): 44–46.
Whalen, Charles, and Barbara Whalen. *The Longest Debate: A Legislative History of the 1964 Civil Rights Act.* New York: Mentor, 1986.
White House Conference. "Civil Rights: Can Any Program Satisfy Everyone? [Highlights of White House Conference, 'To Fulfill These Rights,' June 1–2, 1966]." *U.S. News and World Report* 60 (June 13, 1966): 60–62.
———. *Speeches from the White House Conference, "To Fulfill These Rights," June 1–2, 1966* [includes addresses by President Johnson, Vice President Humphrey, A. Philip Randolph, Thurgood Marshall, and Roy Wilkins]. Washington, D.C.: U.S. Gov't. Printing Office, 1966.
"Why Goldwater Said 'No' to the Civil Rights Bill." *U.S. News and World Report* 58 (June 29, 1964): 67–68.
"With the New Civil-Rights Law—How Negroes See the Future." *U.S. News and World Report* 56 (June 29, 1964): 38–39.
Wrong, Elaine Gale. "A Study of Arbitrators' Awards in Cases Involving Discrimination since the Passage of the Civil Rights Act of 1964." New York: New York University, 1980. Ph.D. dissertation. University Microfilms No. 80-27498.
Zarefsky, David H. "Lyndon Johnson Redefines 'Equal Opportunity': The Beginning of Affirmative Action." *Central States Speech Journal* 31 (Summer 1980): 16.

D. EDUCATION

Ashbrooke, John. "Education Bill Strong-Armed through House." *Human Events* 25 (April 17, 1965): 15.
Bailey, Stephen K. *The Office of Education and the Education*

Act of 1965. Indianapolis: Bobbs-Merrill, ICP Case Series No. 100, 1966.

———, and Edith K. Mosher. *ESEA: The Office of Education Administers a Law.* Syracuse, N.Y.: Syracuse University Press, 1968.

"Billions for Schools: Who Gets Them." *U.S. News and World Report* 61 (October 31, 1966): 48.

Citron, Henry. "The Study of the Arguments of Interest Groups which Opposed Federal Aid to Education from 1949–1965." New York: New York University, 1977. Ph.D. dissertation. University Microfilms No. 77-20739.

Cohen, Wilbur J. "Education Legislation 1963–1968: Various Vantage Points." *Educational Researcher* 1 (March 1972): 4–10.

Coleman, James, et al. "Equal Educational Opportunity." *Harvard Education Review* 38 (Winter 1968): 3–175.

Coleman, Robert Boykin. "Federal Legislation and Educational Change: An Analysis of the House Committee on Education and Labor, 1961–1967." New Brunswick, N.J.: Rutgers University, 1979. ED.D. dissertation. University Microfilms No. 8000839.

"Critics Appear Won Over to 'Localized' Teacher Corps [U.S. Office of Education Teacher Corps]." *Congressional Quarterly Weekly Report* 25 (June 23, 1967): 1068–70.

Cronin, Thomas E., and N. C. Thomas. "Educational Policy Advisors and the Great Society." *Public Policy* 19 (Fall 1970): 659–86.

Davenport, Sally Ann. "Smuggling-In-Reform: Equal Opportunity and the Higher Education Act, 1965–80." Baltimore: Johns Hopkins University, 1983. Ph.D. dissertation. University Microfilms No. 8302653.

De Toledano, Ralph. "Education in the Great Society." *Human Events* 25 (May 1, 1965): 8.

———. "The Myths of Federal Aid to Education and the Facts." *Human Events* 25 (March 20, 1965): 9.

"Education: The GOP Flunks Out [1964 Democratic and Republican Party Platforms]." *AFL-CIO American Federationist* 71 (October 1964): 21–24.

"Education Bill Skirts Church-State Conflict." *Congressional Quarterly Weekly Report* 23 (February 5, 1965): 199–201+.

"Elementary Education Bills Passed by House and Senate."

Congressional Quarterly Weekly Report 24 (October 14, 1966): 2463–65.
Exton, Elaine. "Education: A Weapon in the War on Poverty." *American School Board Journal* 148 (May 1964): 40–42.
———. "Issues Churned Up by Federal Aid [to Education]." *American School Board Journal* 149 (September 1964): 42–43+.
———. "More Federal Funds: More Politics in Education." *American School Board Journal* 150 (May 1965): 13–14.
———. "New Education Emphasis in the Federal Budget." *American School Board Journal* 152 (March 1966): 29–31.
———. "Politics in the White House Conference [on Education, Washington, D.C., July 20–21, 1965]." *American School Board Journal* 151 (September 1965): 61–63.
———. "The U.S. Office of Education in Transition." *American School Board Journal* 151 (October 1965): 12+.
Ezell, Macel D. "Two Sides of Lyndon Johnson's Commitment to Education." *University College Quarterly* 25 (January 1980): 20–29.
"Federal Aid to Education Rammed through House." *Human Events* 25 (April 10, 1965): 12.
"The Fight over Federal Aid to Schools." *Changing Times* 19 (February 1965): 43–46.
Finn, Chester E., Jr. *Education and the Presidency.* Lexington, Mass.: D. C. Heath, 1977.
Fister, J. Blaine. "The Elementary and Secondary Education Act of 1965." *Information Service* (National Council of Churches) 44 (April 24, 1965): 1–4.
"The Forgotten Youth in Today's America: The 'Just Average' Majority." *U.S. News and World Report* 60 (February 21, 1966): 52–54+.
Freeman, Roger A. "Federal Aid to Schools: 1965 Model." *Tax Digest* (California), vol. 43, First Quarter, 1965: 9–11+.
Graham, Hugh Davis. "Short-Circuiting the Bureaucracy in the Great Society, Policy Origins in Education." *Presidential Studies Quarterly* 12 (Summer 1982): 407–20.
———. *The Uncertain Triumph: Federal Education Policy in the Kennedy and Johnson Years.* Chapel Hill: University of North Carolina Press, 1984.
Graham, Richard A. "The [U.S. Office of Education] Teacher Corps—It Works." *AFL-CIO American Federationist* 74 (April 1967): 5–7.

Grant, Gerald. "President Johnson's Education Package." *Progressive* 29 (March 1965): 27–29.
Harris, Seymour E., and Alan Levensohn, eds. *Education and Public Policy.* Berkeley, Cal.: McCutchan, 1965.
"Higher Education Bill: Provisions." *Congressional Quarterly Weekly Report* 23 (September 3, 1965): 1763–66.
"House Passes Elementary-Secondary Education Bill." *Congressional Quarterly Weekly Report* 23 (April 2, 1965): 573–77.
Howe, Harold II. "Federal Money in Public Schools: An Interview with Harold Howe, Commissioner of Eduction." *U.S. News and World Report* 61 (December 5, 1966): 68–74.
———. *Meet the Press: Guest, Harold Howe II, United States Commissioner of Education* (Interview). Washington, D.C.: Merkle Press, vol. 11, no. 36, 1967.
Iannaccone, Laurence. *Politics in Education.* New York: Center for Applied Research in Education, Inc., 1967.
———, and Frank W. Lutz. "The Changing Politics of Education." *AAUW Journal* [American Assn. of University Women] 60 (May 1967): 160–62+.
Kerr, Janet C. "From Truman to Johnson: Ad Hoc Policy Formulation in Higher Education." Charlottesville: University of Virginia, 1985. Ph.D. dissertation.
———. "From Truman to Johnson: Ad Hoc Policy Formulation in Higher Education." *The Review of Higher Education* 8 (Fall 1984): 15–54.
"LBJ Pushes $250-Million Sleeper in College Aid Bill." *Human Events* 25 (October 2, 1965): 1.
"LBJ's Education Plans Rebuked." *Human Events* 27 (December 2, 1967): 4.
Loeb (Carl M.) Rhoades and Co. *Book Publishing and Federal Aid to Education* [Impact on publishing industry of ESEA of 1965 and proposed Higher Education Act of 1965] New York: Carl M. Loeb Rhoades and Co., May 1965.
Meier, Deborah. "Head Start or Dead End?" *Poverty: Views from the Left,* edited by Jeremy Larner and Irving Howe, pp. 124–35. New York: William Morrow, 1969.
Meranto, Philip. *The Politics of Federal Aid to Education in 1965: A Study in Political Innovation.* Syracuse, N.Y.: Syracuse University Press, 1967.
Miller, S. M., and Pamela Roby. "Education and Redistribution: The Limits of a Strategy [Education as a Panacea for Reduc-

ing Poverty in the U.S.]." *Poverty and Human Resources Abstracts* 4 (March/April 1969): 5–13.
Morse, Wayne. "The Education Act of 1965: What Did $1 Million Buy?" *American County Government* 32 (January 1967): 15–16+.
National Education Association. "What Teachers Think: A Summary of Teacher Opinion Poll Findings, 1960–1965 [Summarized from NEA *Journal*]." Washington, D.C.: National Education Association, Research Division, Research Report 1965-R13, September 1965.
Norton, John K., comp. and ed. *Dimensions in School Finance*. Washington, D.C.: National Education Association, 1966.
Oslo, Kenneth, ed. *Educating a Nation: The Changing American Commitment*. Austin: Lyndon Baines Johnson School of Public Affairs, University of Texas, 1973.
Pagano, Jules. "New Education for Adults: Two New Federal Programs, One to Overcome Adult Illiteracy, Another to Aid College and University Programs Dealing with Urban Problems." *AFL-CIO American Federationist* 74 (February 1967): 5–7.
Pfeffer, Leo. "The Price We Pay for Federal Aid [Constitutional Aspects in Federal Aid to Parochial and Sectarian Schools]." *Midstream* 11 (March 1965): 38–42.
President's Task Force on Higher Education. *Priorities in Higher Education* (The Hester Report). Washington, D.C.: U.S. Gov't. Printing Office, 1970.
"President's Cuts in School Programs Face Opposition." *Congressional Quarterly Weekly Report* 24 (March 18, 1966): 617–26.
"Primary Education Bill Clears Congress, Becomes Law." *Congressional Quarterly Weekly Report* 23 (April 16, 1965): 665–68.
Ravitch, Diane. *The Troubled Crusade: American Education, 1945–1980*. New York: Basic Books, 1983.
Rockler, Michael J. "Lyndon Baines Johnson and Education." Paper presented at Fifth Annual Hofstra University Presidential Conference: Lyndon Baines Johnson, A Texan in Washington. Hempstead, New York, April 10–12, 1986.
Rogin, Lawrence. "Education: A Way Out of Poverty [President Johnson's Aid-to-Education Program]." *AFL-CIO American Federationist* 72 (March 1965): 1–10.

Schmidt, John T. "The Elementary and Secondary Education Act—The Implications of Title I." *Michigan Law Review* 65 (April 1967): 1184–1223.
Seib, Shirley M., ed. *Federal Role in Education: History of 1965 Acts, 1966 Amendments*. 2nd ed. Washington, D.C.: Congressional Quarterly, Inc., 1967.
Smith, Nancy Kegan. "Higher Education Act of 1965: Implications for the 1980s?" Paper presented to Meeting of Council on Student Loans, 28 February 1984, Austin, Texas (c/o Lyndon B. Johnson Library).
Southwest Texas State University. *Proceedings: 20th Anniversary, Higher Education Act 1965–85*. San Marcos: Southwest Texas State University, November 7–8, 1985.
Stanley, James David. "A Study of the U.S. Office of Education, with Special Emphasis on the Lyndon B. Johnson Presidency." Denton: North Texas State University, 1976. Ed.D. dissertation. University Microfilms No. 7623775.
Stevens, C. R. "The Church-State Booby Trap in the President's Education Bill." *Human Events* 25 (February 13, 1965): 12, 13.
Stevens, Frank. "ESEA Title II: The First Year in Review." *Library Journal* 92 (January 15, 1967): 311–17.
Sutherland, James Harrison. "Federal Grants to State Departments of Education for the Administration of the Elementary and Secondary Education Act of 1965." University of Michigan Social Foundations of Education Monograph Series, No. 6, 1974. Ph.D. dissertation. University Microfilms No. 75-00829.
Thomas, Norman C. *Education in National Politics*. New York: David McKay, 1975.
United States Office of Economic Opportunity. *Education: An Answer to Poverty*. Washington, D.C.: U.S. Gov't. Printing Office, 1966.
United States Office of Education. *The States Report: The First Year of Title 1, Elementary and Secondary Education Act of 1965*. Washington, D.C.: U.S. Gov't. Printing Office, 1967.
"U.S. Schools Getting Better? A Look at What Billions Buy." *U.S. News and World Report* 59 (September 13, 1965): 77–80.
White House Conference on Education. "Contemporary Issues in American Education: Consultants' Papers Prepared for

Use at the White House Conference on Education, July 20–1, 1965." *U.S. Office of Education Bulletin*, no. 3, 1966.
———. "Report of the White House Conference on Education, July 20–1, 1965." *Congressional Quarterly Weekly Report* 23 (August 13, 1965): 1612–14.
"Who Gets the Billions in LBJ's School Plan?" *U.S. News and World Report* 58 (January 25, 1965): 66–67.
"Who'll Get the School Aid Money." *U.S. News and World Report* 58 (April 19, 1965): 40–42.
Willis, Benjamin C. "A Federal Hand on Local Schools? An Interview with Chicago's Superintendent Benjamin C. Willis." *U.S. News and World Report* 59 (November 8, 1965): 54–59.
Woolley, John T. *Monetary Politics: The Federal Reserve and the Politics of Monetary Policy.* Cambridge, England: Cambridge University Press, 1984.

E. THE FEDERAL BUDGET, THE ECONOMY, TAXES

Ackley, Gardner. "Fiscal Policy for a Prosperous Economy [in the Kennedy, Johnson Administrations]." *Baylor Business Studies*, May/July 1966: 7–23.
———. "Lyndon Johnson and the Making of Economic Policy." Paper prepared by former chairman of Council of Economic Advisers, November 24, 1986 [c/o LBJ Library].
———, and R. A. Wallace. "Administration Views on How to Keep the Boat from Rocking: Prices and Labor Rates, Flexible Tax Tactics." *Steel* 159 (October 17, 1966): 55.
"Administration Abandons Strict Wage-Price Guidelines." *Congressional Quarterly Weekly Report* 25 (January 27, 1967): 114–15.
"Administration-Backed Cellar Bill: Are Wage-Price Controls Just around the Corner?" *Human Events* 26 (February 12, 1966): 1.
"Administration Presents New Plan to Cut Spending." *Congressional Quarterly Weekly Report* 25 (December 1, 1967): 2430–32.
Alexander, Holmes. "LBJ's Economic Claims." *Human Events* 24 (April 25, 1964): 1.
"The American [Economic] Recovery: How Big an Upturn?" *Economist* (Great Britain) 224 (July 15, 1967): 228–29.

"The American Economy: Suddenly It's Spring." *Economist* (Great Britain) 223 (May 6, 1967): 578–79.
"The American Economy in 1964." *Survey of Current Business* 45 (January 1965): 1–3.
Anderson, James E. "Economic Policy Formation in the Carter and Johnson Administrations: The Case of Wage-Price Guidelines." Paper presented at Southern Political Science Assn., Birmingham, Ala., November 3–5, 1983.
———, and Jared E. Hazleton. *Managing Macroeconomic Policy: The Johnson Presidency*. Administrative History of the Johnson Presidency Series. Austin: University of Texas Press, 1986.
Asher, Harold. "Impact of Defense Spending on the Economy." *Federal Accountant* 14 (Fall 1964): 100–11.
Babson, R. W. "The New Economics: Its Durability Compared with Truman's and Eisenhower's Policies." *Commercial and Financial Chronicle* 204 (December 29, 1966): 2327.
Berman, Larry. "The Evolution of a Presidential Staff Agency: Variations in How the Bureau of the Budget-Office of Management and Budget Has Responded to Presidential Needs." Princeton, N.J.: Princeton University, 1977. Ph.D. dissertation. University Microfilms No. 77-21436.
———. *The Office of Management and Budget and the Presidency, 1921–1979*. Princeton, N.J.: Princeton University Press, 1979.
———. "The Office of Management and Budget that Almost Wasn't." *Political Science Quarterly* 92 (Summer 1977): 281–303.
Biederman, Paul, ed. *Economic Almanac, 1967–1968: Business Factbook*. New York: Macmillan, 1967.
"The Blow from Texas [Johnson's Proposals to Combat U.S. Deficit May Slow Down World's Economic Expansion and Still Fail]." *Economist* (Great Britain) 226 (January 6, 1968): 41–42.
Boskin, M. J. "Negative Income Tax and the Supply of Work Effort." *National Tax Journal* 20 (December 1967): 353–67.
Bowen, William. "The U.S. Economy Enters a New Era: The Great Boom Has Come to an End." *Fortune* 75 (March 1967): 110–15+.
———. "Vietnam: A Cost Accounting." *Fortune* 73 (April 1966): 119–23+.

Bratter, H. "American Bankers' Association Comments on the President's 1967 Economic Report." *Banking* 59 (April 1967): 46+.
Bronfenbrenner, Martin. "A Guidepost-Mortem [the Problems with Kennedy-Johnson Wage-Price Guideposts]." *Industrial and Labor Relations Review* 20 (July 1967): 637–49.
Brozen, Yale. "The New Mythology of the New Economics [under the Kennedy and Johnson Administrations]." *Banker* (Great Britain) 117 (August 1967): 678–83.
Brundage, Percival F. *The Bureau of the Budget.* New York: Praeger, 1970.
"The Budget: Johnson Calls for $99.7-Billion Spending in Fiscal 1966." *Business Week,* January 30, 1965: 78–80+.
"The Budget Blues." *Human Events* 26 (January 8, 1966): 5.
"Budget Proposes Spending $186.1 Billion in Fiscal 1969— President Repeats Plea for Enactment of 10% Surtax." *Congressional Quarterly Weekly Report* 26 (February 2, 1968): 141–51.
"Budget Reflects Strain of War." *Business Week,* February 3, 1968: 100–01.
"A Budget That's Bound to Bend [Fiscal 1967 Outlays for Vietnam, Space, Farm Programs Could Upset Figures]." *Business Week,* January 29, 1966: 27–29.
"Budget Wins New Role: Charles L. Schultze, Bureau Director, to Make Sure Great Society Gets Off to a Good Start." *Business Week,* August 21, 1965: 128–30+.
"Budget Won't Lie Still: Administration's Plans Are Changing Fast." *Business Week,* May 7, 1966: 27–28.
"Business Feels the Spur: Resumption of Bombing in Vietnam Puts New Pressures on the Economy." *Business Week,* February 5, 1966: 21–23.
"'Butter' Plus Guns: A New Boom Ahead? [Effects of Welfare-Defense Spending on U.S. Economy]." *U.S. News and World Report* 59 (August 16, 1965): 70–72.
Caton, Christopher N. "The Impact of the War in Vietnam on the U.S. Economy." Philadelphia: University of Pennsylvania, 1974. Ph.D. dissertation. University Microfims No. 75–14549.
"Committee for Economic Development's Plan to Nourish the Top Bureaucrats." *Business Week,* July 25, 1964: 70+.

"Congress Cuts Budget 2%, Shuns Tax Increase." *Congressional Quarterly Weekly Report* 25 (October 13, 1967): 2080–83.

"Congress Grabs for Fiscal Reins: The Tax-Bill Battle." *Business Week,* May 18, 1968: 96–98+.

Connor, John Thomas. "Keeping the Economy in Balance.'" *Conference Board Record* 2 (November 1965): 48–50.

"Controversy over the Administration's Proposed 1968 Budget: Pro and Con." *Congressional Digest* 46 (April 1967): 99–123.

Crosby, R. W. "What Will (Johnson's) Great Economy Cost?" *Iron Age* 195 (February 4, 1965): 26–27.

"Danger Signs in Midst of Prosperity: Spiraling Inflation, Swelling Budget Deficits, Soaring Credit Costs." *U.S. News and World Report* 64 (May 13, 1968): 76–77.

Davis, James W., and Randall B. Ripley. "The Bureau of the Budget and Executive Branch Agencies: Notes on Their Interaction." *Journal of Politics* 29 (November 1967): 749–69.

De Toledano, Ralph. "Administration's Big Secret—Rules for Wage-Price Controls Already Drafted." *Human Events* 26 (September 24, 1966): 1.

———. "The 'Great Society' Imposes Tax on Bread." *Human Events* 25 (June 12, 1965): 7.

———. "LBJ Strategy: Switch 'Surtax' to 'War' Tax—'Soak the Rich' Formula." *Human Events* 28 (March 23, 1968): 10.

"Decisions under the Gun: Johnson Faces Bitter Choices in Drafting New Budget." *Business Week,* December 25, 1965: 11–13.

"Defense Expenditures Have Major Influence on the Economy." *Congressional Quarterly Weekly Report* 23 (June 11, 1965): 1131–33.

Diamond, P. A. "Negative Taxes and the Poverty Problem—A Review Article." *National Tax Journal* 21 (September 1968): 288–303.

"Did LBJ Win a Round on Taxes?" *Engineering News-Record* 180 (May 9, 1968): 26–27.

"Disarmament: Economic Effects." *Current History* 47 (August 1964): 81–87.

Eckstein, Otto. "The Unmistakable Brand of LBJ: The Fiscal '65 Budget." *Challenge* 12 (April 1964): 4–7.

"Economic Justification for Administration's Tax Program Is Debated." *Congressional Quarterly Weekly Report* 25 (September 29, 1967): 1964–69.
"Economic Trends in Mid-1967." *Federal Reserve Bulletin* 53 (June 1967): 901–11.
"Economy Wave Rolls on in Congress: Demands for Budget Cuts." *Congressional Quarterly Weekly Report* 25 (October 6, 1967): 1995–99.
Edwards, Willard. "Johnson Must Submit Budget before Leaving." *Human Events* 28 (November 16, 1968): 11.
"The Federal Budget." *Congress and the Nation, 1965–1968.* Washington, D.C.: Congressional Quarterly Service, 1969.
"The Fine Art of Economic Balance: The Johnson Administration's Juggling Act." *Printers' Ink* 292 (March 25, 1966): 3.
"Fiscal Squeeze: The Great Society Plus Vietnam." *First National City Bank of New York Monthly Letter*, December 1965: 136–40.
"The $40 Billion the Budget Leaves Out—Spending Few People Know About." *Business Week*, February 25, 1967: 55–56+.
Gallaway, Lowell E. "Negative Income Tax Rates and the Elimination of Poverty." *National Tax Journal* 19 (September 1966): 298–307 [for reply and comment, see Taussig, M. K.].
Goldwater, Barry. "LBJ's Sham Battle against Inflation." *Human Events* 26 (October 15, 1966): 1.
Goodwin, Craufurd D., ed. *Exhortation of Controls: The Search for a Wage-Price Policy, 1945–1971.* Washington, D.C.: Brookings Institution, 1975.
"GOP Digs in Its Heels: Republicans under House Minority Leader Ford Challenge Administration's 1968 Budget Proposals." *Business Week*, June 24, 1967: 42+.
"Guns vs. Butter Poses a Budget Problem." *Engineering News-Record* 176 (January 6, 1966): 14–15.
Harris, T. George. "Do We Owe People a Living? [Negative Income Tax]" *Look* 32 (April 30, 1968): 24–29.
Hayes, Alfred. "A Tax Increase Is Essential [Support for Administration's 10% Surcharge Proposal]." *Federal Reserve New York Monthly Review* 49 (October 1967): 187–90.
Hazlitt, Henry. "Another Planned Deficit." *Human Events* 27 (February 11, 1967): 5.
———. "Johnson Has Hit on Perfect Way to Endanger Eco-

nomic Prosperity." *Human Events* 26 (November 5, 1966): 13.

———. "LBJ Makes Good Move in Restoring Investment Tax Credit." *Human Events* 27 (March 25, 1967): 7.

———. "[LBJ's] Tax Hike Is False Remedy." *Human Events* 28 (April 6, 1968): 10.

Heller, Deane, and David Heller. "The Extraordinary Power of the Bureau of the Budget." *American Legion Magazine* 79 (August 1965): 8–12+.

Heller, Walter W. "Taxes and the State of the Economy: An Interview with Chairman of CEA." *Challenge* 12 (May 1964): 20–24.

"How Federal Spending Will Soar in '66, War or No War." *U.S. News and World Report* 60 (January 10, 1966): 75–77.

"How LBJ Wins at the Budget Game." *Business Week*, June 26, 1965: 30–31.

"If Spending Is Cut 7 Billions: Tax Policy, Spending, 'Great Society,' the Business Boom—All Is at Stake in the Impasse between LBJ and Congress." *U.S. News and World Report* 63 (October 23, 1967): 31–33.

"Income Tax That Pays the Poor: How a Negative Income Tax Plan Might Work." *Business Week*, November 13, 1965: 105–06.

"Is a 'Money Crisis' Near? President Johnson's Anti-Inflation Plan." *U.S. News and World Report* 61 (September 19, 1966): 29–33.

"It's Still a One-Way Budget: Up." *U.S. News and World Report* 58 (February 1, 1965): 75–78.

Jacoby, Neil H. "Economic Policy Problems Facing the New Administration." *California Management Review* 7 (Summer 1965): 3–10.

Janeway, Eliot. *The Economics of Crisis: War, Politics, and the Dollar.* New York: Weybright and Talley, 1968.

Javits, Jacob K., Charles J. Hitch, and Arthur F. Burns. *The Defense Sector and the American Economy.* New York: New York University Press, 1968.

"Johnson Budget [for Fiscal 1965] Cuts Spending, Renews Kennedy Quests." *Congressional Quarterly Weekly Report* 22 (January 24, 1964): 139–42+.

"Johnson Charts His Economics." *Business Week*, January 30, 1965: 25–26.

"The Johnson Gambit." *Financial World* 129 (April 10, 1968): 3–4+.
"Johnson Tries for Fresh Formula: Need for Wage-Price Guidepost Reinforcement." *Business Week*, August 13, 1966: 25–26.
"Johnson's Celebrated Budget Cutting: A Triumph of Illusion over Reality." *Human Events* 24 (May 16, 1964): 11.
"Johnson's Economics." *Business Week*, October 31, 1964: 47–48+.
"Johnson's First Budget—To Break All Records." *U.S. News and World Report* 55 (December 23, 1963): 30–31.
"Johnson's Gear Shift [on Economic Policy]." *Statist* 191 (February 3, 1967): 151–52.
"Johnson's Newest Economics: Special Report." *Business Week*, September 17, 1966: 35–39.
Jones, Jenkin Lloyd. "'Great Society' Spending Orgy Ignores National Debt Growth." *Human Events* 25 (June 26, 1965): 13.
Jones, Robert V. "The Great Tax Cut: Where the Money Is Coming From." *Modern Age* 9 (Spring 1965): 152–64.
Kaufman, K. A. "LBJ on Wages, Price, Import Quotas." *Iron Age* 201 (February 8, 1968): 48–49.
———. "Spending Spree by Congress Worries Even L.B.J." *Iron Age* 197 (May 5, 1966): 30.
Kettl, Donald F. "The Econmic Education of Lyndon Johnson: Guns, Butter, and Taxes." *The Johnson Years, Volume Two: Vietnam, the Environment, and Science*, edited by Robert A. Divine, pp. 54–78. Lawrence: University Press of Kansas, 1987.
King, Ronald F. "The President and Fiscal Policy in 1966: The Year Taxes Were Not Raised." *Polity*, vol. 42, no. 4 (1985): 685–714.
Kuhn, James. "The Tax Surcharge: Paying for the War." *Christianity and Crisis* 27 (November 13, 1967): 257–58.
"LBJ Blocks Tax [Surcharge] Bill." *Human Events* 28 (May 18, 1968): 4.
"LBJ Clamps Down—A Bit: Fiscal Restraint." *Business Week*, September 10, 1966: 37–38.
"LBJ Must Decide if Post Office, IRS Budgets Will Be Cut in '68." *Advertising Age.* 38 (October 23, 1967): 1+.
"LBJ Reneges on Cutback Promises: Taxes, Spending Go Up." *Human Events* 27 (January 21, 1967): 1, 15.

THE FEDERAL BUDGET 177

"LBJ Walks Economic Tightrope." *Engineering News-Record* 178 (February 2, 1967): 11–12.
"LBJ's Brand Goes on the Economy." *Business Week*, January 25, 1964: 71–74+.
"LBJ's Economics Meets the Critics." *Business Week*, February 11, 1967: 32–33.
"LBJ's First Three Months: Spending Hits a Record." *U.S. News and World Report* 56 (April 13, 1964): 95–96.
"LBJ's Swollen Budget." *Human Events* 27 (February 4, 1967): 4.
Lekachman, Robert. "Blunting the Great Society: Johnson's Economic Program." *New Leader* 49 (February 14, 1966): 10–12.
———. "Cost-Push or Demand-Pull: The Johnson Budget." *New Leader* 51 (February 12, 1968): 9–11.
———. "Too Little of Everything: The Johnson Budget." *New Leader* 48 (February 15, 1964): 3–5.
Lewis, Ted. "LBJ's Dilemma: Would He Pay for a Tax Hike?" *Human Events* 26 (December 3, 1966): 5.
Lloyd, Lewis E. "Big Factor in the Dollar Drain: The Foreign Aid Program." *Challenge* 12 (February 1964): 34–37.
Makinin, G. E. "Economic Stabilization in Wartime: A Comparative Study of Korea and Vietnam." *Journal of Political Economy* 79 (November-December 1971): 1216–44.
Margolis, Howard. "McNamara's New Budget." *Bulletin of the Atomic Scientists* 21 (March 1965): 54–56.
Maynard, P. J. "Where Our Economy Is in a Squeeze between Unbridled Inflation and Federal Control." *Magazine of Wall Street* 117 (February 19, 1966): 528–31+.
McCarthy, Terence. "The Garrison Economy [Impact of Vietnam War on American Economy]." *Columbia University Forum* 9 (Fall 1966): 27–32.
McKaig, J. E. "Evaluating the President's Economic Report and the Course He Advocates to Meet Our Needs in a Stormy World." *Magazine of Wall Street* 117 (February 19, 1966): 520–23.
McKinley, Gordon W. "The Oversimplified Economics of Wage-Price Guidelines." *Business Economics* 2 (Spring 1967): 29–33.
"A McNamara-Style Budget Bureau: LBJ's No. 1 Watchdog Is Being Reshaped to Coordinate Federal Programs." *Business Week*, September 23, 1967: 129+.

Miller, Glenn H., Jr. "The Budget, Fiscal Action, and Short-Run Economic Change." *Federal Reserve Kansas City Monthly Review*, January/February 1967: 3–11; March/April 1967: 3–10.

"Miscalculations Almost Killed Tax Surcharge: Legislative History of President's Tax Increase Proposal." *Congressional Quarterly Weekly Report* 26 (July 26, 1968): 1969–74.

"Money, Interest Rates, Prices, and Output: 1964–67." *Federal Reserve St. Louis Review* 49 (November 1967): 2–6.

"Mounting a Long War on Inflation: White House Battle Plan." *Business Week*, February 3, 1968: 102+.

"Moves by Administration against Softening the Economy." *Engineering News-Record* 178 (March 9, 1967): 11.

Mowery, David C., and Mark S. Kamlet. "Coming Apart: Fiscal and Budgetary Policy Processes in the Johnson Administration." *Budgeting and Finance* 2 (Summer 1982): 16–34.

National Industrial Conference Board. *The Federal Budget: Its Impact on the Economy, Fiscal 1969 Edition*. New York: National Industrial Conference Board, 1968.

"New Economics Gets Its Lumps." *Business Week*, May 13, 1967: 96–98.

"The 'New Economics' Takes Over the Budget." *U.S. News and World Report* 62 (February 6, 1967): 90–92.

"The New Push for Protection: 'Import Quota' Is the New Magic Term, But Administration Still Face Tough Battle." *Business Week*, October 21, 1967: 124–25+.

"Next: A Tax Break for Lower Incomes?" *U.S. News and World Report* 58 (April 19, 1965): 101–03.

"1966 Economic Report of the President." *Monthly Labor Review* 89 (March 1966): 278–82.

"1967 Outlook on Trade: Will the White House Stand Pat While Protectionists Run Free? (Kennedy-Round Decision)." *Business Abroad* 92 (January 9, 1967): 7–8.

Novick, David. "Brief History of Program Budgeting." *Current Practice in Program Budgeting*, edited by David Novick, pp 19–28. New York: Crane, Russak, 1973.

Nyitray, Joseph Paul. "The President's Economic Responsibilities: An Analysis of Four Cases." Columbus: Ohio State University, 1971. Ph.D. dissertation. University Microfilms No. 71-22, 515.

Paradiso, L. J. "Summaries of the 1966 Economic Outlook." *Banking* 58 (January 1966): 41–42.

Peterson, Svend. "How the 89th Congress Has Increased Federal Spending." *Human Events* 25 (November 20, 1965): 12.
Poole, Kenjon E. "Fingers Crossed on the Tax Cut: Inflation and Unemployment—To What Extent Will President Johnson's Economic Policy Rectify this Imbalance." *Challenge* 12 (May 1964): 31–34.
"The President and Aluminum: Another Price Fixing Attempt." *Human Events* 25 (November 13, 1965): 12.
"President Johnson Sends Fiscal 1968 Budget to Congress: Estimates Spending at $169.2 Billion, Deficit at $2.1 Billion." *Congressional Quarterly Weekly Report* 25 (January 27, 1967): 109–13.
"President Presents $112.8 Billion Budget with Special Viet Nam Costs of $10.5 Billion [for 1967]." *Congressional Quarterly Weekly Report* 24 (January 28, 1966): 271–76.
President's Committee on the Economic Impact of Defense and Disarmament. *Report*. Washington, D.C.: Gov't. Printing Office, 1965.
"President's Dilemma: Inflation." *Business Week*, March 19, 1966: 33–35.
"President's Economic Report Predicts Boom from Tax Cut." *Congressional Quarterly Weekly Report* 22 (January 24, 1964): 143+.
"President's $99.7 Billion Budget Emphasizes Health, Education, Welfare." *Congressional Quarterly Weekly Report* 23 (January 29, 1965): 121–28+.
"Prosperity Wears an Uneasy Smile." *Business Week*, March 26, 1966: 43–45.
"Putting a Dollar Sign on Everything: Washington Is Applying McNamara's Once Controversial Cost-Effectiveness Budgeting to the Civilian Sector." *Business Week*, July 16, 1966: 122–24+.
Randall, Ronald. "Presidential Uses of Management Tools from PPB to ZBB [Program Budgeting from LBJ to Carter]." *Presidential Studies Quarterly* 12 (April 1982): 186–94.
Riddell, Thomas. "The Vietnam War and Inflation Revisited." Paper presented at Fifth Annual Hofstra University Presidential Conference: Lyndon Baines Johnson, A Texan in Washington. Hempstead, New York, April 10–12, 1986.
Rinta, Eugene F. "The Federal Budget and Expenditure Control." *Annals of the American Academy of Political and Social Sciences* 379 (September 1968): 22–29.

"Road for '67: Bumpy But Upward: Reports by Johnson and CEA [Council of Economic Advisors]." *Business Week,* January 28, 1967: 156–58.

Roberts, Ben. "Tying the Imperial Purse Strings. *Washington Monthly* 7 (September 1975): 27–30.

Robertson, Norman. "The U.S. Economy—A New Look at 1968." *Banker (Great Britain)* 118 (March 1968): 214–21+.

Rosen, Gerald R. "Is There a New Economy?" *Dun's Review and Modern Industry* 85 (June 1965): 38–41+.

———. "Negative Income Tax?" *Dun's Review and Modern Industry* 92 (August 1968): 38–39.

"Runaway Spending: Can LBJ Check It?" *U.S. News and World Report* 61 (December 19, 1966): 29–30.

Schick, Allen. "The Budget Bureau That Was." *The Institutionalized Presidency,* edited by Norman C. Thomas and Hans W. Baade, pp. 91–113. Dobbs Ferry, N.Y.: Oceana, 1972.

Schienbaum, Kim Ezra, and Ervin Shienbaum. "Public Perceptions of Presidential Economic Performance: From Johnson to Carter." *Presidential Studies Quarterly* 12 (Summer 1982): 421–27.

Schultze, Charles. "New Look at the Budget Bureau" (Interview). *Challenge* 14 (January/February 1966): 14–16.

Seib, Shirley M., ed. *Federal Economic Policy, 1945–1967.* 2nd ed. Washington, D.C.: Congressional Quarterly Service, July 1967.

"Self-Restraint or Else: Johnson Attacks the Dollar Drain." *Business Week,* February 13, 1965: 25–26.

Shannon, William V. "The Surtax Scrimmage." *Commonweal* 87 (October 27, 1967): 107–108.

"Shaping a Simpler Budget: Efforts of President's Commission on Budget Concepts." *Business Week,* August 5, 1967: 95–96+.

Siegel, Barry N. "A New Kind of Economy: Consequences of the Cold War—Defense and Space Expenditures and Their Impact on Social and Economic Institutions." *Challenge* 12 (November 1963): 3–6.

Simpson, Phillip M. "Lyndon B. Johnson and the 1964–68 Revenue Acts: Congressional Politics and 'Fiscal Chickens Coming Home to Roost'." Paper presented at Fifth Annual Hofstra University Presidential Conference: Lyndon Baines Johnson, A Texan in Washington. Hempstead, New York, April 10–12, 1986.

Slesinger, Reuben E. "The Budget and the Numbers Game." *Banking* 60 (August 1967): 59+.

Sloan, John W. "President Johnson, the Council of Economic Advisers, and the Failure to Raise Taxes in 1966 and 1967." *Presidential Studies Quarterly* 15 (Winter 1985): 89–98.

Sommers, Albert T. "The Economic Environment of the Middle Sixties." *Conference Board Record* 1 (September 1964): 1–56.

Stans, Maurice H. "Federal Expenditures—Goals and Priorities [1968 Federal Budget]." *Tax Review* 27 (December 1966): 45–48.

Stein, Herbert. *Presidential Economics: The Making of Economic Policy from Roosevelt to Reagan and Beyond.* New York: Simon and Schuster, 1984.

Stiles, Lynn A. "Aiding the Poor: The Negative Income Tax." *Federal Reserve Chicago*, September 1968: 9–15.

Taussig, M. K. "Reply and Comment: Negative Income Tax Rates and the Elimination of Poverty." *National Tax Journal* 20 (September 1967): 328–43.

"Tax Bill [Passed by Congress]." *Human Events* 28 (June 29, 1968): 4.

"Tax Plan that Pays People Is Newest Plan to Wipe Out Poverty in U.S.: 'Negative Income Tax'." *U.S. News and World Report* 60 (February 14, 1966): 63.

Taylor, Henry J. "Budget Hides Real Foreign Aid Figure." *Human Events* 27 (February 11, 1967): 1.

———. "Can the LBJ Boom Economy Last?" *Human Events* 25 (December 4, 1965): 1.

Teigen, Robert L. "Trends and Cycles in Compositions of the Federal Budget, 1947–1978." *Policy Studies Journal* 9 (Autumn 1980): 11–19.

Thompson, A. A. "The Utopian Economics of the Great Society." *Commercial and Financial Chronicles* 204 (July 7, 1966): 51+.

"United States: Why the Bankers Are Worried—Why President Johnson Needs a Quick Disinflationary Cut." *Economist* (Great Britain) 226 (March 23, 1968): 78+.

United States Executive Office of the President, Bureau of the Budget. *The Bureau of the Budget during the Administration of Lyndon B. Johnson.* 2 vols. Washington, D.C.: OMB Library, November 14, 1968. Mimeographed.

———. *The Bureau of the Budget: What It Is, What It Does.* Washington, D.C.: U.S. Gov't. Printing Office, 1966.

———. *Career Staff to the President.* Washington, D.C.: U.S. Gov't. Printing Office, 1965.

"Viet Requirements Boost Budget: Special Report." *Aviation Week and Space Technology* 86 (January 30, 1967): 21–22.

Waite, Charles A. "The Federal Budget for Fiscal 1966." *Survey of Current Business* 45 (February 1965): 8–12.

———. "Federal Programs for Fiscal 1967." *Survey of Current Business* 46 (February 1966): 4–8+.

———. "Federal Programs for Fiscal Year 1969." *Survey of Current Business* 48 (February 1968): 11–16.

———. "Federal Programs in Fiscal Year 1968." *Survey of Current Business* 47 (February 1967): 11–16.

"'Watchdog' Agency Tugs on Leash: General Accounting Office." *Business Week*, June 12, 1965: 76.

Webb, William R. "LBJ and Government Spending." Course paper for Lewis L. Gould, University of Texas at Austin, May 14, 1986 [c/o LBJ Library].

"What LBJ Wants on Taxes and Money: President Hopes His Policy Will Keep the Economy Stimulated Despite An Increase in Taxes." *Business Week*, January 14, 1967: 26–27.

"What's $172 Billion? War and 'Great Society' Have Run the Budget Up to Unprecedented Levels." *U.S. News and World Report* 62 (February 6, 1967): 25–27.

"Where Johnson Stands on Financial Issues." *U.S. News and World Report* 55 (December 9, 1963): 117–19.

"Where the Money Goes: President Johnson's New Budget and Economic Policies." *Chemical Week* 98 (February 5, 1966): 15.

"Who Are the Big Spenders? What the Record Shows in Two Administrations over the Past 8 Years." *U.S. News and World Report* 57 (August 3, 1964): 74–76.

"Why Cutting the Budget Isn't Easy." *Business Week*, November 28, 1964: 32–33.

Wildavsky, Aaron. *The Politics of the Budgetary Process.* 2nd ed. Boston: Little, Brown, 1974.

"Will the Real Budget Please Stand Up?" *Human Events* 26 (February 5, 1966): 8–9.

Woelflein, Kevin G. "1967: A New Spending Mix [Economic Impact of Increased Government Spending—Especially Defense—and Decreased Consumer Spending]." *Federal Reserve Philadelphia Business Review*, January 1967: 14–19.

F. HEALTH CARE AND SOCIAL SECURITY

"Administration Makes Sweeping Changes in Health Aid Spending." *Human Events* 27 (January 7, 1967): 16.
"American Medical Assn. Rallies Troops for Aged Care Fight." *AFL-CIO News* 9 (December 5, 1964): 1, 7.
"Biggest Change since the New Deal [Medicare]." *Newsweek* 65 (April 12, 1965): 88.
Burns, Eveline M. "Social Policy and the Health Services: Health Legislation of 1965." *American Journal of Public Health* 57 (February 1967): 199–212.
Cohen, Wilber J. "Improving the Status of the Aged." *Social Security Bulletin* 29 (December 1966): 3–8.
"Congress Achieves Substantial Health Record in 1965." *Congressional Quarterly Weekly Report* 23 (December 3, 1965): 2436–38.
Corning, Peter. *The Evolution of Medicare: From Idea to Law.* Washington, D.C.: U.S. Gov't. Printing Office, 1969.
David, Sheri Iris. "Medicare: Hallmark of the Great Society." Paper presented at Fifth Annual Hofstra University Presidential Conference: Lyndon Baines Johnson, A Texan in Washington. Hempstead, New York, April 10–12, 1986.
―――. "To Lift a Heavy Burden: The Story of the Medicare and Medicaid Law." New York: City University of New York, 1982. Ph.D. dissertation. University Microfilms No. 8222938.
Feingold, Eugene. *Medicare: Policy and Politics.* San Francisco: Chandler Publishing Co., 1966.
"$500-Million HEW Plan for Neighborhood Health Centers." *Human Events* 26 (October 1, 1966): 5.
Forgotson, Edward H. "1965: The Turning Point in Health Law—1966 Reflections." *American Journal of Public Health* 57 (June 1967): 934–46.
Helms, Jesse. "Health Booklet Is Latest LBJ Propaganda." *Human Events* 26 (April 2, 1966): 14.
"How Red Tape Is Strangling Medicare." *Human Events* 27 (April 1, 1967): 7.
Humphrey, Hubert H. "The Future of Health Services for the Poor." *Public Health Reports* 83 (January 1968): 1–10.

Kilpatrick, James Jackson. "More Government Medicine Ahead." *Human Events* 27 (February 18, 1967): 1.
Kissick, William L., ed. "Dimensions and Determinants of Health Care Policy." *Milbank Memorial Fund Quarterly* 46 (January 1968): Part 2, pp. 3–269.
Lasby, Clarence. "The War on Disease." *The Johnson Years, Volume Two: Vietnam, the Environment, and Science,* edited by Robert A. Divine, pp. 183–216. Lawrence: University Press of Kansas, 1987.
"LBJ Plans to Pack Ways and Means Committee with Pro-Medicare Majority." *Human Events* 24 (December 19, 1964): 3.
"LBJ's Big Health Plan: Cradle to Grave." *U.S. News and World Report* 58 (January 18, 1965): 34–35.
Marmor, Theodore R. *The Politics of Medicare.* Chicago: Aldine Publishing Co., 1970.
McKinney, John C., and Frank T. de Vyver, eds. *Aging and Social Policy.* New York: Appleton-Century-Crofts, 1966.
"Medicare Breeds False Hopes." *Human Events* 25 (February 27, 1965): 10.
"The Medicare Boondoggle." *Human Events* 27 (March 18, 1967): 4.
"The 'Medicare' Controversy in the Current Congress: Pro and Con." *Congressional Digest* 44 (March 1965): 67–91.
"Medicare Set for the Next Round." *Business Week,* October 31, 1964: 32.
"The Medicare Steamroller." *Human Events* 25 (March 6, 1965): 12.
"Medicare's Expensive Companion." *Business Week,* June 25, 1966: 38–39.
"Medicoup." *Newsweek* 65 (April 5, 1965): 28.
Meyers, Harold B. "Mr. Mill's Elder-Medi-Bettercare." *Fortune* 71 (June 1965): 166–68.
"Mill's Terms for Medicare." *U.S. News and World Report* 57 (December 21, 1964): 74.
"Metropolitan Life Supports President's Fitness Program." *Insurance* 69 (January 13, 1968): 7.
Portz, Phillip. "The Elderly and Medical Care." *America* 110 (February 27, 1964): 276–78.
"Public Health Service Power Loss a Gain for HEW in Johnson Plan." *Oil, Paint and Drug Reporter* 189 (May 2, 1966): 5.

Sanford, David. "Care for the Not So Poor." *New Republic* 154 (June 4, 1966): 8.

"Scaring Expenses, Crowded Hospitals Mark Medicare's First Year." *Human Events* 27 (June 3, 1967): 9.

Sirgo, Henry B. "Congressional Liaison Operations during the Johnson Administration: The Case of Medicare." *Presidential Studies Quarterly* 15 (Fall 1985): 826–34.

"Social Security LBJ Style." *Human Events* 27 (February 25, 1967): 7.

Spector, Rachel Elsa. "A Description of the Impact of Medicare on Health-Illness Beliefs and Practices of White Ethnic Senior Citizens in Central Texas." Austin: University of Texas, 1983. Ph.D. dissertation.

Stevens, Robert, and Rosemary Stevens. *Welfare Medicare in America: A Case Study of Medicaid.* New York: Free Press, 1974.

Stewart, William H. "The Positive Impact of Medicare on the Nation's Health Care Systems." *Social Security Bulletin* 30 (July 1967): 9–12+.

"Ways and Means Holds Up Social Security, Medicare Expansions." *Human Events* 27 (April 22, 1967): 5.

"White House Conference on Public Health, November 3–4, 1965, Washington, D.C." *Public Health Reports* 81 (February 1966): 111–20.

"Wrapping Up the Medicare Bill." *Business Week*, March 27, 1965: 132.

Zarefsky, David H. "*Welfare Medicine in America: A Case Study of Medicaid,* by Robert Stevens and Rosemary Stevens [Book Review Essay]." *Texas Law Review* 53 (March 1975): 636–52.

G. THE SPACE PROGRAM, SCIENCE POLICY, DEFENSE

"After Spending 30 Billions—How U.S. Stands in Space." *U.S. News and World Report* 59 (September 6, 1965): 41–43.

Agapos, A. M., and Lowell E. Gallaway. "Defense Profits and the Renegotiation Board in the Aerospace Industry [1945–1969]." *Journal of Political Economy* 78 (September/October 1970): 1093–1105.

"Air Force in Orbit: Military Objectives of American Space Efforts." *Economist* (Great Britain) 216 (September 4, 1965): 873–74.

Alexander, Charles C. "Manned Spacecraft Center." *The Handbook of Texas: A Supplement*, edited by Eldon Stephen Branda, vol. 3, pp. 567–69. Austin: Texas State Historical Association, 1976.

Alexander, G. "White House Push Seen in Extra-Vehicular Decision." *Aviation Week and Space Technology* 82 (May 31, 1965): 17.

Alexander, Louis. "Space Flight News: NASA's Press Relations and Media Reaction." *Journalism Quarterly* 43 (Winter 1966): 722–28.

Alexander, Tom. "The Unsuspected Payoff of Project Apollo." *Fortune* 80 (July 1969): 114–17+.

"America's Lag in Space Race: Slowdown and Discouragement Have Replaced Success and Glamour in the Space Program." *U.S. News and World Report* 63 (November 6, 1967): 43–45.

Anderson, Frank W., Jr. *Orders of Magnitude: A History of NACA and NASA, 1915–1980.* Washington, D.C.: U.S. Gov't. Printing Office, 1981.

Angel, William D., Jr. "The Politics of Space: NASA's Decision to Locate the Manned Spacecraft Center in Houston." *The Houston Review*, 1984, pp. 62–81.

"Arms Race Shifts to Space: And Reds Have a Head Start." *U.S. News and World Report* 58 (June 21, 1965): 40–43.

"As U.S. 'Moonport' Takes Shape [John F. Kennedy Space Center, Merritt Island, Florida]." *U.S. News and World Report* 59 (August 30, 1965): 27–30.

Asher, Harold. "Impact of Defense Spending on the Economy." *Federal Accountant* 14 (Fall 1964): 100–11.

Averch, Harvey. *The Logic of American Science and Technology Policy.* Baltimore: Johns Hopkins University Press, 1984.

Barro, Stephen M. "Economic Impact of Space Expenditures." *Business Horizons* 10 (Summer 1967): 71–80.

Benson, Charles D., and William B. Faherty. *Moonport: History of Apollo Launch Facilities and Operations.* Washington, D.C.: U.S. Gov't. Printing Office, 1978.

Bisplinghoff, Raymond L. "After Apollo, Where Do We Go? Interview with Dr. Raymond L. Bisplinghoff, Associate Administrator for Advanced Research and Development, NASA." *Date* 10 (June 1965): 22–25.

Brendlinger, Nancy. "Lyndon Johnson's Involvement in the American Space Program." Paper presented at Fifth Annual Hofstra University Presidential Conference: Lyndon Baines Johnson, A Texan in Washington. Hempstead, New York, April 10–12, 1986.

Brooks, Courtney G., James M. Grimwood, and Lloyd S. Swenson, Jr. *Chariots for Apollo: A History of Manned Lunar Spacecraft.* Washington, D.C.: U.S. Gov't. Printing Office, 1979.

Burke, William. "Defense Spending: '68." *Federal Reserve San Francisco Monthly Review,* March 1967: 78–80.

Cafiero, L. H. "Defense R & D, Fiscal 1968 Stress on Tactical Hardware: Johnson's $73 Billion Defense Budget." *Electronic News* 12 (January 23, 1967): 1+.

Chapman, Richard L. *Project Management in NASA: The System and the Men.* Washington, D.C.: U.S. Gov't. Printing Office, 1973.

Clark, John J. "The New Economics of National Defense." *University of Washington Business Review* 24 (October 1964): 28–50.

"Congress Weighs Soundness of Present U.S. Space Policy: Pro and Con." *Congressional Digest* 44 (February 1965): 35–57.

Connolly, R. "Message from Batman: Presidential Threat to Reduce Spending for Nation's Space Program." *Electronic News* 11 (August 15, 1966): 8.

Cooper, John Cobb. "The Manned Orbiting Laboratory: President Johnson's 'Peaceful Use' of Space Includes Military Defense." *American Bar Association Journal* 51 (December 1965): 1137–40.

David, Heather M. "House Group Spurs Military Space: Governmental Operations Committee Recommends Immediate MOL [Manned Orbiting Lab] Development." *Missiles and Rockets* 16 (June 7, 1965): 16.

———. "Soviet Moon Statements Give Congress Pause on Proposed NASA Budget Cuts." *Missiles and Rockets* 16 (March 29, 1965): 22+.

"Defense Cuts Bring New Kind of Job Crisis: Professional Specialists—Engineers, Scientists, Technicians—Losing Jobs and Arms Contracts Are Cancelled." *U.S. News and World Report* 56 (May 18, 1964): 80–83.

"Defense Expenditures Have Major Influence on the Economy."

Congressional Quarterly Weekly Report 23 (June 11, 1965): 1131–33.
Divine, Robert A. "LBJ and the Politics of Space." *The Johnson Years, Volume Two: Vietnam, the Environment, and Science*, edited by Robert A. Divine, pp. 217–53. Lawrence: University Press of Kansas, 1987.
Elswit, J. "New Trends in Defense Spending: Space and Aircraft Programs, Research, Development." *Magazine of Wall Street* 115 (February 6, 1965): 476–79.
Frank, Frederick. *The Manned Space Flight Programs: Some Elements of Organizational Philosophy and Management Decisions in Historical Perspective.* Fort Lauderdale, Fla.: Nova University, June 1978.
Frutkin, Arnold. "America's Space Effort." *European Review (Great Britain)* 16 (Summer 1966): 12–14.
Fulton, Joseph F. "Employment Impact of Changing Defense Programs." *Monthly Labor Review* 87 (May 1964): 508–16.
Goldstein, Walter. "The Science Establishment and Its Political Control." *American Government and Political Change*, edited by William R. Nelson, pp. 248–58. New York: Oxford University Press, 1967.
Haley, Andrew G., and Mortimer D. Schwartz, eds. *Colloquium on the Law of Outer Space: Proceedings of the International Institute of Space Law of the International Astronautical Federation, September 14–15, 1965, Athens, Greece.* New Jersey: Rothman, and Norman: University of Oklahoma Research Institute, 1966.
"He Keeps the Space Shots Zooming: William Pickering, Director of the Jet Propulsion Laboratory." *Business Week*, August 14, 1965: 118–20.
"Is the Moon Program in Real Trouble?" *U.S. News and World Report* 62 (February 13, 1967): 29–32.
Johnsen, K. "President's Committee Optimistic on Impact of Defense Fund Shifts." *Aviation Week and Space Technology* 83 (October 11, 1965): 105+.
Kerr, James R. "Congress and Space." *Public Administration Review* 25 (September 1965): 185–92.
Kozar, Paul Michael. "The Politics of Deterrence: A Comparative Assessment of American and Soviet Defense Policy, 1960–1964." Washington, D.C.: Georgetown University, 1984. Ph.D. dissertation.

Lambright, W. Henry. "Lyndon Johnson and National Science Policy: The Continuing Issues." Paper presented at Fifth Annual Hofstra University Presidential Conference: Lyndon Baines Johnson, A Texan in Washington. Hempstead, New York, April 10–12, 1986.

———. *Presidential Management of Science and Technology: The Johnson Presidency.* Administrative History of the Johnson Presidency Series. Austin: University of Texas Press, 1985.

Lane, Thomas A., Gen. "Outer Space Treaty Jeopardizes U.S. Security." *Human Events* 27 (March 18, 1967): 7.

Leopold, Robert L. "Apollo 1: Disaster and Its Effects on the Space Program." Course paper for Lewis L. Gould, University of Texas at Austin, May 14, 1986 [c/o LBJ Library].

Levine, Arnold S. *Managing NASA in the Apollo Era.* Washington, D.C.: Government Printing Office, 1983.

Ley, Willy. *Rockets, Missiles, and Men in Space.* New York: Viking Press, 1968.

Library of Congress Report. *United States Civilian Space Programs, 1958–1978.* Washington, D.C.: U.S. Gov't. Printing Office, prepared for House Committee on Science and Technology, 97th Congress, 1981.

"Lyndon B. Johnson Space Center." *The Historical Encyclopedia of Texas,* edited by Thomas S. Chamberlin, pp. 33–35. Austin?: Texas Historical Institute, 1982.

Mancuso, Thomas George. "An Organizational History of the Lyndon B. Johnson Space Center: The First Ten Years, 1958–1967." Denver: University of Colorado Graduate School of Public Affairs, 1984. D.P.A. dissertation. University Microfilms No. 8418255.

"Manned Orbiting Lab Gets Push from LBJ." *Business Week,* August 28, 1965: 27.

Margolis, Milton, and Stephen Barro. "The Space Program." *Program Budgeting,* edited by David Novick, pp. 120–45. Cambridge, Mass.: Harvard University Press, 1965.

Mazlish, Bruce, ed.*The Railroad and the Space Program: An Exploration in Historical Analogy.* Cambridge, Mass.: M.I.T. Press, 1965.

McDougall, Walter A. . . . *The Heavens and the Earth: A Political History of the Space Age.* New York: Basic Books, 1985.

"McNamara Presents Defense Posture Briefing [U.S. Global Defense Policies]." *Congressional Quarterly Weekly Report* 23 (February 26, 1965): 313–16.

"McNamara Presents Defense Posture Briefing." *Congressional Quarterly Weekly Report* 24 (February 25, 1966): 447–48.

McNamara, Robert S. "McNamara on U.S. Nuclear Strategy." *Congressional Quarterly Weekly Report* 25 (October 6, 1967): 2010–14.

———. "McNamara's Plan for Defending the U.S. in a Nuclear Age: What Is the Official Line on the Danger of Nuclear War?" *U.S. News and World Report* 62 (February 6, 1967): 38–39.

Mecklin, John. "Jim Webb's Earthly Management of Space [NASA Administrator James Edwin Webb]." *Fortune* 76 (August 1967): 82–87+.

Miernyk, William H., et al. *Impact of the Space Program on a Local Economy* [Boulder, Colorado]. Morgantown: West Virginia University Press, 1967.

"Missiles and Rockets 5th Annual NASA Issue." *Missiles and Rockets* 17 (November 29, 1965): all.

"The Moon Treaty with the Soviets." *Human Events* 26 (June 25, 1966): 13.

Murphy, Charles J. V. "The Desperate Drive to Cut Defense Spending: Before Sizable Cuts Can Be Made, Johnson Will Have to Re-Examine Strategy." *Fortune* 69 (January 1964): 94–97+.

"A New Hard Look at the Space Race: Is America Pushing Too Hard to Outrace Russia?" *U.S. News and World Report* 60 (March 28, 1966): 34+.

"New Look at Defense: Why Congress Worries: Growing Debate—Are U.S. Military Cutbacks Going Too Far?" *U.S. News and World Report* 58 (March 1, 1965): 37–41.

"On the Road to the Moon." *Economist* (Great Britain) 223 (May 20, 1967): 791–92.

Piland, Robert Owens. "The Promotion of Engineers at the NASA Johnson Space Center from 1960 to 2000." Denver: University of Colorado Graduate School of Public Affairs, 1984. Ph.D. dissertation. University Microfilms No. 84–18254.

"Pitchman for NASA's Trip to the Moon: James E. Webb." *Business Week*, May 27, 1967: 70–72+.

"Political Chief [Clark Clifford] at the Pentagon: Congress Is

Heating Up Its Opposition to the Administration on Defense." *Business Week,* January 27, 1968: 96–98+.
"President Johnson Hails U.N. Accord on Treaty Governing Exploration of Outer Space." *Current History* 52 (March 1967): 175–77.
"Ready to Launch a Lab: NASA's First Major Research Center [Cambridge, Massachusetts]." *Business Week,* September 11, 1965: 72+.
"The Real Story of the Space Race: National Security" *U.S. News and World Report* 58 (April 6, 1965): 33–36.
"Report Blasts Aerospace 'Violations'." *Missiles and Rockets* 17 (August 23, 1965): 14.
Root, Eugene. "The [Economic] Return on Our Investment in Space Exploration." *Looking Ahead* 13 (September 1965): 1–4+.
Shelton, William. "For Ten Years—Neck and Neck in the Space Race: U.S. and Soviet Space Efforts, 1957–1967." *Fortune* 76 (October 1967): 166–68+.
———. "The Russians Mean to Win the Space Race." *Fortune* 73 (February 1966): 140–42.
Siegel, Barry N. "A New Kind of Economy: Consequences of the Cold War—Defense and Space Expenditures and Their Impact on Social and Economic Institutions." *Challenge* 12 (November 1963): 3–6.
Skardon, James A. "The Apollo Story: The Grissom-White-Chaffee Tragedy." *Columbia Journalism Review* 6 (Fall 1976): 11–15; (Winter 1967/68): 34–39.
Smith, Michael L. "Selling the Moon: The U.S. Manned Space Program and the Triumph of Commodity Scientism." *The Culture of Consumption,* edited by Richard Wightman Fox and T.J. Jackson Lears, pp. 175–209. New York: Pantheon Books, 1983.
"Space for What? [U.S. Space Program]." *Economist* (Great Britain) 219 (June 18, 1966): 1307–08.
"Space Race Hits Economy Hurdle: White House Cost-Cutting Drive." *Business Week,* January 13, 1968: 41–42.
"Special Report: The Budget [1966 Space Program Budget]." *Missiles and Rockets* 16 (February 1, 1965): 10–11+.
Stares, Paul B. *The Militarization of Space: U.S. Policy, 1945–1984.* Ithaca, N.Y.: Cornell University Press, 1985.
"Status of Major U.S. Defense, Aerospace Programs." *Aviation Week and Space Technology* 84 (March 7, 1966): 64–66.

Swenson, Loyd S., Jr. "The Fertile Crescent: The South's Role in the National Space Program." *Southwestern Historical Quarterly* 71 (January 1968): 377–92.
Taylor, Hal. "Voskhod Shows Big Soviet Lead: But Administration Officials Say U.S. Can Still Catch Up." *Missiles and Rockets* 15 (October 19, 1964): 13–14.
"Treaty on Outer Space Clears Senate Unanimously." *Congressional Quarterly Weekly Report* 25 (April 28, 1967): 661–63.
"Treaty on Principles Governing the Activities of State in the Exploration and Use of Outer Space, Including the Moon and Other Celestial Bodies." *New Times* (Moscow), February 8, 1967: 37–40.
United States Aeronautics and Space Council. *Report to the Congress from the President of the United States: United States Aeronautics and Space Activities, 1965.* Washington, D.C.: U.S. Gov't. Printing Office, 1966.
"U.S. and Russia in Space: The Pace Quickens." *U.S. News and World Report* 59 (August 30, 1965): 25–26.
Von Hippel, Frank, and Joel Primack. *The Politics of Technology.* Stanford, Cal.: Stanford University Press, 1970.
Warnock, Charles F. "An Analysis and Evaluation of the NASA Organizational Structure at Cape Kennedy, Florida, from July 1, 1962, to July 31, 1966." Tallahassee: Florida State University, 1968.
"Way Station to the Moon: Mississippi Test Facility." *Business Week,* April 2, 1966: 62–64+.
Weidenbaum, Murray L. "Adjusting to Defense Cutback: Government Policy toward Big Business." *Quarterly Review of Economics and Business* 4 (Spring 1964): 7–14.
———. "Measurements of the Economic Impact of Defense and Space Programs." *American Journal of Economics and Sociology* 25 (October 1966): 415–26.
"What Comes after the Moon?" *Business Week,* December 10, 1966: 130–31.
"What Comes after the Moon? NASA Worries about Future Funds from Congress." *Business Week,* July 2, 1966: 36–38.
"What Houston Won When NASA Came to Town." *Business Week,* September 11, 1965: 90–91+.
"Where the Space Race is Bringing a '25-Year Boom' [Manned

Spacecraft Center, Houston, Texas]." *U.S. News and World Report* 59 (September 6, 1965): 44–47.
"Why LBJ Holds the Arms Line." *Business Week*, January 23, 1965: 28–29.
Wilson, George C. "Major Aerospace Decisions Face Johnson." *Aviation Week and Space Technology* 81 (November 9, 1964): 22.
Zhukov, G. "The Moon, Politics and Law." *International Affairs* (Moscow), September 1966: 32–37.

H. THE SUPREME COURT, THE FEDERAL COURTS

Abraham, Henry J. *Justices and Presidents: A Political History of Appointments to the Supreme Court.* 2nd ed. New York: Oxford University Press, 1985.
American Jewish Congress. *Civil Rights and Civil Liberties Decisions of the United States Supreme Court for the 1966–1967 Term: A Summary and Analysis.* New York: American Jewish Congress, October 1967.
Atkins, Burton M., and Terry Sloope. "The 'New' Hugo Black and the Warren Court." *Polity* 18 (Summer 1986): 621–37.
Bartholomew, Paul C. "The Supreme Court of the United States, 1964–1965." *Western Political Quarterly* 18 (December 1965): 741–54.
———. "The Supreme Court of the United States, 1965–1966." *Western Political Quarterly* 19 (December 1966): 705–18.
———. "The Supreme Court of the United States, 1966–1967." *Western Political Quarterly* 20 (December 1967): 841–55.
Benson, Paul R., Jr. *The Supreme Court and the Commerce Clause, 1937–1970.* New York: Dunellen, 1970.
Berg, Larry L. "The Supreme Court and Congress: Conflict and Interaction, 1947–1968." Santa Barbara: University of California, 1972. Ph.D. dissertation. University Microfilms No. 72-26826.
Bickel, Alexander M. *Politics and the Warren Court.* New York: Harper, 1965.
———. "Voting the Court Up or Down: Fortas, Johnson and the Senate." *New Republic* 159 (September 28, 1968): 21–23.
Bigel, Alan I. *The Supreme Court on Emergency Powers, Foreign Affairs, and Protection of Civil Liberties, 1935–1975.* Lanham, Md.: University Press of America, 1986.

Black, Hugo L., and Elizabeth Black. *Mr. Justice and Mrs. Black: The Memoirs of Hugo L. Black and Elizabeth Black.* New York: Random House, 1986.
Bland, Randall W. *Private Pressure on Public Law: The Legal Career of Justice Thurgood Marshall.* Port Washington, N.Y.: Kennikat, 1973.
Bozell, L. Brent. *The Warren Revolution: Reflections on the Consensus Society.* New Rochelle, N.Y.: Arlington House, 1966.
Carter, John D. *The Warren Court and the Constitution: A Critical View of Judicial Activism.* Gretna, La.: Pelican, 1973.
Chase, Harold W. *Federal Judges: The Appointing Process.* Minneapolis: University of Minnesota Press, 1972.
"Civil Rights Cases Dominate 1964–65 Court Term." *Congressional Quarterly Weekly Report* 23 (September 17, 1965): 1892–96.
Congressional Quarterly Service. *Congressional Quarterly's Guide to the U.S. Supreme Court.* Washington, D.C.: Congressional Quarterly, Inc., 1979.
———. *CQ Guide to Current American Government* [the Presidency, Congress, Key Issues 1965, Supreme Court, Politics 1964–66]. Washington, D.C.: Congressional Quarterly Service, Fall 1965.
Countryman, Vern. *The Judicial Record of Justice William O. Douglas.* Cambridge, Mass.: Harvard University Press, 1974.
"The Courts, HEW, and Southern School Desegregation." *Yale Law Journal* 77 (December 1967): 321–65.
Dunne, Gerald T. *Hugo Black and the Judicial Revolution.* New York: Simon and Schuster, 1977.
Edwards, Willard. "Behind [Earl] Warren's Resignation." *Human Events* 28 (July 13, 1968): 11.
"Fortas: LBJ's 'Mr. Fixit'." *Human Events* 28 (July 6, 1968): 3.
Friedman, Leon, and Fred L. Israel, eds. *The Justices of the U.S. Supreme Court, 1789–1978.* 5 vols. New York: Chelsea House, 1979.
Gill, Robert L. "Shaping the Negro Revolution through Court Decisions, 1964–1966" *Journal of Human Relations*, vol. 15, Fourth Quarter (1967): 423–42.
Goldman, Sheldon. "Johnson and Nixon Appointees to the Lower Federal Courts: Some Socio-Political Perspectives." *Journal of Politics* 34 (August 1972): 934–42.

Goulden, Joseph C. *The Benchwarmers: The Private World of the Powerful Federal Judges.* New York: Weybright and Talley, 1974.
Howard, A. E. Dick. "Mr. Justice Black: The Negro Protest Movement and the Rule of Law." *Virginia Law Review* 53 (June 1967): 1030–90.
"In the 13th Year of the 'Warren Revolution': How the Supreme Court Is Changing the U.S." *U.S. News and World Report* 60 (June 20, 1966): 48–53.
Jacob, Bernard E. "Supreme Court Justices: Presidential Advising and Other Non-judicial Roles." Paper presented at Fifth Annual Hofstra University Presidential Conference: Lyndon Baines Johnson, A Texan in Washington. Hempstead, New York, April 10–12, 1986.
Johnson, Nicholas, et al. "Symposium: Mr. Justice Black: Thirty Years in Retrospect." *UCLA Law Review* 14 (January 1967): 397–552.
Jones, Hugh E. "The Defeat of the Nomination of Abe Fortas as Chief Justice of the United States: A Case Study in Judicial Politics." Baltimore: Johns Hopkins University, 1976. Ph.D. Dissertation. University Microfilms No. 76-22928.
Katcher, Leo. *Earl Warren: A Political Biography.* New York: McGraw-Hill, 1967.
Kirk, Russell. "Fortas Defeat a Conservative Victory." *Human Events* 28 (October 12, 1968): 1.
Kurland, Philip B., ed. *Supreme Court Review, 1965.* Chicago: University of Chicago Press, 1965.
———. *Supreme Court Review, 1966.* Chicago: University of Chicago Press, 1966.
Lazarus, Simon. "End of the Warren Court: The New Jurisprudence of Justice [Hugo L.] Black." *New Leader* 50 (January 16, 1967): 6–8.
"LBJ 'Packs' the Court." *Human Events* 27 (June 24, 1967): 4.
Mason, Alpheus Thomas. "Understanding the Warren Court: Judicial Self-Restraint and Judicial Duty." *Political Science Quarterly* 81 (December 1966): 523–63.
———. "The Warren Court and the Bill of Rights." *Yale Review* 56 (December 1966): 197–211.
McCloskey, Robert G. "Reflections on the Warren Court: 'Judicial Activism'." *Virginia Law Review* 51 (November 1965): 1229–70.
McFeeley, Neil D. *Appointment of Judges: The Johnson Presi-*

dency. An Administrative History of the Johnson Presidency Series. Austin: University of Texas Press, 1987.
Miles, Edward W. "The Jurisprudence of the Warren Court v. The Post-Reconstruction Court." *News for Teachers of Political Science,* no. 41, Spring 1984: 24–25.
Mishkin, Paul J. "The Supreme Court, 1964 Term." *Harvard Law Review* 79 (November 1965): 56–211.
Mizell, Winton R. "The U.S. Senate Committee on the Judiciary and Presidential Nominations to the Supreme Court, 1965–1971: A Study of Role and Function of a Legislative Subsystem." Norman: University of Oklahoma, 1974. Ph.D. dissertation. University Microfilms No. 75-6538.
Murphy, Bruce. "Abe Fortas: The Justice and The Friend." Paper presented at Fifth Annual Hofstra University Presidential Conference: Lyndon Baines Johnson, A Texan in Washington. Hempstead, New York, April 10–12, 1986.
"Now a Changing Supreme Court." *U.S. News and World Report* 65 (July 8, 1968): 31–33.
O'Brien, David M. "LBJ and Supreme Court Politics in the Light of History." Paper presented at Fifth Annual Hofstra University Presidential Conference: Lyndon Baines Johnson, A Texan in Washington. Hempstead, New York, April 10–12, 1986.
———. *Storm Center: The Supreme Court in American Politics.* New York: Norton, 1986.
Packer, Herbert L., et al. "A Symposium on the Supreme Court and the Police: 1966." *Journal of Criminal Law, Criminology and Police Science* 57 (Septebmer 1966): 237–311; (December 1966): 379–425.
Read, Frank T., and Lucy S. McGough. *Let Them Be Judged: The Judicial Integration of the Deep South.* Metuchen, N.J.: Scarecrow, 1978.
"Review of 1966–1967 Supreme Court Term." *Congressional Quarterly Weekly Review* 25 (June 23, 1967): 1071–74.
Robison, Joseph B. "The Civil Rights and Civil Liberties Decisions of the U.S. Supreme Court for the 1964–1965 Term: A Summary and Analysis." *Law in Transition Quarterly* 2 (Fall 1965): 191–261.
———, and Carol Weisbrod. "The Civil Rights and Civil Liberties of the United States Supreme Court for the 1965–1966 Term." *Law in Transition Quarterly* 3 (Fall 1966): 236–51.

Rossiter, Clinton. *The Supreme Court and The Commander in Chief.* Ithaca, N.Y.: Cornell University Press, 1976.

Rowland, C. K., Robert A. Carp, and Ronald A. Stidham. "Judges' Policy Choices and the Value Basis of Judicial Appointments: A Comparison of Support for Criminal Defendants among Nixon, Johnson, and Kennedy Appointees to the Federal District Courts." *Journal of Politics* 46 (August 1984): 886–902.

Schwartz, Bernard. *Super Chief: Earl Warren and His Supreme Court—A Judicial Biography.* New York: New York University Press, 1983.

———, and Stephen Lesher. *Inside the Warren Court.* Garden City, N.Y.: Doubleday, 1983.

Scigliano, Robert. *The Supreme Court and the Presidency.* New York: Free Press, 1971.

"A Shift in the Supreme Court—What One New Justice Can Mean." *U.S. News and World Report* 62 (April 24, 1967): 67–68.

Shogan, Robert. *A Question of Judgement: The Fortas Case and the Struggle for the Supreme Court.* Indianapolis: Bobbs-Merrill, 1972.

Strickland, Stephen Parks, ed. *Hugo Black and the Supreme Court.* Indianapolis: Bobbs-Merrill, 1967.

"The Supreme Court: 1965 Term." *Harvard Law Review* 80 (November 1966): 91–272.

"The Supreme Court: 1966 Term." *Harvard Law Review* 81 (November 1967): 69–262.

"The Supreme Court, 1967–68 Term in Review." *Congressional Quarterly Weekly Report* 26 (June 28, 1968): 1595–1600.

"Supreme Court Upholds Public Accomodation Law." *Congressional Quarterly Weekly Report* 22 (December 18, 1964): 2812–13.

Swindler, William F. *Court and Constitution in the Twentieth Century: The New Legality, 1932–1968.* Indianapolis: Bobbs-Merrill, 1970.

Teger, Stuart Henry. "Presidential Strategy for the Appointment of Supreme Court Justices." Rochester, N.Y.: University of Rochester, Ph.D. dissertation, 1976. University Microfilms No. 7624027.

Trohan, Walter. "Politics Still Dominate Selection of U.S. Justices." *Human Events* 27 (July 1, 1967): 13.

———. "President Called 'Trail Boss' over Appointment Handling." *Human Events* 25 (August 28, 1965): 10.
Warren, Earl. *Memoirs of Chief Justice Earl Warren.* Garden City, N.Y.: Doubleday, 1977.
Weaver, John D. *Warren: The Man, The Court, The Era.* Boston: Little, Brown, 1967.
"What High Court Rules Now on School Integration." *U.S. News and World Report* 63 (October 23, 1967): 49.

I. URBAN DEVELOPMENT

Abrams, Charles. *The City Is the Frontier.* New York: Harper, 1965.
"America the Un-beautiful [Discussion of Johnson's Conservation Program, Air and Water Pollution, and Urban Planning]." *I.U.D. Agenda* (Industrial Union Department) 1 (March 1965): 5–13.
Barnes, Peter. "Demonstration in the Cities [Urban Renewal]." *New Leader* 49 (February 28, 1966): 18–20.
Bellush, Jewel, and Murray Hausknecht, eds. *Urban Renewal: People, Politics, and Planning.* Garden City, N.Y.: Doubleday, 1967.
Bergman, Ralph M. "The Effectuation of the Grebgy Plan: A Case Study of the Utilization of Federal Aid Programs to Revitalize the Central Business District of Green Bay [Wisconsin]." *Municipality* (Wisconsin) 61 (March 1966): 64+.
"Business Joins War on Urban Ills: The Urban Coalition Now Headed by John W. Gardner." *Business Week,* April 27, 1968: 84+.
"Caesar's Urban Putsch: The Urban Development Program." *Human Events* 26 (March 12, 1966): 4.
"Citizen Participation in Urban Renewal." *Columbia Law Review* 66 (March 1966): 485–607.
"City Aid Still in Trouble." *Nation's Cities* 5 (May 1967): 10–15+.
"Community Development Law Passes after Nine-Month Debate: Demonstration Cities Act of 1966." *Journal of Housing* 23 (November 1966): 562–70.
"Controversial Urban Program's Starting Slowly: Model Cities and Rent Supplements." *Congressional Quarterly Weekly Report* 26 (May 31, 1968): 1271–75.
"Controversy over Federal Urban Renewal: Pro and Con." *Congressional Digest* 43 (April 1964): 99–125.

"Controversy over the New Federal Program for 'Demonstration Cities': Pro and Con." *Congressional Digest* 46 (February 1967): 33–64.

"Crisis in the Cities: LBJ's Plan—A Complete Overhaul of Metropolitan United States." *U.S. News and World Report* 60 (February 7, 1966): 55–57.

Davies, Clarence J. *Neighborhood Groups and Urban Renewal.* Metropolitan Politics Series. New York: Columbia University Press, 1966.

Dillon, Conley H. *The Area Redevelopment Administration: New Patterns in Developmental Administration.* College Park: University of Maryland, Bureau of Governmental Research, 1964.

Doxiadis, C. A. *Urban Renewal and the Future of the American City.* Chicago: Public Administration Service, 1966.

"Drive Begins to Save President Johnson's Rent Supplements and 'Model Cities' Programs." *Congressional Quarterly Weekly Report* 25 (July 28, 1967): 1317–19+.

"Economic Opportunity Act Puts Housing, Renewal in Front Lines of Anti-Poverty War." *Journal of Housing* 21 (August 1964): 352–63.

Edwards, John, and Richard Batly. *The Politics of Positive Discrimination: Evaluation of the Urban Program, 1967–77.* London: Tavistock Publications, 1978.

"Final Provisions of the Housing and Urban Development Act of 1965." *Congressional Quarterly Weekly Report* 23 (August 6, 1965): 1550–53.

Fishman, Robert Alan. "The Development of the Model Cities Program." Cambridge, Mass.: Harvard College, 1970. Undergraduate thesis.

Goldschmidt, Leopold A. "Urban Planning: Developments in 1965." *Municipal Year Book, 1966,* pp. 306–38. Chicago: International City Managers Assn., 1966.

Greer, Scott. *Urban Renewal and American Cities: The Dilemma of Democratic Intervention.* Indianapolis: Bobbs-Merrill, 1965.

"Housing for All: The Housing and Urban Development Act of 1965." *Federal Aid Reporter,* November 1966: 1–11.

"HUD at Two: Sec. [Robert C.] Weaver Reviews the First Two Years of Urban Program Development of the Department of Housing and Urban Development." *Nation's Cities* 5 (November 1967): 7–9.

Hudson, Anne Mooney. "Urban Redevelopment in American Cities, 1950–1965." Ann Arbor: University of Michigan, 1973. Ph.D. dissertation. University Microfilms No. 74-15759.
Johnson, Thomas F. "Government, Housing, and Urban Renewal: Interrelated Problems and Politics." *Michigan Business Review* 19 (November 1967): 24–29.
"Lack of Areawide Planning Threatens Federal Urban Aid: Implications of Section 204 of the Demonstration Cities Act, 1966." *Congressional Quarterly Weekly Review* 25 (April 28, 1967): 676–77.
"LBJ Insists on Quick Passage of 'Demonstration Cities' Bill." *Human Events* 26 (August 6, 1966): 10.
"LBJ's New Institute [for Urban Development]." *Human Events* 27 (December 16, 1967): 3.
Levitan, Sar A. "Area Redevelopment: An Analysis of the Program [under the Area Redevelopment Act]." *Industrial Relations* 3 (May 1964): 79–95.
Lowe, Jeanne R. *Cities in a Race—with Time: Progress and Poverty in America's Renewing Cities.* New York: Random House, 1967.
"Major Housing Bill to Help Poor Purchase Homes: The Housing and Urban Development Act of 1968." *Congressional Quarterly Weekly Report* 26 (August 2, 1968): 2031–36.
Mao, James C. *Efficiency in Public Urban Renewal Expenditures through Capital Budgeting.* Berkeley: Center for Real Estate and Urban Economics, Institute of Urban and Regional Development, University of California, Research Report No. 27, 1965.
Meltzer, Jack. "The Urban Conflict." *Urban Affairs Quarterly* 3 (March 1968): 3–20.
Menges, Gary L. "Model Cities: A Bibiliography." Monticello, Ill.: Council of Planning Librarians, May 1968. Mimeograph.
Mollenkopf, John H. *The Contested City.* Princeton, N.J.: Princeton University Press, 1983.
Morris, Eugene J. "The Quiet Legal Revolution: Eminent Domain and Urban Redevelopment." *American Bar Association Journal* 52 (April 1966): 355–59.
Northrup, Graham T. "An Analysis of the Demonstration Cities Act of 1966." *Mortgage Banker* 27 (February 1967): 16–22.

URBAN DEVELOPMENT 201

Nourse, Hugh O. "The Economics of Urban Renewal." *Land Economics* 42 (February 1966): 65–74.

Patman, Wright. "Demonstration Cities: How the Program Will Work." *American County Government* 32 (January 1967): 22–23+.

Plager, Sheldon J., and Joel F. Handler. "The Politics of Planning for Urban Redevelopment." *Wisconsin Law Review* 19 (Summer 1966): 724–75.

"Planning for Metropolis." *Economist* (Great Britain) 218 (March 26, 1966): 1233–34.

"President Johnson Signs Demonstration Cities Bill Provision." *Congressional Quarterly Weekly Report* 24 (November 11, 1966): 2817–24.

"[Rep. Louis] Wyman Aids LBJ [Model Cities Program]." *Human Events* 27 (June 24, 1967): 3.

Rogers, Donald I. "Two Trillion Dollars Asked for Federal Urban Renewal." *Human Events* 24 (May 9, 1964): 2.

Rothenberg, Jerome. *Economic Evaluation of Urban Renewal.* Washington, D.C.: Brookings Institution, September 1967.

Schermbeck, C. E. "A New Era in Urban Development." *Public Affairs Commentary* 12 (March 1966): 1–4.

Schnore, Leo F., and Henry Fagin, eds. *Urban Research and Policy Planning.* Beverly Hills, Cal.: Sage Publications, 1967.

Schulz, Bill. "Urban Renewal under Attack." *Human Events* 25 (January 9, 1965): 12.

Slayton, William L. "Community Renewal Program." *Journal of Housing* 21 (September 1964): 419–24.

Taylor, H. Ralph. "Model Neighborhoods and Demonstration Cities." *Michigan Municipal Review* 40 (March 1967): 62–64.

"Urban Problems and Civil Disorder: Background, Events, Programs." *Congressional Quarterly Weekly Report* 25 (September 8, 1967): 1707–67.

Warner, Sam Bass, Jr., ed. *Planning for a Nation of Cities.* Cambridge, Mass.: M.I.T. Press, 1966.

Weaver, Robert C. "The First Twenty Years of HUD." *APA Journal* [American Planning Association], Autumn 1985, pp. 463–74.

Wheaton, William L. C., et al. "Housing Renewal and Development Bibliography." Monticello, Ill.: Council of Planning Librarians, 1968. Mimeograph.

"Which Plan for Slum Renewal? Johnson's, Percy's, Kennedy's." *Business Week*, August 26, 1967: 77–78.

Willmann, John B. *The Department of Housing and Urban Development.* New York: Praeger, 1967.

Wilson, James Q., ed. *Urban Renewal: The Record of the Controversy.* Cambridge, Mass.: M.I.T. Press, 1966.

Wolf, Eleanor P., and Charles N. Lebeaux. "On the Destruction of Poor Neighborhoods by Urban Renewal." *Social Problems* 15 (Summer 1967): 3–8.

Wood, Robert C. "Rebuilding the Cities." *AFL-CIO American Federationist* 74 (February 1967): 1–5.

J. THE WAR ON POVERTY

Aaron, Henry J. "Foundations of the War on Poverty Reexamined." *American Economic Review* 57 (December 1967): 1229–43.

"Administration Has Raised Poverty Line." *Human Events* 25 (May 8, 1965): 10.

"Administrative History of the Office of Economic Opportunity." 3 vols. Austin: Lyndon B. Johnson Library, unpublished manuscript.

"[Administrative and Political] Problems Follow Rapid Expansion of 'War on Poverty'." *Congressional Quarterly Weekly Report* 24 (January 21, 1966): 256–58.

Ahart, Gregory J. "Examining Antipoverty and Welfare Programs." *Tax Review* 30 (June 1969): 25–28.

Alexander, Holmes. "LBJ Boosts Shriver." *Human Events* 23 (February 1, 1964): 8.

Alinsky, Saul, and Hyman G. Bookbinder. "Alinsky vs. Bookbinder: A Debate between War on Poverty Critic, Saul Alinsky, and U.S. Office of Economic Opportunity Official, Hyman G. Bookbinder." *Communities in Action* 1 (May 1966): 22–27.

Allen, Robert S. "House Rebelling against 'War on Poverty' Measures." *Human Events* 27 (October 21, 1967): 7.

———. "Job Corps to Be Abolished?" *Human Events* 27 (April 29, 1967): 1.

American Municipal Association. "Poverty—The War that Needs to Be Fought: 1964 Economic Opportunities Act Offers Substantial Aid to Municipalities." *South Carolina City* 5 (Winter 1964): 6–10+.

Anderson, James E. "Poverty, Unemployment and Economic Development: The Search for a National Antipoverty Policy." *Journal of Politics* 28 (February 1967): 310–30.
Anderson, John. "Inflation: How Government Sabotages War on Poverty." *Human Events* 27 (September 2, 1967): 6.
"Antipoverty Community Corporations." *Columbia Journal of Law and Social Problems* 3 (June 1967): 94–104.
"Anti-Poverty Legislation: The Economic Opportunity Act." *Washington Bulletin* 18 (April 13, 1964): 241–43.
"Anti-Poverty Program: Provisions." *Congressional Quarterly Weekly Report* 23 (July 30, 1965): 1500–02.
"Anti-Poverty Program Promising Federal Funds to Private Groups." *Human Events* 24 (August 8, 1964): 1.
"Arm Twisting the Poverty Bill through Congress." *Human Events* 24 (August 29, 1964): 1.
Arnold, Mark R. "The Good War that Might Have Been [War on Poverty]." *New York Times Magazine,* September 29, 1974: 56–73 passim.
Arnstein, George E. "Implementation of the Economic Opportunity Act: The Neighborhood Youth Corps." *Parks and Recreation* 48 (January 1965): 7–9.
"As the Poverty Program Gets into Gear: After Months of Talk about a 'War on Poverty,' What Is Actually Being Done?" *U.S. News and World Report* 58 (March 8, 1965): 56–58.
Ascoli, Max. "The High Cost of Poverty." *The Reporter* 30 (March 29, 1964): 16.
Baker, G. H. "Unions Applaud LBJ's Move on Right-To-Work." *Iron Age* 196 (August 5, 1965): 30.
"Battling against Poverty: U.S. Office of Economic Opportunity." *Economist* (Great Britain) 215 (April 17, 1965): 297–98.
Bauman, John F. "The Scope of the Poverty Program." *Current History* 61 (November 1971): 284–89.
Beck, Susan Abrams. "The Limits of Presidential Activism: Lyndon Johnson and the Implementation of the Community Action Program." New York: Columbia University, 1985. Ph.D. dissertation. University Microfilms No. 8511481.
Becker, Joseph M., ed. *In Aid of the Unemployed.* Baltimore: Johns Hopkins University Press, 1965.
———, William Haber, and Sar A. Levitan. *Programs to Aid the Unemployed in the 1960's.* Kalamazoo, Mich.: W. E.

Upjohn Institute for Employment Research, 1965.
"Beware of LBJ's Poverty Package." *Human Events* 23 (January 11, 1964): 12.
Bibby, John F., and Roger H. Davidson. "The Economic Opportunity Act of 1964." *On Capitol Hill: Studies in the Legislative Process*, edited by John F. Bibby and Roger H. Davidson, 2nd ed., pp. 225–47. Hinsdale, Ill.: Dryden Press, 1972.
"Birth Pangs Receding: Shriver Says of the Poverty War." *Texas Observer*, February 17, 1967: 7+.
Blakely, Edward James. "Toward a Theory of Training People for the War on Poverty—A Qualitative Comparative Study of Three Anti-Poverty Training Centers." Los Angeles: University of California, 1971. Ph.D. dissertation. University Microfilms No. 71-23000.
Blodgett, Terrell. "The Economic Opportunity Act in Texas." *Public Affairs Commentary* (Institute of Public Affairs, University of Texas at Austin) 11 (July 1965): 1–6.
Bluestein, Iris W. "Housing-Poverty War Relationships Found Too Weak to Make Impact on Slum Conditions." *Journal of Housing* 23 (June 1966): 321–24.
Blumenthal, Richard. "The Bureaucracy: Antipoverty and the Community Action Program." *American Political Institutions and Public Policy*, edited by Allan P. Sindler, pp. 128–79. Boston: Little, Brown, 1969.
Bookbinder, Hyman, et al. "Symposium: Johnson's War on Poverty." *New Politics* 3 (Fall 1964): 7–25.
Brecher, Charles M. The Impact of Federal Anti-Poverty Policies." New York: City University of New York, 1973. Ph.D. dissertation. University Microfilms No. 73-11349.
Brown, Clarence. "Poverty Waste." *Human Events* 25 (May 15, 1965): 15.
Browning, Robert X. *Politics and Social Welfare Policy in the United States*. Knoxville: University of Tennessee Press, 1986.
Burke, Edmund M. "Have the Poor Wrecked Johnson's War on Poverty?" *Antioch Review* 26 (Winter 1966/1967): 443–58.
Burlage, Robb K. *This Is War! An Analysis of the War on Poverty with Special Emphasis on Appalachia*. New York: Students for a Democratic Society, 1964? Pamphlet.
"Business Wages Private War on Poverty and Unemployment." *Human Events* 25 (May 22, 1965): 12.

Cahn, Edgar S., and Jean C. Cahn. "The War on Poverty: A Civilian Perspective." *Yale Law Journal* 73 (July 1964): 1317–52.

Carlson, Robert J. "Unemployment and Public Policy: The Effect of Government Measures on Different Types of Unemployment." *Business and Economics Review* [University of South Carolina] 14 (January 1968): 3–9.

Carter, Barbara. "Can the Job Corps Do the Job?" *Reporter* 32 (March 25, 1965): 21–26.

———. "Sargent Shriver and the Role of the Poor." *Reporter* 34 (May 1966): 17–20.

Cepuran, Joseph. "CAP [Community Action Program] Expenditures in the Fifty States: A Comparison." *Urban Affairs Quarterly* 4 (March 1969): 325–42.

"Change in Community Action Program Studied." *Congressional Quarterly Weekly Report* 25 (June 16, 1967): 1035–37.

"Changing Liabilities to Assets: That's the Job Corps Mission with School Dropout." *Business Week*, March 20, 1965: 156+.

Chazen, Leonard B. "Participation of the Poor: Section 202(a)(3) Organization under the Economic Opportunity Act of 1964." *Yale Law Journal* 75 (March 1966): 599–629.

"Civil Rights Groups and Other Activists Plan to Become Channels for 'Poverty Funds'." *Human Events* 25 (October 19, 1965): 12.

Clark, Dennis. "'The Poor' Identified and Their Prospects Predicted in Context of Poverty War and Housing." *Journal of Housing* 21 (December 1964): 578–84.

Clark, Kenneth B., and Jeanette Hopkins. *A Relevant War against Poverty: A Study of Community Action Programs and Observable Social Change.* New York: Harper and Row, 1969.

Cloward, Richard. "The War on Poverty—Are the Poor Left Out?" *Nation* 201 (August 1965): 55–58.

Cohen, Eli E., et al. "The Job Corps." *American Child* 48 (Winter 1966): 1–32.

Cohen, S. E. "FTC's Battle in the War on Poverty, It Seems, Is an Exercise in Futility." *Advertising Age* 37 (May 30, 1966): 4+.

———. "Poverty War Tries New Ways: Critics Ask, Is It Really a War on Business?" *Advertising Age* 37 (February 7, 1966): 6+.

Combs, Paul William. "Job Corps to 1973." Blacksburg: Virginia Polytechnic Institute and State University. Ed.D. dissertation, 1985. University Microfilms No. 8521304.

Community Action Programs Field Reports. "Work with the Economically Deprived [Neighborhood Youth Corps, Work Study, Job Corps, Head Start]." *YWCA Magazine Special Program Issue* 60 (June 1966): 2–31+.

"Congress Clears Johnson's Anti-Poverty Bill." *Congressional Quarterly Weekly Report* 22 (August 14, 1964): 1729–30.

"Congress Clears Two-Year Antipoverty Program." *Congressional Quarterly Weekly Report* 25 (December 15, 1967): 2546–51.

"Controversy over Federal Programs to Relieve Unemployment in the U.S.—The New 'Poverty Program': Pro and Con." *Congressional Digest* 43 (October 1964): 225, 231–51.

"Controversy over the Federal Antipoverty Community Action Program: Pro and Con." *Congressional Digest* 47 (October 1968): 35–59.

"Controversy over the Federal Job Corps: Pro and Con." *Congressional Digest* 47 (January 1968): 1–32.

"Controversy over the Johnson Administration's Rent Subsidy Program: Pro and Con." *Congressional Digest* 45 (January 1966): 1–32.

"The Controversy over Expanding the Federal Food Stamp Program: Pro and Con." *Congressional Digest* 43 (June/July 1964): 161–92.

"The Controversy over the Federal Anti-Poverty Program: Pro and Con." *Congressional Digest* 45 (March 1966): 67–96.

Couart, A. T. "Antipoverty Expenditures in the American States: A Comparative Analysis." *Midwest Journal of Political Science* 13 (May 1969): 219–36.

Crosby, R. W. "Will Industry Join the Poverty War?" *Iron Age* 193 (January 16, 1964): 40–41.

Davidson, Roger H. "'Creative Federalism' and the War on Poverty." *Poverty and Human Resources Abstracts* 1 (November-December 1966): 5–16.

———. "Poverty and the New Federalism." *Dimensions of Manpower Policy: Program and Research*, edited by Sar Levitan and Irving Siegel, pp. 61–78. Baltimore: Johns Hopkins University Press, 1966.

———, and Sar A. Levitan. *Antipoverty Housekeeping: The*

Administration of the Economic Opportunity Act. Ann Arbor: Institute of Labor and Industrial Relations, University of Michigan and Wayne State University, Policy Papers in Human Resources and Industrial Relations No. 9, September 1969.

Davis, Rennard. *The War on Poverty: Notes on Insurgent Response.* New York: Students for a Democratic Society, 1965? Pamphlet.

De Toledano, Ralph. "Camp Atterbury in Indiana Shows What's Wrong with the Job Corps." *Human Events* 25 (August 28, 1965): 12.

Democratic National Committee. "LBJ: War on Poverty." *The Democrat* 4 (January 13, 1964): 1–8.

——. "120 New Projects for Poverty War." *The Democrat* 4 (December 8, 1964): 2.

Devine, Samuel. "Rent Subsidies in the Great Society." *Human Events* 25 (May 22, 1965): 15.

Dierenfield, Bruce Jonathan. "Congressman Howard W. Smith: A Political Biography." Charlottesville: University of Virginia, 1981. Ph.D. dissertation. University Microfilms No. 82-19058.

Dubnoff, Caren. "The Lost War on Poverty: The Dynamics of a Federal Program in an Urban Political System." New York: Columbia University, 1974. Ph.D. dissertation. University Microfilms No. 77-15279.

"East Texas and the OEO." *Texas Observer*, September 26, 1969: 1+.

"Evaluating the War on Poverty." *Annals of the American Academy of Political and Social Sciences* 385 (September 1969): 1-174. [Special issue]

Everett, Robinson O., ed. "Antipoverty Programs: Symposium." *Law and Contemporary Problems* 31 (Winter 1966): 1–249.

"Federal Legislation and Programs for Underprivileged Young People." *American Library Association Bulletin* 58 (September 1964): 705–11.

Fenn, Richard K. "The CAP [Community Action Program]: An American Gospel." *Science and Society* 33 (Spring 1969): 209–22.

"Field Marshal in Poverty War: Appointment of R. Sargent Shriver to Spearhead the President's New Program Raises

Speculation over the Political Future of the Peace Corps Director." *Business Week,* March 7, 1964: 28–29.
"Finding Jobs that Will Last: The Washington Dilemma." *Texas Observer,* April 1, 1966: 7+.
Fisher, Linda L. "Presidential Implementation: Johnson, the War on Poverty, and Civil Rights." Paper presented to the annual meeting of the Midwest Political Science Assn., Cincinnati, Ohio, April 16–18, 1981.
Freeman, Roger A. "Phoney Baloney in Welfare Spending." *National Review* 17 (September 21, 1965): 823–26.
Friedman, Rose D. *Poverty: Definition and Perspective* [Analysis of CEA]. Washington, D.C.: American Enterprise Institute for Public Policy Research, 1965.
Gagnon, John H., and William Simon. "The War on the Poor." *Motive* 27 (December 1966): 4–11.
Galbraith, John Kenneth. "Let Us Begin: An Invitation to Action on Poverty." *Harper's Magazine* 228 (March 1964): 16–26.
Gelfand, Mark I. "The War on Poverty." *Exploring the Johnson Years,* edited by Robert A. Divine, pp. 126–54. Austin: University of Texas Press, 1981. Republished in paperback as *The Johnson Years, Volume One: Foreign Policy, the Great Society, and the White House.* Lawrence: University Press of Kansas, 1987.
Gish, Tom. *This Is the War that Is: The Failures of the Poverty Program in Eastern Kentucky.* Chicago: Students for a Democratic Society, 1965? Pamphlet.
Gould, Alan E. "Economic Opportunity Act: Impact on Economic Institutions, New York City as an Example." *Catholic Charities Review* 50 (October 1966): 11–18.
Graham, Elinor. "The Politics of Poverty." *Poverty As A Public Issue,* edited by Ben B. Seligman, pp. 231–50. New York: Free Press, 1965.
———. "Poverty and the Legislative Process." *Poverty as a Public Issue,* edited by Ben B. Seligman, pp. 251–71. New York: Free Press, 1965.
Green, Edith. "Who Should Administer the War on Poverty?" *American County Government* 33 (January 1968): 8–10.
Greenleigh Associates. *Evaluation of the VISTA Summer Associates Program.* New York: Greenleigh Associates, Inc., October 1967.

Greenstone, J. David, and Paul Peterson. "Reformers, Machines and the War on Poverty." *City Politics and Public Policy*, edited by James Q. Wilson, pp. 267–92. New York: Wiley, 1968.

Haddad, William F. "Mr. Shriver and the Savage Politics of Poverty." *Harper's Magazine* 231 (December 1965): 43–50.

Hannon, Philip J. "National Policy vs. Local Control: The Legal Services Dilemma [Role of U.S. Office of Economic Opportunity]." *California Western Law Review* 5 (Spring 1969): 223–31.

Harper, Dean. "The Other War [War on Poverty]." *Journal of Human Relations*, vol. 17, Second Quarter (1969): 242–59.

"Harassed Poverty Agency [U.S. Office of Economic Opportunity] Faces Crucial Year." *Congressional Quarterly Weekly Report* 24 (December 23, 1966): 3060–62.

Harrington, Michael. "Politics of Poverty." *Poverty: Views from the Left*, edited by Jeremy Larner and Irving Howe, pp. 13–38. New York: William Morrow, 1969.

Hartman, Chester W. "Politics of Housing." *Poverty: Views from the Left*, edited by Jeremy Larner and Irving Howe, pp. 149–67. New York: William Morrow, 1969.

Harvard Business School. *Jobs Corps*. Cambridge, Mass.: Harvard Business School, Harvard College, Case Study 9-375-152, 1974.

Hayden, Tom. *A View of the Poverty Program*. New York: New York University Graduate School of Social Work, 1966.

Hencke, Paul. "Is War on Poverty Becoming War on Businesses?" *Nation's Business* 54 (March 1966): 40–41+.

Herman, Melvin, and Michael Munk. *Decision Making in Poverty Programs*. New York: Columbia University Press, 1968.

Hersey, John. "Our Romance with Poverty." *American Scholar* 33 (Autumn 1964): 525–36.

Hoffman, Richard Lee. "Community Action: Innovative and Coordinative Strategies in the War on Poverty." Chapel Hill: University of North Carolina, 1969. Ph.D. dissertation. University Microfilms No. 70-02345.

Hofmann, Roger H. "A Study of Business Attitudes toward Poverty during the Johnson Administration." Unpublished paper, November 27, 1972, quoted in Michael Munk, "Policy Priorities in the War on Poverty." New York Uni-

versity, 1974. Ph.D. dissertation. University Microfilms No. 74-30023.
Holloran, Daniel F. "Progress against Poverty: The Governmental Approach." *Public Administration Review* 28 (May/June 1968): 205–13.
Hough, Robbin R. "Casualty Rates and the War on Poverty." *American Economic Review* 58 (May 1968): 528–32, 540–46.
"House Set to Act on Anti-Poverty Bill." *Congressional Quarterly Weekly Report* 22 (July 31, 1964): 1639–41.
"How Goes the War on Poverty?" *Economist* (Great Britain) 216 (September 4, 1965): 878–80+.
"How One Poverty Project Went Broke in West Virginia." *Human Events* 24 (December 19, 1964): 11.
"How Tax Dollars Are Wasted in LBJ's 'War on Poverty'." *Human Events* 24 (December 12, 1964): 11.
Howard, Irving E., Rev. "Capitalism's War on Poverty." *Human Events* 24 (March 14, 1964): 2.
Howard, Jack, et al. "The Neighborhood Youth Corps: Help or Handout?" *American Child* 49 (Spring 1967): 1–32.
Humphrey, Hubert H. "'The Rule of the Jungle Must Not, and It Will Not, Prevail': An 'American Plan' for Impoverished Areas." *American County Government* 22 (September 1967): 26–29.
———. "Social Change through the Legislative and Administrative Process." *The Social Welfare Forum*, National Conference on Social Welfare, pp. 18–21. Boulder: Colorado University Press, 1965.
———. "This Is Your War—The Crusade against Poverty." *I.U.D. Agenda* [Industrial Union Dept.] 1 (March 16, 1965): 16.
———. *War on Poverty*. New York: McGraw Hill, 1964.
Hutcheson, John Dabney, Jr. "Social Position, Alienation and the Impact of the War on Poverty." Athens: University of Georgia, 1969. Ph.D. dissertation. University Microfilms No. 70-10198.
James, Dorothy Buckton, ed. *Analyzing Poverty Policy*. Lexington, Mass.: D. C. Heath, 1975.
James, Edward. *America Against Poverty*. London: Routledge and Kegan Paul Ltd., 1970.
"Job Corps Comes Up to a Test." *Business Week*, October 14, 1967: 36.

"Job Corps Program Seen Entering Crucial Period." *Congressional Quarterly Weekly Report* 24 (July 1, 1966): 1389–93.
"Jobs for the Hard-Core Poor." *Business Week*, March 18, 1967: 48.
"Johnson's Anti-Poverty Bill." *Human Events* 24 (May 31, 1964): 2.
Kafoglis, Madelyn L. "The Economics of the Community Action Program." *Tennessee Survey of Business* 3 (December 1967): 1–7+.
Kershaw, Joseph. *Government Against Poverty.* Washington, D.C.: Brookings Institute, 1970.
Keyserling, Leon H. "Progress or Poverty: The U.S. at the Crossroads." Paper presented at the Conference on Economic Progress, Washington, D.C., December 1964.
Kilpatrick, James Jackson. "Right to Work Laws Uphold Individual's Freedom." *Human Events* 25 (January 30, 1965): 7.
Knoll, Erwin. "Progress on Poverty." *Progressive* 29 (July 1965): 11–14.
———. "The War on Poverty: Some Hope, Some Hoopla." *Progressive* 29 (November 1965): 11–14.
Komatsu, David. "Mr. Johnson's Little War on Poverty." *New Politics* 3 (Spring 1964): 5–29.
Kramer, Ralph M. *Participation of the Poor: Comparative Cases in the War on Poverty.* Englewood Cliffs, N.J.: Prentice Hall, 1969.
Kravitz, Sanford L., et al. "Which Way Community Action." *American Child* 47 (November 1965): 1–23.
"Laredo, Texas: Case History in 'War on Poverty': Some Gains, Some Doubts about the Future." *U.S. News and World Report* 59 (November 1965): 74–76.
"LBJ Moves on Housing, Poverty." *Engineering News-Record* 172 (January 9, 1964): 13–14.
Lenman, Cordelia Snow. "A Selective Integrative Analysis of the War on Poverty." Louisville, Ky.: University of Louisville, 1972. M.A. thesis. University Microfilms No. 13-03956.
Levine, Marvin J. "State and Local Retaining Programs and Legislation: A Case for Federal Action [in Unemployment]." *Labor Law Journal* 16 (January 1965): 27–43.
Levitan, Sar A. "Is This Poverty War 'Different'?" *Dimensions of Manpower Policy: Program and Research,* edited by Sar

Levitan and Irving Siegel, pp. 43–60. Baltimore: Johns Hopkins University Press, 1966.

———. "Minimum Wages—A Tool to Fight Poverty." *Labor Law Journal* 17 (January 1966): 53–60.

———. "Planning the Anti-Poverty Strategy." *Poverty and Human Resources Abstracts* 2 (January/February 1967): 5–15.

———. "Planning the Anti-Poverty Strategy—Part Two." *Poverty and Human Resources Abstracts* 2 (March/April 1967): 5–15.

———. *Programs in Aid of the Poor.* Washington, D.C.: W. E. Upjohn Institute for Employment Research, December 1965.

———. "What's Happening, Baby?—Essential Research for the War on Poverty." *Poverty and Human Resources Abstracts* 1 (September/October 1966): 13–17.

———, et al. *Towards Freedom from Want.* Madison: Industrial Relations Research Assn., University of Wisconsin, 1968.

Lewis, A. "Shriver Moves into the Front Rank." *New York Times Magazine,* March 15, 1964: 21.

Lewis, Fulton, Jr. "Bureaucrats Are Big Winners in Shriver-LBJ 'War on Poverty'." *Human Events* 25 (August 14, 1965): 6.

———. "Despite Scandals, Shriver Still Says Poverty War 'Going Great'." *Human Events* 25 (August 7, 1965): 2.

———. "The High Paid 'Poverty' Army." *Human Events* 25 (April 10, 1965): 14.

Lewis, Ted. "Sargent Shriver: The Administration's Glibbest Salesman." *Human Events* 25 (December 11, 1965): 12.

———. "Shriver's Poverty War." *Human Events* 25 (July 3, 1965): 14.

"Life in the Job Corps: What a Camp Is Like." *U.S. News and World Report* 63 (August 14, 1967): 58–59.

Lindsey, Almont. "Can Poverty Be Abolished?" *Virginia Quarterly Review* 43 (Spring 1967): 177–95.

Ling, Ta-Tseng. "The War on Poverty and the Concept of Participatory Administration." Knoxville: University of Tennessee, 1972. Ph.D. dissertation. University Microfilms No. 73-12417.

Long, Gillis W., et al. "The Economic Opportunity Act of 1964." *Tennessee Planner* 24 (December 1964): 33–64.

Long, Norton. "Urban Poverty and Public Policy." *University of Missouri Business and Government Review* 5 (July/August 1964): 31–38.

MacIver, R. M., ed. *The Assault on Poverty.* New York: Harper, 1965.

Malabre, Alfred L., Jr. "The War on Poverty: The First Skirmish." *Reporter* 31 (December 17, 1964): 27–29.

March, Michael S. "Poverty: How Much Will the War Cost?" *Social Service Review* 39 (June 1965): 141–56.

Marcuse, Peter. "The Anti-Poverty Program: Attack on the Symptom or Attack on the Source?" *Pratt Planning Papers* 3 (October 1965): 21–36.

Marris, Peter, and Martin Rein, eds. *Dilemmas of Social Reform: Poverty and Community Action in the United States.* New York: Atherton Press, 1967.

Marshall, Dale Rogers. *The Politics of Participation in Poverty: A Case Study of the Board of the Economic and Youth Opportunities Agency of Greater Los Angeles.* Berkeley and Los Angeles: University of California Press, 1971.

Martire, D. "Realistic Appraisal of the War on Poverty Program." *Magazine of Wall Street* 114 (April 4, 1964): 68–71.

Matusow, Allen J. "Lyndon B. Johnson's War on Poverty: The Limits of Liberal Reform." Paper presented to the Southern Historical Annual Meeting, Houston, Texas, November 14–16, 1985.

McGraith, Thomas C. "Some Aspects of the 1968 Housing Act." *Journal of Property Management* 34 (January/February 1969): 9–13.

"The 'Mess' in the 'Poverty War' [Mismanagement, Inefficiency, Unethical Practices]." *U.S. News and World Report* 60 (May 16, 1966): 67–69.

"Metals Will Fight War on Poverty." *Iron Age* 198 (December 8, 1966): 175.

Metropolitan Applied Research Center. *A Relevant War against Poverty.* New York: MARC, 1968.

Miller, S. M. "The Politics of Poverty." *Dissent* 12 (Spring 1964): 114–32.

———, and Martin Rein. "Participation, Poverty and Administration." *Public Administration Review* 29 (January/February 1969): 15–25.

———. "The War on Poverty: Perspectives and Prospects." *Poverty as a Public Issue*, edited by Ben B. Seligman, pp. 272–320. New York: Free Press, 1965.

———, and Pamela Roby. "The War on Poverty Reconsidered." *Poverty: Views from the Left*, edited by Jeremy Larner and Irving Howe, pp. 68–82. New York: William Morrow, 1969.

"Minimum Wage for Youth Corps." *Human Events* 25 (February 6, 1965): 2.

"Minority Housing: A Puzzling Market Starts to Shape Up." *House and Home* 27 (February 1965): 76–83.

Moody, Kimberly. "Poverty in the Interests of Big Business?" *New Politics* 6 (Spring 1968): 37–42.

"More Scandals in Poverty War." *Human Events* 25 (December 4, 1965): 8.

Moynihan, Daniel Patrick. "Crisis in Welfare." *Public Interest*, no. 10, Winter 1968: 3–29.

———. "Poverty and Progress." *American Scholar* 33 (Autumn 1964): 594–606.

———. "What Is Community Action?" *The Public Interest* 5 (Fall 1966): 3–8.

Munk, Michael. "Policy Priorities in the War on Poverty: The Funding of 81 Big City Community Action Agencies, 1964–1968." New York: New York University, 1974. Ph.D. dissertation. University Microfilms No. 74-3003.

Murphy, Anne Austin. "Involving the Poor in the War against Poverty." Chapel Hill: University of North Carolina, 1970. Ph.D. dissertation. University Microfilms No. 70-21215.

Murray, Charles. "The War on Poverty: 1965–1980." *Wilson Quarterly* 8 (Autumn 1984): 97–139.

"The Nation's Poorest City and the Poverty War's Crucial Issue." *Texas Observer*, March 31, 1967: 6+.

"New Kind of Poverty War: Farms and Small Towns." *Business Week*, December 16, 1967: 44.

"New Poverty Plan: Move Families to Training Camps." *Human Events* 25 (December 4, 1965): 14.

"900 Millions to Start—Who'll Get the Poverty Dollars: What the New Poverty Law Provides." *U.S. News and World Report* 57 (August 24, 1964): 36–38.

Nolan, David. *The Peace Called War: Lyndon Johnson's Pov-*

erty Program. Nashville: Southern Student Organizing Committee, 196? Pamphlet.

Northrup, Graham. "The Housing Act of 1968." *Urban Land* 27 (October 1968): 3–9.

Nourse, Hugh O. "Redistribution of Income from Public Housing." *National Tax Journal* 19 (March 1966): 27–37.

"Now the War on Poverty Is Called 'Political Grab Bag': Power Struggle Could Kill Whole Program." *U.S. News and World Report* 58 (April 26, 1965): 67–68.

"Now Your Taxes Train Pickets—Unions Are Infiltrating Poverty Programs." *Nation's Business* 55 (March 1967): 37–39.

Oberdorfer, Don. "The Proliferating Appalachias [War on Poverty]." *Reporter* 33 (September 9, 1965): 22–23 +.

"$1.75 Billion Antipoverty Bill Sent to President: Provisions." *Congressional Quarterly Weekly Report* 24 (October 21, 1966): 2561–64.

"Operation of Poverty Program under Sharp Attack [Who Should Control Local 'Community Action' Programs and Expenditures?]." *Congressional Quarterly Weekly Report* 23 (May 21, 1965): 991–94.

Opitz, Edmund A. "The War on Poverty: A Critical Review." *Freeman* 18 (August 1968): 451–61.

"The Other Side of Affluence: Economist Galbraith Sees No Conflict between His Book and the Anti-Poverty Program." *Business Week,* April 18, 1964: 190 +.

Ott, Attiat F., and Paul Hughes-Cromwick. "The War on Poverty: Two Decades Later." Paper presented at Fifth Annual Hofstra University Presidential Conference: Lyndon Baines Johnson, A Texan in Washington. Hempstead, New York, April 10–12, 1986.

"Pa and Ma and LBJ: Or How to Become a Casualty in the Government's War on Poverty." *Nation's Business* 54 (April 1966): 48–49 +.

Pascal, Anthony H. "Reconnaissance for the War on Poverty." Paper Presented at a faculty seminar on poverty, University of California at Los Angeles, March 19, 1965. Santa Monica, Cal.: Rand Corp., P-3092, 1965.

"Peaceniks, Beatniks, and Smutniks: Weird Warriors in the War on Poverty." *Nation's Business* 54 (March 1966): 42–44.

Perry, Constance. "The Community Action Program." *Science and Society* 29 (Fall 1968): 94–109.

Peterson, Paul Elliott. "City Politics and Community Action: The Implementation of the Community Action Program in Three American Cities." Chicago: University of Chicago, 1967. Ph.D. dissertation.
Pilisuk, Marc, and Phyllis Pilisuk, eds. *How We Lost the War on Poverty*. New York: Transition Books, 1973.
Pino, Ricardo. "The Nature of Rural Areas Development (RAD)." *New Mexico Business* 17 (October 1964): 15–21.
Poirot, Paul L. "The War on Poverty: Against Property, against the Poor?" *Freeman* 17 (October 1967): 579–90.
"Politics and the 'Poverty War'." *U.S. News and World Report* 59 (September 6, 1965): 61–63.
Pollitt, Frederick Anthony. "Participation of the Poor in the War on Poverty." University Park: Pennsylvania State University, 1972. Ph.D. dissertation. University Microfilms No. 73-21275.
"Poor Find a Friend in Court: American Bar Association's Program to Supply Legal Aid with Federal Anti-Poverty Funds." *Business Week*, December 10, 1966: 92–94.
"Poverty Contracts Not Competitive." *Human Events* 25 (August 28, 1965): 12.
"Poverty War Draws Business' Best: Companies, after Some Early Coolness, Preparing to Run Massive Urban Training Center." *Business Week*, December 19, 1964: 23–24.
"Poverty War Has Wars of Its Own [Local Battles to Control Funds, while Business Pushes Job Corps Program]." *Business Week*, April 3, 1965: 30–31.
"Poverty War Out of Hand? Agencies Overstaffed, Funds Wasted." *U.S. News and World Report* 59 (August 23, 1965): 48–52.
"Poverty Warriors." *Barron's* 47 (July 31, 1967): 1.
"Pres. Johnson Wars on Poverty; AFL-CIO Pres. George Meany Pledges Labor's Aid." *AFL-CIO News* 9 (January 11, 1964): 1, 11, 12.
"President Declares War on Poverty, Submits Omnibus Bill." *Congressional Quarterly Weekly Report* 22 (March 20, 1964): 554–57.
"President's Action Spurs Debate of Guaranteed Income." *Congressional Quarterly Weekly Report* 25 (March 10, 1967): 349–52.
"President's Pledge: War on Want at Home." *Business Week*, January 11, 1964: 19–21.

"President's Poverty Plan Approved with Limited Changes." *Congressional Quarterly Weekly Report* 22 (May 29, 1964): 1037–42.

Pressman, Jeffrey L., and Aaron Wildavsky. *Implementation: How Great Expectations in Washington Are Dashed in Oakland . . . A Saga of the Economic Development Administration as Told to Two Sympathetic Observers Who Seek to Build Morals on a Foundation of Ruined Hopes.* Berkeley and Los Angeles: University of California Press, 1973.

Prinz, Jonathan. "Community Action and the Poverty War." *Congressional Bi-Weekly* 33 (January 10, 1966): 8–10.

Purcell, Francis. "Troubles in the Job Corps—Report from a Showplace [Camp Kilmer, N.J.]" (Interview). *U.S. News and World Report* 59 (December 27, 1965): 51–55.

"Pushing Harder for Ghetto Jobs: The Administration's Hopes." *Business Week*, January 20, 1968: 123–24+.

"The Question of a Separate Federal Program for the Development of 'Appalachia': Pro and Con." *Congressional Digest* 43 (December 1964): 289–311.

"The Question of [Federal Government] Guaranteed Annual Incomes: Pro and Con." *Congressional Digest* 46 (October 1967): 225–53.

Raskin, A. H. "Generalissimo of the War on Poverty." *New York Times Magazine*, November 22, 1964: 39+.

"The Real Story of the Poverty War: What Actually Is Being Done to Help the Poor?" *U.S. News and World Report* 58 (June 14, 1965): 37–40.

Reiley, Linda Cobb. "Attempting to Achieve Public Consent for the War on Poverty: An Historical Study of the Public Relations Program of the Office of Economic Opportunity Compared to Newspaper Response to the Program from August 20, 1964 to July 1, 1968." Washington, D.C.: The American University, 1969. M.A. thesis. University Microfilms No. 13-02157.

Reissman, Frank. "A Strategy for Antipoverty Community Action Programs." *Social Work* 11 (April 1966): 3–12.

———, Arthur Pearl, and Ray Johnston, eds. *Politics and the Poor.* Evanston, Ill.: Charles and Merrill, 1970.

Rentashler, William H. "Poverty 'War' Finding Jobs for Collegians." *Human Events* 25 (August 21, 1965): 6.

Riesel, Victor. "GAO to Make Sweeping Poverty Probe." *Human Events* 28 (March 2, 1968): 1.

———. "Reuther Launches 'Citizens' Crusade against Poverty." *Human Events* 24 (November 7, 1964): 15.
"'Right-to-Work' Statistics." *Human Events* 25 (June 5, 1965): 9.
Rogers, Donald I. "Private 'War on Poverty'." *Human Events* 24 (May 16, 1964): 10.
———. "Welfare: $4,400 Per Poor Family." *Human Events* 24 (April 4, 1964): 8.
Rogers, John. "Poverty Behind the Cactus Curtain: Programs to Aid Mexican-Americans in Southern Texas." *Progressive* 30 (March 1966): 22–25.
Rose, Stephen M. *The Betrayal of the Poor: The Transformation of Community Action.* Cambridge, Mass.: Schenkman, 1972.
Rosenbaum, Karen J. "Curricular Innovations in Federal Youth Programs: A Comparison of New Deal and War on Poverty Education Efforts." Baltimore: Johns Hopkins University, 1973. Ph.D. dissertation. University Microfilms No. 73-16662.
Rosenblum, Victor. "Controlling the Bureaucracy of the Antipoverty Program." *Law and Contemporary Problems* 31 (Winter 1966): 187–210.
Rothman, Julius F. "A Look at the War on Poverty." *AFL-CIO American Federationist* 74 (November 1967): 1–8.
Russell, James W. "The Economic Opportunity Act and Legal Aid: Bane of the Bar or Savior of the Indigent?" *Baylor Law Review* 18 (Spring 1966): 369–79.
"The Scandal Ridden 'Mobilization for Youth'." *Human Events* 25 (January 2, 1965): 8, 9.
Scheibla, Shirley. *Poverty Is Where the Money Is.* New Rochelle, N.Y.: Arlington House, 1968.
———. "Suffer Little Children: Anti-Poverty Funds Are Financing Public School Boycotts." *Barron's* 47 (May 8, 1967): 9–10+.
Schmidt, Ronald John. "Nongovernmental Policy Implementation: A Case Study in the War on Poverty." Riverside: University of California, 1971. Ph.D. dissertation. University Microfilms No. 72-17064.
Schultz, Theodore W., et al. "The Economics of Poverty." *American Economic Review* 55 (May 1965): 510–48.
Schulz, Bill. "House Starts Nationwide Probe of Scandal-Ridden 'Youth Corps'." *Human Events* 25 (November 20, 1965): 3.

Schwarz, John E. *America's Hidden Success: A Reassessment of Twenty Years of Public Policy.* New York: Norton, 1983.

Scott, Paul. "LBJ Preparing $3,000 Minimum Income Proposal (Pushed in Riot Commission Report)." *Human Events* 28 (March 16, 1968): 1.

"Senate, House Pass Antipoverty Authorizations." *Congressional Quarterly Weekly Report* 24 (October 7, 1966): 2393–2400.

"Senate Passes Anti-Poverty Bill." *Human Events* 24 (August 8, 1964): 11.

"Senate Passes Bill to Extend Anti-Poverty Program." *Congressional Quarterly Weekly Report* 23 (August 27, 1965): 1730–32.

"Senate Passes Johnson's Anti-Poverty Bill, 61–34." *Congressional Quarterly Weekly Report* 22 (July 23, 1964): 1533–34.

Sennholz, Hans. "LBJ's Fallacy-Based War on Poverty." *Human Events* 24 (May 2, 1964): 18.

———. "'War on Poverty': Marxism or Political Football?" *Human Events* 24 (June 13, 1964): 11.

Shaffer, Helen B. "Status of War on Poverty." *Editorial Research Reports,* January 25, 1967: 63–80.

Shanahan, E. K. "Drumming Up Votes for the Poverty Program." *New Republic,* June 17, 1967:

Sherman, Annabelle S. "War on Poverty: A Challenge to Home Economics." *Journal of Home Economics* 57 (June 1965): 434–36.

Shriver, Sargent. "First-Hand Report on 'Poverty War'" (Interview). *U.S. News and World Report* 60 (February 28, 1966): 64–69.

———. *Meet the Press: Guest, Sargent Shriver* (Interview). Washington, D.C.: Merkle Press, vol. 8, no. 9, 1964.

———. *Meet the Press: Guest, Sargent Shriver, Director, Office of Economic Opportunity, Director, Peace Corps* (Interview). Washington, D.C.: Merkle Press, vol. 9, no. 45, 1965.

———. *Meet the Press: Guest, Sargent Shriver, Director, Office of Economic Opportunity* (Interview). Washington, D.C.: Merkle Press, vol. 11, no. 13, 1967.

———. *Meet the Press: Guest, Sargent Shriver, Director, Office of Economic Opportunity* (Interview). Washington, D.C.: Merkle Press, vol. 8, no. 4, 1964.

———. *Point of the Lance.* New York: Harper and Row, 1964.

———. "Towards a National Purpose: The War on Poverty." *Public Relations Journal* 23 (January 1967): 10–12.
———. "The War on Poverty." *American County Government* 31 (September 1966): 22–24+.
———. "The War on Poverty: A 'Giant Stride' Forward." *AFL-CIO American Federationist* 73 (April 1966): 6–9.
Silberman, Charles E. "The Mixed-Up War on Poverty: Some Fear the Proposed 'Community Action' by the Poor Will Disrupt Society; Others Fear There Won't Be Any Action at All." *Fortune* 72 (August 1965): 156–61+.
Singletary, Otis. "The Job Corps: Its Purpose, Its Beginnings, Its Success." *Banking* 58 (January 1966): 49–50+.
Sloan, Jerome S. "The Community Action Program and the Social Responsibility of the Local Lawyer." *Virginia Law Review* 51 (December 1965): 1545–85.
Social Dynamics Research Institute, City University of New York. *A Relevant War against Poverty: A Study of Community Action Programs and Observable Social Change.* New York: Metropolitan Applied Research Center, 1968.
Specht, Harry. "Community Development in Low-Income Negro Areas." *Social Work* 11 (October 1966): 78–89.
"Special Poverty Issue: The War on Poverty." *Washington Bulletin*, April 25, 1966: all.
Spencer, Scott, et al. *Johnson's Skirmish with Poverty.* Chicago: Young People's Socialist League, 196? Pamphlet.
Starr, Roger. "Housing for the Poor." *New Leader* 51 (March 11, 1968): 11–14.
"State Department Personnel Transferred to Office of Economic Opportunity." *Human Events* 28 (February 24, 1968): 11.
Steiner, Gilbert Y. *Social Insecurity: The Politics of Welfare.* Chicago: Rand McNally, 1966.
Stewart, Eugene L. *The Impact of U.S. Foreign Economic Policy on the War on Poverty: A Study of the Implications of Foreign Trade Developments for the Capabilities of U.S. Industries to Create New Job Opportunities for the Nation's Poverty-Stricken Unemployed.* New York: Trade Relations Council of the United States, 1964.
"Sudden Drive on 'Poverty'—Why?" *U.S. News and World Report* 56 (January 20, 1964): 36–39.
Tax Foundation, Inc. *Antipoverty Programs under the Economic Opportunity Act.* New York: Tax Foundation, Inc., Research Publication no. 17, 1968.

Terhorst, Jerald. "The Business Role in the Great Society [Job Corps Program]." *Reporter* 33 (October 21, 1965): 26–30.

"A Think Tank that Thinks for the Poor: University of Wisconsin's Institute of Research on Poverty." *Business Week*, June 22, 1968: 106–08 +.

Thompson, Kenneth. "Presidential Commission Declares War on Poverty Owners." *Human Events* 27 (October 14, 1967): 8–9.

———. "Texas Governor Connally Battles LBJ in Poverty War." *Human Events* 26 (February 19, 1966): 16.

Tucker, James F. "The First 50,000 Neighborhood Youth Corps Enrollees." *Monthly Labor Review* 88 (December 1965): 1442+.

United States Chamber of Commerce. *Analysis in Depth: The 'War on Poverty': A Discussion of the Issues Involved in the Proposed Economic Opportunity Act of 1964, and Constructive Alternatives to Minimize the Problem of Poverty.* Washington, D.C.: U.S. Chamber of Commerce, 1964.

———. *Youth and the War on Poverty: An Evaluation of the Job Corps, Neighborhood Youth Corps, and Project Head Start.* Washington, D.C.: U.S. Chamber of Commerce, U.S. Gov't. Printing Office, 1967.

———. Task Force on Economic Growth and Opportunity. *The Concept of Poverty: First Report.* Washington, D.C.: U.S. Gov't. Printing Office, 1965.

United States Office of Economic Opportunity. *A Nation Aroused: First Annual Report.* Washington, D.C.: U.S. Gov't. Printing Office, 1965.

———. *Community Action Program Guide.* 2 vols. Washington, D.C.: U.S. Gov't. Printing Office, 1965.

———. *Poverty Program Information* [Quarterly Summary of All Programs Initiated under Economic Opportunity Act of 1964]. 2 vols. Washington, D.C.: U.S. Gov't. Printing Office, 1966.

———. *The Quiet Revolution: Second Annual Report.* Washington, D.C.: U.S. Gov't. Printing Office, 1966.

———. *Upward Bound.* Washington, D.C.: U.S. Gov't. Printing Office, 1965.

United States. Manpower Administration. Bureau of Work Training Programs. *The Neighborhood Youth Corps: Three*

Years of Success. Washington, D.C.: U.S. Gov't. Printing Office, 1968.

"U.S. Low-Income Housing Efforts Stir Controversy." *Congressional Quarterly Weekly Report* 25 (October 20, 1967): 2134–36.

"Vicious Circle of Poverty: The Administration Launches a Concerted Attack—A Special Report." *Business Week,* February 1, 1964: 38–40+.

Viles, Robert M. "The War on Poverty: What Can Lawyers (Being Human) Do?" *Iowa Law Review* 53 (August 1967): 122–68.

"VISTA Poverty Program Still Lags." *Human Events* 25 (October 9, 1965): 3.

Wald, Patricia M. "Law and Poverty: 1965." Working Paper for the National Conference on Law and Poverty, sponsored by Sargent Shriver, Director, Office of Economic Opportunity, and Nicholas DeB. Katzenbach, Attorney General of the United States, Washington, D.C., June 23–25, 1965. Washington, D.C.: Distributed by U.S. Gov't. Printing Office, 1965.

"The War on Poverty in Texas." *Texas Observer,* March 19, 1965: 1+; April 2, 1965: 10.

"The War on Poverty—Washington vs. City Hall." *U.S. News and World Report* 59 (November 22, 1965): 54–56.

"The War that Has Yet to Be Fought: State of U.S. Anti-Poverty Programs." *Economist* (Great Britain) 226 (February 24, 1968): 43–44.

"Waste in Poverty War—An Official Appraisal." *U.S. News and World Report* 66 (March 31, 1969): 58.

Waterman, Kenneth. "Local Issues in the Urban War on Poverty." *Social Work* 2 (January 1966): 61+.

Waxman, Chaim Issac, ed. *Poverty: Power and Politics.* New York: Grosset and Dunlap, 1968.

Weeks, Christopher. *Jobs Corps: Dollars and Dropouts.* Boston: Little, Brown and Co., 1967.

Weinberger, Bernard. "Jews and the War on Poverty." *Jewish Life* 34 (September/October 1967): 18–24.

Welch, Wayne. "Experiment at Camp Kilmer [New Jersey—Training Center for Job Corps]." *Reporter* 33 (October 21, 1965): 30–32.

Wells, Paul. "The Problem of Poverty [and Federal Government

Anti-Poverty Programs]." *Business Review* 21 (December 1964): 6–8.
"What Leading Americans Have Said on Right-to-Work." *Human Events* 25 (June 19, 1965): 1.
"What's Going On in the Job Corps." *U.S. News and World Report* 59 (July 26, 1965): 57–60.
"Where $1-Billion Will Go—Poverty Program Outline Goes to Congress." *Business Week*, March 21, 1964: 29–30.
"Where the Poverty Program Is Doing Poorly." *Nation's Business* 55 (October 1967): 52+.
"Who Gets the Cash in the War on Poverty." *U.S. News and World Report* 56 (March 30, 1964): 33–35.
"Why Poverty War Stirs Debate." *Business Week*, May 4, 1968: 76+.
"Why the 'Poverty Package' Is Criticized." *Human Events* 24 (May 31, 1964): 2.
Wickenden, Elizabeth. "The Legal Right to a Minimum But Equal Level of Living." *Journal of Home Economics* 59 (January 1967): 14–19.
Widner, Ralph R. "Experiment in Appalachia." *Pittsburgh Business Review* 37 (March 1967): 1–7+.
Wilson, Beclee Newcomer. "The Role of Symbols in Forming the Public Policy of the War on Poverty." Minneapolis: University of Minnesota, 1979. Ph.D. dissertation. University Microfilms No. 79-26193.
Witcover, Jules, and Erwin Knoll. "Politics and the Poor: Shriver's Second Thoughts." *Reporter*, December 30, 1965:
Wolfenstein, E. Victor. "The Two Wars of Lyndon Johnson [Vietnam and War on Poverty]." *Politics and Society*, vol. 4, no. 3 (1974): 357–96.
Worsnop, Richard L. "Public Housing in the War on Poverty." *Editorial Research Reports*, July 22, 1964: 523–40.
Wrigley, Robert L., Jr. "Area Redevelopment Programs for Economic Growth: Area Redevelopment Administration." *Journal of the American Institute of Planners* 30 (November 1964): 287–95.
"Wrong War: In 1964 Communism, Not Poverty, Is the Real Enemy." *Barron's* 44 (February 17, 1964): 1.
Young, Whitney M. "Whitney Young Reviews Poverty War, Urges NAHRO to Work for Integrated Housing." *Journal of Housing* 22 (December 1965): 583–88.

Younger, George D. "An Object Lesson for the War on Poverty: Mobilization for Youth, Inc." *Christianity and Crisis* 25 (March 22, 1965): 52–54.

Zarefsky, David H. *President Johnson's War on Poverty: Rhetoric and History.* University, Ala.: University of Alabama Press, 1986.

Zimbalist, Sidney E. "Drawing the Poverty Line." *Social Work* 9 (July 1964): 19–26.

Zurcher, Louis, Jr. *Poverty Warriors: The Human Experience of Planned Social Interaction.* Austin: University of Texas Press, 1970.

K. MISCELLANEOUS PROGRAMS

"Air Pollution Bill Clears Congress." *Labor* (Railroad Labor Organizations) 49 (November 25, 1967): 3.

"America the Un-beautiful [Discussion of Johnson's Conservation Program, Air and Water Pollution, and Urban Planning]." *I.U.D. Agenda* (Industrial Union Department) 1 (March 1965): 5–13.

Baughman, James L. *Television's Guardians: The FCC and the Politics of Programming, 1958–1967.* Knoxville: University of Tennessee Press, 1985.

Blake, William. "A Summary of the President's Message on Consumer Interests." *Credit World* 52 (March 1964): 6–7.

Burt, Richard, and Geoffrey Kemp, eds. *Congressional Hearings on American Defense Policy, 1947–1971: An Annotated Bibliography.* Lawrence: University Press of Kansas, 1974.

"The Business of the Nation and the Nation's Business: Toward a New Partnership." Transcript of Business Symposium, Lyndon B. Johnson Library, Austin, March 1–2, 1979.

Calder, James Douglas. "Presidents and Crime Control: Some Limitations on Executive Policy Making." Claremont, Cal.: Claremont Graduate School, 1978. Ph.D. dissertation. University Microfilms No. 78-23817.

Castro, Nash. "LBJ, Man of the Land." *The Lyndon Baines Johnson Memorial Grove on the Potomac: A Tribute to Lyndon B. Johnson, Conservationist.* National Geographic Society, pp. 4–16. Washington, D.C.: Eastern National Park and Monument Assn., 1977.

Chamberlain, John. "Can We Trust Government to Beautify Us?" *Human Events* 25 (February 27, 1965): 10.
Chayes, Abram, and Jerome Weisner, eds. *ABM: An Evaluation of the Decision to Deploy an Anti-Ballastic Missile System*. New York: Harper and Row, 1969.
Cohen, S. E. "Expect LBJ to Remain Moderate on Business." *Advertising Age* 35 (November 9, 1964): 1+.
"Consumerism Losing White House Foothold." *Advertising Age* 38 (January 16, 1967): 1+.
"Controversy over the Johnson Proposal to Change U.S. Immigration Laws: Pro and Con." *Congressional Digest* 44 (May 1965): 131–59.
Crosby, R. W. "LBJ Seeks Industry-Labor Partnership." *Iron Age* January 14, 1965: 30.
Dague, Paul B. "What's Wrong with LBJ's Farm Bill?" *Human Events* 25 (May 8, 1965): 8.
Elliff, John T. *The Reform of FBI Intelligence Activities*. Princeton, N.J.: Princeton University Press, 1979.
Enthoven, Alain C., and K. Wayne Smith. *How Much Is Enough? Shaping the Defense Program, 1961–1968*. New York: Harper and Row, 1971.
"The Fight for Clean Air Continues." *AFL-CIO American Federationist* 74 (June 1967): 17–22.
"Freeman's Newest ['Food for Freedom'] Farm Plan." *Human Events* 26 (March 12, 1966): 5.
"Great Redwoods Saved from Ax [Joint Action by Pres. Johnson and U.S. Rep. Thomas H. Kuchel]." *Labor* (Railroad Labor Organizations) 47 (September 17, 1966): 3.
"Hearings on Beautification Act." *Texas Highways* 13 (May 1966): 28.
Hurt, Henry. *Reasonable Doubt: An Investigation into the Assassination of John F. Kennedy*. New York: Holt, Rinehart & Winston, 1985.
"Johnson Asks Campaign to Cleanse Rivers, Air." *AFL-CIO News* 11 (February 26, 1966): 1, 12.
"[Johnson] Hails 'Milestone in Conservation' [Congress Passes Seven Conservation Bills]." *Labor* (Railroad Labor Organizations) 48 (October 22, 1966): 3.
Jones, Jenkin Lloyd. "LBJ Urges Liberalized Immigration." *Human Events* 25 (February 6, 1965): 16.
Jones, Penn, Jr. *Forgive My Grief: A Critical Review of the War-*

ren Commission Report of the Assassination of President John F. Kennedy. Midlothian, Texas: Midlothian Mirror, Inc., 1966.

Kent, Richard J., Jr. *Safe, Separated, and Soaring: A History of Federal Civil Aviation Policy, 1961–1972.* Washington, D.C.: U.S. Dept. of Transportation, FAA, 1980.

"LBJ Considers Requesting Study of New Assassination Evidence." *Human Events* 27 (April 29, 1967): 11.

"LBJ Pledges Hearty Support to Consumer Advisory Council." *Advertising Age* 34 (December 30, 1963): 36.

"LBJ's Anti-Crime Bill." *Human Events* 27 (April 8, 1967): 4.

"LBJ's Gifts to Labor." *Human Events* 24 (September 26, 1964): 10.

Margolius, Sidney. "Consumer Rights: The Battle Continues." *AFL-CIO American Federationist* 74 (April 1967): 1–4.

Melosi, Martin. "Lyndon Johnson and Environmental Policy." *The Johnson Years, Volume Two: Vietnam, the Environment, and Science,* edited by Robert A. Divine, pp. 113–49. Lawrence: University Press of Kansas, 1987.

Nash, Gerald D. *United States Oil Policy: Business and Government in Twentieth Century America.* 1968. Reprint. Westport, Conn.: Greenwood Press, 1976.

"'New Conservation' Drive and Pollution Controls Backed [by AFL-CIO]." *AFL-CIO News* 10 (March 6, 1965): 4.

Nocera, Joseph. "The Oil Depletion Allowance." *Texas Monthly* 13 (February 1985): 106–07.

"Poverty Program Joins Forces with Buyer Education: The Consumer Action Conference." *Advertising Age* 36 (August 16, 1965): 1+.

"Pres. Johnson Prods Bills to Aid Consumers, Including a Meat Inspection Bill and a Truth in Lending Bill." *AFL-CIO News* 12 (November 25, 1967): 1, 8.

"President Johnson's Immigration Plan." *Human Events* 24 (July 18, 1964): 1.

Ridgeway, James. *The Politics of Ecology.* New York: Dutton, 1970.

Riesel, Victor. "Commitments LBJ Has Given Top Labor Leaders." *Human Events* 25 (January 9, 1965): 1.

———. "Johnson Has 'Closed-Door' Talk with Labor." *Human Events* 23 (January 4, 1964): 10.

———. "Johnson Phones George Meany and Embraces Labor's

Program." *Human Events* 25 (February 6, 1965): 12.
———. "Johnson Wants Labor Law Changes: Keeping Pledge to Union Chiefs." *Human Events* 25 (May 8, 1965): 9.
———. "LBJ Demands Help from Labor Leaders." *Human Events* 24 (May 31, 1964): 11.
———. "LBJ Has 3 Brain Trusts Working on Anti-Strike Formula." *Human Events* 26 (December 24, 1966): 6.
———. "LBJ Promises Union Chiefs He Will Back 35-Hour Week." *Human Events* 24 (September 26, 1964): 7.
———. "LBJ to Deal Directly with Union Chiefs." *Human Events* 24 (April 18, 1964): 10.
Rosenthal, Harvey Daniel. "Their Day in Court: A History of the Indian Claims Commission." Kent, Ohio: Kent State University, 1976. Ph.D. dissertation. University Microfilms No. 76-25373.
Schrepfer, Susan R. *The Fight to Save the Redwoods: A History of Environmental Reform, 1917–1978.* Madison: University of Wisconsin Press, 1983.
Scott, Paul. "Presidential Commission [on Civil Disorders] Studies Militants' 'Battle Plans'." *Human Events* 28 (February 24, 1968): 7.
"Should Kennedy-Khrushchev Letters Be Published? LBJ Must Soon Decide." *Human Events* 27 (June 27, 1967): 1.
Siegel, Stanley. "The United States Post Office, Incorporated: A Blueprint for Reform." *Michigan Law Review* 66 (February 1968): 615–69.
Sirgo, Henry B. "Water Policy Decision-Making and Implementation in the Johnson Administration." *Journal of Political Science* 12 (Spring 1985): 53–63.
Specter, Arlen. "Truth about Kennedy's Assassination. Interview with Arlen Specter, Assistant Counsel, President's Commission to Investigate the Assassination of President Kennedy." *U.S. News and World Report* 61 (October 10, 1966): 44–50.
"The Steel Imbroglio." *Human Events* 26 (January 15, 1964): 5.
Swankin, David A. "'A Marketplace Built on Quality'—The Consumer Protection Program of Lyndon B. Johnson." Paper presented to the Lyndon B. Johnson Library, Austin, Texas, April 1985.
Towne, Anthony. "The Assassination, The Warren Report and the Public Trust." *Motive* 27 (February 1967): 6–14.

"Training vs. Double-Time Overtime Penalty: President Johnson's Proposal to Spur Creation of Jobs by His Industry Officials." *Steel* 157 (July 19, 1965): 25–26.
Vietor, Richard H. *Energy Policy in America since 1945: A Study of Business-Government Relations and Recognition Controversy.* New York: Columbia University Press, 1983.
"Voice for Consumer [Johnson Creates New Post of Special Assistant to President for Consumer Affairs]." *AFL-CIO American Federationist* 71 (March 1964): 13–18.
"The War against Pollution." *Machinist* (Internat'l. Assn. of Machinists and Aerospace Workers) 21 (November 10, 1966): 4.
"What Unions Asked of LBJ—And What They Got." *U.S. News and World Report* 58 (May 31, 1965): 67–69.
Whitnah, Donald R. *Safer Skyways: Federal Control of Aviation, 1926–1966.* Ames: Iowa State Unversity Press, 1966.
"Widens War on Pollution and Acts to Save Resources [Summary of Johnson's Conservation and Anti-pollution Programs]." *Labor* (Railroad Labor Organizations) 47 (March 5, 1966): 6.
Wilcox, Walter W. "Farm Policy Issues, 1966–1970." *Social Action* 32 (November 1965): 6–13.

3. FOREIGN POLICY

A. GENERAL

Andrews, James R. "The Rhetoric of Alliance." *Today's Speech* 16 (February 1968): 20–24.
"Around the World—Puzzle over U.S.: Era of Relative Calm Has Given Way to Crisis—How Does the Outside World Measure Johnson's Ability to Cope with It.?" *U.S. News and World Report* 56 (February 24, 1964): 39–41.
Barilleaux, Ryan John. "The Presidential Ordeal: Evaluating Presidential Performance in Foreign Affairs." Austin: University of Texas, 1983. Ph.D. dissertation. University Microfilms No. 83–29807.
Barnet, Richard J. *Intervention and Revolution: The United States in the Third World.* New York: World Publishing, 1968.
Beckman, Peter R. "The Influence of the American Military Establishment on American Foreign Policy, 1946–1970."

FOREIGN POLICY—GENERAL 229

Madison: University of Wisconsin, 1974. Ph.D. dissertation. University Microfilms No. 74-24709.
Belman, Murray J. "The Power of the President to Use Military Force Abroad." *Virginia Journal of International Law* 10 (December 1969): 37-57.
Berger, Raoul. "Presidential Monopoly of Foreign Relations." *Michigan Law Review* 71 (November 1972): 1-58.
————. "The Tug-of-War between Congress and the Presidency—Foreign Policy and the Power to Make War." *Washburn Law Journal* 16 (Fall 1976): 1-11.
Berkowitz, Morton, P. G. Bock, and Vincent J. Fuccillo. *The Politics of American Foreign Policy: The Social Context of Decisions.* Englewood Cliffs, N.J.: Prentice-Hall, 1977.
Berry, John M. "Foreign Policy Making and the Congress." *Editorial Research Reports,* April 19, 1967: 283-300.
Black, Eugene R. "The Domestic Dividends of Foreign Aid." *Columbia Journal of World Business* 1 (Fall 1965): 21-27.
Bock, Joseph G. "The National Security Assistant and the White House Staff, 1947-1984: Foreign Policy Implications." Washington, D.C.: American University, 1985. Ph.D. dissertation. University Microfilms No. 85-13644.
"Bobby Kennedy's Speeches Are Serving as 'Trial Balloons' on U.S. Foreign Policy." *Human Events* 25 (November 13, 1965): 11.
Boettiger, John R., ed. *Vietnam and American Foreign Policy.* Boston: Heath, 1968.
Brindley, Thomas A. "American Goals in the Educational Policy of UNESCO, 1946-1964." Ann Arbor: University of Michigan, 1968. Ph.D. dissertation. University Microfilms No. 69-12056.
Brown, Donald Eugene. "Fulbright and the Premises of American Foreign Policy." Binghamton: State University of New York, 1982. Ph.D. dissertation. University Microfilms No. 8208554.
Bundy, McGeorge, and William P. Bundy. "How Foreign Policy Is Made—Logic and Experience." *University of Pittsburgh Law Review* 30 (Spring 1969): 437-57.
Burns, Richard Dean. *Arms Control and Disarmament: A Bibliography.* Santa Barbara, Cal.: ABC-Clio, 1977.
————. *Guide to American Foreign Relations since 1700: A Bibliography.* Santa Barbara, Cal.: ABC-Clio, 1983.
Cabot, John Moors. *First Line of Defense: 40 Years' Experience*

of a Career Diplomat. Lanham, Md.: University Press of America, 1979.
Carroll, John M., and George C. Herring, eds. *Modern American Diplomacy.* Wilmington, Del.: Scholarly Resources, 1986.
Carter, Ralph G. "Congressional Foreign Policy Behavior: Persistent Patterns of the Postwar Period [1946–1982]." *Presidential Studies Quarterly* 16 (Spring 1986): 329–59.
Chamberlain, John. "Lynda Bird and Foreign Aid." *Human Events* 26 (June 25, 1966): 14.
———. "1967: Crucial Test of Foreign Policy." *Human Events* 27 (January 7, 1967): 1.
"A Close Look at the Peace Corps and Its Volunteers: An Interview with Sargent Shriver." *U.S. News and World Report* 56 (January 6, 1964): 38–41.
"Coming: a Subtle Shift in Dealing with the World [under President Johnson]." *U.S. News and World Report* 55 (December 9, 1963): 38–42.
"Congress Votes Lowest Foreign Aid Bill in 20 Years." *Congressional Quarterly Weekly Report* 25 (November 24, 1967): 2373–79.
"Controversy in Congress over U.S. Foreign Aid." *Congressional Digest* 44 (June/July 1965): 161–92.
Cooper, Chester L. "The CIA and Decision Making." *Foreign Affairs* 50 (January 1972): 223–36.
Crabb, Cecil V., Jr., and Pat M. Holt. *Invitation to Struggle: Congress, the President and Foreign Policy.* Washington, D.C.: Congressional Quarterly Press, 1980.
Craft, James Pressley, Jr. "The Role of Congress in the Determination of Naval Strategy in Support of United States Foreign Policy, 1956–1966." Philadelphia: University of Pennsylvania, 1969. Ph.D. dissertation. University Microfilms No. 70–16136.
"Current Controversy over U.S. Foreign Aid: Pro and Con." *Congressional Digest* 45 (August–September 1966): 193–224.
Cutler, Neal E. "Generational Succession as a Source of Foreign Policy Attitudes: A Cohort Analysis of American Opinion, 1946–1966." *Journal of Peace Research* (Norway) 7 (1970): 33–48.
Dallek, Robert. *The American Style of Foreign Policy: Cultural Politics and Foreign Affairs.* New York: Knopf, 1983.

FOREIGN POLICY—GENERAL

Deadline Data on World Affairs Editors. "United States Key Foreign Policy Issues—1964." *On Record*, vol. 2, no. 4/5 (1964): 1–148.

Destler, Irving McArthur. "Presidents and Bureaucrats: Organizing the Government for Foreign Policy." Princeton, N.J.: Princeton University, 1971. Ph.D. dissertation. University Microfilms No. 72–13739.

Duke, Paul. "The Foreign Aid Fiasco." *Reporter* 30 (January 16, 1964): 20–25.

"Foreign Policy: Same Goals, Sterner Style—President Johnson Moves at Once." *Business Week*, November 30, 1963: 31–32.

Foreign Policy Association. *Great Decisions, 1966* [regarding Vietnam, Israel, Western Europe, Africa, Russia, Japan, Latin America]. New York: Foreign Policy Assn., 1966.

Fulbright, J. William. "'The Arrogance of Power'—A Clash over U.S. Policy." *U.S. News and World Report* 60 (May 23, 1966): 113–21.

———. *The Crippled Giant: American Foreign Policy and Its Domestic Consequences*. New York: Random House, 1972.

———. *Meet the Press: Guest, Senator J. W. Fulbright, Chairman, Foreign Relations Committee* (Interview). Washington, D.C.: Merkle Press, vol. 9, no. 9, 1965.

———. *Meet the Press: Guest, Senator J. W. Fulbright, Chairman, Senate Foreign Relations Committee* (Interview). Washington, D.C.: Merkle Press, vol. 9, no. 37, 1965.

Galbraith, John Kenneth. "Plain Lessons of a Bad Decade." *Foreign Policy*, no. 1, Winter 1970–71: 31–45.

Gallois, Pierre M. "America's Getting Tough—And It's All to Our Good [Defense of LBJ's Foreign and Military Policy]." *Réalitiés* (Canada; English edition), November 1965: 33–37.

———. "U.S. Foreign Policy: A Study in Military Strength and Diplomatic Weakness." *Orbis* 9 (Summer 1965): 338–57.

Gardner, Lloyd C. *A Covenant with Power: America and World Order from Wilson to Reagan*. New York: Oxford University Press, 1984.

George, Alexander L., and Richard Smoke. *Deterrence in American Foreign Policy*. New York: Columbia University Press, 1974.

Gerberding, William P. "The Foreign Aid Controversy." *American Government Annual, 1964–1965*, pp. 44–68.

"The 'Get Rusk' Movement—Is It Aimed at LBJ?" *U.S. News and World Report* 63 (November 20, 1967): 51–52.

Goldberg, Arthur J. *Meet the Press: Guest, Ambassador Arthur J. Goldberg, United States Representative to the United Nations* (Interview). Washington, D.C.: Merkle Press, vol. 9, no. 34, 1965.

Goldwater, Barry M. "LBJ's 'Telephone Diplomacy'." *Human Events* 25 (February 13, 1965): 8.

———. "The President's Constitutional Primacy in Foreign Relations and National Defense." *Virginia Journal of International Law* 13 (Summer 1973): 463–89.

Graber, Doris A. *Public Opinion, the President, and Foreign Policy.* New York: Holt, Rinehart and Winston, 1968.

Grant, Donald. "Goldberg at the UN." *Progressive* 29 (November 1965): 47–52.

———. "The War against U Thant: Johnson and Rusk have Undertaken an Underground War against United Nations Secretary General because of His Stand on Viet Nam." *Progressive* 31 (March 1967): 19–22.

Hall, David Kent. "Implementing Multiple Advocacy in the National Security Council, 1947–1980." Stanford, Cal.: Stanford University, 1982. Ph.D. dissertation. University Microfilms No. 8220466.

Halper, Thomas. *Foreign Policy Crises: Appearance and Reality in Decision-Making.* Columbus, Ohio: Charles E. Merrill, 1971.

Hamilton, Harry. "The Senate Lets L.B.J. Down." *America* 115 (July 16, 1966): 56.

Hamilton, William Alexander. "The Influence of the American Military upon United States Foreign Policy, 1965–1968," Lincoln: University of Nebraska, 1978. Ph.D. dissertation. University Microfilms No. 79-00316.

Hero, Alfred O., Jr. "American Public Opinion versus Official U.S. Foreign Policy, 1936–68." *Public Opinion Quarterly* 34 (Fall 1970): 446–47.

Herring, George C., ed. *The Secret Diplomacy of the Vietnam War: The Negotiating Volumes of the Pentagon Papers.* Austin: University of Texas Press, 1983.

Hilsman, Roger. *The Politics of Policy Making in Defense and Foreign Affairs.* New York: Harper and Row, 1971.

———, and R. D. Good, eds. *Foreign Policy in the Sixties.* Baltimore: Johns Hopkins University Press, 1965.

Hinton, Harold C. "The United States and Its Two Chinas." *Johns Hopkins Magazine* 15 (June 1964): 4–7+.
Hoffman, Stanley. *Gulliver's Troubles, Or the Setting of American Foreign Policy.* New York: McGraw Hill, 1968.
Holsti, Ole R., and James N. Rosenau. *American Leadership in World Affairs: Vietnam and the Breakdown of Consensus.* Boston: Allen and Unwin, 1984.
Hoopes, Roy, ed. *The Peace Corps Experience.* Preface by Hubert H. Humphrey. New York: Clarkson N. Potter, Inc., 1968.
"House Permits Johnson's Full Foreign Aid Request." *Congressional Quarterly Weekly Report* 22 (June 12, 1964): 1173–76.
"How Helpful Are U.S. Allies? Mood Is to Let U.S. Do It." *U.S. News and World Report* 59 (September 13, 1965): 50–52.
"How Johnson Plans to Export His 'Great Society' Overseas." *Human Events* 25 (November 20, 1965): 7.
Humphrey, Hubert H. *The Cause Is Mankind: A Liberal Program for Modern America.* New York: Praeger, 1964.
Hyson, Charles D., and Alan M. Strout. "The Impact of Foreign Aid on U.S. Exports, 1960–1965." *Harvard Business Review* 46 (January/February 1968): 63–71.
Jewett, Robert. *The Captain America Complex: The Dilemmas of Zealous Nationalism.* Philadelphia: Westminster Press, 1973.
"Johnson Shows a Different Style: Foreign and Domestic Policies." *Business Week,* November 4, 1967: 27–29.
"Johnson Takes the Slow Road: No Radical Change in Either Domestic or Foreign Policy." *Business Week,* November 19, 1966: 37–38.
"Johnson Will Deal from Strength." *Business Week,* November 7, 1964: 142+.
Johnson, H. G. "United States Policy and the Problems of Developing Countries." *Journal of Business* 38 (October 1965): 337–43.
Kamath, P. M. *Executive Privilege versus Democratic Accountability: The Special Assistant to the President for National Security Affairs, 1961–1969.* New Delhi, India: Radiant Publishers, 1981.
Kattenburg, Paul M. "Viet Nam and U.S. Diplomacy, 1940–1970." *Orbis* 15 (Fall 1971): 818–41.

———. *The Vietnam Trauma in American Foreign Policy, 1945–1975*. New Brunswick, N.J.: Transaction Books, 1980.

Kauffman, Kenneth M., and Helena Stalson. "U.S. Assistance to Less Developed Countries." *Foreign Affairs* 45 (July 1967): 715–25.

Kaufman, Burton I. "Foreign Aid and the Balance-of-Payments Problem: Vietnam and Johnson's Foreign Economic Policy." *The Johnson Years, Volume Two: Vietnam, the Environment, and Science*, edited by Robert A. Divine, pp. 79–109. Lawrence: University Press of Kansas, 1987.

Kaufman, Frank L. "United States Developmental Foreign Aid: An Examination of the Needs of Under-Developed Nations as Represented in the Statements of the Policy-Makers [1949–1966]." Washington, D.C.: George Washington University, 1969. DBA dissertation. University Microfilms No. 69–07593.

Kissinger, Henry. *American Foreign Policy*. New York: Norton, 1969.

Kolko, Gabriel. *Anatomy of a War: Vietnam, the United States, and the Modern Historical Experience*. New York: Pantheon, 1986.

Lane, Thomas A., Gen. "Outer Space Treaty Jeopardizes U.S. Security." *Human Events* 27 (March 18, 1967): 7.

"LBJ Holds Secret Meeting on Foreign Aid." *Human Events* 23 (February 22, 1964): 3.

"LBJ's Foreign Policy: Mirror of the Man." *Business Week*, July 19, 1966: 38–40.

"LBJ's Policy of Aiding Unfriendly Nations Receives Bipartisan Congressional Blast." *Human Events* 25 (April 24, 1965): 13.

"LBJ's War on World Poverty." *Human Events* 24 (May 23, 1964): 1.

"The Legislative-Executive Foreign Policy Relationship in the 90th Congress." *Congressional Digest* 47 (October 1968): 225–51.

Lent, Henry B. *The Peace Corps: Ambassadors of Goodwill*. Philadelphia: Westminster Press, 1966.

Linowitz, Sol M. *The Making of a Public Man: A Memoir*. Boston: Little, Brown & Co., 1985.

Liska, George. *Imperial America: The International Politics of Primacy*. Baltimore: Johns Hopkins University Press, 1967.

Lloyd, Lewis E. "Big Factor in the Dollar Drain: The Foreign Aid Program." *Challenge* 12 (February 1964): 34–37.

McGuire, Edna. *The Peace Corps: Kindlers of the Spark.* New York: Macmillan, 1966.

Meyerhoff, Arthur E. *The Strategy of Persuasion: The Use of Advertising Skills in Fighting the Cold War.* New York: Coward-McCann, 1965.

Morse, Wayne. "American Foreign Policy and Vietnam." *North American Review* 4 (September 1967): 6–10.

"Nationalism: A Global Headache for Johnson." *Business Week*, January 4, 1964: 22–23.

"The New LBJ: A Tougher Line—Countries that Want American Friendship Are Expected to Earn It." *U.S. News and World Report* 58 (May 3, 1965): 29–33.

Niebuhr, Reinhold. "Roosevelt and Johnson: A Contrast in Foreign Policy." *New Leader* 48 (July 19, 1965): 5–8.

"Not the First nor the Last: President Johnson on the Eventful Week of Khrushchev's Downfall, Red China's Nuclear Blast, and Labor's Victory in Britain." *Business Week*, October 24, 1964: 29–30.

O'Brien, W. V. "International Law, Morality, and American Interventions." *Catholic World*, September 1965: 388–93.

Oliver, James K. "United States Foreign Policy Formulation and the Budgetary Process in the 1960s." Washington, D.C.: American University, 1970. Ph.D. dissertation. University Microfilms No. 71-8622.

Orekhov, F. T., et al. "U.S. Foreign Policy Today." *International Affairs* (Moscow), February 1968: 60–76.

Packenham, Robert A. "Political-Development Doctrines in American Foreign Aid Program." *World Politics* 18 (January 1966): 194–235.

Parmer, J. Norman, ed. "The Peace Corps." *Annals of the American Academy of Political and Social Science* 365 (February 1966): 1–146.

Phillips, Charles F. "Three Wars: Poverty, Civil Rights, and the Cold War." *Vital Speeches* 30 (October 1, 1964): 757–59.

Plischke, Elmer. "Lyndon Johnson as Diplomat-in-Chief." Paper presented at Fifth Annual Hofstra University Presidential Conference: Lyndon Baines Johnson, A Texan in Washington. Hempstead, New York, April 10–12, 1986.

Poole, Peter A. *Profiles in American Foreign Policy: Stimson,*

Kennan, Acheson, Dulles, Rusk, Kissinger, and Vance. Lanham, Md.: University Press of America, 1981.
Prados, John Frederick. *Presidents' Secret Wars: CIA and Pentagon Covert Operations since World War II.* New York: Morrow, 1986.
"President Cites New Trade Talks in Annual Report." *International Commerce* 74 (February 12, 1968): 5.
"The President Now Must Find the Answers: Johnson Has to Chart a Course for Vietnam, the Congo, UN, other Trouble Spots." *Business Week*, December 5, 1964: 29–30.
"President to Congress: World Economics." *International Commerce* 72 (February 7, 1966): 6.
Ranelagh, John. *The Agency: The Rise and Decline of the CIA, from Wild Bill Donovan to William Casey.* New York: Simon and Schuster, 1986.
Ranis, Gustav. "The Crisis in Foreign Aid." *Yale Review* 53 (June 1964): 522–32.
Rice, Gerard T. *The Bold Experiment: JFK's Peace Corps.* Notre Dame, Ind.: University of Notre Dame Press, 1985.
Roseman, Alvin. "Foreign Aid under Lyndon Johnson." In: "U.S. Foreign Aid: An Overview." *Current History* (Special Issue) 50 (June 1966): 321–66.
Rosenau, James N., ed. *Domestic Sources of Foreign Policy.* New York: Free Press, 1967.
Rostow, Walt W. "Domestic Determinants of U.S. Foreign Policy." *Armed Forces Journal* 27 (June 1970): 16A-17.
———. *View from the Seventh Floor* [U.S. Foreign Affairs Strategy]. New York: Harper, 1964.
Rubin, Barry. *Secrets of State: The State Department and the Struggle over U.S. Foreign Policy.* New York: Oxford University Press, 1985.
Rusk, Dean. "The Anatomy of Foreign Policy Decisions." *Military Review* 46 (July 1966): 73–81.
Schulzinger, Robert D. *American Diplomacy in the Twentieth Century.* New York: Oxford University Press, 1984.
Shelton, Willard. "It's Your Washington—President Johnson's Views on Foreign Policy." *AFL-CIO News* 8 (December 28, 1963): 5.
Shriver, Sargent. "A New Breed of American [Peace Corps Volunteers]." *Occupational Outlook Quarterly* 8 (February 1964): 1–4.

———, and Jack H. Vaughn. "Introductions." *The Complete Peace Corps Guide*, by Roy Hoopes. 3rd ed. New York: Dial Press, 1966.

Simon, Jeffrey D. "Public Opinion and American Foreign Policy, 1952–1972." Los Angeles: University of Southern California, 1978. Ph.D. dissertation.

Small, Melvin. "Public Opinion on Foreign Policy: The View from the Johnson and Nixon White Houses." *Politica*, vol. 16, no. 2 (1984): 184–200.

Smith, Myron J., Jr. *The Secret Wars. Vol. 2, Propaganda and Psychological Warfare, Covert Operations, 1945–1980* [A Bibliography]. Santa Barbara, Cal.: ABC-Clio, 1981.

Spanier, John, and Joseph Nogee, eds. *Congress, the Presidency and American Foreign Policy*. New York: Pergamon Press, 1981.

Stocking, Thomas E. "The Political Objectives of American Foreign Trade Policy, 1948–1973." Minneapolis: University of Minnesota, 1977. Ph.D. dissertation. University Microfilms No. 78-02719.

Taylor, George E., and Ben Cashman. *The New United Nations: A Reappraisal of United States Policies*. Washington, D.C.: American Enterprise Institute for Public Policy Research, 1965.

Taylor, Henry J. "Budget Hides Real Foreign Aid Figure." *Human Events* 27 (February 11, 1967): 1.

Thompson, Kenneth W. "The Johnson Presidency and Foreign Policy: The Unresolved Conflict between National Interest and Collective Security." Paper presented at Fifth Annual Hofstra University Presidential Conference: Lyndon Baines Johnson, A Texan in Washington. Hempstead, New York, April 10–12, 1986.

Toynbee, Arnold J. "The Failure of American Foreign Policy." *Fact* 2 (September-October 1965): 2–7.

"The 'Trigger-Happy' Charge and the U.S. Answer: Faultfinding Allies Are Sniping at U.S. [regarding Vietnam, Dominican Republic]." *U.S. News and World Report* 58 (June 29, 1965): 34–35.

Tucker, Robert W., et al. "Commentary: Experts Respond to the President's Foreign Policy Speech at Johns Hopkins." *Johns Hopkins Magazine* 15 (April 1965): 5+.

United States Peace Corps. *Peace Corps Factbook, 1967*. Washington, D.C.: U.S. Gov't. Printing Office, 1967.

———. *Peace Corps Factbook, 1968.* Washington, D.C.: U.S. Gov't. Printing Office, 1968.

Wallace, James N. "Five Years of the Peace Corps—A Progress Report." *U.S. News and World Report* 61 (July 18, 1966): 72–73.

Wallich, Henry C. "U.S. Aid Is Battered, But It's Here to Stay [as a Diplomatic Tool]." *Journal of Commerce and Commercial* 279 (February 6, 1964): 1+; (February 7, 1964): 13+.

Washburn, Michael A., and Willard H. Mitchell. *Walt Rostow, Vietnam, and Future Tasks of American Foreign Policy.* Princeton, N.J.: Center of International Studies, Woodrow Wilson School of Public and International Affairs, Princeton University, Policy Memorandum no. 33, September 1967.

"The Way U.S. Leaders Size Up the World Now: First-Hand Reports on How the President's Most Intimate Advisers Are Measuring the World's Key Areas." *U.S. News and World Report* 59 (November 15, 1965): 42–44.

Ways, Max. "What U.S. Foreign Policy Has Done Right." *Fortune* 77 (March 1968): 100–05.

"Where U.S. Is Winning in the World (Despite Criticism of LBJ's Policies)." *U.S. News and World Report* 61 (June 11, 1966): 48–51.

"Why Aid? Disenchantment about Aid to Developing Countries Presents a Challenge to President Johnson." *Economist* (Great Britain) 209 (November 1963): 885–86.

"Why the U.S. Is in Trouble in the World: Foreign Policy under Sharp Attack." *U.S. News and World Report* 58 (January 25, 1965): 48–53.

Wilcox, Francis O. *Congress, the Executive, and Foreign Policy.* New York: Harper and Row, 1971.

"The World's Size-Up of LBJ Now." *U.S. News and World Report* 59 (December 27, 1965): 26–29.

Yost, Charles W. *The Conduct and Misconduct of Foreign Affairs.* New York: Random House, 1972.

B. ASIA AND INDIA

"Aid to Red China?" *Human Events* 26 (February 12, 1966): 4.

Allen-Scott Report. "Johnson Tries 'Building Bridges' to the East." *Human Events* 27 (January 14, 1967): 16.

"America and Asia." *Far Eastern Economic Review* (Hong Kong) 45 (July 9, 1964): 55–57+.

"The 'Asian Doctrine': What It's All About: President Pledges a Permanent Military 'Shield', Plus Billions in Aid to Spur Regional Development." *U.S. News and World Report* 61 (August 8, 1966): 30–32.

Ayub, Khan. "The Pakistan-American Alliance: Stresses and Strains." *Foreign Affairs* 42 (January 1964): 195–209.

Ben, Philippe. "The Dead End of Nonalignment [African and Asian Attitude toward Vietnam and the Emerging Relationship between the U.S. and Communist China]." *Reporter* 32 (May 20, 1965): 19–22.

Braz, Rita. "Indo–U.S. Relations: 1965–1975." Boston: University of Massachusetts, 1982. Ph.D. dissertation. University Microfilms No. 8210300.

Chang, C. C. "The Impact of Phasing Out of U.S. Economic Aid on China's [Formosa's] Economy." *Bank of China Economic Review*, July/August 1964: 8–12.

Chang, Jim Park. "American Foreign Policy in Korea and Vietnam: Comparative Case Studies." *Review of Politics* 37 (January 1975): 20–47.

Clough, Ralph. *East Asia and U.S. Security.* Washington, D.C.: Brookings Institution, 1974.

Congressional Quarterly Service. *China and U.S. Far Eastern Policy, 1945–1967.* Washington, D.C.: Congressional Quarterly Service, October 1967.

Council on Foreign Relations. *The United States and China in World Affairs: The American Public's View of U.S. Policy toward China.* Ann Arbor: University of Michigan Survey Research Center, 1964.

Daswani, P. R. "Foreign Aid: Beneficial and Harmful Effects of American Aid to India." *Modern Review* (India) 120 (October 1966): 268–70.

Fleming, Denna Frank. "What Is Our Role in East Asia [Korea, Vietnam, China]." *Western Political Quarterly* 18 (March 1965): 73–86.

Goldstein, Martin E. *American Policy toward Laos.* Rutherford, N.J.: Fairleigh Dickinson University Press, 1973.

Gordon, Bernard K. "Thailand: Its Meaning for the U.S." *Current History* 52 (January 1967): 16–21, 53–54.

Goswami, P. K. *Ups and Downs of Indo-U.S. Relations, 1943–1983.* Columbia, Mo.: South Asia Books, 1984.

Greene, Fred. *U.S. Policy and the Security of Asia.* New York: McGraw-Hill, 1968.
Harrison, Selig S. *The Widening Gulf: Asian Nationalism and American Policy.* New York: Free Press, 1978.
Hasluck, Paul. "Vietnam and SEATO." *Current Notes on International Affairs* (Australia) 37 (May 1966): 257–60.
Hunter, Robert E., and Philip Windsor. "Vietnam and United States Policy in Asia." *International Affairs* (Great Britain) 44 (April 1968): 202–13.
Jain, R. K. *U.S.-South Asian Relations, 1947–1982.* 3 vols. Atlantic Highlands, N.J.: Humanities Press International, 1983.
"Johnson Builds Up Our Asian Allies . . . As Laos Fades." *Saturday Evening Post,* April 4, 1964: 34–34A.
"Johnson Pulls Aid Strings." *Far Eastern Economic Review* (Hong Kong) 43 (January 16, 1964): 99–101.
"Johnson Uses New Authority to Activate Reservists following Pueblo Incident." *Congressional Quarterly Weekly Report* 26 (February 2, 1968): 176–77.
Johnstone, William C. "United States Policy in Southern Asia." *Current History* 46 (February 1964): 65–70+.
Karnow, Stanley. "Up in Arms: Thailand and the U.S." *Far Eastern Economic Review* (Hong Kong) 58 (December 28, 1967): 583–85.
Kesavan, K. V. "The Vietnam War as an Issue in Japan's Relations with the United States." *International Studies* (India) 16 (October-December 1977): 501–20.
Kim Benedict Sang-Joon. *The United States and SEATO.* New Haven, Conn.: Yale University, 1964. Ph.D. dissertation.
Kirk, Russell. "Foreign Aid to Taiwan and Egypt." *Human Events* 25 (July 17, 1965): 8.
Kusnitz, Leonard A. *Public Opinion and Foreign Policy: America's China Policy, 1949–1979.* Westport, Conn.: Greenwood Press, 1984.
Lockwood, David E. "The U.S. Aid Program in Asia." *Current History* 49 (November 1965): 257–61+.
Lyon, Peter. "SEATO in Perspective." *Yearbook of World Affairs, 1965,* pp. 113–36. London: Stevens, 1965.
Marks, Thomas A. "Thai Security during the 'American Era', 1960–1976." *Issues and Studies* 15 (Spring 1979): 61–88.
Marshall, S. L. A., Charles Burton Marshall, and Robert Sandoz.

"The Pueblo Affair." *New Leader* 51 (February 12, 1968): 3-8.
Melby, John F. "The Philippines: A Unique Effort [U.S. Aid Program]." *Current History* 49 (November 1965): 278-83 +.
Mendel, Douglas H. "Japan Reviews Her American Alliance." *Public Opinion Quarterly* 30 (Spring 1966): 1-18.
"More on the Strange Story of the *Pueblo*." *U.S. News and World Report* 66 (February 10, 1969): 33-34.
Nairn, Ronald C. "SEATO: A Critique." *Pacific World Affairs* 41 (Spring 1968): 5-18.
"A New Worry for the U.S.—Trouble with an Old Ally [the Philippines]." *U.S. News and World Report* 57 (October 12, 1964): 77-79.
"Now a Bigger War Threat in Asia? Seizure of a U.S. Warship [*Pueblo*] by Koreans Sets Off a New Crisis." *U.S. News and World Report* 64 (February 5, 1968): 23-26.
Pace, Eric. "Laos: Continuing Crisis." *Foreign Affairs* 43 (October 1964): 64-74.
"Pacific Consensus: Johnson Doctrine for Asia." *Economist* (Great Britain) 221 (October 29, 1966): 445-46.
Palmer, Norman D. "India and Pakistan: The Major Recipients [of U.S. Aid]." *Current History* 49 (November 1965): 262-70+.
―――. *South Asia and United States Policy*. Boston: Houghton-Mifflin, 1966.
Park, Chang Jin. "American Foreign Policy in Korea and Vietnam: Comparative Case Studies." *Review of Politics* 37 (January 1975): 20-47.
Pollard, Vincent K. "ASA and ASEAN, 1961-1967: South-East Asia Regionalism." *Asian Survey* 10 (March 1970): 244-55.
―――. "Pacific Strategy." *Far Eastern Economic Review* (Hong Kong) 74 (October 9, 1971): 59.
"*Pueblo* Captain Tells His Story of Capture—and Captivity." *U.S. News and World Report* 66 (January 6, 1969): 30-31.
"*Pueblo* Surrender: Who Made the Mistakes?" *U.S. News and World Report* 66 (February 24, 1969): 58-59.
"The *Pueblo* Seizure." *U.S. News and World Report* 64 (February 12, 1968): 26.
Pyong Choon Hahm. "Korea's 'Mendicant Mentality'? A Critique of U.S. [Foreign and Economic] Policy." *Foreign Affairs* 43 (October 1964): 165-74.

Randolph, Raymond Sean. "Diplomacy and National Interest: Thai-American Security Cooperation in the Vietnam Era." Medford, Mass.: Fletcher School of Law and Diplomacy, Tufts University, 1978. Ph.D. dissertation.

——. "The Limits of Influence: American Aid to Thailand, 1965–1970." *Asian Affairs* 6 (March/April 1979): 243–63.

"Red China: Behind LBJ's Push for Long-Term Foreign Aid." *Human Events* 26 (July 2, 1966): 5.

Reday, Joesph Z., et al. "America and Asia: Annual Survey." *Far Eastern Economic Review* (Hong Kong) 49 (July 8, 1965): 57–61+.

Rusk, Dean, and Robert S. McNamara. *Meet the Press: Guests, Secretary of State Dean Rusk, Secretary of Defense Robert S. McNamara [Pueblo Incident] (Interviews)*. Washington, D.C.: Merkle Press, vol. 12, no. 5, 1968.

Sato, Eisaku. "Japan, the U.S., and the War in South Vietnam: An Interview with Japan's New Prime Minister, Eisaku Sato." *U.S. News and World Report* 58 (January 11, 1965): 42–43.

Scalapino, Robert. "The New Asia and U.S.-Japan Relations." *University of Missouri Business and Government Review* 7 (September/October 1966): 30–38.

Schlesinger, Arthur M., Jr., ed. *The Dynamics of World Power*. Vol. 4: *The Far East*. New York: McGraw-Hill, 1973.

Scott, Paul. "LBJ Withholds Full 'Pueblo' Report." *Human Events* 28 (February 17, 1968): 1.

——. "'Pueblo' Seizure: Provocation for 2nd Front in Korea?" *Human Events* 28 (April 13, 1968): 6.

——. "Trial of 'Pueblo' Crew Likely in North Korea: Administration Split on Paying Ransom." *Human Events* 28 (March 23, 1968): 1.

Shee Poon-Kim. "A Decade of ASEAN, 1967–1977." *Asian Survey* 17 (August 1977): 753–70.

Starner, Frances L. "LBJ's Doctrine for Asia." *Far Eastern Economic Review* (Hong Kong) 53 (September 29, 1966): 635–37.

——. "Reluctant Partnership [U.S.-Philippines]." *Far Eastern Economic Review* (Hong Kong) 47 (February 25, 1965): 326–28.

Stevenson, Charles A. *The End of Nowhere: American Policy toward Laos since 1954*. Boston: Beacon, 1972.

"The Strange Tale of the *Pueblo*." *U.S. News and World Report* 66 (February 3, 1969): 50–51.

"A Success for the U.S.: The Story in Non-Communist Asia." *U.S. News and World Report* 62 (May 8, 1967): 38–40.

Thompson, W. Scott. *Unequal Partners: Philippine and Thai Relations with the United States, 1965–1975.* Lexington, Mass.: Heath, 1975.

"Threat of New War and Trouble with an Ally: Why LBJ Went to Hawaii [*Pueblo* Incident]." *U.S. News and World Report* 64 (April 29, 1968): 26–27.

Toru Yano. "Sarit and Thailand's 'Pro-American Policy'." *Developing Economics* 6 (September 1968): 284–99.

Trager, Frank N. "American Foreign Policy in Southeast Asia." In *Studies on Asia, 1965*, pp. 17–59.

———. "The United States and Pakistan: A Failure of Diplomacy." *Orbis* 9 (Fall 1965): 613–29.

"Trouble in Korea: More Light on the *Pueblo*." *U.S. News and World Report* 64 (February 19, 1968): 44.

"[U.S.] Aid that Works: South Korea and Formosa." *Economist* (Great Britain) 222 (February 11, 1967): 508+.

"U.S. and the Philippines—Drawing Closer?" *U.S. News and World Report* 60 (April 4, 1966): 84–85.

Viksnins, George J. "United States Military Spending and the Economy of Thailand, 1967–1972." *Asian Survey* 13 (May 1973): 441–57.

Wallace, Paul. "U.S. Foreign Policy and Asia." *University of Missouri Business and Government Review* 7 (March/April 1966): 5–13.

Whiting, Allen S. "How We Almost Went to War with China [1964–1967]." *Look* 33 (April 29, 1969): 76–79.

"Why Russia and China Now Fear U.S. [Nuclear Arsenals Compared]." *U.S. News and World Report* 57 (November 30, 1964): 66–70.

Wilson, Dick. "Reluctant Donors: U.S. Aid to Asia." *Far Eastern Economic Review* (Hong Kong) 59 (January 25, 1968): 152+.

Yim, Kwan H., ed. *China and the United States, Nineteen Sixty-four to Nineteen Seventy-two.* Ann Arbor, Mich.: Books on Demand, UMI, n.d.

C. EUROPE AND THE SOVIET UNION

"Adenauer Talks about Johnson: Exclusive Interview with the Former Chancellor of West Germany." *U.S. News and World Report* 55 (December 16, 1963): 44–47.

"Administration Policies Help Increase Trade with Russia, Cuba." *Human Events* 24 (December 26, 1964): 3.

"Agreement between the U.S. and U.S.S.R. on Exchanges in the Scientific, Technical, Educational, Cultural and Other Fields in 1964–1965." *International Legal Materials* 3 (March 1964): 339–55.

Armstrong, John A. "The Soviet-American Confrontation: A New Stage?" *Russian Review* 23 (April 1964): 97–115.

Aron, Raymond. "Europe and the United States." *Commentary* 38 (August 1964): 54–60.

"At the Summit and After [President Johnson Meets with Premier Kosygin]." *U.S. News and World Report* 63 (July 3, 1967): 29–31.

Atkins, Thomas. "Rebuilding the Bridge to Poland." *Reporter* 32 (February 25, 1965): 39–41.

"Back from the Brink: Middle East Fighting Cemented A Tacit Understanding that Neither U.S. or Soviet Union Will Let Such a Crisis Provoke It to a Nuclear War." *Business Week*, June 10, 1967: 35–36.

"Basic U.S. Foreign Policy Commitments and the Question of Reduction of U.S. Troops in Europe: Pro and Con." *Congressional Digest* 45 (October 1966): 222–56.

Baylis, John. *Anglo-American Defense Relations, 1939–1979: The Special Relationship*. New York: St. Martin's Press, 1981.

Brown, John A., Jr. "De Gaulle's France: Is It Really against U.S.?" *Freedom and Union* 21 (January 1966): 12–15.

"Cabinet-Level Trips to Moscow Part of 'Bridge-Building' Plans." *Human Events* 27 (March 18, 1967): 13.

Caldwell, Dan. *American-Soviet Relations: From Nineteen Forty-seven to the Nixon-Kissinger Grand Design*. Westport, Conn.: Greenwood Press, 1981.

Campbell, John C. "Soviet-American Relations [in the 1960s]: Conflict and Cooperation." *Current History* 53 (October 1967): 193–202+.

Cerny, P. G. "The Fall of Two Presidents and Extraparliamen-

tary Opposition: France and the United States in 1968." *Government and Opposition* 5 (Summer 1970): 287–306.
Church, Frank. *Meet the Press: Guest, Senator Frank Church* [Senate Foreign Relations Committee European Fact-Finding Tour] (Interview). Washington, D.C.: Merkle Press, vol. 10, no. 20, 1966.
Collins, John M. *U.S.-Soviet Military Balance: Concepts and Capabilities, 1960–1980*. New York: Aviation Week, 1980.
Dallin, Alexander. "Moscow and Vietnam: Hazards of U.S. Policy." *New Leader* 48 (May 10, 1965): 5–8.
De Toledano, Ralph. "LBJ's Aid-to-Soviets Policy." *Human Events* 25 (September 18, 1965): 7.
Dobriansky, Lev E. "Review of U.S. Policy toward the USSR: A Major Theme for the 1967 Captive Nations Week." *Ukrainian Quarterly* 23 (Spring 1967): 27–42.
"Down from the [U.S.-Soviet] Summit: Johnson Gains Some More Political Kudos." *Business Week*, July 1, 1967: 13–15.
Etzioni, Amitai. "Beyond the Arms Race: Despite Current Détente, the Arms Spiral Continues Upward." *Columbia University Forum* 7 (Spring 1964): 4–11.
"Europe's New Mood—Its Meaning for U.S.: Changing Relationship between U.S. and Europe." *U.S. News and World Report* 60 (June 20, 1966): 39–41.
Fergusson, A. "Wilson and Johnson: Project Europe." *Statist* 190 (August 5, 1966): 335–36.
"First [Soviet] Reactions to Johnson's [April 7, 1965] Speech on Vietnam." *Current Digest of the Soviet Press* 17 (April 28, 1965): 12–13.
"From LBJ to NSK: The NATO Mixed-Manned Nuclear Force." *Economist* (Great Britain) 212 (August 8, 1964): 534–35.
Herken, Gregg F. *Counsels of War* [Atomic Diplomacy and Soviet-American Relations from Truman to Reagan]. New York: Knopf, 1984.
"How U.S. Taps Soviet Missile Secrets." *Aviation Week and Space Technology* 67 (October 1967): 26–27.
Hudson, Richard. "A Warning from Moscow [Russian vs. American Interests in Asia]." *War/Peace Report* 5 (June 1965): 3–7.
Humphrey, Hubert H. "Humphrey Reports on Europe Mission." *Editor and Publisher* 100 (April 29, 1967): 96.

"Humphrey in Europe: Salute the Warrior." *Statist* 191 (April 14, 1967): 751–52.

Ilgen, Thomas L. *Autonomy and Interdependence: U.S.-Western European Monetary and Trade Relations, 1958–1984.* Totowa, N.J.: Rowman, 1985.

"Is It to Be a Truce with Russia? A Far Different Cold War Is Now Taking Place." *U.S. News and World Report* 56 (May 4, 1964): 35–37.

Isaacson, Walter, and Evan Thomas. *The Wise Men: Six Friends and the World They Made.* New York: Simon and Schuster, 1986.

"Johnson Over Elbe [Eastern Europe Trip]." *Economist* (Great Britain) 211 (May 30, 1964): 924–26.

"Johnson's Bunch of Carrots Dangling before Russia's Leaders." *Statist* 190 (October 14, 1966): 901.

"Johnson's Choice: General de Gaulle's Latest Declaration Points to a Balkanized Europe." *Economist* (Great Britain) 216 (September 18, 1965): 1074–75.

Korbonski, Andrzej. "U.S. Policy in East Europe." *Current History* 48 (March 1965): 129–34+.

Kozar, Paul Michael. "The Politics of Deterrence: A Comparative Assessment of American and Soviet Defense Policy, 1960–1984." Washington, D.C.: Georgetown University, 1984. Ph.D. dissertation.

"LBJ and Disarmament." *Human Events* 24 (May 2, 1964): 4.

"LBJ Doesn't Want to 'Antagonize' the Russians." *Human Events* 26 (January 29, 1966): 1.

"LBJ Has Trouble Lowering Red Trade Barriers." *Human Events* 26 (March 5, 1966): 11.

"LBJ Lets Great Britain Trade with North Vietnam." *Human Events* 25 (March 13, 1965): 10.

"LBJ Quietly Pushes Gimmick to Finance Increased Red Trade." *Human Events* 27 (April 1, 1967): 11.

"LBJ Splits with (German Chancellor) Erhard." *Human Events* 24 (July 4, 1964): 5.

"Life with LBJ [U.S.-British Relations]." *Economist* (Great Britain) 215 (May 22, 1965): 883–84.

Louis, William Roger, and Hedley Bull, eds. *The Special Relationship: Anglo-American Relations since 1945.* London: Oxford University Press, 1986.

Mares, Vaclav E. "U.S. Aid to East Europe." *Current History* 51 (July 1966): 36–44.

Markovich, Stephen C. "The Influence of American Foreign Aid on Yugoslav Policies, 1948–1966." Charlottesville: University of Virginia, 1968. Ph.D. dissertation. University Microfilms No. 68-18221.

McNamara, Robert S. "Is Russia Slowing Down in the Arms Race? An Interview with the Defense Secretary." *U.S. News and World Report* 58 (April 12, 1965): 52–56.

———. "The Long Road to Reykjavík [Glassboro Summit Conference of 1967]." *Time* 128 (October 20, 1986): 34–35.

Meyer, Karl E. "End of 'Atlantic Partnership'?" *New Leader* 48 (January 18, 1965): 16–17.

Miller, Mark Emory. "The Interplay of Politics and Economics in the U.S.-U.S.S.R. Relationship, 1969–1976." Coral Gables, Fla.: University of Miami, 1978. Ph.D. dissertation. University Microfilms No. 7818725.

"The Moon Treaty with the Soviets." *Human Events* 26 (June 25, 1966): 13.

Mosely, Philip E. "Present Trends in U.S.-Soviet Relations." *International Studies* (India) 6 (October 1964): 117–32.

"New President's Message [Soviet Views on LBJ's 1965 State of Union Message]." *Current Digest of the Soviet Press* 17 (January 27, 1965): 17–18.

"New Strains on Old Alliance: U.S.-British Summit Meeting [between President Johnson and Prime Minister Sir Alec Douglas-Home]." *U.S. News and World Report* 56 (February 24, 1964): 42.

"90th Congress in Early Fight over [U.S.-Soviet] Consular Treaty." *Congressional Quarterly Weekly Report* 25 (February 10, 1967): 205–06+.

"Now at Washington: What [British Prime Minister Harold] Wilson Should Tell LBJ." *Statist* 190 (July 22, 1966): 210.

"Over to Washington: The Cyprus Crisis." *Economist* (Great Britain) 211 (June 20, 1964): 1343.

Prados, John Frederick. "Analysis, Organizations and Politics: The Case of National Intelligence Estimates on Soviet Strategic Forces, 1945–1975." New York: Columbia University, 1982. Ph.D. dissertation. University Microfilms No. 84-06536.

Richman, Alvin. "The Changing American Image of the Soviet Union [1940–1965]." Philadelphia: University of Pennsylvania, 1968. Ph.D. dissertation. University Microfilms No. 69-05660.

Roubatis, Yiannis P. "The United States Involvement in the Army and Politics of Greece, 1946–1967." Baltimore: Johns Hopkins University, 1981. Ph.D. dissertation. University Microfilms No. 81–16125.

"Running Scared: Khrushchev's Foreign Policy If Goldwater Is Elected." *Economist* (Great Britain) 212 (July 25, 1964): 344.

"Rusk Pushes Nuclear Accord in Talks with Gromyko." *Human.Events* 25 (October 23, 1965): 11.

Schiff, Martin. "The United States and Sweden: A Troubled Relationship. *American Scandinavian Review*, vol. 61, no. 4 (1973): 367–72.

Schlesinger, Arthur M., Jr., ed. *The Dynamics of World Power*. Vol. 1: *Western Europe*. Vol 2: *Eastern Europe and the Soviet Union*. New York: McGraw-Hill, 1973.

Scott, Paul. "LBJ Has Begun Secret Correspondence with Kosygin." *Human Events* 28 (June 29, 1968): 12.

———. "LBJ Places Curb on Spying on Soviets." *Human Events* 28 (November 30, 1968): 11.

———. "Lyndon B. Johnson and Espionage on Russia." *Human Events* 28 (November 30, 1968): 11.

"Secret Rusk-Gromyko Accord Explains Viet Nam Sanctuary." *Human Events* 27 (October 28, 1967): 1.

Stevens, Francis B. "Is a 'Deal' with Russia Stirring? Despite Vietnam, There's a Noticeable Thaw in the Diplomatic Climate between U.S. and Russia." *U.S. News and World Report* 61 (November 7, 1966): 46–49.

Stromseth, Jane. "The Conventional Defense of Western Europe: Lessons from the 1960s." *Reassessing Arms Control*, edited by David Carlton and Carlo Schaerf, pp. 193–206. London: Macmillan Press LTD, 1985.

"Summitry in Spring? A Johnson-Khrushchev Meeting Seems Probable." *Economist* (Great Britain) 213 (October 3, 1964): 19–20.

Talbot, Ross B. *The Chicken War: An International Trade Conflict between the United States and the European Economic Community, 1961–1964*. Ames: Iowa State University Press, 1978.

Taylor, Henry J. "LBJ's 'Unconscionable Hoax' on Nuclear Weapons to NATO." *Human Events* 24 (October 24, 1964): 1.

———. "Now Is No Time for a Summit Meeting: LBJ Should

Resist Temptation." *Human Events* 29 (January 11, 1969): 14.
"To Russia with Love: Rostow." *Human Events* 27 (March 11, 1967): 3.
Weeks, Stanley B. "United States Defense Policy toward Spain, 1950–1976." Washington, D.C.: American University, 1977. Ph.D. dissertation. University Microfilms No. 77-27445.
Weihmiller, Gordon R. *U.S.-Soviet Summits: An Account of East-West Diplomacy at the Top, 1955–1985.* Lanham, Md.: University Press of America, 1986.
Whalen, Richard J. "The Shifting Equation of Nuclear Defense: A Swift Soviet Buildup Is Forcing the U.S. to New Decisions." *Fortune* 75 (June 1, 1967): 84–87+.
"What's LBJ Now Offering the Russians." *Human Events* 26 (October 8, 1966): 1.
"What's Really Going On Between U.S. and Russia." *U.S. News and World Report* 62 (March 27, 1967): 46–50.
"Where U.S. Patience Is Getting Thin: Europe." *U.S. News and World Report* 58 (April 5, 1965): 50–53.
"Why Russia and China Now Fear U.S. [Nuclear Arsenals Compared]." *U.S. News and World Report* 57 (November 30, 1964): 66–70.
"Why the Vietnam War Worries U.S. Allies." *U.S. News and World Report* 60 (June 13, 1966): 38–39.
"The Whys of a Treaty with the Russians [Consular Treaty]." *U.S. News and World Report* 62 (March 13, 1967): 51–52.
Wicker, Tom. "Lyndon 'N' Ludwig [West German Chancellor Erhard]." *Texas, Our Texas: 150 Moments that Made Us the Way We Are.* Texas Monthly Magazine Editors, p. 50. Austin: Texas Monthly Press, 1986.
"Will U.S. Liberals Ever Learn? [Soviet Seizure of Czechoslovakia]." *Human Events* 28 (August 31, 1968): 1.

D. LATIN AMERICA AND THE CARIBBEAN

"Administration Policies Help Increase Trade with Russia, Cuba." *Human Events* 24 (December 26, 1964): 3.
"Alliance for Progress: How It Looks after Five Years." *U.S. News and World Report* 61 (August 29, 1966): 66–69.
Augelli, J. P. "Dominican Republic." *Focus*, May 1965: 1–6.

Baver, Sherrie Lynn. "Policy-Making for Industrialization in Puerto Rico, 1947–1976." New York: Columbia University, 1979. Ph.D. dissertation. University Microfilms No. 80-09679.

Berle, Adolf A. "A Stich in Time [U.S. Intervention in Dominican Republic]." *Reporter* 32 (May 20, 1965): 22–23.

Bhana, Surendra. *The United States and the Development of the Puerto Rican Status Question, 1936–1968.* Lawrence: University Press of Kansas, 1975.

Bielenberg, Douglas Georg. "The Dominican Crisis, 1965: Imperialism or Benign Intervention?" Boca Raton, Fla.: Florida Atlantic University, 1974. M.A. thesis. University Microfilms No. M-5791.

Black, Jan K. *The Dominican Republic: Politics and Development in an Unsovereign State.* Winchester, Mass.: Allen & Unwin, 1986.

Blasier, Cole. *The Hovering Giant: U.S. Responses to Revolutionary Change in Latin America, 1910–1985.* Rev. ed. Pittsburgh: University of Pittsburgh Press, Pittsburgh Latin America Series, 1985.

Bosch, Juan. "A Tale of Two Nations: Dominican-American Diplomacy." *New Leader* 48 (June 21, 1965): 3–7.

"Brazil, Latin America and the United States." *Monthly Review* 16 (June 1964): 65–84.

Brennan, Paul Edward. "The War-Making Powers of the American President as Commander-in-Chief of the Armed Forces." Fullerton: California State College, 1968. M.A. thesis. University Microfilms No. M-1537.

"Bundy Group Using U.S. Aid to Pressure Dubious Coalition in Dominican Republic." *Human Events* 25 (June 5, 1965): 6.

"Can LBJ Help Latin America Solve Its Problems?" *U.S. News and World Report* 55 (December 30, 1963): 32–33.

"Castro's Turn Next?" *U.S. News and World Report* 58 (May 17, 1965): 44–47.

Chamberlain, John. "The Cuban Issue and LBJ." *Human Events* 23 (January 4, 1964): 10.

Davis, Saville. "Patterns and Problems in U.S. Foreign Policy [Vietnam, Dominican Republic, and Post World War II Attitudes]." *International Affairs* (Great Britain) 41 (October 1965): 624–36.

De Toledano, Ralph. "The Real Story of the Dominican Crisis." *Human Events* 25 (May 15, 1965): 1.

"Degrees for Two Presidents—and a Degree of Accord [U.S. and Mexico]." *Life,* March 6, 1964: 45.
"Dominican Puzzle: Reds Halted, But How to Win the Peace?" *U.S. News and World Report* 58 (May 24, 1965): 37–39.
"Dominican Republic: [U.N. Security] Council Considers Situation." *United Nations Monthly Chronicle* 2 (July 1965): 3–11.
Draper, Theodore. "The American Crisis: Vietnam, Cuba and the Dominican Republic." *Commentary* 43 (January 1967): 27–43.
———. "The Dominican Crisis: A Case Study in American Policy." *Commentary* 40 (December 1965): 33–68.
———. "The New Dominican Crisis." *New Leader* 49 (January 31, 1966): 3–8.
Farnsworth, David, and James McKenney. *U.S.-Panama Relations, 1903–1978: A Study in Linkage Politics.* Boulder, Col.: Westview Press, 1983.
Firfer, Alexander. "U.S. Aid while Bullets Fly—The Real Dominican Story." *U.S. News and World Report* 59 (July 19, 1965): 48–50.
Garrett, William Bruce. "Arms Transfers, Congress, and Foreign Policy: The Case of Latin America, 1967–1976." Baltimore: Johns Hopkins University, 1982. Ph.D. dissertation. University Microfilms No. 8219542.
Geyelin, Philip. "The Irksome Panama Wrangle." *Reporter* 30 (April 9, 1964): 14–17.
Gonionsky, S. "Post-Kennedy U.S. Policy in Latin America." *New Times* (Moscow), June 24, 1964: 8–11.
Gordon, Lincoln. "Punta del Este Revisited [Review of Alliance for Progress]." *Foreign Affairs* 45 (July 1967): 624–38.
Halper, Sam. "The Dominican Upheaval: A Revolution Delayed." *New Leader* 48 (May 10, 1965): 3–4.
Handleman, Howard. "And Now—What Next in Santo Domingo?" *U.S. News and World Report* 58 (June 7, 1965): 41.
———. "Another U.S. Problem That Just Will Not Go Away [Dominican Republic]." *U.S. News and World Report* 60 (February 28, 1966): 52+.
Hanson, Simon G. "The Alliance for Progress: The Fourth Year." *Inter-American Economic Affairs* 20 (Autumn 1966): 3–96.
———. "The Alliance for Progress: The Third Year." *Inter-American Economic Affairs* 18 (Spring 1965): 3–112.

Hill, Robert C. "U.S. Policy toward Latin America." *Orbis* 10 (Summer 1966): 390–407.
Humphrey, Hubert H. "U.S. Policy in Latin America." *Foreign Affairs* 42 (July 1964): 585–601.
"Johnson's Men: Brazilian Stand on American Intervention in Dominican Republic." *Economist* (Great Britain), 215 (June 5, 1965): 1138.
Jorden, William J. *Panama Odyssey*. Austin: University of Texas Press, 1984.
Kaplan, Stephen S. "U.S. Arms Transfers to Latin America, 1945–1974: Rational Strategy, Bureaucratic Politics, and Executive Parameters." *International Studies Quarterly* 19 (1975): 399–431.
Kelso, Quinten Allen. "The Dominican Crisis of 1965: A New Appraisal." Boulder: University of Colorado, 1982. Ph.D. dissertation. University Microfilms No. 8221093.
Kilpatrick, James Jackson. "Johnson Is Playing a Losing Game in Latin America." *Human Events* 25 (October 16, 1965): 8.
Kirk, Russell. "Rusk Seeks the Impossible in Santo Domingo." *Human Events* 25 (June 19, 1965): 6.
LaFeber, Walter. *Inevitable Revolutions: The United States in Central America*. Expanded ed. New York: Norton, 1984.
Langley, Lester D. *The United States and the Caribbean in the Twentieth Century*. Rev. ed. Athens: University of Georgia Press, 1985.
Laurence, Edward J. "Arms Transfers and Influence in Latin America: 1961–1973." Paper presented at the Annual Meeting of the International Studies Assn., Toronto, Canada, February 25–29, 1976.
Listov, Vadim. "Report on Dominica: Big Stick against a Small Nation." *New Times* (Moscow), May 17, 1965: 8–11.
Luan-Miller, Patricia D. "U.S. Direct Involvement in Mexico, 1876–1978: An Historical, Theoretical and Empirical Analysis." Austin: University of Texas, 1980. Ph.D. dissertation. University Microfilms No. 81-00932.
Martinez, Julio Cesar, et al. "Revolution and Counter Revolution in the Dominican Republic." *New Politics* 4 (Spring 1965): 47–77.
McVittie. W. W. "The Rough Road to Santo Domingo." *Venture* 17 (September 1965): 10–14.
Montalva, Eduardo Frei. "The Alliance That Lost Its Way [Alliance for Progress]." *Foreign Affairs* 45 (April 1967): 437–48.

Niemeyer, E. V., Jr. "Personal Diplomacy: Lyndon B. Johnson and Mexico, 1963–1968." *Southwestern Historical Quarterly* 90 (October 1986): 159–87.

"Panama: Security Council Takes Up Complaint against the United States on January 10, 1964." *United Nations Review* 11 (February 1964): 6–8.

"Panama—No U.S. Backdown." *U.S. News and World Report* 56 (January 27, 1964): 29–31.

"Panama Is First Big Test: Johnson Must Make Some Concessions, Yet Watch Out for 'Appeaser' Charge." *Business Week*, January 18, 1964: 23–25.

Rabe, Stephen G. "The Johnson (Eisenhower?) Doctrine for Latin America." *Diplomatic History* 9 (Winter 1985): 95–100.

Riga, Peter. "The Alliance for Progress: An Appraisal." *World Justice* (Belgium) 6 (March 1966): 296–316.

Rodman, Selden. "A Close View of Santo Domingo." *Reporter* 33 (July 15, 1965): 20–27.

Ruddy, T. Michael. *The Cautious Diplomat: Charles E. Bohlen and the Soviet Union, 1929–1969.* Kent, Ohio: Kent State University Press, 1986.

"Safety First in the Caribbean: The First Rule of Self-Defense Is to Hit First—But Whom Have the Americans Hit?" *Economist* (Great Britain) 215 (May 8, 1965): 617–18, 625–26.

Schlesinger, Arthur M., Jr., ed. *The Dynamics of World Power.* Vol. 3: *Latin America.* New York: McGraw-Hill, 1973.

Schmitt, Karl M. *Mexico and the United States, 1821–1973: Conflict and Coexistence.* New York, 1974.

Schneider, Ronald M. "U.S. Policy in Latin America." *Current History* 51 (November 1966): 257–63.

Sclanders, Ian. "The Backwater War That Could Shake the World [Dominican Republic]." *MacLean's* (Canada) 78 (July 24, 1965): 20–21+.

Scranton, Margaret E. "Senate Versus the Executive: The 1967 [American Republics] Summit at Punta Del Este and An Early Lesson of Vietnam." Paper presented at the annual meeting of the Southern Political Science Assn., Nashville, Tenn., November 17–19, 1985.

"Summit Meeting Reviews Alliance's First Six Years [Alliance for Progress]." *Congressional Quarterly Weekly Report* 25 (April 14, 1967): 594–99.

Tarango, Jose R. "The Chamizal Dispute [History of U.S.-

Mexican Boundary Dispute at El Paso, Texas]." *The Junior Historian of the Texas State Historical Association* 29 (March 1969): 20–23.
Taylor, Henry J. "Brazil Should Provide Foreign Policy Bright Spot." *Human Events* 27 (January 14, 1967): 5.
"U.S.-Panama Pact: Double Gain." *Business Week*, October 2, 1965: 29.
"U.S. Policy toward Communist Activities in Latin America: Pro and Con." *Congressional Digest* 44 (November 1965): 257–88.
"U.S. Steps into Another Hornet's Nest: Sending Troops to Santo Domingo." *Business Week*, May 8, 1965: 28–29.
"U.S. Tries Armed Force and Persuasive Power in Dominican Republic and Vietnam." *Business Week*, May 22, 1965: 26.
Van Cleve, John V. "The Political Use of Military Aid: The United States and the Latin American, 1945–1965." Irvine: University of California, 1976. Ph.D. dissertation. University Microfilms No. 76–29268.
Veliz, Claudio. "Crisis in Panama." *World Today* 20 (February 1964): 77–83.
Walterhouse, Harry F. "Good Neighbors in Uniform [Civic Action Programs and U.S. Armed Forces in Latin America." *Military Review* 45 (February 1965): 10–18.
"What the Squabble in Panama Is All About: Interview with Rep. Armistead I. Selden, Jr., Chairman of the House Subcommittee on Inter-American Affairs." *U.S. News and World Report* 56 (January 27, 1964): 34–37.
"Who Incited Riot in Panama: Findings of International Commission of Jurists Clears U.S. of Charges of Aggression." *U.S. News and World Report* 56 (June 22, 1964): 37.
Wilgus, A. Curtis, ed. *The Caribbean: Current United States Relations*. Gainsville: University of Florida Press, Series One, Vol. XVI, 1966.
Wilson, Larman C. "The Monroe Doctrine, Cold War Anachronism: Cuba and the Dominican Republic." *Journal of Politics* 28 (May 1966): 322–46.
———. "The United States Dominican Intervention of 1965: Illicit or Licit Exercise of Force?" Paper prepared for the Institute of World Policy, Georgetown University, Washington, D.C., 1966.
———. "U.S. Military Assistance to the Dominican Republic,

1916–1967." Paper presented at the Center for International Affairs, Harvard University, April 26, 1967.

"The World Isn't Waiting: Critical Foreign Issues Are Crowding in on President Johnson [Panama Crisis]." *Business Week*, February 22, 1964: 23–25.

E. THE MIDDLE EAST AND AFRICA

Ables, Gisela Renate. "Foreign Policy and Domestic Politics: Lyndon Baines Johnson's View of the Middle East." Houston: University of Houston, 1984. M.A. thesis. University Microfilms No. 1324035.

Alexander, Yonah, and Allan Nanes, eds. *The United States and Iran: A Documentary History*. Lanham, Md.: University Press of America, 1980.

"All Sell All Round: Johnson's Recipe for the Middle East." *Jewish Observer—Middle East Review* 13 (March 27, 1964): 4.

Badeau, John S. "U.S.A. and U.A.R. [United Arab Republic]: A Crisis in Confidence." *Foreign Affairs* 43 (January 1965): 281–96.

Bard, Mitchell. "Domestic Policies and the 1968 Phantom Jet Sale: Explaining the Evolution of the U.S.-Israel Alliance." Paper prepared for 1987 Annual Meeting of Western Political Science Assn., Anaheim, California, March 26–28, 1987.

Ben-Horin, Eliahu. "Cairo Aftermath: 'Johnson the Jew'; Arab Reaction to President Johnson's Speech." *Reconstructionist* 30 (February 21, 1964): 28–30.

Bill, James Alban. *U.S.-Arab Relations: The Iranian Dimension*. Washington, D.C.: National Council on U.S.-Arab Relations, 1984.

———, and Robert W. Stookey. *Politics and Petroleum: The Middle East and the United States*. Brunswick, Ohio: King's Court Communications, 1975.

Burns, William J. *Economic Aid and American Policy toward Egypt, 1955–1981*. Albany: State University of New York Press, 1984.

Chester, Edward W. *U.S. Oil Policy and Diplomacy: A 20th Century Overview*. Westport, Conn.: Greenwood Press, 1983.

"Controversy over Present U.S. Policy toward Rhodesia: Pros and Cons." *Congressional Digest* 46 (March 1967): 65–96.
Dickson, David. *U.S. Foreign Policy towards Sub-Saharan Africa: Change, Continuity, and Restraint.* American Values Projected Abroad Series, vol. 18. Lanham, Md.: University Press of America, 1985.
Druks, Herbert J. *The U.S. and Israel, Nineteen Forty-five to Nineteen Eighty-five.* New York: Robert Speller and Sons, 1986.
Duignan, Peter, and Lewis H. Gann. *The United States and Africa: A History.* New York: Cambridge University Press, 1984.
Emerson, Rupert. *Africa and the United States' Policy* [Truman to Johnson]. Englewood Cliffs, N.J.: Prentice-Hall, 1967.
Findley, Paul. *They Dare to Speak Out: People and Institutions Confront Israel's Lobby.* Westport, Conn.: Lawrence Hill & Co., 1984.
Gan, Andrew Carter. "Johnson and the Six Day War." Course Paper, Professor Robert A. Divine, University of Texas at Austin, February 2, 1982 [c/o LBJ Library]."
Green, Stephen. *Taking Sides: America's Secret Relations with a Militant Israel.* New York: Morrow, 1984.
Herz, Martin F. *A View from Tehran: A Diplomatist Looks at the Shah's Regime in June, 1964.* Lanham, Md.: University Press of America, 1985.
Hoskins, Halford L. "The U.S. in the Middle East: Policy in Transition." *Current History* 48 (May 1965): 257–62.
"[Israeli Prime Minister] Eshkol Pleased with Texas Talks; Johnson Pledges Alliance for Peace." *Jewish Observer—Middle East Review* 17 (January 12, 1968): 3–4.
Jackson, Henry F. *From the Congo to Soweto: U.S. Foreign Policy toward Africa since 1960.* New York: Morrow, 1982.
"Johnson and [Israel Prime Minister] Eshkol agree on 'Broad Area of Understanding'." *Israel Digest* 7 (June 5, 1964): 1–2.
"Johnson Declaration: Israel's Nuclear Capacity Recognized." *Jewish Observer—Middle East Review* 13 (February 14, 1964): 3–4.
Kerr, Malcolm. "'Coming to Terms with Nasser': Attempts and Failures [in Anglo-Egyptian and American-Egyptian Relations since the 1956 Suez Crisis]." *International Affairs* (Great Britain) 43 (January 1967): 65–84.

Kilpatrick, James Jackson. "The Campaign against Rhodesia." *Human Events* 25 (December 11, 1965): 3.
———. "Illusion Yields to Reality in the Middle East." *Human Events* 27 (July 1, 1967): 16.
———. "Why Did LBJ Send U.S. Troops to the Congo?" *Human Events* 27 (July 29, 1967): 5.
"King Hussein's Sobering Encounter with President Johnson." *Jewish Observer—Middle East Review* 13 (April 24, 1964): 5–7.
Kirk, Russell. "Foreign Aid to Taiwan and Egypt." *Human Events* 25 (July 17, 1965): 8.
Lake, Anthony. "Caution and Concern: The Making of American Policy toward South Africa, 1946–1971." Princeton, N.J.: Princeton University, 1974. Ph.D. dissertation. University Microfilms No. 75–06653.
Lamb, Morris. "Vietnam Dove and Israel Hawk." *Conservative Judaism* 22 (Winter 1968): 77–78.
Landau, Julian J. "Middle East or Vietnam? Johnson's Financial Dilemma." *Jewish Observer and Middle East Review* 17 (February 23, 1968): 10–11.
———. "U.S. Elections and Israel: Vietnam Link Rejected." *Jewish Observer and Middle East Review* 17 (February 2, 1968): 8–9.
"LBJ Admits Hot Line Was Helpful in Arab-Israeli War." *Editor and Publisher* 100 (June 17, 1967): 12.
"LBJ's Rhodesian Blockade." *Human Events* 26 (April 23, 1966): 5.
Lefever, Ernest W. *Crisis in the Congo: A United Nations Force in Action.* Washington, D.C.: Brookings Institution, 1965.
Maheshwari, B. "American Aid to Africa." *African Quarterly* 7 (October/December 1967): 239–50.
Meisler, Stanley. "Peace Corps Teaching in Africa." *Africa Report* 11 (December 1966): 16–20.
Mordechai, Nahumi. "The United States and the Middle East: Will the Trend toward Relaxation of Israeli-Arab Tension and a Regional Détente Continue in 1964?" *New Outlook* (Israel) 7 (February 1964): 25–33.
Neal, Fred Warner. "Foreign Policy—The Vital Difference [Congo Crisis]." *Progressive* 28 (October 1964): 12–15.
Neff, David. *Warriors for Jerusalem: The Six Days That Changed the Middle East.* New York: Linden/Simon & Schuster, 1984.

Nielsen, Waldemar A. *African Battleline: American Policy Choices in Southern Africa.* New York: Harper, for the Council on Foreign Relations, 1965.

Okanla, Mousa Affalabi. "The United States and Southern Africa, 1961 to 1976: A Test of Theories of Foreign Policy." Ann Arbor: University of Michigan, 1982. Ph.D. dissertation. University Microfilms No. 8304564.

Pollock, David. *The Politics of Pressure: American Arms and Israeli Policy since the Six Day War.* Westport, Conn.: Greenwood Press, 1982.

"President Johnson Pledges U.S. Aid to Israel in Changing Salt Water to Fresh Water." *World Over* 25 (February 28, 1964): 4.

Ramazani, R. K. "The Changing United States Policy in the Middle East." *Virginia Quarterly Review* 40 (Summer 1964): 369–82.

"Reassuring Nasser." *Near East Report* 8 (February 11, 1964): 13–14.

Rivkin, Arnold. "Lost Goals in Africa." *Foreign Affairs* 44 (October 1965): 111–26.

Rubenberg, Cheryl A. "United States-Israeli Relations, 1947–1974: A Study in the Convergence and Divergence of Interests." Coral Gables, Fla.: University of Miami, 1979. Ph.D. dissertation. University Microfilms No. 79–21762.

Schlesinger, Arthur M., Jr., ed. *The Dynamics of World Power.* Vol. 5: *United Nations, Middle East, Subsaharan Africa.* New York: McGraw-Hill, 1973.

Spiegel, Steven L. *The Other Arab-Israeli Conflict: Making America's Middle East Policy, from Truman to Reagan.* Chicago: University of Chicago Press, 1985.

Taylor, Henry J. "LBJ Lifts Ban on Trade to Nasser." *Human Events* 25 (July 10, 1965): 10.

"U.S. Economic Aid to Africa, 1950–1964." *Africa Report* 9 (December 1964): 8–12.

"U.S.-Israel Partnership." *Near East Report* 8 (March 10, 1964): 21.

"War on 3 Fronts—New Worry for U.S.: Congo, Vietnam, Cyprus." *U.S. News and World Report* 57 (August 24, 1964): 29–30.

Weissman, Stephen R. *American Foreign Policy in the Congo, 1960–1964.* Ithaca, N.Y.: Cornell University Press, 1974.

Whetten, Lawrence L. *The Canal War: Four-Power Conflict in the Middle East.* Cambridge, Mass.: M.I.T. Press, 1974.
Williams, G. Mennen. "Diplomatic Rapport between Africa and the United States." *Annals of the American Academy of Political and Social Science* 354 (July 1964): 54–64.

F. OTHER NATIONS

Barclay, Glen S. *Friends in High Places: The Australian-American Security Relationship since 1945.* New York: Oxford University Press, 1985.
Clark, Gerald. *Canada: The Uneasy Neighbor.* New York: McKay, 1965.
Collins, Hugh Norman. "Assuming Primacy: the Australian-American Alliance, 1950–1968." Cambridge, Mass.: Harvard University, 1979. Ph.D. dissertation.
Manning, John. "Canadian-American Relationships: Economic and Political." *Midwest Quarterly* 5 (Spring 1964): 181–209.
Millar, Thomas B. "Australia and the American Alliance." *Pacific Affairs* 37 (Summer 1964): 148–60.
Singh, L. P. "Canada, the United States and Vietnam." *Journal of Commonwealth Political Studies* (Great Britain) 6 (July 1968): 125–48.
Taylor, Charles. *Snow Job: Canada, the United States and Vietnam, 1954–1973.* Toronto: Anansi, 1974.

4. THE VIETNAM WAR

A. GENERAL

"ABC's of War in Vietnam: What's It All About?" *U.S. News and World Report* 58 (June 28, 1965): 36–39.
"Aboard the Maddox: From the Files of Navy Intelligence." *Life* 57 (August 14, 1964): 21.
"After Show of Force: Still a Losing War in Vietnam." *U.S. News and World Report* 57 (August 24, 1964): 31–33.
Alter, J. "McNamara Recalls Vietnam." *Newsweek* 103 (May 28, 1984): 31.
Andrus, David J. "The Origins of American Involvement in Vietnam: A Thematic Analysis of the Pentagon Papers." Los

Angeles: University of Southern California, 1975. Ph.D. dissertation.

"Another Enemy in Vietnam—Corruption: Graft, Theft, Bribery, Misuse of U.S. Aid, Black Market, Opium Smuggling, Trade with Enemy." *U.S. News and World Report* 60 (February 14, 1966): 44–45.

Baral, Jaya Krishna. *The Pentagon and the Making of U.S. Foreign Policy: A Case Study of Vietnam, 1960–1968.* Atlantic Highlands, N.J.: Humanities Press International, 1978.

Baritz, Loren. *Backfire: A History of How American Culture Led Us into Vietnam and Made Us Fight the Way We Did.* New York: William Morrow, 1985.

Basich, Thomas. "Vietnam: The Confusion and the Commitment." *Dialog* 6 (Winter 1967): 34–43.

Beisel, David R. "The Vietnam War: A Beginning Psychohistory." *Journal of Psychohistory* 12 (Winter 1985): 371–93.

Bird, Roland. "Barbara Ward [British Economist]." *The Economist* (Great Britain) 279 (June 6, 1981): 35–39.

Boettiger, John R., ed. *Vietnam and American Foreign Policy.* Boston: Heath, 1968.

Boston Publishing Company Editors [Doyle, Edward G. et al]. *The Vietnam Experience.* 20 vols. Boston: Boston Publishing Co., 1981–1986.

Bowman, John S., gen. ed. *The Vietnam War: An Almanac.* Introduction by Fox Butterfield. New York: World Almanac Publications, 1985.

Boyle, Richard. *The Flower of the Dragon: The Breakdown of the U.S. Army in Vietnam.* Palo Alto, Cal.: Ramparts, 1972.

Braestrup, Peter, ed. *Vietnam as History: Ten Years after the Paris Peace Accords.* Lanham, Md.: University Press of America, 1983.

Brendon, Piers. *Ike: His Life and Times.* New York: Harper and Row, 1986.

Brodie, Bernard. "The Tet Offensive." *Decisive Battles of the 20th Century,* edited by Noble Frankland and Christopher Dowling, pp. 321–34. London: Sidgwick and Jackson, 1976.

Brogan, Dennis William. "Americans and the War in Vietnam." *The Listener* (Great Britain) 75 (April 7, 1966): 493–95, 509.

Brooke, Edward W. "The United States and Vietnam." *World Affairs* 130 (April-June 1967): 5–12.

"Brown and Root in Vietnam." *Texas Observer,* June 21, 1968: 11.

Bui Diem. *Meet the Press: Guest, Ambassador Bui Diem, Republic of Vietnam* (Interview). Washington, D.C.: Merkle Press, vol. 11, no. 5, 1967.
Bundy, William P. *Meet the Press: Guest, William P. Bundy, Assistant Secretary of State for East Asian and Pacific Affairs* (Interview). Washington, D.C.: Merkle Press, vol. 11, no. 35, 1967.
———. "The Path to Vietnam: Ten Decisions." *Orbis* 11 (Fall 1967): 647–63.
Bunker, Ellsworth, and Gen. William C. Westmoreland. *Meet the Press: Guests, Ambassador Ellsworth Bunker, General William C. Westmoreland* (Interview). Washington, D.C.: Merkle Press, vol. 11, no. 47, 1967.
Burns, Richard Dean. *The Wars in Vietnam, Cambodia, and Laos, 1945–1982: A Bibliographic Guide.* Santa Barbara, Cal.: ABC-Clio Information Service, 1984.
Butterfield, Fox. "The New Vietnam Scholarship: Challenging the Old Passions." *New York Times Magazine,* February 13, 1983: 26–61.
Buttinger, Joseph. *Vietnam: A Political History.* New York: Praeger, 1969.
Cairns, James F. *The Eagle and the Lotus, Western Intervention in Vietnam: 1847–1968.* Melbourne, Australia: Lansdowne Press, 1969.
Capps, Walter H. "The Vietnam War and American Values." *Center Magazine* 11 (July-August 1978): 17–39.
Castan, Sam. "What Johnson Faces in South Vietnam." *Look* 28 (January 28, 1964): 19–30.
Charlton, Michael, and Anthony Moncrieff. *Many Reasons Why: The American Involvement in Vietnam, 1950–1975.* New York: Hill and Wang, 1978.
Chomsky, Noam. "The Pentagon Papers as Propaganda and as History." *The Pentagon Papers.* Sen. Gravel Edition, vol. 5, pp. 179–201. Boston: Beacon Press, 1972.
———. "Vietnam, the Cold War and Other Matters." *Commentary* 48 (April 1969): 12–26.
———. "Vietnam: How Government Became Wolves." *New York Review of Books,* June 15, 1972: 23–31.
Church, Frank. "Vietnam: Interview [with Sen. Frank Church, Senate Foreign Relations Committee]." *Ramparts* 3 (January/February 1965): 16–22.

Cincinnatus [pseud.]. *Self-Destruction: The Disintegration and Decay of the United States Army during the Vietnam Era.* New York: Norton, 1981.
Clough, Ralph. *East Asia and U.S. Security.* Washington, D.C.: Brookings Institute, 1974.
Committee of Concerned Asian Scholars. *The Indochina Story: A Critical Appraisal of American Involvement in Southeast Asia.* New York: Panthean Books, 1971.
Congressional Research Service [William C. Gibbons]. *The U.S. Government and the Vietnam War: Executive and Legislative Roles and Relationships, Part 2, 1961–1964.* Washington, D.C.: U.S. Gov't. Printing Office, December 1984.
Dallek, Robert. *The American Style of Foreign Policy: Cultural Politics and Foreign Affairs.* New York: Knopf, 1983.
Dallin, Alexander. "Moscow and Vietnam: Hazards of U.S. Policy." *New Leader* 48 (May 10, 1965): 5–8.
Davis, Saville. "Patterns and Problems in U.S. Foreign Policy [Vietnam, Dominican Republic, and Post World War II Attitudes]." *International Affairs* (Great Britain) 41 (October 1965): 624–36.
Dommen, Arthur J. "Laos in the Second Indochina War." *Current History* 59 (December 1970): 326–32+.
———. "Laos: The Troubled 'Neutral'." *Asian Survey* 7 (January 1967): 74–80.
Donovan, Robert. *Nemesis: Truman and Johnson in the Coils of War in Asia.* New York: St. Martin's Press, 1984.
Draper, Theodore. "The American Crisis: Vietnam, Cuba and the Dominican Republic." *Commentary* 43 (January 1967): 27–43.
Dugger, Ronnie. "A Slip of the Tongue: In Lyndon Johnson's Mind, Viet Nam Was Like the Alamo All Over Again." *Texas Monthly* 10 (March 1982): 115.
Dunn, Joe P. "Our Changing Vietnam Retrospect [Reviews Vietnam War Literature]." *Air University Review* 37 (March-April 1986): 115–23.
Eder, Richard. "A Quiet American Goes to Vietnam [Ellsworth Bunker]." *New York Times Magazine,* March 26, 1967: 28+.
Einbinder, Harvey. *Mah Name Is Lyndon: A Play.* New York: Lady Bird Press, 1968.
"The Emerging [American] Victory in Asia." *Fortune* 74 (August 1966): 97+.
Emerson, Gloria. *Winners and Losers: Battles, Retreats, Gains,*

THE VIETNAM WAR—GENERAL

Losses, and Ruins from the Vietnam War. New York: Penguin Books, 1985.
Fall, Bernard B. "Our Options in Vietnam." *Reporter* 30 (March 12, 1964): 17–22.
———. *The Two Vietnams: A Political and Military Analysis.* 2nd ed. New York: Praeger, 1967.
———. "Vietnam: The Agonizing Reappraisal." *Current History* 48 (February 1965): 95–102, 166.
———. "Vietnam: The New Korea." *Current History* 50 (February 1966): 85–90, 117–19.
———. "Vietnam in the Balance." *Foreign Affairs* 45 (October 1966): 1–18.
Fishel, Wesley R., ed. *Vietnam: Anatomy of a Conflict.* Itasca, Ill.: Peacock, 1968.
Fulbright, J. William. *Meet the Press: Guest, J. W. Fulbright, Chairman, Foreign Relations Committee* (Interview). Washington, D.C.: Merkle Press, vol. 12, no. 3, 1968.
Galbraith, John Kenneth. *How to Get Out of Vietnam: A Workable Solution to the Worst Problem of Our Time.* New York: New American Library, 1967.
Gange, John. "Misadventure in Vietnam: The Mix of Fact and Truth." *Nation* 199 (August 24, 1964): 63–66.
Gardner, Lloyd C. *A Covenant with Power: America and World Order from Wilson to Reagan.* New York: Oxford University Press, 1984.
Gettleman, Marvin E., and Jane Franklin, eds. *Vietnam and America: A Documentary History.* New York: Grove, 1985.
Gibbons, William C. *The U.S. Government and the Vietnam War: Executive and Legislative Roles and Relationships. Part 1: 1945–1960. Part 2: 1961–1964.* The U.S. Government and the Vietnam War Series. Princeton, N.J.: Princeton University Press, 1986.
Gibson, James William. "The Perfect War: Technowar in Vietnam." New Haven, Conn.: Yale University, 1985. Ph.D. dissertation. University Microfilms No. 86–01082.
Graff, Henry F. "Teach-In on Vietnam by . . . the President, the Secretary of State, the Secretary of Defense and the Under-Secretary of State." *New York Times Magazine,* March 20, 1966: 25.
Grant, Zalin B. "Report from Laos, the Hidden War." *New Republic* 158 (April 20, 1968): 17–19.
Greene, Jerry. "Reds Achieve Great Propaganda Victory: U.S.

Embassy Attack in South Vietnam." *Human Events* 28 (February 10, 1968): 1.
Griffen, William L. *Teaching the Vietnam War.* Montclair, N.J.: Allanheld, Osmun & Co., 1979.
Grinter, Laurence E. "How They Lost: Doctrines, Strategies and Outcomes of the Vietnam War." *Asian Survey* 15 (December 1975): 114–32.
Gruening, Ernest H. "The Reality of Vietnam." *Progressive* 30 (February 1966): 15–17.
Halberstam, David. *The Making of a Quagmire, 1954–65.* New York: Random House, 1964.
Hammond, William M. *The Unknown Servicemen of the Vietnam Era.* Washington, D.C.: U.S. Dept. of the Army, Center of Military History, 1985.
Hartke, Vance. *The American Crisis in Vietnam.* New York: Bobbs-Merrill, 1968.
Hasluck, Paul. "Vietnam and SEATO." *Current Notes on International Affairs* (Australia) 37 (May 1966): 257–60.
Hellmann, John. *American Myth and the Legacy of Vietnam.* New York: Columbia University Press, 1986.
Herring, George C. *America's Longest War: The U.S. and Vietnam, 1950–1975.* 2nd ed. Philadelphia: Temple University Press, 1986.
———. "Vietnam Remembered [Reviews Vietnam War Literature]." *Journal of American History* 73 (June 1986): 152–64.
Herz, Martin F. *The Vietnam War in Retrospect.* Lanham, Md.: University Press of America, 1985.
Holsti, Ole R., and James N. Rosenau. *American Leadership in World Affairs: Vietnam and the Breakdown of Consensus.* Boston: Allen and Unwin, 1984.
———. "The 'Lessons' of Vietnam: a Study of American Leadership." Paper presented at the 17th Annual Convention of the International Studies Assn., Toronto, Canada, February 25–29, 1976.
Holt, Harold. "Why Australia Backs U.S. in the Vietnam War: Interview with Prime Minister Harold Holt." *U.S. News and World Report* 62 (January 2, 1967): 58–61.
"House Democrats Plan Revolt against Speaker [McCormack]." *Business Week*, April 6, 1968: 41.
"How Johnson Meets the Challenge in Vietnam." *Business Week*, March 13, 1965: 28–29.

Isaacs, Arnold R. *Without Honor: Defeat in Vietnam and Cambodia.* Baltimore, Md.: Johns Hopkins University Press, 1983.
Jain, R. K. *U.S.-South Asian Relations, 1947–1982.* 3 vols. Atlantic Highlands, N.J.: Humanities Press International, 1983.
Jewett, Robert. *The Captain America Complex: The Dilemmas of Zealous Nationalism.* Philadelphia: Westminister Press, 1973.
Johnson, Harold K., Gen. "End of Vietnam War in Sight? Size-Up by the Army's Chief of Staff, General Harold K. Johnson" (Interview). *U.S. News and World Report* 63 (September 11, 1967): 44–48.
Johnson, Ralph William. "Confucian Political Influence on the South Vietnamese Government of President Ngo Dinh Diem: 1954–1963." Washington, D.C.: The American University, 1978. M.A. thesis. University Microfilms No. 13-11399.
"Johnson's Prison." *Texas Observer*, February 3, 1967: 13.
Kahin, George McTurnan. *Intervention: How America Became Involved in Vietnam.* New York: Knopf, 1986.
Karnow, Stanley. *Vietnam: A History: The First Complete Account of Vietnam at War.* New York: Viking Press, 1983.
Kattenburg, Paul M. "Reflections of Vietnam: Of Revisionism and Lessons Yet to Be Learned." *Parameters: Journal of the U.S. Army War College* 14 (Autumn 1984): 42–50.
Kennedy, Edward M. "A Fresh Look at Vietnam." *Look* 30 (February 8, 1966): 21–23.
———. "Halt the Bombing: Mutual Withdrawal." *Vital Speeches* 34 (September 15, 1966): 717–19.
———. "The 'Other War' in Vietnam." *New Leader* 50 (November 20, 1967): 6–9.
Keyserling, Leon H. "Fables and Foibles on Vietnam." *AFL-CIO Free Trade Union News* 23 (May 1968): 8.
"Know Your Enemy: Vietnam Explodes the Myth of Peaceful Coexistence." *Barron's* 45 (February 22, 1965): 1.
Kolko, Gabriel. *Anatomy of a War: Vietnam, the United States, and the Modern Historical Experience.* New York: Pantheon, 1986.
Kowet, Don. *A Matter of Honor.* New York: Macmillan, 1984.
Langland, S. G. "Laos Factor in a Vietnam Equation." *International Affairs* (Great Britain) 45 (October 1969): 631–47.

Lansdale, Edward G., Gen. *In the Midst of Wars: An American's Mission to Southeast Asia.* New York: Harper and Row, 1972.
———. "Viet Nam: Do We Understand Revolution?" *Foreign Affairs* 43 (October 1964): 75–86.
Larson, Stanley R., and James L. Collins, Jr. *Allied Participation in Vietnam.* Washington, D.C.: U.S. Gov't. Printing Office, 1975.
"LBJ Faces Crisis in Viet Nam." *Human Events* 22 (December 28, 1963): 13.
"LBJ's Story: 5 Critical Decisions on Vietnam." *U.S. News and World Report* 71 (November 8, 1971): 77–80.
"LBJ's Viet Mistakes." *Human Events* 28 (February 17, 1968): 3.
Levantrosser, William F. "Tonkin Gulf Revisited: Vietnam, Military Mirage, and Political Reality in 1964." Paper prepared for the Lyndon B. Johnson Presidential Conference, Hofstra University, Hemstead, New York, April 10–12, 1986.
Levi, Arrige, et al. "Europe and Vietnam." *Interplay of European/American Affairs* 1 (March 1968): 5–13.
Lodge, Henry Cabot. *Meet the Press: Guest, Henry Cabot Lodge, Ambassador at Large* (Interview). Washington, D.C.: Merkle Press, vol. 11, no. 38, 1967.
———. *Meet the Press: Guest, Henry Cabot Lodge, Former U.S. Ambassador to South Vietnam* (Interview). Washington, D.C.: Merkle Press, vol. 9, no. 19, 1965.
———. "How the World's Hottest Spot Looks to Me." *Life* 56 (April 17, 1964): 38D-38F.
Lomperis, Timothy John. "A Conceptual Framework for Deriving the 'Lessons of History': The U.S. Involvement in Vietnam (1960–1975) as a Case Study." Durham, N.C.: Duke University, 1981. Ph.D. dissertation. University Microfilms No. 8114553.
———. *The War Everyone Lost—And Won: America's Intervention in Vietnam's Twin Struggles.* Baton Rouge: Louisiana State University Press, 1984.
"Lyndon Baines Johnson and the Rise of Presidential Militarism." *Social Science Quarterly* 53 (1972): 395–402.
"Lyndon's War." *Human Events* 24 (August 8, 1964): 4.
Mangold, Tom, and John Penycate. *The Tunnels of Cu Chi: The Untold Story of Vietnam.* New York: Random House, 1985.

Martin, Robert P. "What the Vietnam War Means to the U.S.: The Brink of All-Out War [post-Pleiku]." *U.S. News and World Report* 58 (February 22, 1965): 35–39.

McGovern, George S. "Affirmative Alternative in Vietnam." *Progressive* 29 (March 1965): 12–14.

———. "The Lessons of Vietnam." *Progressive* 31 (May 1967): 12–17.

———. "We Can Solve the Vietnam Dilemma." *Saturday Review* 48 (October 1965): 37–38.

McLintock, Robert. *The Meaning of Limited War.* Boston: Houghton-Mifflin, 1967.

Mecklin, John, Walter Guzzardi, Jr., and Charles J. V. Murphy. "Vietnam 1967: The Struggle to Rescue the People." *Fortune* 75 (April 1967): 125–45+.

Melanson, Richard A. *Writing History and Making Policy: The Cold War, Vietnam, and Revisionism: Volume VI, American Values Projected Abroad.* Lanham, Md.: University Press of America, 1983.

Mezerik, A. G., ed. *Viet Nam and the U.N., 1967: National and International Policy.* New York: International Review Service, 1967.

Montagu, Ivor. "The Other War—Laos." *Labour Monthly* (Great Britain) 48 (July 1966): 322–38.

Morgenthau, Hans J. *Meet the Press: Guest, Professor Hans Morgenthau, University of Chicago* (Interview). Washington, D.C.: Merkle Press, vol. 9, no. 18, 1965.

———. "Vietnam: Shadow and Substance." *New York Review of Books,* September 16, 1965: 3–7.

———. *Vietnam and the United States.* Washington, D.C.: Public Affairs Press, 1965.

National Broadcasting Corporation. "NBC White Paper: Vietnam—Lessons of a Lost War." Executive Producer, Anthony Potter; reported by Marvin Kalb, April 27, 1985.

Neustadt, Richard E., and Ernest R. May. *Thinking in Time: The Uses of History for Decision-Makers.* New York: Free Press, 1986.

Nixon, Richard M. *Meet the Press: Guest, Richard M. Nixon, Former Vice President of the United States* [U.S. situation in Vietnam] (Interview). Washington, D.C.: Merkle Press, vol. 9, no. 32, 1965.

———. *No More Vietnams.* New York: Arbor House, 1985.

Pace, Eric. "Laos: Continuing Crisis." *Foreign Affairs* 43 (October 1964): 64–74.
Palmer, Gregory. *McNamara Strategy and the Vietnam War: Program Budgeting in the Pentagon, 1960–1968.* Westport, Conn.: Greenwood, 1978.
Park, Chang Jin. "American Foreign Policy in Korea and Vietnam: Comparative Case Studies." *Review of Politics* 37 (January 1975): 20–47.
Podwal, Mark H. *The Decline and Fall of the American Empire.* New York: Darien House, 1971.
Pollard, Vincent K. "ASA and ASEAN, 1961–1967: South-East Asia Regionalism." *Asian Survey* 10 (March 1970): 244–55.
———. "The Association of Southeast Asia (ASA), 1961–1967: Regionalsim, Ideology, and Declaratory Foreign Policy." Chicago: University of Chicago, Committee on International Regulations. M.A. thesis, December 1968. Reprinted, Zug, Switzerland: Inter Documentation Co., 1973, SE-DISS-1, South East Asia Project.
———. "Meeting Whose Need?" *Far Eastern Economic Review* (Hong Kong) 73 (September 18, 1971): 25–26.
———. "South East Asian Regionalism—Containment, Counterinsurgency and the Nixon Doctrine." *Journal of Contemporary Asia* (Stockholm), vol. 1, no. 4, 1971: 45–54.
Pratt, John Clark, comp. *Vietnam Voices: Perspectives on the War Years, 1941–1982.* New York: Viking Penguin, 1984.
"President Faces Dilemma in South Viet Nam." *Human Events* 24 (September 26, 1964): 3.
Rajagopal, D. R. "Report from Hanoi: Hanoi's View of the Vietnamese War." *Far Eastern Economic Review* (Hong Kong) 50 (December 30, 1965): 601–03.
Riddell, Thomas Allen. "The $676 Billion Quagmire." *Progressive* 37 (October 1973): 33–37.
Roberts, Adam. "The Fog of Crisis: The 1964 Tonkin Gulf Incidents." *World Today* (Great Britain) 26 (May 1970): 209–17.
Roskin, Michael. "From Pearl Harbor to Vietnam: Shifting Generational Paradigms and Foreign Policy." *Political Science Quarterly* 89 (Fall 1974): 563–88.
Rostow, Walt W. "Dangers that Remain in the Vietnam War." *U.S. News and World Report* 71 (November 8, 1971): 80–85.

———. *The Diffusion of Power: An Essay in Recent History.* New York: Macmillan, 1972.

———. "LBJ, Asia, and Vietnam." Paper presented to Lyndon Baines Johnson Presidential Conference, Hofstra University, Hempstead, New York, April 10–12, 1986.

Rubin, Barry. *Secrets of State: The State Department and the Struggle over U.S. Foreign Policy.* New York: Oxford University Press, 1985.

Rubin, Richard Alan. "Foreign Policy, Secrecy, and the First Amendment: The Pentagon Papers in Retrospect." *Howard Law Journal,* vol. 17, no. 3 (1972): 579–612.

Salisbury, Harrison E., ed. *Vietnam Reconsidered: Lessons from a War.* New York: Harper and Row, 1984.

Sanders, Sol W. "Can the U.S. Win in Vietnam? An Inside Report." *U.S. News and World Report* 58 (January 11, 1965): 44–47.

Schlesinger, Arthur M., Jr. "The Quagmire Papers." *New York Review of Books,* December 16, 1971: 41–42.

Schlight, John, ed. *Second Indochina War Symposium: Papers and Commentary: Proceedings of a Symposium Held at Airlie, Virginia, November 7–9, 1984.* Washington, D.C.: U.S. Army, Center of Military History, 1986.

"Secret Rusk-Gromyko Accord Explains Viet Nam Sanctuary." *Human Events* 27 (October 28, 1967): 1.

Senate Republican Policy Committee. *The War in Vietnam.* Washington, D.C.: Public Affairs Press, 1967.

Shaplen, Robert. "Letter from Laos." *New Yorker* 44 (May 4, 1968): 136+.

———. "Letter from Saigon" [series]. *New Yorker* 43 (January 20, 1968): 35–38+; 44 (March 2, 1968): 44–46+; 44 (March 23, 1968): 114+; 44 (June 29, 1968): 37–40+; 44 (January 11, 1969): 66–72+; 45 (September 20, 1969): 110.

———. "Letter from South Vietnam." *New Yorker* 45 (April 12, 1969): 134+.

———. *Lost Revolution: The U.S. in Vietnam, 1946–1966.* Revised Edition. New York: Harper and Row, 1966.

———. *The Road from War: Vietnam, 1965–1971.* Revised Edition. New York: Harper and Row, 1971.

———. "Viet Nam: Crisis of Indecision." *Foreign Affairs* 46 (October 1967): 95–110.

Sharp, U.S. Grant, and William C. Westmoreland. *Report on the*

War in Vietnam. Washington, D.C.: U.S. Gov't. Printing Office, 1969.
Shizuo, Maruyama. "Japanese Opinion and the Vietnam War." *Japan Quarterly* (Japan) 12 (July/September 1965): 303–10.
Sigelman, Lee, and Dixie Mercer McNeil. "White House Decision-Making under Stress: A Case Analysis [of the Tet Offensive]." *American Journal of Political Science* 24 (November 1980): 652–73.
Simmonds, E. H. S. "Laos and the War in Vietnam." *World Today* (Great Britain) 22 (May 1966): 199–206.
Skorov, A. "McNamara's Dirty War." *International Affairs* (Moscow), August 1964: 61–64.
Smith, Myron J., Jr. *Air War Southeast Asia, 1961–1973: A Bibliography and 16mm Film Guide.* Metuchen, N.J.: Scarecrow, 1979.
Sorenson, Theodore C. "The War in Vietnam: How We Can End It." *Saturday Review* 50 (October 21, 1967): 19–21.
Stanton, Shelby L. *The Rise and Fall of an American Army: U.S. Ground Forces in Vietnam, 1965–1973.* Novato, Cal.: Presidio Press, 1985.
Stegenga, J. A. "Books on Vietnam [Reviews Vietnam War Literature]." *America* 155 (November 29, 1986): 348–51.
Stevenson, Charles A. *The End of Nowhere: American Policy toward Laos since 1954.* Boston: Beacon, 1972.
Stone, I. F. "The Tonkin Bay Mystery." *New York Review of Books,* March 28, 1968: 5–12.
Stuckey, John D., and Joseph H. Pistorius. "Mobilization for the Vietnam War: A Political and Military Catastrophe." *Parameters: Journal of the U.S. Army War College* 15 (Spring 1985): 26–38.
Sullivan, Marianna P. "DeGaulle's Policy toward the Conflict in Vietnam, 1963–1969." Charlottesville: University of Virginia, 1971. Ph.D. dissertation. University Microfilms No. 72-07179.
Summers, Harry G., Jr. "The Bitter Triumph of Ia Drang." *American Heritage* 35 (February/March 1984): 50–57.
"Symposium: The National Interest and the Pentagon Papers." *Partisan Review* 39 (Summer 1972): 336–75.
Tanham, George K., et al. *War without Guns: American Civilians in Rural Vietnam.* New York: Praeger, 1966.
Taylor, Charles. *Snow Job: Canada, the United States and Vietnam, 1954–1973.* Toronto: Anansi, 1974.

Taylor, Henry J. "Johnson Speaks of Peace while Fighting a Losing War." *Human Events* 24 (October 17, 1964): 10.
Taylor, Maxwell D., Gen. "The Cause in Vietnam Is Being Won." *New York Times Magazine*, October 15, 1967: 36–37.
———. "The Lessons of Vietnam: Exclusive Interview with General Maxwell D. Taylor, USA (Ret.) Adviser to Three Presidents." *U.S. News and World Report*, November 27, 1972: 22–26.
———. *Meet the Press: Guest, General Maxwell D. Taylor, U.S. Ambassador to South Vietnam* (Interview). Washington, D.C.: Merkle Press, vol. 9, no. 29, 1965.
———. "Top Authority Looks at Vietnam War: Exclusive Interview with Gen. Maxwell D. Taylor." *U.S. News and World Report* 60 (February 21, 1966): 38–42+.
Thompson, Kenneth W. "The Johnson Presidency and Foreign Policy: The Unresolved Conflict between National Interest and Collective Security." Paper presented at Fifth Annual Hofstra University Presidential Conference: Lyndon Baines Johnson, A Texan in Washington. Hempstead, New York, April 10–12, 1986.
Trager, Frank N. "American Foreign Policy in Southeast Asia." In *Studies on Asia, 1965*, pp. 17–59.
"Truce, or Bigger War: Showdown Ahead in Vietnam." *U.S. News and World Report* 60 (January 10, 1966): 27–28.
Truscott, Lucian K. III. "Body Count: The Degrading Illusion." *Nation* 211 (November 16, 1970): 487–89.
Tuchman, Barbara W. *The March of Folly from Troy to Vietnam*. New York: Knopf, 1984.
Tucker, Robert W. *The Radical Left and American Foreign Policy*. Baltimore: Johns Hopkins University Press, 1971.
Turner, Nicholas. "Saigon Shivers: South Vietnam-U.S. Relations." *Far Eastern Economic Review* (Hong Kong) 59 (January 18, 1968): 111–14.
"The United States and the Situation in Vietnam: Pro and Con." *Congressional Digest* 44 (April 1965): 99–128.
United States Marine Corps. *The Marines in Vietnam, 1954–1973: An Anthology and Annotated Bibliography*. Washington, D.C.: U.S. Gov't. Printing Office, 1974.
"Untold Story of the Road to War in Vietnam [Special Section]." *U.S. News and World Report* 95 (October 10, 1983): VN1-VN24.

Urrows, Elizabeth. "Recurring Problem in Laos." *Current History* 57 (December 1969): 361–63, 367.
Van Klaveren, Tricia. "Annotated Bibliography: Books on Vietnam." *Teaching Political Science* 12 (Summer 1985): 195+.
Verba, Sidney, and Richard A. Brody. "Participation, Policy Preferences, and the War in Vietnam." *Public Opinion Quarterly* 34 (Fall 1970): 325–32.
"Vietnam as History." *The Wilson Quarterly* 7 (Summer 1983): 94–139.
"Vietnam as History." *The Wilson Quarterly* 2 (Spring 1978): 178–87.
"The Vietnam War: An Indictment." *Texas Observer*, December 9, 1966: 27+.
"Vietnam War—Special Issue." *Texas Observer*, November 10, 1967: all.
Warner, Denis. "The Catastrophic Non-War in Laos." *Reporter* 30 (June 13, 1964): 21–24.
———. *Certain Victory: How Hanoi Won the War.* Kansas City, Kan.: Sheed Andrews and McMeel, 1978.
———. "Drawing the Line in Southeast Asia." *Reporter* 31 (September 10, 1964): 33–36.
———. "Vietnam: General Taylor Faces an All-Out War." *Reporter* 31 (August 13, 1964): 50–53.
Warner, Geoffrey. "The United States and Vietnam, 1945–65." *International Affairs* (Great Britain) 48 (July 1972): 379–94; (October 1972): 593–615.
Washburn, Michael A., and Willard H. Mitchell. *Walt Rostow, Vietnam, and Future Tasks of American Foreign Policy.* Princeton, N.J.: Center of International Studies, Woodrow Wilson School of Public and International Affairs, Princeton University, Policy Memorandum no. 33, September 1967.
"The Way Congress Sizes Up the War." *U.S. News and World Report* 60 (January 31, 1966): 28–31.
Wechsler, James A. "Vietnam: A Study in Deception." *Progressive* 29 (February 1965): 14–17.
Westmoreland, William, Gen. "What General Westmoreland Told Congress." *U.S. News and World Report* 62 (May 8, 1967): 44–45.
"What Congressmen Found in Vietnam: Personal Reports from 25 Members of Congress." *U.S. News and World Report* 60 (January 3, 1966): 24–31.

"What [Defense Secretary] McNamara Learned in Vietnam." *U.S. News and World Report* 61 (October 24, 1966): 41–42.

White, Ralph K. "Misperception and the Vietman War." *Journal of Social Issues* 22 (July 1966): 1–54.

———. *Nobody Wanted War: Misperception in Vietnam and Other Wars*. New York: Doubleday, 1968.

"Why Is the U.S. in a War." *U.S. News and World Report* 58 (April 5, 1965): 42–44.

"Why the Viet Nam Crisis." *Human Events* 26 (April 16, 1966): 4.

Williams, William A. et al. *America in Vietnam: A Documentary History*. Garden City, N.Y.: Doubleday, 1985.

Wilmer, Harry A., and James F. Veninga, eds. *Vietnam in Remission*. [Published papers from Symposium on Understanding Vietnam, Salado, Texas, October 29–31, 1982.] College Station: Texas A&M University Press, 1985.

Wolfenstein, E. Victor. "The Two Wars of Lyndon Johnson [Vietnam and War on Poverty]." *Politics and Society*, vol. 4, no. 3 (1974): 357–96.

Zinn, Howard. *Vietnam: The Logic of Withdrawal*. Boston: Beacon Press, 1967.

———. "Vietnam: The Logic of Withdrawal." *Nation* 204 (February 6, 1967): 170–75.

B. THE MEDIA

Adams, Samuel A. "Vietnam Cover-Up: Playing War with Numbers—A CIA Conspiracy against Its Own Intelligence." *Harper's Magazine* 250 (May 1975): 41–44, 62–73.

Adler, Renata. "Annals of Law: Two Trials—I and II [CBS v. Westermoreland]." *New Yorker* 62 (June 16, 1986): 42–96; and (June 23, 1986): 34–83.

Aiken, George D. "The Triumph of Media over Matter: Vietnam and the '68 Elections." *War/Peace Report* 89 (March 1968): 14–16.

Alter, J. "The General's Retreat [Westmoreland Ends Suit against CBS]." *Newsweek* 105 (March 4, 1985): 59–60.

Arlen, Michael J. "The Falklands, Vietnam, and Our Collective Memory (Television Coverage)." *New Yorker* 58 (August 16, 1982): 70+.

———. *Living-Room War*. New York: Viking, 1969.

Bailey, George A. "Television War: Trends in Network Coverage of Vietnam, 1965–1970." *Journal of Broadcasting* 20 (Spring 1976): 147–58.

Baldwin, Hanson W. "The Information War in Saigon." *Reporter* 34 (February 24, 1966): 29–31.

Braestrup, Peter. *Big Story: How the Press and Televison Reported and Analyzed the Crisis of Tet in 1968 in Vietnam and Washington.* Rev. ed. New Haven: Yale University Press, 1983.

Brewin, Bob, and Sydney Shaw. *Vietnam on Trial: Westmoreland vs. CBS.* New York: Atheneum, 1986.

Chandler, Robert W. *War of Ideas: The U.S. Propaganda Campaign in Vietnam, 1965–1972.* Boulder: Westview, 1981.

Chomsky, Noam. "Reporting Indochina: The News Media and the Legitimation of Lies." *Social Policy* 4 (September-October 1973): 4–19.

"The Credibility Gap." *Nation* 204 (April 17, 1967): 484.

D'Costa, Carlos. "Media Coverage of the Tet Offensive, 1968." Boca Raton: Florida Atlantic University, 1981. M.A. thesis. University Microfilms No. 1316670.

Docking, Robert. "Viet Nam: An Observer's Report." *Washburn Law Journal* 7 (Winter 1968): 187–93.

Dodd, Thomas J. "Needed: More Balanced Press Coverage of Vietnam." *Human Events* 25 (June 12, 1965): 8.

Elterman, Howard A. "The State, the Mass Media and Ideological Hegemony: United States Policy Decisions in Indochina, 1954–1975—Historical Record, Government Pronouncements and Press Coverage." New York: New York University 1978. Ph.D. dissertation. University Microfilms No. 78-18414.

Emery, Edwin. "The Press in the Vietnam Quagmire." *Journalism Quarterly* 48 (Winter 1971): 619–26.

Erskine, Hazel. "The Polls: Is War a Mistake?" *Public Opinion Quarterly* 34 (Spring 1970): 34–50.

Faulkner, Francis D. "Bao Chi: The American News Media in Vietnam, 1960–1975." Amherst: University of Massachusetts, 1981. Ph.D. dissertation. University Microfilms No. 81-10327.

Fox, Tom. "The Word from the Front: The Unreported War, Army vs. the Press." *Commonweal* 90 (August 8, 1969): 485–86.

Hallin, Daniel C. "The Mass Media and the Crisis in American Politics: The Case of Vietnam." Berkeley: University of California, 1980. Ph.D. dissertation. University Microfilms No. 81-13056.

———. "The Media, the War in Vietnam, and Political Support: A Critique of the Thesis of an Oppositional Media." *Journal of Politics* 46 (February 1984): 2–24.

———. *The "Uncensored War": The Media and Vietnam.* New York: Oxford University Press, 1986.

"History on Trial [Westmoreland Ends Suit against CBS]." *Nation* 240 (March 2, 1985): 227–28.

Hollander, Neil. "Adolescents and the War: The Sources of Socialization." *Journalism Quarterly* 48 (Autumn 1971): 472–79.

"Indo-Camera War: President Johnson Still Hasn't Found the Best Way of Explaining Vietnam to the American People." *Economist* (Great Britain) 222 (March 4, 1967): 802.

Kaplan, H. J. "The American Press in Vietnam." *Commentary* 73 (May 1982): 42–49.

Kelly, J. "Live, from Vietnam." *Time* 125 (May 13, 1985): 57.

MacDonald, Glenn. *Report or Distort? The Inside Story of the Media's Coverage of the Vietnam War.* New York: Exposition, 1973.

Marshall, S. L. A., Gen., Malcolm W. Browne, et al. "Press Failure in Vietnam: America's Sedentary War Correspondents." *New Leader* 49 (October 12, 1966): 3–5; and (November 21, 1966): 3–16.

Moise, Edwin E. "Why Westmoreland Gave Up." *Pacific Affairs* 58 (Winter 1985–86): 663+.

Pfeiffer, Richard Norton. "The Popular Periodical Press and the Vietnam War, 1954–1968." Louisville, Ky.: University of Louisville, 1978. M.A. thesis. University Microfilms No. 13-11825.

Podhoretz, Norman. "Vietnam: The Revised Standard Version." *Commentary* 77 (April 1984): 35–41; 78 (August 1984): 4–7.

Polsby, Nelson W. "Political Science and the Press: Notes on the Coverage of a Public Opinion Survey on the Vietnam War." *Western Political Quarterly* 22 (March 1969): 47–60.

Rollins, Peter C. "Television's Vietnam: The Visual Language of Vietnam News." *Journal of American Culture*, vol. 4, no. 2 (1981): 114–35.

Sheehan, Neil. "The Press and the Pentegon Papers." *Naval War College Review* 24 (November-December 1972): 8–12.
Showalter, Stuart W. "Coverage of Conscientious Objectors to the Vietnam War: An Analysis of Editorial Content of American Magazines, 1964–1972." Austin: University of Texas, 1975. Ph.D. dissertation. University Microfilms No. 76–08108. [For a summary, see *Journalism Quarterly*, vol. 53, no. 4, 1976: 648–53.]
Singer, Benjamin D. "Violence, Protest, and War in Television News: The U.S. and Canada Compared." *Public Opinion Quarterly* 34 (Winter 1970–1971): 611–16.
Sullivan, Marianna P. "Presidential Rhetoric on Vietnam: Kennedy, Johnson and Nixon." *International Interactions*, vol. 9, no. 2 (1982): 125–46.
"The Truth about War in Vietnam: Facts vs. Propaganda." *U.S. News and World Report* 63 (July 31, 1967): 40–43.
Turner, Kathleen J. *Lyndon Johnson's Dual War: Vietnam and the Press.* Chicago: University of Chicago Press, 1985.
———. "Presidential-Press Interaction: Media Influences on the Johns Hopkins Address." Paper presented at Fifth Annual Hofstra University Presidential Conference: Lyndon Baines Johnson, A Texan in Washington. Hempstead, New York, April 10–12, 1986.
"Vietnam and the Press: A Critical Analysis." *Columbia Journalism Review* 9 (Winter 1971): 7–47.
"Wartime Office of Censorship Already Set Up." *Human Events* 25 (August 21, 1965): 7.
Weintraub, Arnold Norman. "The Public Statements and Speeches of Robert F. Kennedy on the Vietnam War Issue." Lincoln: University of Nebraska, 1975. Ph.D. dissertation. University Microfilms No. 76-04502.
"Westmoreland Takes on CBS [Special Section]." *Newsweek* 104 (October 22, 1984): 60–62+.
"Westmoreland vs. CBS: The Story Behind the Battle." *U.S. News and World Report* 97 (October 1, 1984): 44–47.
Westmoreland, William, Gen. "The Commanding General Reports on the Vietnam War." *U.S. News and World Report* 62 (May 8, 1967): 42–44.

C. MILITARY POLICY AND STRATEGY

Air War Study Group, Cornell University. *The Air War in Indochina*. Rev. ed. Boston: Beacon, 1972.

Andrews, Bruce. *Public Constraint and American Policy in Vietnam*. Beverly Hills, Cal.: Sage Progressional Papers no. 4, 1976.

Arnold, Hugh M. "Official Justification for America's Role in Indo-China, 1949–67." *Asian Affairs* 3 (September/October 1975): 31–48.

Baldwin, Hanson W. "The Case for Mobilization." *Reporter* 34 (May 19, 1966): 20–33.

Ball, George W. "Top Secret: The Prophecy the President Rejected [Assumptions of the Administration's Vietnam Policy]." *Atlantic Monthly* 230 (July 1972): 33–49.

Blaufarb, Douglas. *The Counter-Insurgency Era: U.S. Doctrine and Performance*. Glencoe, Ill.: Free Press, 1977.

Braestrup, Peter. "'The Uncounted Enemy: a Vietnam Deception'—A Dissenting View." *Washington Journalism Review*, April 1982: 46–48.

Brands, Henry William, Jr. "Johnson and Eisenhower: The President, the Former President, and the War in Vietnam." *Presidential Studies Quarterly* 15 (Summer 1985): 589–601.

Branfman, Fred. "The President's Secret Army: A Case Study; the CIA in Laos, 1962–1972." *The CIA File*, edited by R. L. Borosage and J. D. Marks, pp. 46–78. New York: Grossman, 1976.

Brodie, Bernard. "Why Were We So [Strategically] Wrong [in Vietnam]." *Foreign Policy*, no. 5, Winter 1971–72: 151–62. Reprinted in *Military Review* 52 (June 1972): 40–46.

Brogan, Dennis William. "Naivete versus Reality in Vietnam." *Atlantic Monthly* 220 (July 1967): 48–55.

Brown, D. E. "The Use of Herbicides in War: A Political-Military Analysis. *The Control of Chemical and Biological Weapons*, pp. 39–63. New York: Carnegie Endowment for International Peace, 1971.

Brownlow, C. "Johnson Facing Critical Vietnam Decisions." *Aviation Week and Space Technology* 83 (July 19, 1965): 18–19.

Buckley, K. "Front Man for an Unpopular War [Westmoreland's

Relationship with LBJ]." *Nation* 240 (March 30, 1985): 367–69.
Bundy, William P. "Why the U.S. Is in Vietnam: An Official Explanation." *U.S. News and World Report* 63 (December 18, 1967): 48–49.
Burke, John P. "Responsibilities of Presidents and Advisers: A Theory and Case Study of Vietnam Decision Making." *Journal of Politics* 46 (August 1984): 818–45.
Burnham, James. "South Vietnam: The United States Policy." *Vital Speeches* 30 (April 15, 1964): 394–99.
Buzzanco, Bob. "The American Military's Rationale against the Vietnam War." *Political Science Quarterly*, vol. 101, no. 4 (1986): 559–76.
Cable, Larry E. *Conflict of Myths: The Development of American Counterinsurgency Doctrine and the Vietnam War.* New York: New York University Press, 1986.
Cecil, Paul Frederick. *Herbidical Warfare: The Ranch Hand Project in Vietnam.* New York: Praeger, 1986.
Center for Naval Analyses. *Naval Operations in Southeast Asia, 1964–1973: A Bibliography.* Arlington, Va.: Center for Naval Analyses, May 1974.
Collins, James L., Jr. *The Development and Training of the South Vietnamese Army, 1950–1972.* Washington, D.C.: U.S. Gov't. Printing Office, 1975.
Collins, John M. "Vietnam Postmortem: A Senseless Strategy." *Parameters: Journal of the U.S. Army War College* 8 (March 1978): 8–15.
Dawson, William W. "A Value Analysis of Four Major Addresses of President Lyndon B. Johnson on the Subject of the United States Involvement in Vietnam." Stillwater: Oklahoma State University, 1967. M.A. thesis.
Denno, Bryce F. "New War in Vietnam: Introduction of U.S. Combat Forces Has Precipitated a Fourth Distinct Phase of the Vietnam War." *U.S. Naval Institute Proceedings* 92 (March 1966): 70–79.
Dommen, Arthur J. "Neutralization Experiment in Laos." *Current History* 48 (February 1965): 89–94.
Drummond, S. "Korea and Vietnam: Some Speculations about the Possible Influences of the Korean War on American Policy in Vietnam." *Army Quarterly and Defense Journal* (Great Britain), vol. 97, no. 1, 1968: 65–71.

Eliot, George Fielding. "Lyndon Johnson's Get-Tough Policy: Historic Landmark." *American Legion Magazine* 79 (September 1965): 10–13+.

Fishel, Wesley R. "American Aid to Vietnam." *Current History* 49 (November 1965): 294–99.

Ford, Gerald R. "Why More Troops If There's No Victory Plan?" *Human Events* 27 (August 19, 1967): 1, 15.

Friedman, Alvin, and Henry Steele Commager. "Debate on Vietnam Policy." *Massachusetts Review* 7 (Spring 1966): 407–19.

"Gearing Up for Vietnam: A Tough Ground War Multiplies the Costs [McNamara's Return from Saigon]." *Business Week*, July 24, 1965: 22–25.

Gilster, Herma L. "Air Interdiction in Protracted War: An Economic Evaluation." *Air University Review* 28 (May-June 1977): 2–18.

Ginsburgh, Robert N. "Strategy and Air Power: The Lessons of Southeast Asia." *Strategic Review* 2 (Summer 1973): 18–25.

Girling, J. L. S. "Vietnam and the Domino Theory." *Australian Outlook* (Australia) 21 (April 1967): 61–70.

Goldwater, Barry. "President Johnson Overrides the Military on Viet Nam Fighting." *Human Events* 25 (July 10, 1965): 13.

"Guns and Butter: Failure of a Policy." *U.S. News and World Report* 64 (February 12, 1968): 27–29.

"Guns vs. Butter Poses a Budget Problem." *Engineering News-Record* 176 (January 6, 1966): 14–15.

Halberstam, David. *The Best and the Brightest*. New York: Random House, 1972.

"Hanoi's Threat to Execute Captured U.S. Pilots Triggers New Consideration of Naval Blockade." *Human Events* 25 (October 16, 1965): 7.

Hatcher, Patrick Lloyd. "Tonkin to Tet: The U.S. National Security System and Vietnam." Berkeley: University of California, 1985. Ph.D. dissertation. University Microfilms No. 86-1004.

Hodgson, Gordon S. "Of Hawks and Doves [U.S. Vietnam Policy]." *United States Naval Institute Proceedings* 93 (May 1967): 30–37.

Hood, Donald Eugene. "'Lessons' of the Vietnam War: Henry Kissinger, George F. Kennan, Richard Falk and the Debate over Containment, 1965–1980." Seattle: University of Washington, 1982. Ph.D. dissertation. University Microfilms No. 8218231.

"How the State Department Tried to Explain Away the Use of 'Non-Lethal' Gases." *I.F. Stone Weekly* 13 (March 29, 1965): 2–3.

Humphrey, David C. "Tuesday Lunch at the Johnson White House: A Preliminary Assessment." *Diplomatic History* 8 (Winter 1984): 81–101.

Humphrey, Hubert H. "'We Do Not Want a Group to Shoot Its Way into Power': Vice President Humphrey Presents Another Side of the Vietnam Debate" (Interview). *U.S. News and World Report* 60 (March 14, 1966): 71–72+.

Huynk, Kim Khanh. "The War in Vietnam: The U.S. Official Line: A Review Article." *Pacific Affairs* 42 (Spring 1969): 58–67.

"Into the Delta—Decision Is Made for Bigger War in Vietnam." *U.S. News and World Report* 61 (October 3, 1966): 40–42.

Isaacson, Walter, and Evan Thomas. *The Wise Men: Six Friends and the World They Made*. New York: Simon and Schuster, 1986.

"Johnson Builds Up Our Asian Allies . . . As Laos Fades." *Saturday Evening Post*, April 4, 1964: 34–34A.

"Johnson Is Still Playing to Win in Vietnam." *Business Week*, December 23, 1967: 14–17.

"Johnson Puts Vietnam Policy in the Wringer." *Business Week*, March 16, 1968: 34–35.

Johnson, Harold K., Gen. "End of Vietnam War in Sight? Size-Up by the Army's Chief of Staff, Gen. Harold K. Johnson" (Interview). *U.S. News and World Report* 63 (September 11, 1967): 44–48.

Johnson, R. H. "Escalation Then and Now." *Foreign Policy* 60 (Fall 1985): 130–47.

Johnson, Ralph William. "Phoenix/Phung Hoang: A Study of Wartime Intelligence Management [Vietnam War Counterinsurgency]." Washington, D.C.: American University, 1985. Ph.D. dissertation. University Microfilms No. 85-14487.

"Johnson's Dilemma: Coping with a Half-War." *Business Week*, December 4, 1965: 27–28.

Kahn, Herman. "Escalation as a Strategy." *Fortune* 71 (April 1965): 110–12+.

Kennan, George F. "Kennan on Vietnam." *New Republic* 154 (February 26, 1966): 19–30.
―――, and Maxwell D. Taylor. "The Vietnam Debate." *Survival* 8 (April 1966): 108–14.
"Key Senators [on Foreign Relations Committee and Armed Services Committee] Tell What to do about Vietnam." *U.S. News and World Report* 58 (February 15, 1965): 68–72.
Kissinger, Henry. "What Should We Do in Vietnam." *Look*, August 9, 1966: 26.
Komer, Robert W. *Bureaucracy Does Its Thing: Institutional Constraints on U.S.-GVN Performance in Vietnam.* Chicago: Rand, 1972.
Krepinevich, Andrew Francis. "The Army Concept and Vietnam: A Case Study in Organizational Failure." Cambridge, Mass.: Harvard University, 1984. Ph.D. dissertation. University Microfilms No. 84-10945.
Lane, Thomas A., Gen. "LBJ Can't Win Viet War with Present Advisers." *Human Events* 27 (December 30, 1967): 11.
―――. "LBJ Has Surrendered to Diplomats: Why War Goes Badly." *Human Events* 28 (March 9, 1968): 1.
Lansdale, Edward G. "Viet Nam: Still the Search for Goals." *Foreign Affairs* 47 (October 1968): 92–98.
"LBJ Asked to Call Up Reserves." *Human Events* 27 (June 10, 1967): 5.
"LBJ's Strange Viet Strategy." *Human Events* 26 (March 5, 1966): 5.
"Limits of Clobbering: What May Work in S. Vietnam Almost Certainly Will Not Work in Laos." *Economist* (Great Britain) 211 (May 23, 1964): 812–13.
Lodge, Henry Cabot. "Go on Fighting in Vietnam?" (Interview). *U.S. News and World Report* 58 (February 15, 1965): 62–67.
―――. "If We Are Persistant, the Outlook Is Good: Ambassador Lodge Reports on Southeast Asia." *Army* 15 (August 1964): 80–81.
―――. "Outlook Now for War in Vietnam: Exclusive Interview with Ambassador Henry Cabot Lodge." *U.S. News and World Report* 61 (November 21, 1966): 66–68.
Martin, Graham. "Why U.S. Is in Asia: A Top Diplomat Explains" (Interview). *U.S. News and World Report* 64 (February 19, 1968): 46–48.
Martin, Robert P., and Sol W. Sanders. "U.S. Bungle in Viet-

nam? The Inside Story." *U.S. News and World Report* 57 (September 14, 1964): 56–58.

McCarthy, Joseph E. *Illusion of Power: American Policy toward Vietnam, 1954–1966*. New York: Carlton Press, 1967.

"McNamara's Third Task: President Johnson Announces a Bigger Call-Up to Complete 'The McNamara Strategy'." *Economist* (Great Britain) 216 (July 31, 1965): 418–19.

Meany, Neville. "From the Pentegon Papers: Reflections on the Making of America's Vietnam Policy." *Australian Outlook* (Australia) 26 (August 1972): 163–92.

"Military Experts Tell Why 'Gradualism' Failed in Vietnam: Report of the Republican Task Force on National Security." *U.S. News and World Report* 64 (April 29, 1968): 56–58.

Morgenthau, Hans J. "Bundy's Doctrine of War without End." *New Republic* 159 (November 2, 1968): 18–20.

Moulton, Harland B. "The McNamara General War Strategy." *Orbis* 8 (Summer 1964): 238–54.

Nguyen-van-Thieu. "U.S. Pullback in Vietnam: Interview with Vietnam President." *U.S. News and World Report* 65 (August 5, 1968): 42–46.

Nighswonger, William Asa. "Rural Pacification in Vietnam, 1962–1965." Washington, D.C.: American University, 1966. Ph.D. dissertation. University Microfilms No. 66-12813.

O'Ballance, Edgar. "Strategy in Viet Nam [American, Vietnamese, Viet Cong Strategy]." *Army Quarterly* 93 (January 1967): 160–67.

"Outlook for Vietnam: Johnson Is Still Playing to Win." *Business Week*, December 23, 1967: 14–17.

Palmer, Bruce, Jr., Gen. *The 25-Year War: America's Military Role in Vietnam*. Lexington: University Press of Kentucky, 1984.

Pollard, Vincent K. "Pacific Strategy." *Far Eastern Economic Review* (Hong Kong) 74 (October 9, 1971): 59.

Prados, John Frederick. *Presidents' Secret Wars: CIA and Pentagon Covert Operations since World War II*. New York: Morrow, 1986.

"Pressure Goes Up: Johnson Is Heating Up War, But His Basic Strategy Is the Same." *Business Week*, July 9, 1966: 37–38.

Pryor, Bernard Bruce. "Role and Perception: A Case Study of a President's Use of the Concept of Democracy as the Rationale for the Conduct of War in Vietnam." Claremont, Cal.: Claremont Graduate School, 1975. Ph.D. dissertation. University Microfilms No. 75-25827.

"Pull Out of Vietnam? What Key Senators Say about Next Moves in the War." *U.S. News and World Report* 62 (January 23, 1967): 40–45.

"Quick Passage of Asian Development Bank Is Central to Johnson's Viet Nam Strategy." *Human Events* 26 (February 19, 1966): 6.

"Record of Recent Review in Congress of U.S. Policy in Vietnam." *Congressional Digest* 45 (April 1966): 99–128.

"Robert McNamara Talks about Vietnam." *Newsweek* 104 (December 17, 1984): 49.

Rostow, Walt W. "Will We Snatch Defeat form the Jaws of Victory?" *Naval War College Review* 24 (September 1971): 3–18.

"Rusk and McNamara Urge New Bombing Phase: Would Be Unannounced." *Human Events* 27 (May 27, 1967): 7.

Rusk, Dean. "As Told by Secretary Rusk—Why U.S. Fights in Viet Nam." *U.S. News and World Report* 60 (February 28, 1966): 76–78+.

———. "Communist Aggression: Vietnam." *Vital Speeches* 35 (October 15, 1968): 2–6.

———, and Gen. Maxwell Taylor. *Heart of the Problem: Secretary Rusk and General Taylor Review Viet-Nam Policy in Senate Hearings.* Washington, D.C.: U.S. Gov't. Printing Office, 1966.

———, and Robert McNamara. "Political and Military Aspects of U.S. Policy in Viet-Nam" (Interview). *U.S. Department of State Bulletin* 53 (August 30, 1965): 342–56.

Shapley, Deborah. *Robert McNamara: Soldier of the American Century.* New York: Morrow, 1986.

Shizuo, Maruyama. "The Other War in Vietnam: The Revolutionary Development Program [South Vietnam Pacification]." *Japan Quarterly* (Japan) 14 (July/September 1967): 297–303.

Shultz, Richard. "Strategy Lessons from an Unconventional War: The U.S. Experience in Vietnam." *Nonnuclear Conflicts in the Nuclear Age,* edited by Sam C. Sarkesian, pp.138–84. New York: Praeger, 1980.

Silverman, Jerry Mark. "The Domino Theory: Alternatives to

a Self-Fulfilling Prophecy." *Asian Survey* 15 (November 1975): 915–39.
Smith, Melden E., Jr. "The Strategic Bombing Debate: The Second World War and Vietnam." *Journal of Contemporary History* 12 (October 1976): 175–93.
Smith, Myron J., Jr. *The Secret Wars.* Vol. 2, *Propaganda and Psychological Warfare, Covert Operations, 1945–1980* [A Bibliography]. Santa Barbara, Cal.: ABC-Clio, 1981.
Taylor, Maxwell D., Gen. *Meet the Press: Guest, General Maxwell D. Taylor, Special Consultant to the President and President, Institute for Defense Analysis* (Interview). Washington, D.C.: Merkle Press, vol. 12, no. 13, 1968.
"This Is Really War: Johnson Announces Doubling of Draft Quotes and Heavier Commitment of Regular Forces." *Business Week*, July 31, 1965: 15–16.
Thompson, James C. *Rolling Thunder: Understanding Policy and Program Failure.* Chapel Hill: University of North Carolina Press, 1980.
Trager, Frank N. "The Importance of Laos in Southeast Asia." *Current History* 46 (February 1964): 107–11.
"U.S. Winning a Battle on Vietnam Economy: Massive Doses of Aid Are Slowing Inflation and Lifting Civilian Morale." *Business Week*, December 4, 1965: 30–31.
"Vietnam War's New Strategy: Will It Work?" *U.S. News and World Report* 60 (February 21, 1966): 31–36.
Volsky, D. "McNamara's Saigon Equation." *New Times* (Moscow), April 3, 1964: 11–12.
Walt, Lewis W., Gen. *Strange War, Strange Strategy.* New York: Funk and Wagnells, 1970.
"War at Crisis—Mobilization Ahead? The President's Biggest Decision on Vietnam." *U.S. News and World Report* 62 (June 12, 1967): 29–31.
"War Take-Over by South Vietnam—LBJ Is Pushing the Idea." *U.S. News and World Report* 64 (May 13, 1968): 58–59.
Warner, Denis. "Our Secret War in Laos." *Reporter* 32 (April 22, 1965): 23–26.
"What It Would Take to Turn the Tide in Vietnam." *U.S. News and World Report* 59 (July 12, 1965): 46–48.
"What Next in Vietnam? [LBJ's 1965 Escalation Decision]." *U.S. News and World Report* 59 (August 9, 1965): 33–40.
Wheeler, Earle G., Gen. "How to Fight the War in Vietnam: Inteview with Gen. Earle G. Wheeler, Chairman, U.S. Joint

Chiefs of Staff." *U.S. News and World Report* 62 (February 27, 1967): 38–45.
"Who Runs the Whole U.S. Show in the World? Johnson's Reliance on Civilian Staff for Formation of Military Strategy." *U.S. News and World Report* 62 (June 5, 1967): 37–39.
"Why LBJ Holds the Arms Line." *Business Week*, January 23, 1965: 28–29.
"Why No War Declaration? Growing Mystery of Vietnam." *U.S. News and World Report* 62 (May 22, 1967): 31–33.
Wilson, George C. "Manpower Squeeze: Vietnam War Challenges McNamara." *Aviation Week and Space Technology* 84 (April 25, 1966): 27–28.
Wilson, Melford A., Jr. "Criticism and the Policy Maker's Reaction: United States Policy on Vietnam, 1961–1966." Washington, D.C.: American University, 1969. Ph.D. dissertation. University Microfilms No. 69-18813.
Zant, Thomas. "The Concept of National Interest and Its Application to United States Policy in Vietnam." Columbia: University of Missouri, 1973. Ph.D. dissertation. University Microfilms No. 74-18677.

D. PEACE NEGOTIATIONS

Acheson, Dean. "Negotiate with the Reds?" *U.S. News and World Report* 63 (December 18, 1967): 50–51.
"After the First Round—Truce Outlook Now." *U.S. News and World Report* 64 (May 27, 1968): 31–32.
"And a New Plan for Peace—What Was Decided in Manila." *U.S. News and World Report* 61 (November 7, 1966): 33–34.
"Are Negotiations a Mistake? LBJ and Vietnam." *Human Events* 28 (April 13, 1968): 1.
Barnet, Richard J. "The North Vietnamese in Paris: The Impasse." *New York Review of Books*, October 24, 1968: 7.
Belovski, Dince. "The Paris Talks." *Review of International Affairs* (Yugoslavia) 19 (June 5, 1968): 6–8.
"A Bid for Peace—And a Rebuff [LBJ's Peace Initiative of February 2, 1967]." *U.S. News and World Report* 62 (April 3, 1967): 26–27.
Browne, Malcolm W. "Are Negotiations Possible? No." *War/Peace Report* 7 (January 1967): 6–7.
Bundy, William P. *Meet the Press: Guest, William P. Bundy,*

Assistant Secretary of State for East Asian and Pacific Affairs (Interview). Washington, D.C.: Merkle Press, vol. 12, no. 8, 1968.

Burchett, Wilfred G. "Negotiations on Vietnam? How It Looks from the 'Other Side'." *War/Peace Report* 6 (November 1966): 3–5.

———. "A Neutral Peace?" (Interview). *Far Eastern Economic Review* (Hong Kong) 60 (June 27, 1968): 638–40.

———. "The Paris Talks: Report." *New World Review* 36 (Fall-Winter 1968): 3–16.

———. "The Paris Talks and the War." *Liberation* 13 (October 1968): 29–31.

———. "Vietnam: One Year of the Peace Talks." *New World Review*, vol. 37, no. 2 (1969): 2–9.

———. "Why North Vietnam Rejects 'Unconditional' Negotiations." *War/Peace Report* 5 (December 1965): 7–9.

"The Chances for Peace: When LBJ Had to Choose on Vietnam." *U.S. News and World Report* 64 (April 15, 1968): 49–52.

"Chances for Peace in Vietnam." *U.S. News and World Report* 59 (August 16, 1965): 29–31.

Cheshire, H. "Construction Escalates in Vietnam as Washington Peace Offensive Fails." *Engineering News-Record* 176 (February 3, 1966): 11–14; (February 10, 1966): 60–62; (February 17, 1966): 99–100+.

Clark, Mark W. "Do Truce Talks Mean Peace?" (Interview). *U.S. News and World Report* 62 (March 20, 1967): 42–44.

Cutchley, Julian, and Betty Hunt. *The Vietnam War Negotiations*. London: World and School Crisis Papers, 1968.

Cutrona, Joseph F. H. "Peace in Vietnam: An Acceptable Solution." *Military Review* 46 (November 1966): 60–68.

Davis, Derek. "What Price Peace at Paris?" *Far Eastern Economic Review* (Hong Kong) 60 (May 26–June 1, 1968): 473–76.

Draper, Theodore. "How Not to Negotiate." *New York Review of Books*, May 4, 1967: 17–29.

"Facts about Truce Talks: U.S. Terms for 'Productive' Negotiations Go Far Beyond Anything Hanoi Has Agreed To." *U.S. News and World Report* 64 (January 22, 1968): 29–31.

Falk, Richard A. *A Vietnam Settlement: The Views from Hanoi*. Princeton, N.J.: Princeton University Press, 1968.

Fraleigh, Arnold. "How to Fail in Negotiations without Really Trying." *New Republic* 154 (January 1, 1966): 9.
Fulbright, J. William. "We Must Negotiate Peace in Vietnam." *Saturday Evening Post* 239 (April 9, 1966): 10–14.
Goldberg, Arthur J. "The Search for Peace." *Thought: Fordham University Quarterly*, vol. 41, no. 160 (1966): 45–51.
Grant, Zalin B. "The Bombing Halt." *New Republic* 159 (November 9, 1968): 13–15.
Great Britain Foreign Office. *Recent Exchange Concerning Attempts to Promote a Negotiated Settlement of the Conflict in Viet-Nam*. London: HMSO, 1965.
Gregory, Gene. "Paris Talks: First Round to Hanoi." *Far Eastern Economic Review* (Hong Kong) 60 (June 20, 1968): 611–12+.
Halberstam, David. "Bargaining with Hanoi." *New Republic* 158 (May 11, 1968): 14–16.
Harriman, W. Averell. "Vietnam Peace Talks: Harriman Gives the Official U.S. Position." *U.S. News and World Report* 64 (May 27, 1968): 90–91.
Hartke, Vance. "Where Are the Peace Makers?" *Progressive* 30 (September 1966): 13–14.
Hayden, Tom. "The Impasse in Paris." *Ramparts* 7 (August 24, 1968): 18–21.
Heller, Walter W. "Getting Ready for Peace." *Harper's Magazine* 236 (April 1968): 57–62.
Heren, Louis. "Peace and U.S. Politics." *Atlas*, May 1968: 14–16.
Herring, George C., ed. *The Secret Diplomacy of the Vietnam War: The Negotiating Volumes of the Pentagon Papers*. Austin: University of Texas Press, 1983.
"Ho Keeps Saying 'No': Two Years, 45 Peace 'Feelers'." *U.S. News and World Report* 62 (April 10, 1967): 42.
Honick, Morris. "The French Initiatives of 1966." Paper presented at Fifth Annual Hofstra University Presidential Conference: Lyndon Baines Johnson, A Texan in Washington. Hempstead, New York, April 10–12, 1986.
Hopkins, Waring C. "An Historical Analogy: Geneva 1954 and Paris 1968." *Naval War College Review* 21 (September 1968): 88–91.
Hudson, Richard. "The Nearest to Negotiations Yet." *War/Peace Report* 7 (March 1967): 3–4.

Ikle, Fred C. "The Real Negotiations on South Vietnam." *Reporter* 32 (June 3, 1965): 15–19.
"In Vietnam, Still No Answer: Hanoi and Peking Denounce President Johnson's Efforts." *Business Week*, January 8, 1966: 367.
"Johnson and Ho Edge toward the Peace Table." *Business Week*, April 6, 1968: 22–23.
Kahin, George McT. "Impasse at Paris." *New Republic* 159 (October 12, 1968): 23–26.
Kahn, Herman. "If Negotiations Fail." *Foreign Affairs* 46 (July 1968): 627–41.
Kelman, Steven J. "'Viet-Report' and [Staughton] Lynd Mission: Launching a Parallel Peace Offensive." *New Leader* 49 (January 17, 1966): 12–14.
Kissinger, Henry. "The Vietnam Negotiations." *Foreign Affairs* 47 (January 1969): 211–34.
Langer, Paul F. "Laos: Preparing for a Settlement in Vietnam." *Asian Survey* 9 (January 1969): 69–74.
———. "Laos: Search for Peace in the Midst of War." *Asian Survey* 8 (January 1968): 80–86.
"LBJ Eleventh-Hour Move: Bombing Halt." *Human Events* 28 (November 9, 1968): 3.
"LBJ's Bomb Pause." *Human Events* 26 (February 5, 1966): 4.
"LBJ's Peace Drive." *Human Events* 26 (October 15,1966): 3.
Lenart, Edith R. "Paris Talks: Stubbornly Last Summer." *Far Eastern Economic Review* (Hong Kong) 63 (December 29, 1968): 18–20.
Lens, Sidney. "What Hanoi Wants." *Progressive* 31 (September 1967): 18–20.
McCullouch, Frank. "Peace Feelers: This Frail Dance of the Seven Veils." *Life* 64 (March 22, 1968): 32–38.
Mowrer, Edgar Ansel. "Just What to Negotiate in Viet Nam Is Unclear." *Human Events* 27 (April 1, 1967): 13.
———. "LBJ Playing Patsy Role in Haste to Make Peace." *Human Events* 26 (November 5, 1966): 12.
Nekach, Larry A. *Cease Fire in Vietnam: A Chronology of Statements by the United States, South Vietnam, North Vietnam, and the NLF/PRG.* Washington, D.C.: Library of Congress, Leg. Ref. Serv., 1970.
"A New Plan for Peace—What Was Decided in Manila." *U.S. News and World Report* 61(November 7, 1966): 33–34.

Nguyen Van Ba. "Bases for a Valid Settlement." *Vietnamese Studies* 18/19 (September 1968): 303–34.
"No Letup in Vietnam: Strategy after Guam [Peace Talks, March 21–22, 1967]." *U.S. News and World Report* 62 (April 3, 1967): 25–28.
"North Vietnamese Peace Proposal." *Current History* 49 (October 1965): 237+.
"Peace Hopes Weaken as Shooting Resumes." *Business Week*, January 29, 1966: 30–31.
"Peace Offer Jolts Vietnamese." *Human Events* 26 (January 22, 1966): 5.
Roberts, Adam. "Hanoi's Offer to Talk." *World Affairs* 24 (May 1968): 176–78.
Sacks, Milton. "Politics in the Jet Age: Effects of the Guam Conference." *New Leader* 50 (April 10, 1967): 3–5.
Sanders, Sol W. "Truce Talks: Edge of Dilemma." *U.S. News and World Report* 65 (July 1, 1968): 21.
———. "Why Vietnam's Reds Scorn Peace Talks" (Interview). *U.S. News and World Report* 59 (November 29, 1965): 50–55.
Scott, Paul. "Humphrey Considers Flight to Paris: Dramatic 'Peace' Move." *Human Events* 28 (October 5, 1968): 1.
———. "Will [New U.N. Ambassador George] Ball End All Bombing of North Viet Nam?" *Human Events* 28 (May 11, 1968): 1.
Shaplen, Robert. "Seats at the Table [Paris Peace Talks]." *New Yorker* 44 (November 16, 1968): 193–206.
Terrill, Ross. "Making Peace at Paris: A Special Report on the Negotiations." *Atlantic Monthly* 222 (December 1968): 4–33.
———. "A Report on the Paris Talks." *New Republic* 159 (July 13, 1968): 15–18.
Thee, Marek. "Vietnam: The Subtle Art of Negotiation." *Peace Proposals*, vol. 3, no. 2 (1972): 163–71.
———. *Vietnam Peace Proposals, Documents 1954–1968.* Oslo: International Peace Research Institute, March 1969.
Thomas, Norman. "Let the President Call for Immediate Cease Fire." *New Politics* 4 (Winter 1965): 4–11.
Tran Chanh Thanh. *From Geneva '54 to Paris '69: Have Words Lost All of Their Meanings?* Saigon: Vietnam Council on Foreign Relations, 1969.

Tran Van Dinh. "Are Negotiations Possible? Yes." *War/Peace Report* 7 (January 1967): 7–10.
"U.S. Peace Plan for Asia: Will It Work? [Johnson's Plan for Ending the War in Vietnam]." *U.S. News and World Report* 58 (April 19, 1965): 35–37.
Warner, Denis. "Vietnam: The Politics of Peace." *Reporter* 32 (April 8, 1965): 40–42.
"Were the Americans Wrong? Alexi Kosygin Would Probably Say No [Failure of Anglo-Russian Efforts to Effect Peace Talks between Hanoi and U.S.]." *Economist* (Great Britain) 222 (February 19, 1967): 591–92.
"What LBJ Will Find in Asia: President Johnson Will Find No 'Doves' at the Asian Summit Meeting in Manila." *U.S. News and World Report* 61 (October 24, 1966): 37–40.
"Why Johnson Is Ready to Talk on Vietnam." *Business Week*, April 10, 1965: 30–31.
"Will It Work? President above Party—Johnson's Position in the U.S.-Vietnam Peace Talks." *Economist* (Great Britain) 227 (April 6, 1968): 13–16+.
"Will There Be a Real Truce?" *U.S. News and World Report* 62 (February 20, 1967): 33–35.
Williams, Geoffrey. "America Seeks to Negotiate." *Contemporary Review* 213 (August 1968): 84–85.

E. POLITICS AND LEGAL ISSUES

Alford, Neill H., Jr. "The Legality of American Military Involvement in Vietnam: A Broader Perspective." *Yale Law Journal* 75 (June 1966): 1109–21.
Allison, Graham T. "Making War: The President and Congress." *Law and Contempory Problems* 40 (Summer 1976): 86.
"The Apostles of Consensus." *Texas Observer*, May 12, 1967: 14+.
Avillo, Philip J., Jr. "'In What Direction Are We Going in Vietnam?' The U.S. Senate, Lyndon Johnson and the Vietnam War, 1964–1965." Paper presented at Fifth Annual Hofstra University Presidential Conference: Lyndon Baines Johnson, A Texan in Washington. Hempstead, New York, April 10–12, 1986.
―――. "Limits of Dissent: Senators Wayne Morse, Ernest

Gruening, and the Vietnam War." Paper presented to the Duquesne History Forum, Duquesne University, Pittsburgh, Pennsylvania, January 1984.

Belman, Murray J. "The Power of the President to Use Military Force Abroad." *Virginia Journal of International Law* 10 (December 1969): 37–57.

Benton, Mary Josephine Griffin. "Wayne Morse and Vietnam: A Study of the Role of Dissenter." Denver: University of Denver, 1968. Ph.D. dissertation. University Microfilms No. 69-07007.

Berger, Raoul. "The Tug-of-War between Congress and the Presidency—Foreign Policy and the Power to Make War." *Washburn Law Journal* 16 (Fall 1976): 1–11.

———. "War Making by the President." *The Vietnam War and International Law,* edited by Richard A. Falk, vol. 4, pp. 604–61. Princeton, N.J.: Princeton University Press, 1976.

———. "War-Making by the President." *University of Pennsylvania Law Review* 29 (November 1972): 29–86.

Bickel, Alexander M. "Congress, the President and the Power to Wage War." *Chicago-Kent Law Review* 48 (Fall-Winter 1971): 131–47.

Brennan, Paul Edward. "The War-Making Powers of the American President as Commander-in-Chief of the Armed Forces." Fullerton: California State College, 1968. M.A. thesis. University Microfilms No. M-1537.

Bromley, Dorothy Dunbar. *Washington and Vietnam: An Examination of the Moral and Political Issues.* Dobbs Ferry, N.Y.: Oceana, 1966.

Brownlow, C. "Republicans Renew Vietnam Policy Attack." *Aviation Week and Space Technology* 81 (August 17, 1964): 22–23.

Burnham, James. "McNamara's Non-War." *National Review* 19 (September 19, 1967): 1012–14.

Burstein, Paul. "Senate Voting on the Vietnam War, 1964–1973: From Hawk to Dove." *Journal of Political and Military Sociology* 7 (Fall 1979): 271–82.

———, and William Freudenburg. "Changing Public Policy: The Impact of Public Opinion, Antiwar Demonstrations, and War Costs on Senate Voting on Vietnam War Motions." *American Journal of Sociology* 83 (July 1978): 99–122.

———. "Ending the Vietnam War: Components of Change in Senate Voting on Vietnam War Bills." *American Journal of Sociology* 82 (March 1977): 991-1006.

Cerny, P. G. "The Fall of Two Presidents and Extraparliamentary Opposition: France and the United States in 1968." *Government and Opposition* 5 (Summer 1970): 287–306.

"Congress Backs President in Viet Nam Crisis." *Congressional Quarterly Weekly Report* 22 (August 7, 1964): 1667–69.

"Congress, the President, and the Power to Commit Forces to Combat." *Harvard Law Review* 81 (June 1968): 1771–1805.

"Congress, the President, and the Power to Commit Forces to Combat." *The Vietnam War and International Law*, edited by Richard A. Falk, vol. 2, pp. 616–60. Princeton, N.J.: Princeton University Press, 1969.

"Connally vs. Sen. Kennedy." *Texas Observer*, April 1, 1967: 3.

"The Constitution, the War, and American Society." *Texas Observer*, September 18, 1970: 17.

Cousins, Norman. "Journeys with Humphrey: Memoir of a Mission that Failed." *Saturday Review* 61 (March 4, 1978): 10–18.

D'Amato, Anthony A., and Robert M. O'Neal. *The Judiciary and Vietnam*. New York: St. Martin's Press, 1972.

Deutsch, Eberhard P. "The Legality of the United States Position in Vietnam." *American Bar Association Journal* 52 (May 1966): 436–42.

Dietz, Terry. *Republicans and Vietnam, 1961–1968*. Westport, Conn.: Greenwood Press, 1986.

"Dissent on LBJ's Viet Policy." *Human Events* 26 (February 12, 1966): 4.

Dorsey, Barry Martin. "The Struggle between the President and Congress over the War-Making Powers." Washington, D.C.: The American University, 1969. M.A. thesis. University Microfilms No. M-1865.

"Double-Edged Criticism Hits Viet Nam Policy ['Dove' and 'Hawk' Factions in Congress]." *Congressional Quarterly Weekly Report* 25 (September 22, 1967): 1865–67.

Elowitz, Larry, and John W. Spainer. "Korea and Vietnam: Limited War and the American Political System." *Orbis* 18 (Summer 1974): 510–34.

Emerson, J. Terry. "The War Powers Resolution Tested: The

President's Independent Defense Power." *Notre Dame Lawyer* 51 (December 1975): 187–216.
Evans, M. Stanton. "Senator Kickenlooper, There's a Dove in Your Kitchen: a Not-Too-Sympathetic Account of the GOP Policy Committee's Staff Report on Viet Nam." *Human Events* 27 (May 27, 1967): 8–9.
Falk, Richard A. "International Law and the United States' Role in Vietnam: A Response to Professor [John Norton] Moore." *Yale Law Journal* 76 (August 1967): 1095–1158.
———. *The Six Legal Dimensions of the Vietnam War.* Princeton, N.J.: Princeton University, Center of International Studies, Research Monography No. 34, 1968.
———. "U.S. in Vietnam: Rationale and Law." *Dissent* 13 (May/June 1966): 275–84.
———, ed. *The Vietnam War and International Law.* 4 vols. Princeton, N.J.: Princeton University Press, 1968–76.
"Falling Away from LBJ: Democrats Split on Viet Nam." *Human Events* 27 (June 3, 1967): 4.
Faulkner, Stanley. "The War in Vietnam: Is It Constitutional?" *Georgetown Law Journal* 56 (June 1968): 1132–43.
Finney, John. "Tonkin Gulf Attack." *New Republic* 158 (January 27, 1968): 19–22.
———. "The Tonkin Verdict." *New Republic* 158 (March 9, 1968): 17–19.
Friedman, Jonathan M. "American Courts, International Law, and the War in Vietnam." *Columbia Journal of Law and Social Problems,* vol. 18, no. 3 (1984): 295–348.
Friedman, Wolfgang. "Law and Politics in the Vietnam War: Commentary." *American Journal of International Law* 6 (July 1967): 776–84.
Fulbright, J. William, ed. *The Vietnam Hearings.* New York: Vintage, 1966.
Gallucci, Robert. *Neither Peace Nor Honor: The Politics of American Military Policy in Vietnam.* Baltimore: Johns Hopkins University Press, 1975.
Garrett, Stephen A. *Ideals and Reality: An Analysis of the Debate over Vietnam.* Lanham, Md.: University Press of America, 1978.
Goldfarb, Ronald L. "Three Conscientious Objectors and the Supreme Court." *American Bar Association Journal* 52 (June 1966): 564–67.

Goldwater, Barry M. "As Goldwater Now Sees the War in Vietnam." *U.S. News and World Report* 60 (April 25, 1966): 44–46.
———. "Despite Liberal Noises, GOP Still Backs Viet War." *Human Events* 27 (October 21, 1967): 14.
———. "The President's Ability to Protect America's Freedoms—The War-Making Power." *Law and Social Order,* 1971: 423–49.
Goodale, James C., ed. *The New York Times Co. vs United States, A Documentary History: The Pentagon Papers Litigation.* 2 vols. New York: Arno, 1971.
Goodman, Allan. *Politics in War: The Bases of Political Community in South Vietnam.* Cambridge, Mass.: Harvard University Press, 1973.
Grant, Donald. "The War against U Thant: Johnson and Rusk have Undertaken an Underground War against the United Nations Secretary General because of His Stand on Viet Nam." *Progressive* 31 (March 1967): 19–22.
Grinter, Lawrence E. "Bargaining between Saigon and Washington: Dilemmas of Linkage Politics during War." *Orbis* 18 (Fall 1974): 837–68.
"Gulf of Tonkin Resolution [Text]." *Current History* 54 (January 1968): 49.
Halperin, Morton H. "The President and the Military [FDR to Nixon]." *Foreign Affairs* 50 (January 1972): 310–24.
Hamre, John J. "Congressional Dissent and American Foreign Policy: Constitutional War-Making in the Vietnam Years." Baltimore: Johns Hopkins University, 1978. Ph.D. dissertation. University Microfilms No. 78-17947.
Henkin, Louis. "Vietnam in the Courts of the United States: 'Political Question'." *American Journal of International Law* 63 (April 1967): 284–89.
Holton, Thomas. "Peace in Vietnam through Due Process: An Unexplored Path." *American Bar Association Journal* 54 (January 1968): 45–47.
Hull, Roger, and J. Novogrod. *Law and Vietnam.* Dobbs Ferry, N.Y.: Oceana, 1968.
Ivie, Robert L. "Presidential Motives for War." *Quarterly Journal of Speech* 60 (October 1974): 337–45.
Janes, Thomas Warham. "Rational Man—Irrational Policy: A Political Biography of John McNaughton's Involvement in

the Vietnam War." Cambridge, Mass.: Harvard University, 1977. B.A. senior honors thesis.
Jenkins, Gerald L. "The War Powers Resolution: Statutory Limitation on the Commander-In-Chief." *Harvard Journal on Legislation* 196 (February 1974): 181–204.
Johnson, Haynes B., and Bernard M. Gwertzman. *Fulbright: The Dissenter.* Garden City, N.Y.: Doubleday, 1976.
Kelly, Wayne. "Senator Russell Vows to Speak His Mind [regarding Vietnam] after a Painful Silence." *Atlanta Journal and Constitution Magazine,* February 4, 1968): 9+.
Kennedy, Robert F. "Comment [on P. Findley's 'End the Vietnam War through the Rule of Law']." *Social Science* 43 (June 1968): 138–39.
———. "Senator Robert Kennedy Explains His Position [on Vietnam—Interview]." *U.S. News and World Report* 60 (March 14, 1966): 68–70.
———. "What We Can Do to End the Agony of Vietnam." *Look* 31 (November 28, 1967): 34–36.
Kennedy, Ross A. "Dissent and Decision-Making: A Study of George Ball's and John McNaughton's Opposition to the Vietnam War." *Fletcher Forum* 9 (Winter 1985): 69–104.
Lawyer's Committee on American Policy towards Vietnam. *Vietnam and International Law: An Analysis of the Legality of U.S. Military Involvement.* Flanders, N.J.: O'Hare Books, 1967.
"LBJ and Congress: Trouble Over Vietnam." *U.S. News and World Report* 59 (August 23, 1965): 30–31.
"LBJ's Vietnam Critics." *Human Events* 26 (February 26, 1966): 4.
"Legality of U.S. Participation in the Defense of Viet-Nam." *American Journal of International Law* 60 (July 1966): 565–85.
Lowe, George E. "'Vietnams and Munichs': The Bombing of Hanoi [as Middle Ground between] the Urgings of the Extreme Left for another Munich [and] the Extreme Right for the Vaporization of North Vietnam." *United States Naval Institute Proceedings* 92 (October 1966): 62–71.
"Majority of Congress Members Backs Viet Nam Course." *Congressional Quarterly Weekly Report* 24 (October 28, 1966): 2661–64+.

Malawer, Stuart S. "The Vietnam War under the Constitution: Legal Issues Involved in the United States Military Involvement in Vietnam." *University of Pittsburgh Law Review* 31 (1969): 205–41.

Manzel, Paul, ed. *Moral Argument and the War in Vietnam.* Nashville: Aurora, 1971.

"McNamara Testifies on Tonkin Gulf Attacks." *Congressional Quarterly Weekly Report* 26 (March 1, 1968): 384–86.

Meeker, Leonard C. "The Legality of United States Participation in the Defense of Viet-Nam." *Yale Law Journal* 75 (June 1966): 1085–1108.

Messing, J. H. "American Actions in Vietnam: Justifiable in International Law?" *Stanford Law Review* 19 (June 1967): 1307–36.

Moore, John Norton. "International Law and the United States' Role in Viet Nam: A Reply [to Richard A. Falk]." *Yale Law Journal* 76 (May 1967): 1051–94.

———. "Law and Politics in the Vietnam War: A Response to Professor [Wolfgang] Friedman." *American Journal of International Law* 61 (October 1967): 1039–53.

———. *Law and the Indo-China War.* Princeton, N.J.: Princeton University Press, 1972.

———. "Lawfulness of Military Assistance to the Republic of Vietnam." *American Journal of International Law* 61 (January 1967): 1–35.

———. "The National Executive and the Use of Armed Forces Abroad." *The Vietnam War and International Law*, edited by Richard A. Falk, vol. 2, pp. 808–21. Princeton, N.J.: Princeton University Press, 1969.

Morse, Wayne. "Humpty Dumpty in Vietnam." *Progressive* 28 (August 1964): 13–16.

———. "Protests against Vietnam Policy." *Vital Speeches* 32 (November 15, 1965): 74–78.

———. *The Truth about Vietnam: Report on the U.S. Senate Hearings.* Analysis by Wayne Morse, edited by F. M. Robinson and E. Kemp. San Diego, Cal.: Greenleaf Classics, 1966.

———. "The U.S. Must Withdraw [from Vietnam]: 'We Are Pursuing Neither Law Nor Peace.'" *Christianity and Crisis* 24 (November 2, 1964): 209–13.

Moyer, Henry W., Jr. "Congressional Voting on Defense in WWII and Viet Nam: Toward a General Ideological Expla-

nation." New Haven, Conn.: Yale University, 1976. Ph.D. dissertation. University Microfilms No. 77-14294.
Myrdal, Gunnar. "The Vietnam War and the Political and Moral Isolation of America." *New University Thought* 5 (Spring 1967): 3–12.
Neal, William Patrick. "Senator Wayne L. Morse and the Quagmire of Vietnam, 1964–1968." Eugene: University of Oregon, 1979. Ph.D. dissertation. University Microfilms No. 80-05787.
O'Brien, W. V. "International Law, Morality, and American Interventions." *Catholic World*, September 1965: 388–93.
Page, Benjamin I., and Richard A. Brody. "Policy Voting and the Electoral Process: The Vietnam War Issue." *American Political Science Review* 66 (September 1972): 979–95.
Pickus, Robert. "Peace, the 'New Politics'—and the Pity of It All: American Viet Nam Policy as an Issue in Domestic Politics." *War/Peace Report* 6 (October 1966): 10–13.
Pollard, Vincent K. "Comment on Gerald Sussman's 'Macapagal, the Sabah Claim and Maphilindo: The Politics of Penetration." *Journal of Contemporary Asia* (Stockholm) vol. 14, no. 3, 1984: 376–78.
Possony, Stefan I. *Aggression and Self-Defense: The Legality of U.S. Action in South Vietnam*. Philadelphia: University of Pennsylvania, Foreign Policy Research Institute, FPRI Monograph Series No. 6, 1966.
Ratner, Leonard G. "The Coordinated Warmaking Power—Legislative, Executive and Judicial Roles." *Southern California Law Review* 44 (1971): 461–89.
"Republicans Say Vietnam Contracts Are LBJ Payoff." *Engineering News-Record* 177 (September 8, 1966): 20–21.
Reveley, W. Taylor III. "Presidential War-Making: Constitutional Prerogative or Usurpation?" *Virginia Law Review* 55 (November 1969): 1243–1305.
Ritchie, Donald A. "Making Fulbright Chairman: Or How the 'Johnson Treatment' Nearly Backfired." *The Society for Historians of American Foreign Relations Newsletter* 15 (No. 3, September 1984): 21–28.
Robertson, D.W. "The Debate among American International Lawyers about the Vietnam War." *Texas Law Review* 46 (July 1968): 898–913.
Roche, John P. "The Liberals and Vietnam." *New Leader* 48 (April 26, 1965): 16–20.

Rogers, William P. "Congress, the President and War Powers." *California Law Review* 59 (September 1971): 1194–1214.
Rosenwasser, Marie. "The Rhetoric of the 'Doves': A Descriptive Analysis of the Strategies and Techniques Used by Eight Senate 'Doves' in Selected Speech Manuscripts from 1964–1968." Lafayette, Ind.: Purdue University, 1969. M.A. thesis.
"Rusk vs Senators: The War Explained." *U.S. News and World Report* 64 (March 25, 1968) 74–78.
Russell, Richard B. "Senator Russell on Vietnam: 'Go In and Win or Get Out' " (Interview). *U.S. News and World Report* 60 (May 2, 1966): 56–57.
Scheer, Robert, and Warren Hinckle. "The 'Vietnam Lobby'." *Ramparts* 4 (July 1965): 16–24.
Schlesinger, Arthur M., Jr. "Vietnam and the 1968 Elections." *New Leader* 50 (November 6, 1967): 5–12.
Schreiber, Eugene M. "Vietnam Demonstrations and Votes in the USA." *Politics* (Australia) 10 (November 1975): 207–09.
———. "Vietnam Policy Preferences and Withheld 1968 Presidential Polls." *Public Opinion Quarterly* 37 (Spring 1973): 91–98.
Schwartz, Warren F., and Wayne McCormack. "The Justiciability of Legal Objections to the American Military Effort in Vietnam." *Texas Law Review* 46 (November 1968): 1033–53.
"Senate Rift over Vietnam Widens." *Business Week*, February 12, 1966: 28–29.
"Senator Morse's Advice and Dissent." *New York Times Magazine*, April 17, 1966: 24+.
Shinn, Roger L. "The President and His War Critics." *Christianity and Crisis* 27 (January 8, 1968): 309–10.
Skolnick, Jerome H. *Politics of Protest*. New York: Simon and Schuster, 1969.
Stevenson, Adlai E. *Reply to Critics of U.S. Vietnam Policy*. New York: Freedom House Reprint Series No. 19, December 16, 1965.
"[Supreme] Court Rejects Case Challenging Legality of the War [in Vietnam]." *Congressional Quarterly Weekly Report* 25 (November 17, 1967): 2357.
"Texas Liberals to LBJ: End War, Leave Vietnam." *Texas Observer*, June 24, 1966: 5.

"Vietnam—Pro and Con of Kennedy's Peace Plan." *U.S. News and World Report* 60 (March 7, 1966): 104–107.

"Vietnam and the Congressional Record: An Analytical Symposium." *Michigan Quarterly Review* 7 (September 1968): 151–65.

"Vietnam Debate: Dirksen vs Fulbright." *New Leader* 50 (October 23, 1967): 9–19.

Wallace, Don, Jr. "The War-Making Powers: A Constitutional Flaw?" *Cornell Law Review* 57 (May 1972): 719–76.

"War Costs, Problems Dominate 1966 Scene in Congress." *Congressional Quarterly Weekly Report* 23 (December 31, 1965): 2503–07.

Waskow, Arthur. "The Politics of the Pentegon Papers." *Peace and Change: A Journal for Peace Research* 17 (Fall 1972): 1–10.

Wechsler, James A. "The Two-Front War: Johnson vs. Kennedy—The Political Rivalry between LBJ and RFK." *Progressive* 31 (May 1967): 21–24.

Wells, John M., and Maria Wilhelm, eds. *The People vs Presidential War*. New York: Dunellen, 1970.

Wilkins, Lillian Claire. "Wayne Morse: An Exploratory Biography." Eugene: University of Oregon, 1982. Ph.D. dissertation. University Microfilms No. 8215323.

Wormuth, Francis D. "The Nixon Theory of the War Power: A Critique." *California Law Review* 60 (May 1972): 623–703.

———. "The Vietnam War: The President versus the Constitution." *The Vietnam War and International Law*, edited by Richard A. Falk, vol. 2, pp. 711–807. Princeton, N.J.: Princeton University Press, 1969.

Worsnop, Richard L. "War Powers of the President [Congress, the President, and Vietnam]." *Editorial Research Reports*, March 14, 1966: 183–200.

Wright, Quincy. "Legal Aspects of the Viet-Nam Situation." *American Journal of International Law* 60 (October 1966): 750–69.

Zeiger, Henry A. *Robert F. Kennedy: A Biography*. New York: Meredith, 1968.

F. PUBLIC RESPONSE AND DOMESTIC IMPACT

"American Jews and Vietnam: President Corrects 'False Impression'." *Jewish Observer and Middle East Review* 15 (September 16, 1966): 4–6.
Anderson, Terry H. "Pop Music and the Vietnam War." *Peace and Change*, vol. 11, no. 2, 1986: 51–66.
Appleton, Sheldon. "The Public, the Polls, and the War." *Vietnam Perspectives* 1 (May 1966): 3–13.
Bachman, Jerald G., and M. Kent Jennings. "The Impact of Vietnam on Trust in Government." *Journal of Social Issues* 31 (Fall 1975): 141–56.
Badillo, Gilbert, and David G. Curry. "The Social Incidence of Vietnam Casualties: Social Class or Race?" *Armed Forces and Society* 2 (Spring 1976): 397–406.
Baral, Jaya Krishna. "The Anti-Vietnam War Student Movement in America, 1965–1971." *Indian Political Science Review* (India), vol. 12, no. 1, 1978: 43–58.
Baskir, Lawrence M., and William A. Strauss. *Chance and Circumstance: The Draft, The War, and the Vietnam Generation.* New York: Vintage, 1978.
Baum, Phil. "Johnson, Vietnam and the Jews." *Congressional Bi-Weekly* 33 (October 24, 1966): 7–9.
Beisner, Robert L. "On Student Reaction to the Indochina Crisis." *North American Review* 255 (Fall 1970): 55–58.
Bell, D. Bruce, and Beverly W. Bell. "Desertion and Antiwar Protest: Findings from the Ford Clemency Program." *Armed Forces and Society* 3 (Spring 1977): 433–44.
"Boom Times—Unhappy People—Why? Results of a Nationwide Survey." *U.S. News and World Report* 60 (March 21, 1966): 64–68+.
Boulding, Kenneth E. "Forum: Reflections on Protest [of Vietnam War]." *Bulletin of Atomic Scientists*, October 1965: 18–24.
Bowen, William. "Vietnam: A Cost Accounting." *Fortune* 73 (April 1966): 119–23+.
Browne, R. S. "The Freedom Movement and the War in Vietnam." *Freedom-Ways* 5 (Fall 1965): 467–80.
"Budget Reflects Strain of War." *Business Week*, February 3, 1968: 100–01.
Burkhead, Jesse. "Vietnam and the Great Income Reshuffle: Unlike WWII and Korea, the Vietnam Conflict Has Not Con-

tributed to Greater Income Equality." *Challenge* 15 (May/ June 1967): 12–13+.

Burnham, Walter Dean. "Vietnam and the Voter." *Commonweal* 84 (September 30, 1966): 635–37.

Burton, Michael G. "Elite Disunity and Political Instability: A Study of American Opposition to the Vietnam War." Austin: University of Texas, 1974. Ph.D. dissertation. University Microfilms No. 74-14675.

"Business Feels the Spur: Resumption of Bombing in Vietnam Puts New Pressures on the Economy." *Business Week*, February 5, 1966: 21–23.

Butwin, Miriam, and Patricia Pirmantgen. *Protest II: Civil Rights and Black Liberation, the Anti-War Movement.* Minneapolis: Lerner, 1972.

Caine, P. D. "The United States in Korea and Vietnam: A Study in Public Opinion." *Air University Review* 20 (January-February 1968): 49–55.

Campbell, Keith E. "Religiosity and Attitudes toward Selected Wars: A Correlation Study." Columbia: University of Missouri, 1977. Ph.D. dissertation. University Microfilms No. 77–31714.

Cantril, Albert H. *The American People, Vietnam, and the Presidency.* Princeton, N.J.: Princeton University Press, 1970.

Caton, Christopher N. "The Impact of the War in Vietnam on the U.S. Economy." Philadelphia: University of Pennsylvania, 1974. Ph.D. dissertation. University Microfims No. 75-14549.

Chamberlain, John. "Demonstrators Abandon Civil Rights for Vietnam and Dominican Protests." *Human Events* 25 (June 5, 1965): 10.

"Civil Rights Militants Plan Protests on Vietnam." *Human Events* 25 (July 31, 1965): 1.

Close, Alexandra. "The Vietnam War: The Peace Movement." *Far Eastern Economic Review* (Hong Kong) 58 (November 30, 1967): 400–03.

"Controversies: Vietnam as Unending Trauma." *Society* (Special Section) 21 (November-December 1983): 4–34.

Converse, Philip E., and Howard Schuman. "Silent Majorities and the Vietnam War." *Scientific American* 222 (June 1970): 17–25.

Cox, James Robert, Jr. "Perspectives in Rhetorical Criticism on Movements: Antiwar Dissent, 1964–1970." *Western Speech* 38 (Fall 1974): 254–68.

———. "The Rhetorical Structure of Mass Protest: A Criticism of Selected Speeches of the Vietnam Antiwar Movement." Pittsburgh: University of Pittsburgh, 1973. Ph.D. dissertation. University Microfilms No. 74-06785.

Dane, Barbara, comp. *The Vietnam Songbook*. New York: The Guardian, dist. by Monthly Review Press, 1969.

Day, Bonner. "The 'War without a Goal': Mood of Americans in Vietnam." *U.S. News and World Report* 64 (June 24, 1968): 31–33.

DeBenedetti, Charles. "Lyndon Johnson and the Antiwar Opposition." *The Johnson Years, Volume Two: Vietnam, the Environment, and Science*, edited by Robert A. Divine, pp. 23–53. Lawrence: University Press of Kansas, 1987.

"Deflating the Fears of a Recession: Economic Impact of Vietnam Reveals Demand Will Continue to Rise." *Business Week*, October 22, 1966: 122–24.

"Draft Bill Cleared: Provisions of Administration-Requested Military Draft Extension Bill." *Congressional Quarterly Weekly Report* 25 (June 23, 1967): 1050–54.

"Draft Card Burnings Decline as Federal Law Is Enforced." *Human Events* 26 (December 10, 1966): 7.

"Draft Law Extension: Provisions of Administration-Backed Military Selective Service Act of 1967." *Congressional Quarterly Weekly Report* 25 (June 2, 1967): 917–20.

"Draft Outlook under the New Law: Key Decisions on Students, Induction Age Are Up to LBJ." *U.S. News and World Report* 62 (June 19, 1967): 70.

"Draft Revision Affects Peace Corps, Other Volunteers." *Congressional Quarterly Weekly Report* 25 (July 21, 1967): 1239–40.

"Draft Steps Up—What It Means." *U.S. News and World Report* 58 (April 12, 1965): 39.

"Drive for Big Change in the Draft—What's Wrong with the Draft as Presidential Advisers See It." *U.S. News and World Report* 62 (March 13, 1967): 44–46.

Eccles, Marriner S. "Vietnam—Its Effect on the Nation: Serious Economic, Financial and Political Problems." *War/Peace Report* 7 (October 1967): 3–5.

"Far-Reaching Consequences Seen for War Dissent: Implica-

tions of Domestic Opposition to Administration's Policies in Vietnam." *Congressional Quarterly Weekly Report* 25 (June 2, 1967): 935–37.
Finman, Ted, and Stewart Macauly. "Freedom to Dissent: The Vietnam Protests and the Words of Public Officials." *Wisconsin Law Review,* Summer 1966: 632–723.
Finn, James. *Protest: Pacifism and Politics; Some Passionate Views on War and Nonviolence.* New York: Random House, 1968.
Fisher, Randall M. *Rhetoric and American Democracy: Black Protest through Vietnam Dissent.* Lanham, Md.: University Press of America, 1985.
Flemming, Karl. "America's Sad Young Exiles." *Newsweek* 77 (February 15, 1971): 28–30.
Flynn, George Q. *Lewis B. Hershey, Mr. Selective Service.* Chapel Hill: University of North Carolina Press, 1985.
Garrett, Banning, and Katherine Barkley, eds. *Two, Three . . . Many Vietnams: A Radical Reader on the Wars in Southeast Asia and the Conflicts at Home.* San Francisco: Canfield, 1971.
Geyelin, Philip. "The Vietnamese Refugee Problem." *Reporter* 33 (September 23, 1965): 43–45.
Goldstein, Jonathan. "Vietnam Research on Campus: The Summit/Spicerack Controversy at the University of Pennsylvania, 1965–67." *Peace and Change,* vol. 11, no. 2 (1986): 27–50.
Hahn, Harlan. "Correlates of Public Sentiments about War: Local Referenda on the Vietnam Issue." *American Political Science Review* 64 (December 1970): 1186–98.
Halstead, Fred. *Out Now! A Participant's Account of the Movement against the Vietnam War (1965–1975).* New York: Monad, 1978.
Hamby, Alonzo L. "Public Opinion: Korea and Vietnam." *Wilson Quarterly* 2 (Summer 1978): 137–41.
Hartke, Vance. "Vietnam Costs More than You Think." *Saturday Evening Post* 240 (April 1967): 10+.
Haskins, James. *The War and the Protest: Vietnam.* Garden City, N.Y.: Doubleday, 1971.
Hauck, Robb J., and Maude A. Stewart. "College Men and the Draft: 1969." *Journal of College Student Personnel* 11 (no. 6, November 1970): 439–44.

Hayashi, Tetsumaro. "John Steinbeck and the Vietnam War (Part I)." Muncie, Ind.: Ball State University, Dept. of English, Steinbeck Research Institute, Steinbeck Monograph Series, No. 12, 1986.

Hayes, James Robert. "The War within a War: Dissent in the Military with an Emphasis upon the Vietnam War." Storrs: University of Connecticut, 1975. Ph.D. dissertation. University Microfilms No. 75-16515.

Health, G. Louis, ed. *Mutiny Does Not Happen Lightly: The Literature of the American Resistance to the Vietnam War.* Metuchen, N.J.: Scarecrow, 1976.

Heirich, Max. *The Beginning: Berkeley, 1964.* New York: Columbia University Press, 1971.

———. "Demonstrations at Berkeley: Collective Behavior during the Free Speech Movement of 1964–1965." Berkeley: University of California, 1967. Ph.D. dissertation. University Microfilms No. 68-00078.

Hensley, William E. "The Vietnam Anti-War Movement: History and Criticism." Eugene: University of Oregon, 1979. Ph.D. dissertation. University Microfilms No. 80-05770.

"Hooray for War or, Peaceniks and the SS Out at the LBJ." *Texas Observer,* April 30, 1965: 8 +.

"House Armed Services Committee Curbs President's Draft Revision." *Congressional Quarterly Weekly Report* 25 (May 26, 1967): 868–69.

"How Big a Mobilization Ahead? The Effect on Business and People." *U.S. News and World Report* 59 (August 2, 1965): 19–29.

"How Does Jewish Opinion on Vietnam Compare with the Rest of the U.S.?" *World Over* 28 (October 28, 1966): 4.

Hubbell, John, et al. *P.O.W.: A Definitive History of the American Prisoner of War Experience in Vietnam, 1964–73.* Pleasantville, N.Y.: Reader's Digest Press, 1976.

"Impact of Vietnam Begins to Register: Increase in Defense Spending Has Brought Some Orders to Contractors." *Business Week,* May 15, 1965: 27–28.

Janeway, Eliot. *The Economics of Crisis: War, Politics, and the Dollar.* New York: Weybright and Talley, 1968.

Jones, Lew. "Report on the American Antiwar Movement." *International Socialist Review* 29 (January/February 1968): 56–64.

Kauffman, J. F. "Vietnam and the Campus." *NASPA Journal* 5 (April 1968): 313–16.
Kelman, Steven J. *Push Comes to Shove: The Escalation of Student Protest.* Boston: Houghton-Mifflin, 1970.
———. "Youth and Foreign Policy: Youth of the 'New Left' and Their Opposition to United States Policies in the Vietnamese War." *Foreign Affairs* 48 (April 1970): 414–26.
King, Christopher T. "The Unemployment Impact of the Vietnam Years." East Lansing: Michigan State University, 1976. Ph.D. dissertation. University Microfilms No. 76-27118.
King, Martin Luther, Jr. "Declaration of Independence from the War in Vietnam." *Ramparts* 5 (May 1967): 32–37.
———, et al. *Dr. Martin Luther King, Dr. John C. Bennet, Dr. Henry Steele Commager, Rabbi Abraham Heschel Speak on the War in Vietnam.* New York: Clergy and Laymen Concerned about Vietnam, 1967.
Krause, Patricia A., ed. *Anatomy of an Undeclared War: Congressional Conference on the Pentegon Papers.* New York: International Universities Press, 1972.
Labin, Suzanne "Survey of American Public Opinion on the Vietnam War." *NATO's Fifteen Nations* 13 (April-May 1968: 46–49+.
Lauter, Paul, et al. "The Draft: Reform or Resistance? A Report on Two University of Chicago Conferences." *Liberation* 11 (January 1967): 34–39.
Lee, D. B., Jr., and J. W. Dyckman. "Economic Impact of the Vietnam War: A Primer." *Journal of the American Institute of Planners* 36 (September 1970): 298–309.
Levine, Mark H., and Serge R. Denisoff. "Draft Susceptibility and Vietnam War Attitudes." *Youth and Society* 4 (December 1972): 169–76.
Lewis, Fulton, Jr. "Radical Churchman Assail U.S. Policy in South Viet Nam." *Human Events* 25 (August 21, 1965): 3.
Lieberman, E. James. "Statement on the Effects of U.S. Casualties in Vietnam on American Families." *Journal of Marriage and the Family* 32 (May 1970): 197–99.
Lipset, Seymour Martin. "Polls and Protests [about Vietnam]." *Foreign Affairs* 49 (April 1971): 548–55.
———. "Rebellion on Campus." *American Education* 4 (October 1968): 28–31.
———. "Student Opposition in the United States." *Government and Opposition* 1 (April 1966): 351–74.

———, ed. *Student Politics.* New York: Basic Books, 1967.
———, and Sheldon S. Wolin, eds. *The Berkeley Student Revolt: Facts and Interpretations.* Garden City, N.Y.: Anchor Books, 1965.
"Long Lectures for LBJ—Teach-in Forums Register Protest in Colleges over Tough Policy in Vietnam." *Business Week,* May 22, 1965: 27.
Long, Ellis E. "Communication and Social Change: The Verbal and Nonverbal Protest of Selected Clerical Activists Opposed to the Vietnam War, 1965–1970." Tallahassee: Florida State University, 1971. Ph.D. dissertation.
Longino, Charles F., Jr. "Draft Lottery Numbers and Student Opposition to War." *Sociology of Education* 46 (Fall 1973): 499–506.
Lovell, John P. "The College Student and Vietnam: a View from the Classroom." *Worldview* 10 (January 1967): 11–15.
Lunch, William M., and Peter W. Sperlich. "American Public Opinion and the War in Vietnam." *Western Political Quarterly* 32 (March 1979): 21–44.
Lynd, Alice. *We Won't Go: Personal Accounts of War Objectors.* Boston: Beacon, 1968.
Makinin, G. E. "Economic Stabilization in Wartime: A Comparative Study of Korea and Vietnam." *Journal of Political Economy* 79 (November-December 1971): 1216–44.
Mangano, R. M., and A. L. Casebeer. "Alarming Parallels in Student Anti-War Activism of the '30s and '60s." *NASPA Journal* 9 (October 1971): 119–26.
Markel, Lester. "Public Opinion and the War in Vietnam." *New York Times Magazine,* August 8, 1965: 9.
"The Marshall Commission Report [National Advisory Commission on the Selective Service]." *Current History* 55 (July 1968): 42–46+.
McCarthy, Terence. "The Garrison Economy [Impact of Vietnam War on American Economy]." *Columbia University Forum* 9 (Fall 1966): 27–32.
McCaughey, Robert A. "American University Teachers and Opposition to the Vietnam War: A Reconsideration." *Minerva* 14 (Autumn 1976): 307–29.
Mueller, John E. "Trends in Popular Support for the Wars in Korea and Vietnam." *American Political Science Review* 65 (June 1971): 358–75.

Nalty, Bernard C. *Strength for the Fight: A History of Black Americans in the Military.* New York: Free Press, 1986.
Nelson, Frederick. "Administration, Not Peaceniks, Has Made War Unpopular." *Human Events* 27 (April 1, 1967): 13.
Neuhaus, Richard J. "The War, Churches, and Civil Religion." *Annals of the American Academy of Political and Social Science* 387 (January 1970): 128–40.
"New [Army] Draft Rules—Who Will Be Called Now." *U.S. News and World Report* 61 (September 5, 1966): 26–27.
O'Donnell, B. "Effects of the War as Seen by a Counseling Director." *NASPA Journal* 5 (April 1968): 324–26.
"Patriotic Americans Counter Peacenik Activities." *Human Events* 25 (November 13, 1965): 3.
Paul, Norman S. "Outlook for the Draft: An Interview with the Assistant Secretary of Defense for Manpower." *U.S. News and World Report* 59 (August 16, 1965): 36–40.
"Paying for the War." *Economist* (Great Britain) 224 (August 12, 1967): 573–74.
"Peace Corps Begins to Feel Effect of Military Draft." *Congressional Quarterly Weekly Report* 26 (August 2, 1968): 2063–65.
Peck, Sideny M. "Notes on Strategy and Tactics: The Movement against the War." *New Politics* 6 (Fall 1967): 42–55.
Perham, John. "Business and Vietnam: Industry Leaders Are Particularly Concerned about the Information Gap." *Dun's Review and Modern Industry* 87 (April 1966): 40–42+.
Powers, Thomas. *Vietnam: The War at Home—The Antiwar Movement, 1964–1968.* Boston: Macmillan, G. K. Hall, 1984.
"The President, the Jews and Viet Nam." *World Over* 28 (October 14, 1966): 4.
"Proposed Changes in the Selective Service System." *Congressional Digest* 46 (May 1967): 131–59.
"Public Opinion and the Vietnam War, 1964–1967." *Gallup Opinion Index*, no. 30, December 1967: 6–35.
"Public Opinion and the Vietnam War, 1964–1969: A Special Report." *Gallup Opinion Index*, no. 52, October 1969: 1–15.
Quinley, Harold E. "The Protestant Clergy and the War in Vietnam." *Public Opinion Quarterly* 34 (Spring 1970): 43–52.
Riddell, Thomas. "The Vietnam War and Inflation Revisited." Paper presented at Fifth Annual Hofstra University Presi-

dential Conference: Lyndon Baines Johnson, A Texan in Washington. Hempstead, New York, April 10–12, 1986.

Robinson, John P., and Solomon G. Jacobson. "American Public Opinion about Vietnam." *Vietnam: Some Basic Issues and Alternatives,* edited by Walter Isard, pp. 63–79. Cambridge, Mass.: Schenkman, 1969.

Roghbart, Myron, and James C. M. Johnson. "Social Class and Vietnam War: Some Discrepant Motives for Supporting or Opposing United States Involvement in Southeast Asia." *Pacific Sociological Review* 17 (January 1974): 46–59.

Rosenberg, Milton J., Sidney Verba, and Philip E. Converse. *Vietnam and the Silent Majortity: The Dove's Guide.* New York: Harper and Row, 1970.

Sax, J. L. "Conscience and Anarchy: The Prosecution of War Resisters." *Yale Review* 57 (June 1968): 481–94.

Schreiber, Eugene M. "Anti-War Demonstrations and American Public Opinion on War in Vietnam." *British Journal of Sociology (Great Britain)* 27 (June 1976): 225–36.

———. "Opposition to the Vietnam War among American University Students and Faculty." *British Journal of Sociology (Great Britain)* 24 (September 1973): 288–302.

Schuyler, George. "Martin Luther King's Ominous Warning: 'Hotter Summer' Ahead: Negro Leader Plans to Combine Civil Rights Drive with Viet Nam Peace Campaign." *Human Events* 27 (April 15, 1967): 10.

"The Selective Service: Structure and Administration." *Yale Law Journal* 76 (November 1966): 160–99.

Sessions, John A. "Education and the Draft." *AFL-CIO American Federationist* 74 (August 1967): 12–14.

Shaw, William Lawrence. "The Selective Service System in 1966." *Military Law Review* 36 (April 1967): 147–48.

Shields, Patricia M. "The Burden of the Draft: The Vietnam Years." *Journal of Political and Military Sociology* 9 (Fall 1981): 215–28.

Sidey, Hugh. "Lyndon Johnson's Personal Alamo [Vietnam]." *Time* 125 (April 15, 1985): 47.

Siemering, William H. "The War and Student Activities." *NASPA Journal* 5 (April 1968): 327–29.

Small, Melvin. "The Impact of the Antiwar Movement on Lyndon Johnson, 1965–1968: A Preliminary Report." *Peace and Change* 10 (Spring 1984): 1–22.

Smith, Robert B. "The Vietnam War and Student Militancy." *Social Science Quarterly* 52 (June 1971): 133–56.

"Spending Escalated in Vietnam Action—Defense Markets." *Steel* 156 (May 10, 1965): 43–44.

Stewart, Maude A., and Robb J. Hauck. "College Men and the Draft." *Journal of College Student Personnel* 9 (November 1968): 371–77.

Stohl, Michael. "War and Domestic Political Violence: The Case of the United States, 1890–1970." *Journal of Conflict Resolution* 19 (September 1975): 379–416.

"Taking War in Its Stride [Effects of Military Spending on U.S. Economy]." *Economist* (Great Britain) 216 (August 21, 1965): 693–94+.

Taylor, Clyde. "Black Consciousness and the Vietnam War." *Black Scholar* 5 (October 1973): 2–8.

———, comp. *Vietnam and Black America: An Anthology of Protest and Resistance.* Garden City, N.Y.: Anchor, 1973.

"Texans, ABM, and Vietnam." *Texas Observer,* May 23, 1969: 20+.

Thorne, Barrie. "Protest and the Problems of Credibility: Uses of Knowledge and Risk-Taking in the Draft Resistance Movement of the 1960s." *Social Problems,* vol. 23, no. 2 (1975): 111–23.

"Turmoil over the Draft: The Effect of LBJ's Plan [on the Public and Congress]." *U.S. News and World Report* 62 (March 20, 1967): 33–34.

"Twenty Questions about the Draft Answered: How the New Law Will Work." *U.S. News and World Report* 63 (July 10, 1967): 36–37.

"Two Senate Panels Study Draft Revision Plans." *Congressional Quarterly Weekly Report* 25 (April 28, 1967): 667–70.

Unseem, Michael. *Conscription, Protest, and Social Conflict: The Life and Death of a Draft Resistance Movement.* New York: Wiley, 1973.

Verba, Sidney, et al. "[American] Public Opinion and the War in Vietnam." *American Political Science Review* 61 (June 1967): 317–33.

———, et al. *Vietnam and the Silent Majority: The Dove's Guide.* New York: Harper, 1970.

"Vietnam [Special Section]." *Time* 125 (April 15, 1985): 16–26+.
"Vietnam: Ten Years After [Special Issue]." *New Republic* 192 (April 29, 1985): 7–25+.
"Vietnam: The Lasting Impact [Special Section]." *U.S. News and World Report* 98 (April 22, 1985): 35–41.
"Vietnam in America: Ten Years after the Fall of Saigon—A Special Issue." *New York Times Magazine,* March 31, 1985: 27–36+.
"Vietnam Puts Squeeze on the Great Society." *Business Week,* December 18, 1965: 31.
"Vietnam's Bitter Legacy [Special Section]." *MacLeans* (Canada) 98 (April 29, 1985): 38–48.
"War Costs Set Pace for Jump in Spending." *Business Week,* December 4, 1965: 28–30.
We Accuse: The Vietnam Day Protest in Berkeley, California. Berkeley, Cal.: Diablo Press, 1965.
Weaver, Gary Rodger. "The American Public and Vietnam: An In-Depth Study of the American People in Times of International Conflict." Washington, D.C.: American University, 1970. Ph.D. dissertation. University Microfilms No. 71-08628.
Weidenbaum, Murray L. *Economic Impact of the Vietnam War.* Washington, D.C.: Center for Strategic Studies, June 1967.
Williams, Roger N. *The New Exiles: American War Resisters in Canada.* New York: Liveright, 1971.
Willis, John M. "Who Died in Vietnam? An Analysis of the Social Background of Vietnam Casualties." Lafayette, Ind.: Purdue University, 1975. Ph.D. dissertation. University Microfilms No. 76-07155.
Wilson, George C. "Asian War May Undermine Budget Hopes." *Aviation Week and Space Technology* 84 (January 31, 1966): 14–15.
Windmiller, Marshall. "U.S. Public Opinion and the Vietnam War." *Review of International Affairs* (Yugoslavia) 18 (January 20, 1967): 5–7.
Wyschogrod, Michael. "Jewish Interest in Vietnam." *Tradition* 9 (Fall 1967): 154–56; condensed in *Jewish Digest* 12 (July 1967): 1–6.
Yoder, Jess. "The Protest of the American Clergy in Opposition to the War in Vietnam." *Today's Speech* 17 (September 1969): 51–59.

Zaroulis, Nancy, and Gerald Sullivan. *Who Spoke Up? American Protest against the War in Vietnam, 1963–1976.* Garden City, N.Y.: Doubleday, 1984.

Zeitlin, Maurice, et al. "Death in Vietnam: Class, Poverty, and the Risks of War." *Politics and Society* 3 (Spring 1973): 313–28.

VIII. The Postpresidential Years, 1969–1973

A. GENERAL

"After LBJ 'Retires' to Texas." *U.S. News and World Report* 65 (December 23, 1968): 40–44.

Alexander, Holmes. "Is Johnson Really Gone for Good?" *Human Events* 29 (February 1, 1969): 1.

Chester, Edward W. "Lyndon Baines Johnson, an American 'King Lear': A Critical Evaluation of His Newspaper Obituaries." Paper presented to the 27th Annual Meeting of the Western Social Science Assn., Ft. Worth, Texas, April 24, 1985.

"Consensus after LBJ." *Southwest Review* 53 (Spring 1968): 113.

"For LBJ, No Roughing It Back on the Ranch." *Human Events* 29 (February 22, 1969): 12.

Gordon, Jennifer. "Talking about L.B.J. [University of Texas Oral History Project on Johnson]." *Texas Highways* 21 (June 1974): 28–31.

Hardesty, Mary. "LBJ's Rambunctious Retirement." *Harper's Weekly*, January 24, 1975: 10–11.

"Has LBJ Forgotten Monk's Most Unforgettable Story? Visiting the LBJ Ranch." *Editor and Publisher* 105 (January 8, 1972): 22.

Hewitt, Don. *Minute by Minute . . .* New York: Random House, 1985.

"Johnson Programs that Will Survive: Much of the 'Great Society' Will Continue under Nixon, but New Programs May Be Few." *Business Week*, January 4, 1969: 16–18.

"The Johnson Complex." *Texas Observer*, January 24, 1969: 2+.

"Last Flight to Johnson City." *Texas Observer*, January 24, 1969: 6+.

"LBJ: A Political Spectator." *U.S. News and World Report* 73 (July 31, 1972): 47.
"LBJ in Retirement: A Close-Up of an Ex-President." *U.S. News and World Report* 70 (April 12, 1971): 71–73.
"LBJ in Retirement—Still a Busy Man." *U.S. News and World Report* 67 (September 29, 1969): 44–47.
"LBJ Memoirs Edited for 12-Part Serial." *Editor and Publisher* 104 (August 21, 1971): 24.
"LBJ Privately Challenges HHH on Party Leadership." *Human Events* 29 (March 8, 1969): 5.
"LBJ's Funeral Oration." *National Review* 35 (March 4, 1983): 232–33.
"Leaders Acclaim LBJ Record." *Crisis* 80 (April 1973): 127–33.
Lisagor, Peter. "Lyndon Johnson Discusses His Failure with Amerian Youth." *True*, March 1969: 34–37.
"Lyndon B. Johnson, 1908–1973." *Human Events* 33 (February 3, 1973): 20.
"McGovern Comes to Texas." *Texas Observer*, September 8, 1972: 6+.
McGowan, Carl "Presidents and Their Papers." *Minnesota Law Review* 68 (December 1983): 409–37.
National Geographic Society. *The Lyndon Baines Johnson Memorial Grove on the Potomac: A Tribute to Lyndon B. Johnson Conservationist.* Washington, D.C.: Eastern National Park and Monument Assn., 1977.
"New Vocation for LBJ." *Texas Observer*, April 23, 1971: 5.
"Oh, Good Grief." *Texas Observer*, May 21, 1971: 8+.
Postal, Bernard. "Some Jewish Jottings about Lyndon Baines Johnson." *Jewish Digest* 18 (March 1973): 13–15.
"President Johnson's Biggest Success." *Jewish Observer—Middle East Review* 18 (January 17, 1969): 3.
"Unpredictible LBJ—Seems Like Old Times in the Perdernales." *U.S. News and World Report* 69 (September 7, 1970): 28.
"Welcome Home, Mr. President." *Texas Observer*, January 24, 1969: 3.

B. THE LYNDON B. JOHNSON LIBRARY AND LBJ STATE PARK

"And a Good Time Was Had by Most [LBJ Library]." *Texas Observer*, June 4, 1971: 4+.

Anderson, Claudia Wilson. "Adolescence to Middle Age: The Maturing of a Presidential Library." Paper presented to the annual meeting of the Society of American Archivists, Austin, Texas, October 31, 1985.
———. "The Lyndon Baines Johnson Library and Museum, Austin, Texas." *A Guide to the History of Texas*, edited by Light T. Cummins and Alvin Bailey. Westport, Conn.: Greenwood Press, 1986.
Banks, Ginger. "A Library Like No Other: Throngs of Tourists, from President Nixon on Down, Find the LBJ Library an Exciting Place." *Texas Star* [*Houston Post*] 1 (September 5, 1971): 4–5.
Barnett, John. *LBJ Country: A Guide to the Lyndon Baines Johnson National Historic Site* [Birthplace and Boyhood Home], *Johnson City, the Texas White House, LBJ State Park, Hye, Stonewall and Fredericksburg*. Fresno, Cal.: Awani Press, 1970.
Berman, Larry. "Presidential Libraries: How Not to Be a Stranger in a Strange Land." *Studying the Presidency*, edited by George C. Edwards III and Stephen J. Wayne, pp. 225–56. Knoxville: University of Tennessee Press, 1983.
Bostic, Elaine. "Recording the Johnson Era: From Texas to President [LBJ Library]." *Texas Parade* 32 (June 1971): 44
Campbell, Douglas G. "The Lyndon Baines Johnson Library: A Museum–Library Monument." *Journal of the West* 23 (January 1984): 97–102.
Carpenter, Liz. "LBJ Library Sharpens Its Focus." *Texas Highways* 29 (September 1982): 3.
"Clippings: [Original] LBJ Library Staff." *Southwestern Historical Quarterly* 75 (October 1971): 234–35.
"Dedication [of LBJ Library]." *Southwestern Historical Quarterly* 75 (July 1971): 88–90.
Divine, Robert A. "Presidential Library." *Discovery: Research and Scholarship at the University of Texas at Austin*, vol. 10, no. 1 (1985): 30–33.
Dreyer, Martin. "Library for Lyndon." *Texas Sunday Magazine* [*Houston Chronicle*], May 16, 1971: 7–9+.
Dunlop, Richard. "Footprints of a President [Lyndon Baines Johnson State Park]." *Southern Living* 9 (April 1974): 142.
"The Education President: National Symposium Marks Opening of Johnson Library's Education Documents." *Texas Times* 4 (February 1972): 1–12.

Elzy, Martin I. "LBJ Library: Local History Resources Found Nowhere Else." *History News* 35 (February 1980): 9–11.

Gordon, Jennifer. "LBJ Country [LBJ Park and Johnson Boyhood Home, Johnson City, Texas]." *Texas Highways* 22 (September 1975): 8–14.

"Grandeur, Piety and Barbecue [LBJ Library]." *Texas Observer*, June 4, 1971: 2.

"The Johnson Library and School." *Texas Times* 3 (April/May 1971): 1A-8A.

"LBJ Library . . . Touchstone with History." *Austin* (Official Publication of the Austin Chamber of Commerce) 12 (May 1971): 12–15.

Lipsius, Frank. "The LBJ Memorial Library." *Diversion*, November 1983: 108–112.

Lowry, M. "LBJ State Park." *Texas Parks and Wildlife* 28 (May 1970): 24–27.

"Lyndon B. Johnson Library Next Right." *Texas Observer*, July 30, 1971: 15.

"Lyndon Baines Johnson Library." *The Handbook of Texas: A Supplement*, edited by Eldon Stephen Branda, vol. 3, p. 549. Austin: Texas State Historical Association, 1976.

"Lyndon Baines Johnson Library Museum." *The Historical Encyclopedia of Texas*, edited by Thomas S. Chamberlin, pp. 36–37. Austin?: Texas Historical Institute, 1982.

"Lyndon Johnson and the University." *Texas Observer*, June 12, 1970: 15.

Middleton, Harry J. "An Invitation to the Lyndon Baines Johnson Library—Editorial." *Texas Historian* 32 (January 1972): 28.

———. "The Lyndon Baines Johnson Presidential Library." *Texas Libraries* 39 (Winter 1977): 181–91.

"Pseudo-Event at the Mausoleum [LBJ Library]." *Texas Observer*, December 29, 1972: 14.

Sidey, Hugh. "One More Call to Reason Together: A Gathering at the Lyndon Baines Johnson Library, University of Texas [the Civil Rights Symposium]." *Life* 73 (December 29, 1972): 16D.

Tyler, Paula Eyrich, and Ron Tyler. *Texas Museums: A Guidebook*. Austin: University of Texas Press, 1983.

"Who Paid for LBJ's Park [Lyndon B. Johnson State Park]." *Texas Observer*, December 13, 1968: 8.

PART 2

LADY BIRD JOHNSON AND FAMILY

I. Lady Bird Johnson, Writings and Interviews

Johnson, Claudia A. T.; Lady Bird Johnson; Mrs. Lyndon B. Johnson; Claudia Taylor. "First Lady Talks about Her Mother-in-Law." *McCalls* 93 (November 1965): 8+.

———. "Foreword." *Texas Wildflowers: A Field Guide,* by Campbell and Lynn Loughmiller, pp. vii–viii. Austin: University of Texas Press, 1984.

———. "Help Your Husband Guard His Heart: Senator Johnson's Wife Tells What She Learned—Almost Too Late—as a Result of His Frightening Illness." *This Week Magazine* [*Washington Sunday Star*], February 12, 1956: 7–9.

———. "I See America First." *National Geographic* 127 (December 1965): 874–904.

———. "In Memoriam" (Interview). *Texas Observer,* March 30, 1973: 14.

———. "Introduction." *Paintings in the White House: A Close Up.* Westinghouse Broadcasting Co., 1965.

———. "New UT [University of Texas] Regents" (Interview). *Texas Observer,* January 29, 1971: 9+.

———. "On Preserving Wilderness." *Southwest Review* 69 (Spring 1984): 194–200.

———. "Personal Interview." *Texas Observer,* September 22, 1972: 9.

———. "Personal Interview." *Texas Observer,* October 6, 1972: 7.

———. "Personal Interview." *Texas Observer,* September 9, 1977: 14.

———. "Remarks." *Proceedings at the Dedication of the Sam Rayburn Statue.* Washington, D.C.: U.S. Gov't. Printing Office, 1965, pp. 25–27.

———. "Text of Television Interview with Mrs. Johnson, August 22, 1964." *Congressional Quarterly Weekly Report* 22 (September 18, 1964): 2190–92.

———. "Welcome." Public Policy Association. The Second Presidential Library Conference on the Public and Public Policy, LBJ Library, Austin, March 22, 1984. Transcript: Kennedy Reporting Service, Austin, Texas, pp. 7–9.

———, and Lyndon B. Johnson. "Television Interview with the President and Mrs. Johnson." *Weekly Compilation of Presidential Documents* 3 (December 18, 1967): 1687–91.

———, as told to Giovanna Breu. "Let a Billion Wildflowers Bloom." *People Weekly* 25 (June 2, 1986): 70–72.

II. Biographical Works (see also Part 1, Section II)

Crawford, Ann Fears, and Crystal Sasse Ragsdale. *Women in Texas: Their Lives, Their Experiences, Their Accomplishments.* Burnet, Texas: Eakin Press, 1982.
Kearns, Doris. *Lyndon Johnson and the American Dream.* New York: Harper and Row, 1976.
"Lyndon Baines Johnson." *Texas Democracy: A Centennial History of Politics and Personalities of the Democratic Party, 1836–1936,* edited by Frank Carter Adams, vol. III, pp. 167–68. Austin: Democratic Historical Assn., 1937.
Smith, Eliz Simpson. *Five First Ladies: A Look into the Lives of Nancy Reagan, Rosalynn Carter, Betty Ford, Pat Nixon, and Lady Bird Johnson.* New York: Walker & Co., 1986.
Steinberg, Alfred. *Sam Johnson's Boy: A Close-Up of the President from Texas.* New York: Macmillan, 1968.
Texas Mothers Committee. "Claudia Alta Taylor Johnson." *Worthy Mothers of Texas.* Texas Mothers Committee, p. 102. Belton, Texas: Stillhouse Hollow Publishers, 1976.
Tolbert, Frank X. *Tolbert's Texas.* Garden City, N.Y.: Doubleday, 1983.

III. The Prepresidential Years, 1912–1963

Bannworth, Deborah. "Lady Bird Johnson's Tenure in the Congressional Office." Course paper for Lewis L. Gould, University of Texas at Austin, May 14, 1986 [c/o LBJ Library].
Caro, Robert A. *The Years of Lyndon Johnson: The Path to Power*. New York: Alfred A. Knopf, 1982.
Dugger, Ronnie. *The Politician: The Life and Times of Lyndon Johnson—The Drive for Power, from the Frontier to Master of the Senate*. New York: Norton, 1982.
Garcia, Elvia. "Lady Bird Johnson: Whistle Stopping through the South." Austin: University of Texas at Austin, 1986. B.A. senior thesis [c/o LBJ Library].
"The Johnsons' TV Interests." *Texas Observer*, December 18, 1959: 1+.
King, C. Richard. "By-Lines of Claudia Alta Taylor on [University of Texas at Austin] *Daily Texan* Newspaper." Paper, Department of Journalism, University of Texas at Austin, May 1, 1964. Typewritten [c/o LBJ Library].
Lane, Dorothy. "A Sketch of Alice Glass." Course paper for Lewis L. Gould, University of Texas at Austin, May 14, 1986 [c/o LBJ Library].
"The Last Family." *Texas Observer*, May 16, 1963: 12.
Louchheim, Katie, ed. *The Making of the New Deal: The Insiders Speak*. Cambridge, Mass.: Harvard University Press, 1983.

IV. The Presidential Years, 1963–1969

A. GENERAL

Behrens, Anne. "The Fashion for First Ladies: From Jackie to Nancy, from Paris to New York." *The Washington Post Magazine*, February 2, 1986: 162+.
Bornet, Vaughn D. *The Presidency of Lyndon B. Johnson*. Lawrence: University Press of Kansas, 1983.
Colt, George Howe, et al. "White House Families." *Life* 7 (November 1984): 32–51.
Divine, Robert A., ed. *The Johnson Years, Volume Two: Viet-*

nam, the Environment, and Science. Lawrence: University Press of Kansas, 1987.
"Down on the Farm." *Newsweek* 63 (May 25, 1964): 32.
"The Fabled Past: Painter of Presidents [Elizabeth Shounatoff]." *The North Shore Journal* [Locust Valley, New York *Leader* supplement] 16 (August 29, 1985): all.
Fawcett, Ruth. "The Wisdom and Wit of Liz Carpenter." *Texas Woman* 1 (January 1980): 25–29.
"First Ladies Have an Impossible Job." *Forbes Magazine* 127 (February 2, 1981): 20.
Gould, Lewis L. "First Ladies." *American Scholar* 55 (Autumn 1986): 528–35.
———. "Keynote Address." First Ladies Symposium, Gerald R. Ford Library, Grand Rapids, Michigan, April 18–20, 1984.
———. "Modern First Ladies in Historical Perspective." *Presidential Studies Quarterly* 15 (Summer 1985): 532–40.
"Inside the White House with Lady Bird Johnson." *Saturday Evening Post*, February 8, 1964: 19–25.
"The Johnsons in the White House." *Look* 28 (March 10, 1964): 15–23.
"Lady Bird's Success in PR Traced to Study, Intuition." *Editor and Publisher* 104 (June 5, 1971): 38.
Louchheim, Katie. "The Spotlight Shifts in Washington." *Ladies' Home Journal* 81 (January 1964): 55.
McCarthy, Dennis V. N., with Philip W. Smith. *Protecting the President: The Inside Story of a Secret Service Agent.* New York: Morrow, 1985.
Sidey, Hugh. "The Second Toughest Job [First Ladies]." *Time*, January 14, 1985: 35.
Small, Melvin. "The Impact of Antiwar Movement on Lyndon Johnson, 1965–1968." *Peace and Change*, vol. 10, no. 1 (1984): 1–22.
Smith, Nancy Kegan. "'A Journey of the Heart' [Lady Bird Johnson and Her Role as First Lady]." *Prologue* 19 (Summer 1987): 126–35.
———. "'A Journey of the Heart': The Papers of Lady Bird Johnson." Paper delivered to the Society of American Archivists, October 29, 1985, Austin, Texas [c/o LBJ Library].
———. "Women and the White House: A Look at Women's Papers in the Johnson Library." *Prologue* 18 (Summer 1986): 123–29.

Starr, Samuel D. *Lady Bird Cha Cha Cha.* Words by Frank H. Keith. Hammond, Ind.: De 'Besth Music Publishing Co., 1968.
Sutherland, John P. "Life on the Ranch: A Day at Home with LBJ." *U.S. News and World Report* 56 (April 13, 1964): 67–68.
Thompson, Pat. *Ladybird's Man.* Los Angeles: Holloway House, 1964.
West, J. Bernard, and Mary Lynn Kotz. *Upstairs at the White House: My Life with the First Ladies* [White House Chief Usher, 1941–1969]. New York: Coward, McCann and Geoghegan, 1973.
"With Lady Bird in the White House." *U.S. News and World Report* 58 (February 1, 1965): 33.
"With the First Lady on Her Farewell Tour." *U.S. News and World Report* 65 (December 9, 1968): 46–47.

B. POLITICS AND POLICY

1. BEAUTIFICATION

Chamberlain, John. "Can We Trust Government to Beautify Us?" *Human Events* 25 (February 27, 1965): 10.
Craig, James B. "Natural Beauty, the Follow Through." *American Forests* 71 (October 1965): 12–15+.
Gould, Lewis L. "First Lady as Catalyst: Lady Bird Johnson and Highway Beautification in the 1960s." *Environmental Review* 10 (Summer 1986): 77–92.
———. "Lady Bird Johnson and Beautification." *The Johnson Years, Volume Two: Vietnam, the Environment, and Science,* edited by Robert A. Divine, pp. 150–80. Lawrence: University Press of Kansas, 1987.
———. *Lady Bird Johnson and the Environment.* Lawrence: University Press of Kansas, 1988.
"Hearings on Beautification Act." *Texas Highways* 13 (May 1966): 28.
"Highway Billboards and Auto Junkyards Target of Drive." *Labor* (Railroad Labor Organizations) 46 (June 5, 1965): 6.
"Lady Bird Johnson Thanks the Clothing Workers for Their Support of the Highway Beautification Act." *Advance* (Amalgamated Clothing Workers of America) 51 (December 1, 1965): 3.

Lewis, Ted. "Lady Bird's 'Beautification' Plan Coupled to Traffic Safety Fund." *Human Events* 27 (February 11, 1967): 6.
Morgan, Edward P. "Beautification Bug Begins to Bite Even the Businessman [in McLean, Virginia]." *AFL-CIO News* 11 (June 18, 1966): 5.
Steinberg, Alfred. *Sam Johnson's Boy: A Close-Up of the President from Texas.* New York: Macmillan, 1968.
Watterson, Joseph. "Beauty USA: The White House Conference on Natural Beauty." *AIA Journal* [American Institute of Architects], July 1965, pp. 61–62.
Weber, Janice. "The Highway Beautification Act of 1965." Course paper for Larry Dodd, University of Texas at Austin, May 1980 [c/o LBJ Library].

2. JOHNSON FAMILY FINANCES

"Baker Case: Potential Election Issues—G.O.P. Criticizes Insurance Man's KTBC Time Purchase." *Broadcasting* 66 (February 3, 1964): 72.
"A Banking Empire in Lyndon Johnson's Fortune? [Johnson Family Interests in Texas Banking]." *U.S. News and World Report* 63 (July 24, 1967): 59–60.
Gelfand, Mark I. "The Johnson Fortune." *Responses of the Presidents to Charges of Misconduct,* edited by C. Vann Woodward, pp. 394–98. New York: Delacorte Press, 1974.
Givens, Ken. [*A Brief History of the Early Years of One Austin, Texas Radio Station, KTBC*]. Austin? s.n., 1981? [booklet; cataloger's title from introduction, c/o Barker Texas History Center, University of Texas at Austin].
"It Isn't Over in Austin Yet—TV Licensee May Not Be Allowed to Buy into Cable System." *Broadcasting* 66 (May 11, 1964): 79.
"Johnson Family Finances." *Congressional Quarterly Weekly Report* 22 (August 21, 1964): 1944–47.
"The Johnsons' Radio-TV Interests." *Texas Observer,* February 21, 1964: 11+.
Kohlmeier, Louis M. "President Johnson's Hometown Coterie Wheels and Deals in Land, Broadcasting, Buy into Austin Banks." *Wall Street Journal,* August 11, 1964: 1.
"Lady Bird's Austin Co. Gets FCC Approval for Another Multi-Million Dollar TV Monopoly." *Human Events* 24 (June 20, 1964): 8.

"Lady Bird's $15 Million Fortune (How Lady Bird Johnson Turned $17,500 into $15 Million)." *Human Events* 24 (July 11, 1964): 2–4.

"LBJ's TV Monopoly." *Human Events* 27 (June 17, 1967): 4.

"Multimillionaire." *Time* 84 (August 21, 1964): 15–16.

"New Chapter in Austin TV Story." *Human Events* 24 (December 12, 1964): 3.

Shapp, M. J. "Austin's CATV's High Value Argued." *Broadcasting* 66 (June 8, 1964): 56–58.

Stern, Laurence M. "LBJ of the FCC [Johnson Family Television Properties]." *Progressive* 28 (June 1964): 21–24.

"Then There's the Little Matter of Propriety (Johnson Family Holdings in TV and Radio)." *Broadcasting* 65 (December 16, 1963: 78–79.

"This Is LBJ Country—Report on a Texas Land Boom: Expanding Empire of Johnson Family." *U.S. News and World Report* 62 (February 20, 1967): 54–58.

3. MISCELLANEOUS POLITICS AND POLICY

"At the Front." *Newsweek* 63 (January 20, 1964): 14.

"Chance to Roam: Lady Bird and Cabinet Wives Tour Landscapes and Landmarks of Virginia." *Time* 85 (May 21, 1965): 27.

Democratic National Committee. "LBJ Carries Campaign into 11 States as First Lady Whistle-Stops in South." *The Democrat* 4 (October 12, 1964): 1–8.

"First Lady in the War Zone." *U.S. News and World Report* 67 (August 11, 1967): 14.

"The First Lady's Poverty Row." *Human Events* 24 (June 20, 1964): 11.

Garcia, Elvia. "Lady Bird Johnson: Whistle Stopping through the South." Austin: University of Texas at Austin, 1986. B.A. senior thesis [c/o LBJ Library].

Gutin, Myra Greenberg. "The President's Partner: The First Lady as Public Communicator, 1920–1976." Ann Arbor: University of Michigan, 1983. Ph.D. dissertation. University Microfilms No. 8324192.

Kirk, Elise K. *Music at the White House: A History of the American Spirit.* Urbana: University of Illinois Press, 1986.

"Lady Bird Becomes Dagak-Deedit-Chish [1964 Election]." *Life*, August 28, 1964: 34.

"Lady Bird's 'Pocket of Poverty' in Alabama." *Human Events* 24 (May 31, 1964): 7, 10.
"LBJ's 'War on Poverty' Should Begin at Home: Lady Bird's Tenants Live in Squalor." *Human Events* 24 (May 31, 1964): 1.
"Leading Campaign Role for Lady Bird." *Human Events* 24 (June 13, 1964): 3.
"Mrs. Lyndon Johnson Honors 42,000 Retired Members of Garment Workers." *Justice* (International Ladies' Garment Workers' Union) 49 (May 15, 1967): 1, 3.
"Reaction to the First Lady's Tour of Wyoming Valley." *Human Events* 23 (February 8, 1964): 2.
Riesel, Victor. "'Lady Bird' and Labor." *Human Events* 22 (December 21, 1963): 12.
Roberts, Dick. "Old Fort Davis [Lady Bird Dedicates National Historic Site]." *Texas Highways* 13 (May 1966): 3–5.
Sidey, Hugh. "The Tortuous Road to Decision, and Lady Bird's Role." *Life* 64 (April 12, 1968): 32–33.
"So Glad, So Glad: First Official Trip Outside Washington." *Time* 83 (April 3, 1964): 24–25.
Wakefield, Beverly Smith. "The Speechmaking of Mrs. Lyndon Baines Johnson, January, 1964–April, 1968." Austin: University of Texas, 1968. M.A. thesis.
"'Whistlestop' Train Tour by First Lady." *Labor* [Railroad Labor Organizations] 46 (September 19, 1964): 10.

V. The Postpresidential Years, 1969–present

A. GENERAL

Alsop, Susan Mary, and Mary E. Nichols. "Architectural Digest Visits: Lady Bird Johnson." *Architectural Digest* 43 (April 1986): 142–51.
Barrineau, Mary. "Laying Down Her Burdens (Life after Lyndon)." *Atlantic Weekly*, November 13, 1983: 29–33.
Bennett, Elizabeth. "Five Winning Women." *Harper's Bazaar* 114 (July 1981): 154–55.
Carpenter, Liz. "The Incomparable Lady Bird." *Ultra Magazine* 3 (November 1983): 86–87.
———. "The Silver Lining: Growing Old Gracefully [Lady Bird]." *Texas Monthly* 13 (March 1985): 126–27, 213.

"The 40 Acres Massacre." *Texas Observer*, October 20, 1974: 3+.
Gilbert, Julie. "Ladybird: Living Life Her Way." *The Magazine of the Houston Post*, May 5, 1985: 7–10, 17.
Klaw, Barbara. "Lady Bird Johnson Remembers." *American Heritage*, vol. 32, no. 1 (1980): 4–17.
"Lady Bird Johnson." *People* 5 (February 23, 1976): 70–71; (May 17, 1976): 56–59.
"Lady Bird Johnson Sets New Mark." *Texas Clubwoman* 43 (November 1970): 6–7.
"Lady Bird's Success in PR Traced to Study, Intuition." *Editor and Publisher* 104 (June 5, 1971): 38.
Levin, Bea. "First Ladies of Fashion." *Texas Weekly Magazine*, May 19–25, 1984: 12–13.
Lyndon B. Johnson Foundation and the Lyndon B. Johnson Library and Museum. *A White House Diary: The Exhibition [at] the Lyndon Baines Johnson Library and Museum, May 1–November 3, 1985*. Austin: Best Printing, 1985.
Matthiessen, Maria Von. "Great Texas Faces." *Ultra Magazine* 5 (December 1985): 102.
"Mrs. Johnson Receives Communication College Honor." *On Campus* (University of Texas at Austin) 13 (April 14–20, 1986): 4.
Pearsall, Joan. "A Conversation with Lady Bird Johnson [about LBJ State Park]." *Texas Parks and Wildlife* 40 (August 1982): 8–9.
Pinkard, Tommie. "Christmas in the [Lyndon B. Johnson State Historic] Park." *Texas Highways* 25 (December 1978): 24–29.
Smith, Nancy Kegan. "'A Journey of the Heart': The Papers of Lady Bird Johnson." Paper delivered to the Society of American Archivists, October 29, 1985, Austin, Texas [c/o LBJ Library].
"Tupperware Party." *Texas Observer*, November 28, 1975: 21+.
United States, 91st Congress, 1st Session. *Tributes to the President and Mrs. Lyndon B. Johnson in the Congress of the United States*. Washington, D.C.: U.S. Gov't. Printing Office, 1969.
Weston, M. "Lady Bird Johnson's Hidden Family Farmhouse." *House and Garden* 155 (January 1983): 126–29.

B. BEAUTIFICATION

Burns, Wendell J. "Let's Beautify America." *Lawn and Garden Marketing,* July 1983: 7–8, 50.
Carpenter, Liz. "First Lady of the Wildflowers [Lady Bird Johnson and the National Wildflower Research Center]." *50 Plus* 25 (July 1985): 20–21+.
"Derrick Wins Lady Bird [Beautification] Award." *Texas Highways* 17 (November 1970): 2–9.
Floyd, Charles F. "Requiem for the Highway Beautification Act." *APA Journal* [American Planning Association], Autumn 1982, pp. 441–53.
"Highway Department's Beautifiers Honored." *Texas Highways* 21 (November 1974): 25.
"Lady Bird and the Beautifiers." *Texas Highways* 19 (September 1972): 28.
"Lady Bird Awards." *Texas Highways* 23 (December 1976): 34.
"Lady Bird Johnson: 'A Passion for American Wildflowers'." *Good Housekeeping* 203 (July 1986): 58.
"Lady Bird Johnson Beautification Award." *Texas Highways* 18 (November 1971): 12–21.
Mathews, Carla. "Lady Bird's Legacy [National Wildflower Research Center]." *Austin Magazine* 27 (June 1985): 37–42.
National Geographic Society. *The Lyndon Baines Johnson Memorial Grove on the Potomac: A Tribute to Lyndon B. Johnson Conservationist.* Washington, D.C.: Eastern National Park and Monument Assn., 1977.
"1972 Lady Bird Johnson Award for Highway Beautification." *Texas Highways* 19 (October 1972): 13–20.
"1978 Lady Bird Johnson Award." *Texas Highways* 25 (December 1978): 34.
Pinkard, Tommie. "Top Beautifier of 1973." *Texas Highways* 20 (November 1973): 9–11.
———. "Winners Speechless at Lady Bird Awards Ceremony." *Texas Highways* 19 (November 1972): 2–4.
Schreiber, Flora Rheta, and Stuart Long. "America, Be Beautiful: A Talk with Lady Bird Johnson." *Modern Maturity* 18 (December/January 1976): 41–43.
"Top Beautifier." *Texas Highways* 24 (November 1977): 34.
"Top Beautifiers Named." *Texas Highways* 22 (December 1975): 32.

Wilson, Amy. "Lady Bird's Legacy: Floral Freeways." *Texas Weekly Magazine*, April 6, 1986: 6–8.

VI. The Family

"Approaching Wedding of Pat [Nugent] and the President's Daughter [Luci Baines Johnson]." *Life* 61 (July 15, 1966): 76–78.
"Bagpipers Play 'The Eyes of Texas' as Lyndon Johnson's Luci Gets Hitched to a Scottish Banker." *People Weekly* 21 (March 19, 1984): 97.
Barnes, Fred. "Ladies and Gentlemen, The Next Vice President . . . [Charles Robb]." *The Washingtonian* 21 (September 1986): 164–67, 202–04.
Chamberlain, John. "Lynda Bird and Foreign Aid." *Human Events* 26 (June 25, 1966): 14.
Colt, George Howe, et al. "White House Families." *Life* 7 (November 1984): 32–51.
Elkin, Sandra. "'A Share of Honour': Virginia's First Lady Lynda Johnson Robb and Women from Businesses and the Humanities Launch a Statewide Celebration of Women's History." *History News* 40 (March 1985): 7–13.
"An End—a Beginning: President Johnson's First Week—Special Issue." *Newsweek* December 9, 1963: 19–48.
"First Family Suitors: Their Military Status." *U.S. News and World Report* 60 (April 25, 1966): 22.
Fowler, George. "'I Never Saw So Many Reporters', Says Pat Nugent before Leaving White House for His Honeymoon." *Editor and Publisher* 99 (August 13, 1966): 64.
"Full Story of Lyndon's World War III Remark." *U.S. News and World Report* 62 (May 29, 1967): 21.
Gilbert, Julie. "Ladybird: Living Life Her Way." *The Magazine of the Houston Post*, May 5, 1985: 7–10, 17.
"In Grandfather Country." *Newsweek* 70 (July 3, 1967): 22.
Johnson, Luci Baines. "I Just Want to Go Bubble around People" (Interview). *Life* 63 (July 7, 1967): 50.
——— [Turpin]. "Life after the White House: How First Families Adjust (Interview)." *U.S. News and World Report* 96 (June 25, 1984): 39–41.

———. "Luci Baines Johnson" (Interview). *Ebony* 20 (February 1965): 40–42+.
———. "Over the River and Through the Woods It's Not [poem]." *Good Housekeeping* 199 (November 1984): 252.
Kirk, Elise K. *Music at the White House: A History of the American Spirit.* Urbana: University of Illinois Press, 1986.
Lasky, Victor. "The Man Who Could Be King [Charles Robb]." *American Politics* 1 (August 1986): 16–19.
"The Last Family." *Texas Observer*, May 16, 1963: 12.
"LBJ and Lyn, Official Word-by-Word Account [Patrick Lyndon Nugent]." *U.S. News and World Report* 63 (July 17, 1967): 8.
McCarthy, Dennis V. N., with Philip W. Smith. *Protecting the President: The Inside Story of a Secret Service Agent.* New York: Morrow, 1985.
"Pat Nugent: Growing Figure in the Expanding Johnson Empire." *U.S. News and World Report* 62 (May 22, 1967): 19.
"Patrick Lyndon." *Time* 89 (June 30, 1967): 17.
Pinkard, Tommie. "Christmas in the [Lyndon B. Johnson State Historic] Park." *Texas Highways* 25 (December 1978): 24–29.
"Presidential Sons-in-Law: Both in Service Soon." *U.S. News and World Report* 64 (March 18, 1968): 22.
Ridder, Marie. "The Middle Man: Chuck Robb Wants to Lead the Democratic Party Back toward the Political Center—and, Perhaps into the White House." *Dossier* 12 (October 1986): 40–43, 66.
Robb, Charles S. "Democratic Legacy: Whither the Future." Paper presented at Fifth Annual Hofstra University Presidential Conference: Lyndon Baines Johnson, A Texan in Washington. Hempstead, New York, April 10–12, 1986.
"Slate-Gray Eyes, Plump and Three Days Old [Patrick Lyndon Nugent]." *Life* 63 (July 7, 1967): 47–50+.
Small, Melvin. "The Impact of the Antiwar Movement on Lyndon Johnson, 1965–1968: A Preliminary Report." *Peace and Change*, vol. 10, no. 1 (1984): 1–22.
Steinberg, Alfred. *Sam Johnson's Boy: A Close-Up of the President from Texas.* New York: Macmillan, 1968.
"Taking Instruction: In the Roman Catholic Faith [Luci Baines Johnson]." *Newsweek* 65 (February 8, 1965): 80–81.
"Who Are the 400? Wedding Invitations [Luci Baines Johnson]." *Newsweek* 68 (July 18, 1966): 22–23.

Appendixes

Appendixes

THE LYNDON BAINES JOHNSON PRESIDENCY
FIRST ADMINISTRATION, NOVEMBER 22, 1963 – JANUARY 20, 1965

Secretary of State	Dean Rusk
Secretary of Treasury	Douglas Dillion
Secretary of Defense	Robert S. McNamara
Attorney General	Robert F. Kennedy
	Nicholas DeB. Katzenbach (1964)
Post Master General	John A. Gronouski
Secretary of Interior	Stewart L. Udall
Secretary of Agriculture	Orville L. Freeman
Secretary of Commerce	Luther H. Hodges
	John T. O'Connor (1965)
Secretary of Labor	W. Willard Wirtz
Secretary of Health, Education and Welfare	Anthony J. Celebrezze

The 88TH CONGRESS, 1963–1965

Speaker of the House	John W. McCormack
President Pro Tempore of the Senate	Carl Hayden
Majority Party, House and Senate	Democratic

THE LYNDON BAINES JOHNSON PRESIDENCY
SECOND ADMINISTRATION, JANUARY 20, 1965 – JANUARY 20, 1969

Vice President	Hubert H. Humphrey
Secretary of State	Dean Rusk
Secretary of Treasury	Douglas Dillion
	Henry H. Fowler (1965)
	Joseph W. Barr (1968)

Secretary of Defense	Robert S. McNamara
	Clark M. Clifford (1968)
Attorney General	Nicholas DeB. Katzenbach
	Ramsey Clark (1967)
Postmaster General	John A. Gronouski
	Lawrence F. O'Brien (1965)
	W. Marvin Watson (1968)
Secretary of Interior	Stewart L. Udall
Secretary of Agriculture	Orville L. Freeman
Secretary of Commerce	John T. O'Connor
	Alexander B. Trowbridge (1967)
	Cyrus R. Smith (1968)
Secretary of Labor	W. Willard Wirtz
Secretary of Health, Education and Welfare	Anthony J. Celebrezze
	John W. Gardner (1965)
	Wilbur J. Cohen (1968)
Secretary of Housing and Urban Development[1]	Robert C. Weaver
	Robert C. Wood (1969)
Secretary of Transportation[2]	Alan S. Boyd

THE 89TH CONGRESS, 1965–1967
THE 90TH CONGRESS, 1967–1969

Speaker of the House	John W. McCormack
President Pro Tempore of the Senate	Carl Hayden
Majority Party, House and Senate	Democratic

---

[1] Created 1965
[2] Created 1967

THE LYNDON BAINES JOHNSON PRESIDENCY
THE SUPREME COURT, 1963–1969

Hugo Black	1937–1971
William O. Douglas	1939–1975
Thomas C. Clark	1949–1967
Earl Warren	1953–1969
John Marshall	1955–1971
William J. Breenan, Jr.	1956–
Potter Stewart	1958–1981
Byron R. White	1962–
Arthur J. Goldberg	1962–1965
Abe Fortas	1965–1970
Thurgood Marshall	1967–

PRESIDENTIAL ELECTIONS, 1956–1968

YEAR	ELECTED (PARTY) ELECTORAL VOTE	DEFEATED (PARTY) ELECTORAL VOTE
1956	Dwight D. Eisenhower (R) 457 Richard M. Nixon (R)	Adlai Stevenson (D) 73 Estes Kefauver (D)
1960	John F. Kennedy (D) 303 Lyndon B. Johnson (D)	Richard M. Nixon (R) 219 Henry Cabot Lodge (R)
1964	Lyndon B. Johnson (D) 486 Hubert H. Humphrey (D)	Barry M. Goldwater (R) 52 William E. Miller (R)
1968	Richard M. Nixon (R) 301 Spiro T. Agnew (R)	Hubert H. Humphrey (D) 191 Edmund S. Muskie (D) George C. Wallace (Am. Independent) 46 Curtis E. LeMay (Am. Independent)

Sources

The following indexes and guides were among the sources used to compile the *Lyndon B. Johnson Bibliography*

ABC POL SCI: A Bibliography of Contents: Political Science and Government
Access: The Supplementary Index to Periodicals
Alternative Press Index
America: History and Life
American Doctoral Dissertations
The American Humanities Index
Applied Science and Technology Index
Arts and Humanities Citation Index
Bibliographic Guide to Latin American Studies
Bibliographic Index
Biography Index
Books in Print
Books in Series
Business Periodicals Index
Catholic Periodical and Literature Index
Combined Retrospective Index to Journals in History
Combined Retrospective Index to Journals in Political Science
Comprehensive Dissertation Index
Comprehensive Index to Little Magazines, 1890–1970
Catalog of the Foreign Relations Library [Council on Foreign Relations, Inc.]
Cumulative Book Index
Cumulative Index to Periodical Literature
Cumulative Subject Index to the P.A.I.S. Annual Bulletins, 1915–1974
Doctoral Dissertations in History
Dissertation Abstracts International
Education Index
Essay and General Literature Index
Forthcoming Books

Historical Abstracts
Humanities Index
Index to Jewish Periodicals
Index to Periodical Articles by and about Blacks
Index to Social Sciences and Humanities Proceedings
International Bibliography of Historical Sciences
International Bibliography of Political Science
International Bibliography of the Social Sciences
International Political Science Abstracts
A London Bibliography of the Social Sciences
Masters Abstracts International
Political Science Abstracts
Political Science, Government and Public Policy Series [Universal Reference System]
Public Affairs Information Service Bulletin
Readers' Guide to Periodical Literature
Recently Published Articles [American Historical Society]
Religion Index One: Periodicals (Index to Religious Periodical Literature)
SSCI: Social Science Citation Index
Social Sciences Index
The Texas Observer Index
The University of Michigan Index to Labor Union Periodicals
Writings on American History

Index

Aaron, Henry J., 202
Abelson, Philip H., 71
Ables, Gisela Renate, 255
Abraham, Henry J., 156, 193
Abrams, Charles, 198
Acheson, Dean G., 39, 285
Ackley, Gardner, 71, 170
Adamany, David, 114
Adams, Bruce, 77-78
Adams, Joey, 47
Adams, Samuel A., 273
Adams, Sherman, 12
Adler, Renata, 273
Agapos, A. M., 185
Agnew, B., 61
Agranoff, Robert, 89
Ahart, Gregory J., 202
Aiken, George D., 115, 273
Air War Study Group, see Cornell University Air War Study Group
Albert, Judith C., 131
Albert, Stewart E., 131
Alexander, Charles C., 186
Alexander, G., 186
Alexander, Herbert E., 82, 102
Alexander, Holmes, 48, 61, 82, 102, 144, 153, 156, 170, 202, 311
Alexander, Louis, 186
Alexander, Tom, 186
Alexander, Yonah, 255
Alford, Neill H., Jr., 290
Alinsky, Saul, 202
Allen, Robert L., 131

Allen, Robert S., 115, 156, 202
Allen-Scott Report, 238
Allison, David, 71
Allison, Graham T., 290
Alsop, Stewart, 71
Alsop, Susan Mary, 322
Alter, J., 259, 273
Altschuler, Bruce E., 82, 115
American Civil Liberties Union, 131
American Council on Education, 131
American Heritage Magazine, 43, 58
American Jewish Congress, 193
American Municipal Association, 202
Anderson, Claudia Wilson, 313
Anderson, Clinton P., 34
Anderson, Frank W., Jr., 186
Anderson, Jack, 12, 34, 39, 48
Anderson, James E., 48, 71, 171, 203
Anderson, Jervis, 131
Anderson, John, 203
Anderson, Ronald E., 106
Anderson, Terry H., 300
Andrain, Charles F., 19, 35
Andrews, Bruce, 277
Andrews, James R., 228
Andrus, David J., 259-260
Angel, William D., Jr., 186
Annunziata, Frank, 102
Appleton, Sheldon, 300
Arien, Michael J., 273

336 INDEX

Armstrong, John A., 244
Arnold, Hugh M., 277
Arnold, Mark R., 203
Arnold, Peri E., 71
Arnstein, George E., 203
Aron, Raymond, 244
Aronowitz, Stanley, 141
Arrendell, Odes Charles, 115
Ascoli, Max, 203
Ashbrooke, John, 164
Asher, Harold, 171, 186
Asher, Herbert B., 25, 102, 115
Atkins, Burton M., 193
Atkins, Thomas, 244
Augelli, J. P., 249
Averch, Harvey, 186
Avillo, Philip J., Jr., 290–291
Ayub, Khan, 239

Babson, R. W., 171
Babu, R. Ramesh, 102
Bachman, Jerald G., 300
Badeau, John S., 255
Badillo, Gilbert, 300
Bailey, Charles W. II, 48
Bailey, F. Lee, Jr., 102
Bailey, George A., 273–274
Bailey, Stephen K., 164–165
Baker, G. H., 203
Baldwin, Hanson W., 274, 277
Ball, George W., 61, 277
Banks, Ginger, 313
Banks, Jimmy, 25
Banks, Louis, 61
Bannworth, Deborah, 317
Baral, Jaya Krishna, 260, 300
Barclay, Glen St. John, 259
Barclay, H. W., 61
Bard, Bernard, 6
Bard, Mitchell, 255
Bardsley, Lance W., 150
Barilleaux, Ryan John, 228
Baritz, Loren, 260
Baritz, Katherine, 303
Barnes, Fred, 325

Barnes, Peter, 198
Barnet, Richard J., 228, 285
Barnett, John, 9, 313
Barrineau, Mary, 322
Barro, Stephen M., 186, 189
Bartholomew, Paul C., 193
Basich, Thomas, 260
Baskir, Lawrence M., 300
Batchelder, Alan, 131
Bates, Stephen, 83
Batly, Richard, 199
Baughman, James Lewis, 82, 224
Baum, Phil, 300
Baum, William, 103
Bauman, John F., 203
Baver, Sherrie Lynn, 250
Baylis, John, 244
Bearss, Edwin C., 9, 10, 12–13, 39
Beck, Susan Abrams, 203
Becker, Joseph M., 203–204
Beckman, Peter R., 228–229
Bedworth, David A., 71
Beebe, Lucius, 48
Behrens, Anne, 317
Beisel, David R., 260
Beisner, Robert L., 300
Belknap, Michael R., 131, 156
Bell, Beverly W., 300
Bell, D. Bruce, 300
Bell, Daniel, 131
Bell, Inge Powell, 131
Bell, Roger, 19
Bellush, Jewel, 198
Belman, Murray J., 229, 291
Belovski, Dince, 285
Ben, Philippe, 239
Benakraitis, NiJole, 156
Benetar, David L., 156
Ben-Horin, Eliahu, 255
Bennett, Elizabeth, 322
Benningfeld, Damond, 48
Benson, Charles D., 186
Benson, George, 145
Benson, Paul R., Jr., 193

INDEX 337

Benton, Mary Josephine Griffin, 291
Benze, James G., 71
Berens, John F., 145
Berg, Larry L., 193
Berger, Raoul, 44, 229, 291
Bergman, Ralph M., 198
Berkowitz, Morton, 229
Berle, Adolf A., 250
Berman, Larry, 44, 72, 171, 313
Berman, Ronald, 153
Berry, John M., 229
Berube, Maurice R., 132
Best, James J., 61–62
Bhana, Surendra, 250
Bibby, John F., 204
Bickel, Alexander M., 44, 156, 193, 291
Biddle, Livingston, 153
Biederman, Paul, 171
Bielenberg, Douglas Georg, 250
Biemiller, Andrew J., 145
Bigel, Alan I., 193
Bill, James Alban, 255
Billington, Monroe L., 13, 89
Bird, Roland, 260
Bisplinghoff, Raymond L., 186
Black, Elizabeth, 194
Black, Eugene R., 145, 229
Black, Hugo L., 194
Black, Jan K., 250
Blake, William, 224
Blakely, Edward James, 204
Blanchard, Robert, 25
Bland, Randall W., 194
Blasier, Cole, 250
Blaufarb, Douglas, 277
Blissett, Marlan, 145
Blodgett, Terrell, 204
Bloom, Kathryn, 153
Bluestein, Iris W., 204
Blum, John Morton, 145
Blum, Zahava, 141
Blumberg, Rhoda Lois, 156
Blumenthal, Fred, 34
Blumenthal, Richard, 204
Bock, Joseph G., 72, 229
Bock, P. G., 229
Boettiger, John R., 229, 260
Boller, Paul F., Jr., 103
Bombardier, Gary, 89
Bookbinder, Hyman G., 202, 204
Booker, Simon, 156
Borklund, Carl W., 62
Bornet, Vaughn D., 317
Borst, Philip W., 95
Bosch, Juan, 250
Boskin, M. J., 171
Bostic, Elaine, 313
Boston Publishing Company Editors, 260
Boulding, Kenneth E., 300
Bourgeois, Christie Lynne, 9
Bowen, David, 132
Bowen, William, 59, 171, 300
Bowles, Nigel P., 39, 72, 95, 145
Bowman, John S., 260
Bowman, LeRoy, 145
Boyd, Alan S., 62
Boyd, James, 12, 39, 48
Boyd, William Austin, 25, 103, 115
Boyle, Richard, 260
Bozell, L. Brent, 194
Brademas, John, 153
Braestrup, Peter, 260, 274, 277
Branden, Anne, 132
Brandon, Henry, 73, 145
Brands, Henry William, Jr., 39, 277
Branfman, Fred, 277
Branyan, Robert L., 13
Bratter, H., 172
Bratton, Daniel L., 44
Brauer, Carl M., 48
Braungart, Richard G., 144
Braz, Rita, 239
Brecher, Charles M., 204
Bremer, Howard F., 6
Brendlinger, Nancy, 19, 187

Brendon, Piers, 13, 260
Brennan, Paul Edward, 44, 250, 291
Breu, Giovanna, 316
Brewin, Bob, 274
Briggs, C. M., 48
Brim, Andrea M., 13
Brindley, Thomas A., 229
Brink, William, 132
Brinton, Howard J., 145
Brinton, John J., 145
Brock, Bernard L., 115
Broder, David S., 13, 115–116
Brodie, Bernard, 260, 277
Brody, Richard A., 84, 272, 297
Brogan, Dennis William, 260, 277
Bromley, Dorothy Dunbar, 291
Bronfenbrenner, Martin, 172
Brooke, Edward W., 260
Brooks, Courtney G., 187
Brophy, William J., 42
Brown, Clarence, 204
Brown, D. Clayton, 35
Brown, D. E., 277
Brown, Donald Eugene, 229
Brown, H. Rap, 132
Brown, Harold, 62
Brown, John A., Jr., 244
Brown, R. L., 103
Brown, Roger O., 89
Browne, Malcolm W., 275, 285
Browne, R. S., 300
Browning, Robert X., 204
Brownlow, C., 277, 291
Brozen, Yale, 172
Brundage, Percival F., 172
Buckley, K., 277–278
Bui Diem, 261
Bull, Hedley, 246
Bullock, Charles S. III, 156, 162
Bundy, McGeorge, 44, 48, 73, 229
Bundy, William P., 44, 62, 229, 261, 278, 285–286

Bunker, Ellsworth, 261
Burchett, Wilfred G., 286
Bureau of National Affairs, 156
Bureau of the Budget, *see* United States Executive Office of the President, Bureau of the Budget
Bureau of the Census, *see* United States, Department of Commerce, Bureau of the Census
Burke, Edmund M., 204
Burke, John P., 73, 278
Burke, William, 187
Burkhead, Jesse, 300–301
Burlage, Robb K., 48, 204
Burner, David, 39–40, 89
Burnham, James, 278, 291
Burnham, Walter Dean, 103, 116, 301
Burns, Arthur F., 175
Burns, Eveline M., 183
Burns, James MacGregor, 145–146
Burns, Richard Dean, 10, 229, 261
Burns, Robert, 56
Burns, Wendell J., 324
Burns, William J., 255
Burnstein, Paul, 291–292
Burt, Eric, 13, 35
Burt, Richard, 224
Burton, Michael G., 301
Butterfield, Fox, 261
Buttinger, Joseph, 261
Button, James Wickham, 132
Butwin, Miriam, 132, 301
Buzzanco, Bob, 278
Byrd, Harry F., 156
Byron, Bruce, 64

Cable, Larry E., 278
Cabot, John Moors, 229
Cafiero, L. H., 187
Cahalan, Joseph M., 82–83

INDEX 339

Cahn, Edgar S., 205
Cahn, Jean C., 205
Caidin, Martin, 10
Caine, P. D., 301
Cairns, James F., 261
Calder, James Douglas, 224
Caldwell, Dan, 244
Califano, Joseph A., Jr., 146
Callaway, Rhonda, 73
Camasso, Michael J., 153
Campbell, Alex, 73
Campbell, David R., 67
Campbell, Douglas G., 313
Campbell, John C., 244
Campbell, Keith E., 301
Cantril, Albert H., 301
Capp, Glenn R., 146
Capps, Walter H., 261
Carbone, Donald J., 44
Carey, William D., 73
Carlson, Robert J., 205
Carney, Francis M., 104, 116
Caro, Robert A., 6–7, 10, 317
Carp, Robert A., 197
Carpenter, Liz, 7, 313, 322, 324
Carroll, John M., 230
Carson, Clayborne, 132
Carter, Barbara, 205
Carter, John D., 194
Carter, Ralph G., 230
Cary, William L., 89
Casebeer, A. L., 306
Cashman, Ben, 237
Castan, Sam, 261
Castro, Nash, 224
Catchpole, Terry, 89, 116
Cater, Douglass, 10, 13, 40
Caton, Christopher N., 172, 301
Cavanagh, Jerome P., 73
Cecil, Paul Frederick, 278
Center for Naval Analyses, 278
Cepuran, Joseph, 205
Cerny, P. G., 244–245, 292
Chamberlain, Henry, 104
Chamberlain, John, 25, 73, 89,

104, 116, 146, 225, 230, 250,
301, 319, 325
Champagne, Anthony, 35
Chandler, Robert W., 274
Chang, C. C., 239
Chang, Jim Park, 239
Chapman, Richard L., 187
Charlton, Michael, 261
Chase, Harold W., 194
Chayes, Abram, 225
Chazen, Leonard B., 205
Cheshire, H., 286
Chester, Edward W., 19, 83, 255, 311
Chodorov, Frank, 35
Chomsky, Noam, 261, 274
Christian, George, 73, 83, 116
Church, Frank, 245, 261
Cincinnatus [pseud.], 262
Citron, Henry, 165
City University of New York,
    Social Dynamics Research Institute, *see* Social Dynamics Research Institute
Claque, Ewan, 132
Clark, Dennis, 205
Clark, Gerald, 259
Clark, John J., 187
Clark, Keith C., 44
Clark, Kenneth B., 205
Clark, Mark W., 286
Clark, Ramsey, 62
Clark, Wayne A., 132
Clarke, Duncan L., 72
Clarke, Newlon, 7
Clayton, James D., 10, 13
Clemons, Cyril, 7
Clifford, Craig Edward, 74
Close, Alexandra, 301
Clough, Ralph N., 239, 262
Cloward, Richard A., 132, 161, 205
Cochrane, James L., 74
Cogley, John, 3
Cogley, Joseph, 3

Cohen, Dan, 26, 35, 59
Cohen, Eli E., 205
Cohen, Jeffrey A., 26, 44–45, 95, 104, 116
Cohen, Jerome, 133
Cohen, Mitchell, 133
Cohen, S. E., 62, 64, 205, 225
Cohen, Wilber J., 49, 165, 183
Colby, Vineta, 133
Coleman, James, 165
Coleman, Robert Boykin, 165
Collier, Peter, 40, 89, 116
Collins, Hugh Norman, 259
Collins, James L., Jr., 266, 278
Collins, John M., 245, 278
Colt, George Howe, 317, 325
Columbia University Fact-Finding Commission, *see* Fact-Finding Commission on Columbia Disturbances
Combs, Paul William, 206
Commager, Henry Steele, 279
Committee of Concerned Asian Scholars, 262
Communist Party of the United States of America, 104
Community Action Programs Field Reports, 206
Condray, Suzanne Elizabeth, 49
Congressional Quarterly Service, 49, 89, 117, 194, 239
Congressional Research Service, 262
Conine, Ernest, 13
Conkin, Paul K., 7
Connolly, R., 62, 187
Connor, John Thomas, 62, 173
Considine, Bob, 4
Converse, Philip E., 301, 308
Cook, Fred J., 35
Cooper, Chester L., 230
Cooper, John Cobb, 187
Cooper, Joseph, 89
Cormier, Frank, 83, 104
Cornell University Air War Study Group, 277

Corning, Peter, 183
Cornwell, Elmer E., Jr., 83
Corwin, Edward S., 45
Cosman, Bernard, 104
Cotter, Cornelius P., 89
Couart, A. T., 206
Council on Foreign Relations, 239
Countryman, Vern, 194
Cousins, Norman, 59, 292
Covington, Cary R., 45
Cox, James Robert, Jr., 301–302
Coyle, David Cushman, 133, 146
Crabb, Cecil V., Jr., 230
Craft, James Pressley, Jr., 230
Craig, James B., 319
Crawford, Ann Fears, 90, 316
Crecine, John P., 78
Crespi, Irving, 86, 117
Cronin, Thomas E., 45, 74, 165
Crosby, R. W., 104, 146, 173, 206, 225
Cummings, Milton C., Jr., 10, 26, 104
Curry, David G., 300
Cutchley, Julian, 286
Cutler, Neal E., 230
Cutrona, Joseph F. H., 286

D'Amato, Anthony A., 292
D'Costa, Carlos, 274
Dague, Paul B., 225
Dallek, Robert, 49, 230, 262
Dallin, Alexander, 245, 262
Dane, Barbara, 302
Danigelis, Nicholas L., 90, 133
Daswani, P. R., 239
Davenport, Sally Ann, 165
David, Heather M., 187
David, Paul, 26
David, Sheri Iris, 183
Davidson, Arthur T., 133, 157
Davidson, Roger H., 13–14, 35, 90, 96, 204, 206–207
Davies, Clarence J., 199
Davis, Derek, 286

INDEX 341

Davis, Eric Lyle, 74
Davis, James W., 14, 173
Davis, John H., 26, 40, 90, 117
Davis, Kenneth S., 26, 35
Davis, Rennard, 207
Davis, Saville, 250, 262
Davis, Vincent, 45
Dawson, William W., 278
Day, Bonner, 302
Day, J. Edward, 62
Daynes, Byron W., 57
Deadline Data on World Affairs Editors, 231
Deakin, James, 83
DeBenedetti, Charles, 302
DeGregorio, William A., 45
Dell, George W., 105
Delli Carpini, Michael X., 133
Democratic National Committee, 26, 96, 105, 146, 207, 321
Denisoff, Serge R., 305
Denno, Bryce F., 278
Derthick, Martha, 90
Destler, Irving McArthur, 45, 231
De Toledano, Ralph, 19, 40, 63, 74, 90, 104, 117, 133, 146, 157, 165, 173, 207, 245, 250
Deutsch, Eberhard P., 292
Devine, Samuel, 207
De Vyver, Frank T., 184
Diamond, Edwin, 83
Diamond, P. A., 173
Dickinson, William B., Jr., 83, 105
Dickson, David, 256
Dickstein, Morris, 133
Dierenfield, Bruce Jonathan, 97, 207
Dies, Martin, 14
Dietz, Terry, 292
Dillon, Conley H., 199
Divine, Robert A., 27, 49, 188, 313, 317–318
Dixler, E., 49
Dobriansky, Lev E., 245

Docking, Robert, 274
Dodd, Thomas J., 274
Doig, Jameson W., 66
Dommen, Arthur J., 262, 278
Donovan, Frank R., 105
Donovan, Hedley, 83
Donovan, Robert, 262
Dorman, Michael, 133
Dorsen, Norman, 134
Dorsey, Barry Martin, 292
Doxiadis, C. A., 199
Doyle, Edward G., 260
Draper, Hal, 134
Draper, Theodore, 251, 262, 286
Dreyer, Martin, 313
Driscoll, Tom, 49
Druks, Herbert J., 256
Drummond, S., 278
Dubnoff, Caren, 207
Duesenberry, James S., 146
Duffey, Joseph, 90
Dugger, Ronnie, 7, 262, 317
Duholm, Beulah F., 9
Duignan, Peter, 256
Duke, Paul, 105, 231
Dulaney, H. G., 35
Duncan, Donald, 117
Dunlap, Carol, 49
Dunlop, Richard, 313
Dunn, Joe P., 262
Dunne, George H., 134
Dunne, Gerald T., 194
Dyckman, J. W., 305
Dye, Thomas, R., 157

Eastwood, Mary, 161
Eccles, Marriner S., 302
Eckstein, Otto, 173
Eder, Richard, 262
Edwards, George C. III, 45, 49
Edwards, Jack, 83
Edwards, John, 199
Edwards, Willard, 27, 117, 174, 194
Einbinder, Harvey, 262
Eisenhower, Dwight David, 134

Eliot, George Fielding, 279
Elkin, Sandra, 325
Elkins, Dov Peretz, 146
Eller, J. N., 90, 146
Elliff, John T., 225
Elowitz, Larry, 292
Elson, Robert R., 63
Elswit, J., 188
Elterman, Howard A., 274
Elzy, Martin I., 74, 314
Emerson, Gloria, 262–263
Emerson, J. Terry, 292–293
Emerson, Rupert, 256
Emerson, Thomas I., 157
Emery, Edwin, 274
Emmert, J. Richard, 97
Emspak, Frank, 134
Emswiler, Marilyn, 35
Engler, Robert, 20
Enthoven, Alain C., 40, 225
Entman, Robert M., 86
Erskine, Hazel, 274
Eszterhas, Joe, 134
Etzioni, Amitai, 146, 245
Evans, Kenneth James, Jr., 134
Evans, M. Stanton, 90, 118, 293
Evans, Rowland, 97
Everett, Robinson O., 207
Ewing, Floyd F., 35–36
Exley, Jo Ella Powell, 7
Exton, Elaine, 166
Ezell, Macel D., 166

Faber, Harold, 118
Fact-Finding Commission on Columbia Disturbances, 134
Fager, Charles E., 134
Fagin, Henry, 201
Faherty, William B., 186
Fairlie, Henry, 36, 40
Falk, Richard A., 286, 293
Fall, Bernard B., 263
Fallaci, Oriana, 90
Fallows, James, 14, 50
Farmer, James, 134

Farnsworth, David, 251
Farrow, Stephen B., 14, 36
Faulk, Odie B., 12
Faulkner, Francis D., 274
Faulkner, Stanley, 293
Fawcett, Ruth, 318
Feagin, Joe R., 156
Featherman, David, 134
Feerick, John D., 40, 59
Feingold, Eugene, 183
Felder, Marvin Ray, 11, 14
Felzenberg, Alvin S., 44
Fenn, Richard K., 207
Fenton, John M., 14
Fenyvesi, Charles, 50
Fergusson, A., 245
Fernandez, Benedict J., 134
Field, John O., 106
Findlay, James, 157–158
Findley, Paul, 84, 256
Finman, Ted, 303
Finn, Chester E., Jr., 166
Finn, James, 303
Finnegan, G. B., 63
Finney, John, 293
Firfer, Alexander, 251
Fishel, Jeff, 45, 50
Fishel, Wesley R., 263, 279
Fishel, Linda L., 158, 208
Fisher, Louis, 45
Fisher, Randall M., 134–135, 303
Fishman, Robert Alan, 199
Fister, J. Blaine, 166
Flacks, Richard, 147
Flacks, Robert, 135
Flash, Edward S., Jr., 45, 74
Fleming, Denna Frank, 239
Fleming, R., 84
Fleming, Thomas J., 59
Flemming, Karl, 303
Floyd, Charles F., 324
Flynn, George Q., 303
Fogelson, Robert M., 135
Forbes, Malcolm S., 106

INDEX 343

Ford, Gerald R., 90, 279
Foreign Policy Association, 231
Forgotson, Edward H., 183
Fowler, George, 84, 325
Fowler, Henry H., 63
Fox, Tom, 274
Frady, Marshall, 118
Fraleigh, Arnold, 287
Frank, Frederick, 188
Frankel, Max, 63, 74
Franklin, Grace A., 46
Franklin, Jane, 263
Frantz, Joe B., 7, 14, 36
Frantz, T. T., 135
Freeburg, Russell, 63
Freedman, Alex S., 135
Freeman, O., 50
Freeman, Roger A., 166, 208
French, Blaire Atherton, 84
Freudenburg, William, 291–292
Fried, Richard M., 20
Friedman, Alvin, 279
Friedman, Jonathan M., 293
Friedman, Leon, 194
Friedman, Rose D., 208
Friedman, Wolfgang, 293
Frommer, Arthur, 106
Frutkin, Arnold, 188
Fuccillo, Vincent J., 229
Fulbright, J. William, 147, 231, 263, 287, 293
Fulton, Joseph F., 188
Fulton, Lewis, Jr., 11, 40, 90
Funkhouser, G. R., 84

Gagnon, John H., 208
Galbraith, John Kenneth, 208, 231, 263
Gallagher, B. G., 135
Gallaway, Lowell E., 135, 174, 185
Gallois, Pierre M., 231
Gallucci, Robert, 293
Gallup, George, 135
Gan, Andrew Carter, 256

Gange, John, 263
Gann, Lewis H., 256
Garcia, Elvia, 317, 321
Gardner, John W., 63–64, 158
Gardner, Lloyd C., 231, 263
Garrett, Banning, 303
Garrett, Stephen A., 293
Garrett, William Bruce, 251
Garrow, David J., 135, 158
Gaskin, Thomas M., 20
Gates, Gary Paul, 88
Gawthrop, Louis, 45
Gelfand, Mark I., 208, 320
George, Alexander L., 231
Gerberding, William P., 231
Germond, Jack W., 118
Geschwender, James A., 135
Getlein, Frank, 154
Gettleman, Marvin E., 263
Geyelin, Philip, 251, 303
Gibbons, William C., 263
Gibson, James William, 263
Gilbert, Julie, 323, 325
Gilder, George F., 58
Gill, Robert L., 194
Gilmore, Susan, 139
Gilster, Herma L., 279
Ginsburgh, Robert N., 279
Girling, J. L. S., 279
Gish, Tom, 208
Gitlin, Todd A., 84
Gittell, Marilyn, 158
Givens, Ken, 320
Glass, Andrew J., 97
Glazer, Nathan, 158
Glick, Edward M., 118
Goehlert, Robert U., 97
Goggin, M. L., 84
Gold, Victor, 118
Goldberg, Arthur J., 232, 287
Goldfarb, Ronald L., 293
Goldman, Eric, 50
Goldman, Sheldon, 194
Goldschmidt, Leopold A., 199
Goldsmith, William M., 45, 50

Goldstein, Joel K., 40, 59
Goldstein, Jonathan, 303
Goldstein, Martin E., 239
Goldstein, Walter, 75, 188
Goldston, Robert, 36
Goldwater, Barry M., 4, 90, 106–107, 118–119, 174, 232, 279, 294
Gonionsky, S., 251
Good, R. D., 232
Goodale, James C., 294
Goodman, Allan, 294
Goodwin, Craufurd D., 174
Goodwin, Richard N., 119
Gordon, Bernard K., 239
Gordon, Jennifer, 311, 314
Gordon, Lincoln, 251
Goswami, P. K., 239
Gould, Alan E., 208
Gould, Lewis L., 7, 318, 319
Goulden, Joseph C., 195
Graber, Doris A., 232
Graff, Henry F., 263
Graham, Elinor, 208
Graham, Hugh Davis, 166
Graham, Richard A., 166
Granberg, Donald, 135
Grant, Donald, 119, 232, 294
Grant, Gerald, 167
Grant, Zalin B., 263, 287
Great Britain Foreign Office, 287
Green, Edith, 208
Green, George Norris, 11
Green, Harry A., 64
Green, Stephen, 256
Greenawalt, Kenneth W., 158
Greenawalt, William S., 158
Greenberg, Sanford D., 45, 74
Greene, Fred, 240
Greene, Jerry, 119, 263–264
Greene, John Robert, 20
Greenfield, Meg, 50, 154
Greenleigh Associates, 208
Greenstein, Fred I., 44
Greenstone, J. David, 209

Greer, Scott, 199
Gregory, Gene, 287
Griffen, William L., 264
Griffith, Robert, 20
Grimwood, James M., 187
Grinter, Lawrence E., 264, 294
Grogan, F. L., 50
Gropman, Alan L., 158
Gross, H. R., 158
Gruberg, Martin, 90
Gruen, Victor, 135
Gruening, Ernest H., 264
Gutin, Myra Greenberg, 84, 321
Guzzardi, Walter, Jr., 267
Gwartney, James, 135
Gwertzman, Bernard M., 295
Gwirtzman, Milton, 91, 119

Haber, Robert Alan, 107
Haber, William, 203–204
Haddad, William F., 209
Hadley, Charles D., 11, 27, 29, 91, 107
Hahn, Harlan, 303
Hahn, Phil, 147
Haight, Timothy, 84
Hajada, Joseph, 27
Halberstam, David, 50, 64, 75, 91, 119, 264, 279, 287
Hale, Dennis, 133
Hale, J. Russell, 147
Haley, Andrew, G., 188
Hall, Chester, Gordon Jr., 50
Hall, David Kent, 232
Hallin, Daniel D., 275
Halper, Sam, 251
Halper, Thomas, 232
Halperin, Morton H., 46, 294
Halstead, Fred, 303
Hamby, Alonzo L., 50, 136, 303
Hamilton, Charles V., 158
Hamilton, Dagmar S., 56, 80, 94
Hamilton, Harry, 158, 232
Hamilton, William Alexander, 232

INDEX 345

Hammond, William M., 264
Hamre, John J., 294
Handleman, Howard, 251
Handler, Joel F., 201
Handlin, Oscar, 136
Hanks, Nancy, 154
Hannon, Philip J., 209
Hanrahan, Jack, 247
Hansen, Donald C., 119
Hanson, Simon G., 251
Hardeman, D. B., 36
Hardesty, Mary, 311
Hardesty, Robert L., 51
Harper, Dean, 209
Harriman, W. Averell, 287
Harrington, Michael, 136, 209
Harris, Gayle T., 75
Harris, Irving D., 9, 51
Harris, Janet, 136
Harris, Louis, 119, 132
Harris, Mark, 154
Harris, Seymour E., 167
Harris, T. George, 174
Harrison, Cynthia Ellen, 136
Harrison, Selig S., 240
Hart, Roderick, 51, 84
Hartke, Vance, 264, 287, 303
Hartley, Robert E., 97
Hartman, Chester W., 209
Harvard Business School, 209
Harvey, Paul, 40, 51
Haskins, James, 303
Hasluck, Paul, 240, 264
Hatcher, Patrick Lloyd, 279
Hauck, Robb J., 303, 309
Hausknecht, Murray, 198
Hauser, Robert, 134
Haveles, Harry P., Jr., 97
Hayashi, Tetsumaro, 304
Hayden, Tom, 209, 287
Hayes, Alfred, 174
Hayes, James Robert, 304
Hazleton, Jared E., 71, 171
Hazlitt, Henry, 75, 136, 147, 174–175

Heady, R., 107
Health, G. Louis, 304
Healy, Paul F., 36, 98
Hecht, Neil, 158
Heckscher, August, 154
Heinlein, Jay Clarke, 75
Heirich, Max, 304
Heller, David, 175
Heller, Deane, 175
Heller, Walter W., 75, 175, 287
Hellmann, John, 264
Helms, Jesse, 183
Hencke, Paul, 209
Henderaker, Ivan, 27
Henderson, Richard B., 9
Henderson, W. L., 147
Henkin, Louis, 294
Henry, John B. II, 64
Hensley, William E., 304
Heren, Louis, 119, 287
Herken, Gregg F., 75, 245
Herman, Melvin, 209
Hero, Alfred O., Jr., 232
Herring, George C., 230, 232, 264, 287
Hersey, John, 209
Herz, Martin F., 256, 264
Herzog, Arthur, 119
Hester Report, see President's Task Force on Higher Education
Hess, Karl, 107
Hess, Thomas B., 154
Heuvel, William V., 91, 119
Hewitt, Don, 311
Higdon, Hal, 119
Hildenbrand, William F., 36, 98
Hill, Robert C., 252
Hilsman, Roger, 40, 232
Hinckle, Warren, 298
Hindell, Keith, 159
Hine, Darlene C., 11
Hinga, Don, 36
Hinton, Harold C., 233
Hirsch, R. G., 147
Hitch, Charles J., 175

Hodgson, Godfrey, 136
Hodgson, Gordon S., 279
Hoffman, Richard Lee, 209
Hoffman, Stanley, 233
Hofmann, Roger H., 209–210
Hofstadter, Richard, 107
Holland, Susan S., 136
Hollander, Neil, 275
Hollomon, J. Herbert, 75
Holloran, Daniel F., 210
Holsti, Ole R., 233, 264
Holt, Harold, 264
Holt, Pat M., 230
Holton, R., 64
Holton, Thomas, 294
Honick, Morris, 287
Hood, Donald Eugene, 279–280
Hoopes, Roy, 233
Hoopes, Townsend, 119
Hopkins, Jeanette, 205
Hopkins, Waring C., 287
Hoppe, Art, 40
Hornig, Donald F., 75
Horowitz, David, 40, 89, 116
Horton, Frank, 107
Hoskins, Halford L., 256
Hough, Robbin R., 210
Houk, Rose, 7
House, James, 28, 91
Howard, A. E. Dick, 195
Howard, Anthony, 76
Howard, Irving E., Rev., 210
Howard, Jack, 210
Howe, Harold II, 167
Howell, Michael J., 28, 108, 120
Howell, Susan E., 11, 27, 107
Hoxie, R. Gordon, 64
Hubbell, John, 304
Huckshorn, Robert J., 91
Hudson, Anne Mooney, 200
Hudson, Richard, 245, 287
Hudson, W. Gail, 28
Hughes-Cromwick, Paul, 215
Hull, Roger, 294
Humphrey, David C., 76, 280

Humphrey, Hubert H., 59–60,
  108, 120, 136, 147, 159, 183,
  210, 233, 245, 252, 280
Hunt, Betty, 286
Hunter, Robert E., 240
Hurley, Robert Michael, 40
Hurt, Henry, 225
Hutcheson, John Dabney, Jr., 210
Hutchison, Bruce, 147–148
Huynk, Kim Khanh, 280
Hyman, Sidney, 28
Hymoff, Edward, 10
Hyson, Charles D., 233

Iannaccone, Laurence, 167
Ikle, Fred C., 288
Ilgen, Thomas L., 246
Inter-University Consortium for
  Political and Social Research,
  108, 120
Isaacs, Arnold R., 265
Isaacson, Walter, 76, 246, 280
Israel, Fred L., 194
Ivie, Robert L., 294

Jackson, Henry F., 256
Jacob, Bernard E., 76, 195
Jacob, Kathryn Allamong, 36, 98
Jacobs, Paul, 136
Jacobson, Solomon G., 308
Jacoby, Neil H., 175
Jain, R. K., 240, 265
James, Dorothy Buckton, 210
James, Edward, 210
James, Peggy A., 98
Jameson, Frederic, 141
Jamieson, Kathleen Hall, 46, 108
Janes, Thomas Warham,
  294–295
Janeway, Eliot, 175, 304
Javits, Jacob K., 175
Jefferis, Frank, 64
Jenkins, Gerald L., 295
Jenkins, Timothy Lionel, 159
Jennings, M. Kent, 300

INDEX

Jetton, Walter, 51
Jewett, Robert, 233, 265
Johnsen, K., 188
Johnson, Claudia A. T., 4, 315–316
Johnson, H. G., 233
Johnson, Harold K., 265, 280
Johnson, Haynes B., 295
Johnson, James C. M., 308
Johnson, Karen S., 85
Johnson, Lady Bird, see Claudia A. T. Johnson
Johnson, Luci Baines, 325–326. See also Turpin, Luci Baines Johnson
Johnson, Lyndon B., 1–6
Johnson, Miles Beardsley, 85
Johnson, Mrs. Lyndon B., see Johnson, Claudia A. T.
Johnson, Nicholas, 195
Johnson, Paul, 85
Johnson, R. H., 280
Johnson, Ralph William, 265, 280
Johnson, Thomas F., 200
Johnson, Walter, 109
Johnson, William, 94
Johnston, Ray, 217
Johnstone, William C., 240
Jones, Augustus Joseph, Jr., 159
Jones, Hugh E., 195
Jones, Jenkin Lloyd, 136, 148, 176, 225
Jones, Lew, 304
Jones, Melvin E., 121
Jones, Penn, Jr., 225–226
Jones, Robert V., 176
Jordan, Barbara C., 52, 148
Jorden, William J., 252
Joyner, Conrad, 121

Kaderlan, Norman, 154
Kafoglis, Madelyn L., 211
Kahin, George McTurnan, 265, 288
Kahl, Mary, 11
Kahn, Herman, 280, 288
Kahn, Tom, 159
Kamath, P. M., 76, 233
Kamlet, Mark S., 78, 178
Kaplan, H. J., 275
Kaplan, Stephen S., 252
Karnow, Stanley, 240, 265
Katcher, Leo, 195
Katona, George, 109
Kattenburg, Paul M., 233–234, 265
Katz, Milton S., 136–137
Katzenbach, Nicholas DeB., 65, 159
Kauffman, J. F., 305
Kauffman, Kenneth M., 234
Kaufman, Burton I., 21, 234
Kaufman, Felice Ann, 76
Kaufman, Frank L., 234
Kaufman, K. A., 148, 176
Kaye, Tony, 8, 52
Kearns, Doris, 316
Keever, Crawford, 11, 15, 41
Keever, Jack, 90
Kehde, Ned, 137
Keith, Frank H., 319
Kellerman, Barbara, 52, 91
Kelly, J., 275
Kelly, O., 46
Kelly, Wayne, 295
Kelman, Steven J., 137, 288, 305
Kelso, Quinten Allen, 252
Kemp, Geoffrey, 224
Kempton, Murray, 121
Kenen, Isaiah L., 52
Kennan, George F., 281
Kennedy, Edward M., 265
Kennedy, John F., 3, 29
Kennedy, Robert F., 41, 121, 295
Kennedy, Ross A., 65, 295
Kennon, Donald R., 36, 98
Kensworthy, E. W., 121
Kent, Richard J., Jr., 226
Keppel, Francis, 154

Kernell, Samuel Houston, 46
Kerr, James R., 188
Kerr, Janet C., 167
Kerr, Malcolm, 256
Kershaw, Joseph, 211
Kesavan, K. V., 240
Kettl, Donald F., 52, 76–77, 176
Keyserling, Leon H., 148–149, 211, 265
Kiker, Douglas, 65
Kilpatrick, James Jackson, 15, 52, 149, 154, 159, 184, 211, 252, 257
Kilson, Martin, 159
Kim Benedict Sang-Joon, 240
Kimball, Penn, 91, 121
King, C. Richard, 317
King, Christopher T., 305
King, James D., 65, 77, 80
King, Martin Luther, Jr., 137, 159, 305
King, Ronald F., 176
Kingsbury, Roger, 58, 121
Kirk, B. A., 137
Kirk, Elsie K., 154, 321, 326
Kirk, John G., 137
Kirk, Russell, 85, 195, 240, 252, 257
Kirkpatrick, Samuel A., 121
Kissick, William L., 184
Kissinger, Henry, 234, 281, 288
Klaw, Barbara, 323
Kluckhorn, Frank, 9, 52, 109
Kluger, Pearl, 149
Knaggs, John R., 41, 91
Knapp, Daniel, 41
Knoll, Erwin, 52, 121, 211, 223
Kohlmeier, Louis, 91, 320
Kolkey, Jonathan Martin, 91, 137
Kolko, Gabriel, 137, 234, 265
Komatsu, David, 211
Komer, Robert W., 281
Kommers, Donald P., 159
Koontz, Hilda E., 52
Kopkind, Andrew, 121

Korbonski, Andrzej, 246
Kornberg, Allan, 109
Kotz, Mary Lynn, 319
Kovenock, David M., 121
Kowert, Bruce, 9
Kowet, Don, 265
Kozar, Paul Michael, 41, 188, 246
Kraft, Joseph, 65, 85
Kramer, Gerald H., 109
Kramer, Ralph M., 211
Kraus, Sidney, 109
Krause, Patricia A., 305
Kravitz, Sanford L., 211
Krepinevich, Andrew Francis, 281
Kress, Paul F., 52
Kristol, Irving, 131
Krock, Arthur, 52
Krosney, Herbert, 137
Krukones, Michael G., 46, 109
Kuhn, James, 176
Kunen, James Simon, 137
Kurland, Gerald, 52
Kurland, Philip B., 195
Kusnitz, Leonard A., 240

Labin, Suzanne, 305
Lachman, Seymour P., 109
Lacy, A. B., 77
Ladd, Everett C., Jr., 11, 29, 91
LaFeber, Walter, 252
Laird, Melvin R., 91
Lake, Anthony, 257
Lalli, F., 65, 121
Lamb, Charles M., 156
Lamb, Morris, 257
Lambert, D. E., 109
Lambright, W. Henry, 77, 189
Lampman, Robert, 137
Landau, Julian J., 257
Landau, Saul, 136
Lane, Dorothy, 11, 317
Lane, Thomas A., 77, 189, 234, 281
Langer, Paul F., 288

Langguth, A. J., 121
Langland, S. G., 265
Langley, Lester D., 252
Lansdale, Edward G., 266, 281
Laocoon, Jr., 21
Larner, Jeremy, 122
Larsen, Lawrence H., 13
Larson, Stanley R., 266
Lasby, Clarence, 184
Lasch, Christopher, 138
Lasky, Victor, 41, 77, 326
Laurence, Edward J., 252
Lauter, Paul, 305
Lawson, Steven F., 160
Lawyer's Committee on American Policy towards Vietnam, 295
Lazarowitz, Arlene, 16, 37
Lazarus, Simon, 195
Lebeaux, Charles N., 202
Lee, D. B., Jr., 305
Lee, Jong R., 46
Lee, Richard W., 86
Lee, Ronald Emery, 122
Lefever, Ernest W., 257
Legere, Lawrence J., 44
Leib, Charles, 77
Lekachman, Robert, 177
Lemann, Nicholas, 53
Lenart, Edith R., 288
Lenman, Cordelia Snow, 211
Lens, Sidney, 288
Lent, Henry B., 234
Leopold, Robert L., 189
Lesher, Stephen, 197
Lester, Robert Leon, 41
Leuchtenburg, William E., 11, 16, 53, 138
Leuthold, David, 109
Levantrosser, William F., 266
Levensohn, Alan, 167
Levi, Arrige, 266
Levin, Bea, 323
Levine, Arnold S., 189
Levine, Mark H., 305

Levine, Marvin J., 211
Levine, Michael L., 53
Levitan, Sar A., 200, 203–204, 206–207, 211–212
Levitas, Mitchell, 138
Levitin, Teresa E., 30, 110, 123
Lewis, A., 212
Lewis, Fulton, Jr., 41, 138, 212, 305
Lewis, Joseph, 122
Lewis, Ted, 30, 53, 65, 77, 86, 91–92, 99, 122, 177, 212, 320
Ley, Willy, 189
Librach, Clifford, 160
Library of Congress Report [House Committee on Science and Technology], 189
Lichtenstein, Nelson, 53
Lichtman, Allan J., 160
Lidtke, Doris, 44
Leiberman, E. James, 305
Light, Paul C., 41, 99
Lindsey, Almont, 212
Ling, Ta-Tseng, 212
Linowitz, Sol M., 234
Lippman, Theodore, Jr., 119
Lipset, Seymour Martin, 305–306
Lipsius, Frank, 314
Lisagor, Peter, 92, 110, 149, 312
Liska, George, 234
Listov, Vadim, 252
Lloyd, Lewis E., 177, 235
Lloyd, Norman, 154
Locander, Robert, 86
Lockard, Duane, 160
Lockwood, David E., 240
Lodge, Henry Cabot, 266, 281
Loeb (Carl M.) Rhoades and Co., 167
Lokos, Lionel, 110
Lomperis, Timothy John, 266
Long, Ellis E., 306
Long, Gillis W., 212
Long, Norton, 213

Long, Stuart, 324
Longino, Charles F., Jr., 306
Louchheim, Katie, 9, 11, 317, 318
Louis, William Roger, 246
Lovell, John P., 306
Lowe, George E., 295
Lowe, Jeanne R., 200
Lowenstein, Allard K., 122
Lowi, Theodore J., 65, 138
Lowry, M., 314
Luan-Miller, Patricia D., 252
Lubell, Samuel, 92, 110
Lubove, Roy, 138
Luce, Phillip Abbott, 138
Luloff, Albert C., 153
Lunch, William M., 306
Lurie, Leonard, 122
Lutz, Frank W., 167
Lynch, Dudley M., 8
Lynd, Alice, 306
Lyndon B. Johnson Foundation, 323
Lyndon B. Johnson Library and Museum, 323
Lyon, Peter, 240
Lyons, Gene, 77

Macalusco, Theodore F., 122
Macauly, Stewart, 303
MacDonald, Glenn, 275
MacIver, R. M., 213
MacLean, Don, 8
Macy, John W., 77–78
Maheshwari, B., 257
Mailer, Norman, 122, 138
Makinin, G. E., 177, 306
Malabre, Alfred L., Jr., 213
Malawer, Stuart S., 296
Malcolm, Donald F., 30
Mancuso, Thomas George, 189
Mangano, R. M., 306
Mangold, Tom, 266
Manheim, Jarol B., 86
Mann, Dean E., 66

Manning, John, 259
Mansfield, Mike, 99
Manzel, Paul, 296
Mao, James C., 200
March, Michael S., 213
Marcuse, Peter, 213
Mares, Vaclav E., 246
Margolis, Howard, 177
Margolis, Milton, 177, 189
Margolius, Sidney, 226
Markel, Lester, 306
Markovich, Stephen C., 247
Marks, Thomas A., 240
Marmor, Theodore R., 184
Marris, Peter, 213
Marrow, A. J., 66
Marsh, Robert, 123
Marshall, Charles Burton, 240–241
Marshall, Dale Rogers, 213
Marshall, S. L. A., 240–241, 275
Martin, Glenn R., 16–17, 99
Martin, Graham, 281
Martin, Harold H., 123
Martin, Howard H., 138
Martin, Janet Marie, 46, 66
Martin, John Bartlow, 110
Martin, John F., 22, 92, 160
Martin, Ralph G., 41, 54
Martin, Robert P., 267, 281–282
Martinez, Julio Cesar, 252
Martire, D., 149, 213
Mashayekhi, Gholam-Hossein, 160
Mason, Alpheus Thomas, 195
Mason, William, 28, 91
Mathews, Carla, 324
Mathews, Dorothy M., 47
Matsunaga, Spark, 99
Matthiessen, Maria Von, 323
Matusow, Allen J., 41, 54, 92, 138, 213
May, Ernest R., 267
Mayhew, David R., 17
Maynard, P. J., 110, 177

Mazlish, Bruce, 189
McCarry, Charles, 123
McCarthy, Dennis V. N., 54, 318, 326
McCarthy, Eugene Joseph, 123
McCarthy, Joseph E., 282
McCarthy, Terence, 177, 306
McCaughey, Robert A., 306
McCloskey, Robert G., 195
McCord, John A., 160
McCord, William, 138
McCormack, Wayne, 298
McCulley, Richard T., 80
McCullouch, Frank, 288
McDonald, Archie P., 8, 54
McDonald, William F., 155
McDougall, Walter A., 22, 42, 189
McFeeley, Neil D., 195–196
McGough, Lucy S., 196
McGovern, George S., 267
McGowan, Carl, 312
McGraith, Thomas C., 213
McGuire, Edna, 235
McKaig, J. E., 149, 177
McKay, Seth Shepard, 10, 11–12, 16, 37
McKenna, William J., 110
McKenney, James, 251
McKinley, Gordon W., 177
McKinney, John C., 184
McKissick, Floyd B., 138
McLintock, Robert, 267
McMenamin, Michael, 92
McNamara, Robert S., 190, 242, 247, 283
McNamara, Walter, 92
McNeil, Dixie Mercer, 163, 270
McNeil, Neil V., 86
McQuaid, Kim, 54
McReynolds, David, 54
McVittie, W. W., 252
McWilliams, Carey, 54
Meany, George, 4
Meany, Neville, 282

Mecklin, John, 190, 267
Meeker, Leonard C., 296
Meier, August, 138, 159, 167
Meier, Deborah, 167
Meisler, Stanley, 257
Melanson, Richard A., 267
Melby, John F., 241
Melosi, Martin, 226
Meltzer, Jack, 200
Mendel, Douglas H., 241
Mendelsohn, Harold, 86
Menges, Garty L., 200
Meranto, Philip, 167
Mermelstein, David, 149
Merriam, Ida C., 149
Merriam, Robert E., 46
Meryman, Richard, 60, 123
Messing, J. H., 296
Metropolitan Applied Research Center, 213
Meyer, Karl E., 247
Meyerhoff, Arthur E., 235
Meyers, David S., 110
Meyers, Harold B., 66, 184
Mezerik, A. G., 267
Middleton, Harry J., 314
Middleton, Neil, 139
Miernyk, William H., 190
Miles, Edward W., 196
Miles, Michael, 123
Milkis, Sidney M., 92
Millar, Thomas B., 259
Miller, Arthur, 54, 92, 123, 139
Miller, Glenn H., Jr., 178
Miller, Mark Emory, 247
Miller, Michael V., 139
Miller, S. M., 167–168, 213–214
Miller, Warren E., 30, 110, 123
Mishkin, Paul J., 196
Mitchell, Willard H., 238, 272
Mizell, Winton R., 196
Moe, Ronald C., 46
Moise, Edwin E., 275
Moley, Raymond, 54, 66, 78

Mollenkopf, John H., 200
Moncrieff, Anthony, 261
Monroe, Kristen R., 46
Montagu, Ivor, 267
Montalva, Eduardo Frei, 252
Montgomery, Roosevelt, 160–161
Montoya, Joseph M., 150
Moody, Kimberly, 214
Moore, John Norton, 296
Mordechai, Nahumi, 257
Morehead, Richard, 17, 30, 92
Morgan Edward P., 320
Morgan, Richard, 162
Morgan, Thomas B., 78
Morgenthau, Hans J., 78, 267, 282
Morley, Felix, 92, 110
Morris, Charles, 139
Morris, Eugene J., 200
Morrow, E. Frederick, 17
Morse, Wayne, 168, 235, 296
Mortensen, C. David (Calvin D.), 30, 86, 110
Mosely, Philip E., 247
Mosher, Edith K., 165
Moskin, J. Robert, 78
Moulton, Harland B., 282
Mowery, David C., 78, 178
Mowrer, Edgar Ansel, 288
Moyer, Henry W., Jr., 296–297
Moyers, Bill D., 54
Moynihan, Daniel Patrick, 66, 139, 214
Mueller, John E., 306
Mullen, James J., 110
Munk, Michael, 209, 214
Munroe, Pat, 78
Murphy, Anne Austin, 214
Murphy, Bruce, 196
Murphy, Charles J. V., 190, 267
Murphy, Thomas E., 161
Murray, Charles, 23, 150, 214
Murray, David, 123
Murray, N., 139
Murray, Pauli, 161

Muste, A. J., 139
Myers, David S., 123
Myers, H. B., 150
Myrdal, Gunnar, 297

Nairn, Ronald C., 241
Nalty, Bernard C., 307
Nanes, Allan, 255
Nash, Bradley D., 78, 226
Nash, Gerald D., 23
Natchez, Peter B., 17, 92
National Broadcasting Corporation, 267
National Education Association, 168
National Geographic Society, 312, 324
National Industrial Conference Board, 178
Natoli, Marie D., 42
Naveh, David, 78
Neal, Fred Warner, 257
Neal, William Patrick, 297
Neff, David, 257
Nekach, Larry A., 288
Nelson, Frederick, 110, 307
Nelson, Michael, 46
Neuhaus, Richard J., 307
Neustadt, Richard E., 54, 267
Nevin, David, 123
Newberry, Anthony Lake, 23, 37
Newfield, Jack, 93, 123
Newman, Dorothy K., 139
Newman, Frank J., 78
Nguyen Van Ba, 282, 289
Nguyen-van-Thieu, 282
Nice, David C., 26, 104, 116
Nicholas, H. G., 123
Nichols, Mary E., 322
Niebuhr, Reinhold, 235
Nielson, Waldemar A., 258
Niemeyer, E. V., Jr., 253
Nighswonger, William Asa, 282
Nixon, Richard M., 31, 37, 60, 93, 124, 267
Nocera, Joseph, 23, 226

Nogee, Joseph, 237
Nolan, David, 214–215
Northrup, Graham T., 200, 215
Norton, Hugh S., 66, 79
Norton, John K., 168
Nourse, Hugh O., 201, 215
Novak, Robert D., 97, 111
Novick, David, 178
Novogrod, J., 294
Nyitray, Joseph Paul, 178

O'Ballance, Edgar, 282
O'Brien, David M., 93, 196
O'Brien, James Putnam, 139
O'Brien, Lawrence F., 66
O'Brien, W. V., 235, 297
O'Donnell, B., 307
O'Donnell, Barbara, 79
O'Mara, Richard, 124
O'Neal, Robert M., 292
O'Reilly, Kenneth, 140
Oates, Stephen B., 42, 140
Oberdorfer, Don, 60, 215
Ogden, Daniel M., Jr., 31
Okamato, Yoichi, 56
Okanla, Mousa Affalabi, 258
Oleszek, Walter J., 13–14, 35, 96
Oliver, James K., 235
Opitz, Edmund A., 215
Orekhov, F. T., 235
Orshansky, Mollie, 140
Orum, Anthony M., 12
Osbourne, Elmo J., 23
Oshinsky, David M., 23, 37
Oslo, Kenneth, 168
Ott, Attiat F., 215
Owens, John E., 10

Pace, Eric, 241, 268
Pack, Lindsy Escoe, 23
Packenham, Robert A., 235
Packer, Herbert L., 196
Pagano, Jules, 168
Page, Benjamin I., 297
Paletz, David L., 86
Palmer, Bruce, Jr., 282

Palmer, Gregory, 268
Palmer, Norman D., 241
Pan American Union Alliance for Progress Special Progress Team, 5–6
Paradiso, L. J., 178
Park, Chang Jin, 241, 268
Parker, Glenn R., 46
Parker, Robert, 17, 161
Parker, Thomas F., 140
Parmer, J. Norman, 235
Parmet, Herbert S., 42
Parrish, John B., 140
Pascal, Anthony H., 215
Paterson, Thomas G., 42
Patman, Wright, 201
Paul, Norman S., 307
Payne, Bruce, 111
Payne, Thomas, 161
Peabody, Robert L., 100
Pearl, Arthur, 217
Pearsall, Joan, 323
Peck, Sidney M., 307
Peirce, Neal R., 93
Penycate, John, 266
Perham, John, 307
Perlo, Victor, 111
Perry, Constance, 215
Peterson, Paul Elliott, 209, 216
Peterson, Richard E., 140
Peterson, Svend, 179
Pfeffer, Leo, 168
Pfeiffer, Richard Norton, 275
Pfiffner, James W., 67
Phillips, Cabell, 31
Phillips, Charles F., 150, 235
Phillips, Donald E., 140
Phillips, Edward Hake, 35, 37
Phillips, Glen D., 87
Pickens, Donald K., 79
Pickus, Robert, 297
Picque, Nicholas D., 150
Pika, Joseph A., 79
Piland, Robert Owens, 190
Pilisuk, Marc, 216
Pilisuk, Phyllis, 216

354 INDEX

Ping Chen, 99
Pinkard, Tommie, 323, 324, 326
Pino, Ricardo, 216
Pipe, G. Russell, 79
Pirmantgen, Patricia, 132, 301
Pistorius, Joseph H., 270
Piven, Frances Fox, 132, 161
Plager, Sheldon J., 201
Plimpton, George, 93, 124
Plischke, Elmer, 235
Podhoretz, Norman, 275
Podwal, Mark H., 140, 268
Poirot, Paul L., 216
Polk, Kenneth, 41
Pollard, Vincent K., 241, 268, 282, 297
Pollitt, Frederick Anthony, 216
Pollock, David, 258
Polsby, Nelson W., 17, 31, 55, 100, 111, 125, 275
Pomper, Gerald, 31, 111, 125
Poole, Kenjon E., 179
Poole, Peter A., 235–236
Portz, Phillip, 184
Possony, Stefan I., 297
Postal, Bernard, 312
Potenziani, David D., 37, 161–162
Potter, Philip, 31
Powers, Richard Gid, 67, 141
Powers, S. P., 150
Powers, Thomas, 307
Prados, John Frederick, 236, 247, 282
Prater, Teresa, 8
Pratt, John Clark, 268
President's Advisory Commission on Civil Disorders, 132
President's Commission on Campus Unrest, 141
President's Committee on the Economic Impact of Defense and Disarmament, 179
President's Science Advisory Board, Panel on Education Innovation (Zacharias Report), 79
President's Task Force on Higher Education [Hester Report], 168
Pressman, Jeffrey L., 217
Primack, Joel, 94, 192
Prinz, Jonathan, 217
Pritchard, Kathleen, 98
Prothro, James W., 121
Provost, Norma Matlock, 23
Pruett, Jakie L., 9
Pryor, Bernard Bruce, 282–283
Pryor, Richard ("Cactus"), 87
Purcell, Francis, 217
Pycior, Julie Leininger, 162
Pyle, Christopher H., 93, 162
Pyong Choon Hahm, 241

Quinley, Harold E., 307
Quirk, John J., 126
Quirk, Paul J., 90

Rabe, Stephen G., 253
Rachlin, Carl, 162
Ragsdale, Crystal Sasse, 316
Ragsdale, Lyn, 87
Ragsdale, Warner, 87
Raines, Edgar F., Jr., 67
Rajagopal, D. R., 268
Ramazani, R. K., 258
Rand, Ayn, 126
Randall, Ronald, 179
Randolph, Raymond Sean, 242
Ranelagh, John, 236
Ranis, Gustav, 236
Rashke, Richard, 17, 161
Raskin, A. H., 162, 217
Ratner, Leonard G., 297
Raveling, Gordon R., 126
Ravitch, Diane, 168
Rayburn, Sam, 32
Read, Frank T., 196
Reagan, Ronald, 126
Reday, Joseph Z., 242
Reddy, John, 126

Redford, Emmette S., 80
Reedy, George E., 46, 55, 87
Reichley, A. James, 126
Reiley, Linda Cobb, 217
Reilly, Richard L., 67
Rein, Martin, 213
Reinhard, David W., 38, 93
Reissman, Frank, 217
Renka, Russell D., 100
Rentashler, William H., 217
Reopel, Michael R., 150
Republican National Convention, 126
Reston, James, 150
Reuther, Walter P., 141
Reveley, W. Taylor III, 297
Riccards, Michael P., 55–56
Rice, Gerard T., 42, 236
Rickman, Alvin, 247
Ridder, Marie, 326
Riddell, Thomas Allen, 179, 268, 307–308
Riddlesperger, James W., Jr., 77, 80
Ridgeway, James, 226
Riesel, Victor, 32, 42, 56, 67, 80, 93, 112, 126–127, 141, 217–218, 226–227, 322
Riga, Peter, 253
Ringer, James A., Jr., 162
Ringquist, Delbert, 14
Rinn, Fauneil, 87
Rinta, Eugene F., 179
Ripley, Randall B., 46, 173
Ritchie, Donald A., 24, 297
Rivkin, Arnold, 258
Robb, Charles S., 326
Roberts, Adam, 268, 289
Roberts, Ben, 180
Roberts, Dick, 322
Roberts, M. D., 134
Roberts, Steven V., 127
Robertson, D. W., 297
Robertson, Norman, 180
Robinson, Donald A., 47

Robinson, John P., 87, 308
Robison, Joseph B., 196
Roby, Pamela, 167–168, 214
Roche, John P., 80, 297
Rockefeller Panel Report [on the Performing Arts], 141
Rockefeller, Nelson, 127
Rockler, Michael J., 168
Rodgers, Harrell R., 162
Rodman, Selden, 253
Rogers, Donald I., 112, 151, 201, 218
Rogers, John, 218
Rogers, Warren, 127
Rogers, William P., 298
Roghbart, Myron, 308
Rogin, Lawrence, 168
Roherty, James M., 67
Rollins, Peter C., 275
Root, Eugene, 191
Rose, Stephen M., 218
Roseman, Alvin, 236
Rosen, Gerald R., 67, 80, 180
Rosenau, James N., 233, 236, 264
Rosenbaum, Karen J., 218
Rosenberg, Benjamin B., 151
Rosenberg, Harold, 155
Rosenberg, Milton J., 308
Rosenblum, Victor, 218
Rosenfeld, Paul, 8
Rosenthal, Harvey Daniel, 227
Rosenwasser, Marie, 298
Roskin, Michael, 268
Ross, Douglas, 93, 127
Rossi, Peter, 141
Rossiter, Clinton, 197
Rossman, Jules, 32, 112
Rostow, Elspeth D., 148
Rostow, Walt W., 127, 236, 268–269, 283
Rothenberg, Jerome, 201
Rothman, Julius F., 218
Rothman, Rozann, 151
Rothschild, Mary Aickin, 141
Roubatis, Yiannis P., 24, 248

Rourke, Francis E., 47
Rowland, C. K., 197
Rowow, I., 141
Rubenberg, Cheryl A., 258
Rubin, Barry, 236, 269
Rubin, Richard Alan, 269
Ruddy, T. Michael, 253
Runyon, John H., 32, 112, 127
Runyon, Sally S., 32, 112, 127
Rusk, Dean, 68, 236, 242, 283
Russell, James W., 218
Russell, Richard B., 298
Rustin, Bayard, 127, 141
Ruth, Robert W., 42
Ryskind, Allan H., 60, 68, 93, 127, 162
Ryskind, Morris, 112, 127, 151

Sabato, Larry J., 93
Sacks, Milton, 289
St. John, Jeffrey, 128
Salisbury, Harrison E., 269
Sampson, Edward E., 141
Samuelson, Paul A., 80
Sanders, Sol W., 269, 281–282, 289
Sandoz, Robert, 240–241
Sanford, David, 185
Sarratt, Reed, 141
Sato, Eisaku, 242
Sax, J. L., 308
Sayre, John R., 97
Sayres, Sohnya, 141
Scalapino, Robert, 242
Scammon, Richard M., 32, 112
Schaffer, William R., 100
Schaffler, Dorothy, 47
Schapsmeier, Edward L., 38, 100
Schapsmeier, Frederick H., 38, 100
Schecter, William, 127
Scheer, Robert, 94, 298
Scheibla, Shirley, 218
Schermbeck, C. E., 201
Schick, Allen, 180

Schienbaum, Ervin, 180
Schienbaum, Kim Ezra, 180
Schiff, Martin, 248
Schlesinger, Arthur M., Jr., 47, 56, 127, 242, 248, 253, 258, 269, 298
Schlight, John, 269
Schmelzer, Janet Louise, 10
Schmidt, John T., 169
Schmidt, Ronald John, 218
Schmitt, Karl M., 253
Schneider, Ronald M., 253
Schneider, Edward, 127
Schnore, Leo F., 201
Schoenebaum, Eleanora W., 53
Schott, Richard L., 56, 80, 94
Schreiber, Eugene M., 298, 308
Schreiber, Flora Rheta, 324
Schrepfer, Susan R., 227
Schulke, Flip, 141
Schultz, Theodore W., 218
Schultze, Charles, 180
Schulz, Bill, 94, 151, 201, 218
Schulzinger, Robert D., 236
Schuman, Howard, 301
Schuyler, George, 141–142, 308
Schuyler, Michael, 56
Schwartz, Bernard, 163, 197
Schwartz, Mortimer D., 188
Schwartz, Tony, 112
Schwartz, Warren F., 298
Schwarz, John E., 151, 219
Scigliano, Robert, 197
Sclanders, Ian, 56, 253
Scott, Paul, 87, 127–128, 142, 219, 227, 242, 248, 289
Scranton, Margaret E., 253
Segal, David R., 112
Seib, Shirley M., 169, 180
Seidel, John, 135
Seligman, Daniel, 68
Senate Republican Policy Committee, 269
Sennholz, Hans, 219
Sessions, John A., 308

INDEX 357

Sevareid, Eric, 32
Sewer, Arnold, 128
Shachtman, Tom, 142
Shadegg, Stephen, 112
Shaffer, Helen B., 142, 163, 219
Shaffer, Samuel, 151
Shanahan, E. K., 219
Shannon, William V., 32, 56, 94, 112, 180
Shaplen, Robert, 269, 289
Shapley, Deborah, 68, 283
Shapp, M. J., 321
Sharp, U. S. Grant, 269–270
Shattuch, Francis M., 33
Shaw, Malcolm, 112–113
Shaw, Sydney, 274
Shaw, William Lawrence, 308
Shee Poon-Kim, 242
Sheehan, Neil, 276
Shelly, Walter Lumley, 128
Shelton, Willard, 236
Shelton, William, 191
Sheppard, Harold L., 142
Sherman, Annabelle S., 219
Sherrard, Thomas D., 142
Sherry, John H., 163
Shields, Patricia M., 308
Shinn, Roger L., 56, 113, 298
Shizuo, Maruyama, 270, 283
Shogan, Robert, 56, 197
Showalter, Stuart W., 276
Shriver, Sargent, 134, 219–220, 236–237
Shultz, Richard, 283
Sidey, Hugh, 56, 80, 308, 314, 318, 322
Siegel, Barry N., 180, 191
Siegel, Frederick F., 56
Siegel, Stanley, 227
Siemering, William H., 308
Sigelman, Lee, 47, 163, 270
Silberman, Charles E., 142, 220
Silver, Howard J., 100
Silverman, Jerry Mark, 283–284
Simchak, Morag, 163

Simmonds, E. H. S., 270
Simms, J. Carroll, 151
Simon, Jeffrey D., 237
Simon, William, 208
Simpson, Phillip M., 180
Singer, Benjamin D., 87, 276
Singh, L. P., 259
Singletary, Otis, 220
Sinise, Jerry, 9
Sirgo, Henry B., 185, 227
Skardon, James A., 191
Skidmore, Max J., 142
Skolnick, Jerome H., 142, 298
Skolnikoff, Eugene B., 68
Skorov, A., 270
Slaiman, Donald, 163
Slayton, William L., 201
Slesinger, Reuben E., 181
Sloan, Jerome S., 220
Sloan, John W., 80, 181
Sloope, Terry, 193
Small, Melvin, 237, 308, 318, 326
Small, William E., 80
Small, William J., 87
Smallwood, James, 38
Smith, Craig Allen, 87–88
Smith, D. L., 147
Smith, Eliz Simpson, 316
Smith, James George, 32–33, 113, 128
Smith, K. Wayne, 225
Smith, Kathy B., 87 88
Smith, Melden E., Jr., 284
Smith, Merriman, 88
Smith, Michael L., 191
Smith, Myron J., Jr., 237, 270, 284
Smith, Nancy Kegan, 80, 151, 169, 318, 323
Smith, Philip W., 54, 318, 326
Smith, Robert B., 308
Smith, Terry, 33, 113
Smith, Tom W., 142–143
Smoke, Richard, 231

Social Dynamics Research Institute, City University of New York, 220
Solberg, Carl, 38, 60
Soloveytchik, George, 56
Sommers, Albert T., 143, 181
Sorenson, Theodore C., 33, 42, 270
Southwest Texas State University, 169
Spanier, John W., 237, 292
Specht, Harry, 220
Specter, Arlen, 227
Spector, Rachel Elsa, 185
Speer, John W., 10
Spencer, Scott, 220
Sperlich, Peter W., 306
Spiegel, Steven L., 258
Spragens, William C., 88
Stafford, Walter W., 143
Stalson, Helena, 234
Stanley, David T., 68
Stanley, James David, 169
Stans, Maurice H., 181
Stanton, Shelby L., 270
Stares, Paul B., 191
Stark, John R., 151
Starner, Frances L., 242
Starr, Roger, 220
Starr, Samuel D., 319
Steele, John L., 56, 100
Steely, Jim, 38
Stegenga, J. A., 270
Stein, Herbert, 181
Stein, Jean, 93, 124
Steinberg, Alfred, 316, 320, 326
Steiner, Gilbert Y., 220
Stempel, Guido H. III, 33, 113
Stephanson, Anders, 141
Stern, Laurence M., 56, 321
Stern, Sol, 68
Stevens, C. R., 169
Stevens, Francis B., 248
Stevens, Frank, 169
Stevens, Robert, 185
Stevens, Roger L., 155
Stevens, Rosemary, 185
Stevenson, Adlai E., 298
Stevenson, Charles A., 242, 270
Stewart, Eugene L., 220
Stewart, John G., 18, 101, 163
Stewart, Malcolm, 57
Stewart, Maude A., 303, 309
Stewart, William H., 185
Stidham, Ronald A., 197
Stieber, Jack, 80
Stiles, Lynn A., 181
Stocking, Thomas E., 237
Stohl, Michael, 309
Stolley, Richard B., 151
Stone, I. F., 57, 143, 270
Stookey, Robert W., 255
Straight, Michael, 155
Strauss, William A., 300
Strickland, Stephen Parks, 197
Striner, Herbert C., 142
Stringfellow, William, 151
Stromseth, Jane, 248
Strout, Alan M., 233
Strout, Richard L., 57
Stuart, Anthony, 88, 94
Stuckey, John D., 270
Stupak, Donald J., 69
Suffridge, James A., 42–43
Sullivan, Gerald, 311
Sullivan, Marianna P., 270, 276
Sullivan, Terry, 101
Sultan, Allen, 163
Summers, Harry G., Jr., 270
Sundquist, James L., 18, 101
Sung, Kayser, 155
Sutherland, James Harrison, 169
Sutherland, John P., 319
Swados, Harvey, 38
Swankin, David A., 227
Sweeney, Paul, 12, 57
Swenson, Loyd S., Jr., 187, 192
Swindler, William F., 197
Symington, Stuart, 3, 29
Sypher, Alden H., 69

Taft, Walter J., 69
Talbot, Ross B., 248
Tananbaum, Duane A., 38
Tanham, George K., 270
Tanzer, Lester, 43
Tarango, Jose R., 253–254
Tatalovich, Raymond, 47, 57
Taussig, M. K., 181
Tax Foundation, Inc., 220
Taylor, Charles, 259, 270
Taylor, Claudia, see Johnson, Claudia A. T.
Taylor, Clyde, 309
Taylor, George E., 237
Taylor, George, 143
Taylor, H. Ralph, 201
Taylor, Hal, 192
Taylor, Harold, 155
Taylor, Henry J., 69, 81, 94, 113, 128, 151, 181, 237, 248–249, 254, 258, 271
Taylor, Maxwell D., 271, 281, 283, 284
Taylor, T. V., 9
Tebbel, John, 88
Teger, Stuart Henry, 197
Teigen, Robert L., 181
Terhorst, Jerald, 221
Terrill, Ross, 289
Texas Monthly Magazine, 57
Texas Mothers Committee, 316
Thee, Marek, 289
Thimmesch, Nick, 94
Thomas, David Allen, 33, 128–129
Thomas, Evan, 76, 246, 280
Thomas, Helen, 83
Thomas, Norman, 289
Thomas, Norman C., 74, 165, 169
Thompson, A. A., 181
Thompson, Frank, Jr., 155
Thompson, James C., 284
Thompson, Kenneth, 94, 221
Thompson, Kenneth W., 47, 57, 88, 237, 271

Thompson, Pat, 319
Thompson, W. Scott, 243
Thomson, Charles A. H., 33
Thorne, Barrie, 309
Tobin, James, 81
Toffler, Al, 18
Tolbert, Frank X., 316
Toru Yano, 243
Towne, Anthony, 227
Toynbee, Arnold J., 237
Trager, Frank N., 243, 271, 284
Tran Chanh Thanh, 289
Tran Van Dinh, 290
Trask, Roger R., 69
Trent, Judith, 34, 129
Trewhitt, Henry L., 69
Trohan, Walter, 43, 57, 81, 94, 101, 152, 197–198
Truscott, Lucian K. III, 271
Tuchman, Barbara W., 271
Tucker, James F., 221
Tucker, Robert W., 237, 271
Tugwell, Rexford G., 81
Turesky, Stanley Fred, 101
Turner, Donald R., 69
Turner, Kathleen J., 88, 276
Turner, Nicholas, 271
Turner, Russell, 38
Turner, W. Earl, 24
Turpin, Luci Baines Johnson, 325
Tyerman, D., 57–58
Tyler, Gus, 58, 113, 129, 143
Tyler, Paula Eyrich, 314
Tyler, Ron, 314

Udall, Stewart L., 69
United Press International, 43, 58
United States Aeronautics and Space Council, 192
United States Chamber of Commerce, 221
United States Chamber of Commerce, Task Force on Economic Growth and Opportunity, 221

360 INDEX

United States Commission on Civil Rights, 143, 163
United States Conference of Mayors, 143
United States Congress, 12, 38–39, 101, 323
United States Congress, House Committee on Science and Technology, see Library of Congress Report
United States Congress, Senate, 18, 39
United States Congress, Senate, Republican Policy Committee, 269
United States Department of Commerce, Bureau of the Census, 113–114, 129
United States Department of Labor, 152
United States Executive Office of the President, Bureau of the Budget, 181–182
United States Manpower Administration, Bureau of Work Training Programs, 221–222
United States Marine Corps, 271
United States National Advisory Commission on Civil Disorders, 143
United States Navy, Center for Naval Analyses, see Center for Naval Analyses
United States Office of Economic Opportunity, 143, 169, 221
United States Office of Education, 169
United States Peace Corps, 237–238
University of Texas, School of Architecture, 143
Unseem, Michael, 309
Urrows, Elizabeth, 272
Ustinov, Peter, 155

Valenti, Jack, 81
Van Cleve, John V., 254
Van den Bosch, Govert W., 114
Van Klaveren, Tricia, 272
Vance, Cyrus R., 69–70
Vaughn, Jack H., 237
Veliz, Claudio, 254
Velvel, Lawrence R., 143
Veninga, James F., 273
Verba, Sidney, 272, 308, 309
Verdini, Jennefer, 32, 112, 127
Vietor, Richard H., 228
Viksnins, George J., 243
Viles, Roberty M., 222
Viorst, Milton, 34, 70
Volsky, D., 284
Von Eckardt, Wolf, 155
Von Hippel, Frank, 94, 192
Voorhis, Jerry, 39

Wainstock, Dennis Dean, 129
Waite, Charles A., 182
Wakefield, Beverly Smith, 322
Wald, Patricia M., 222
Wallace, Don, Jr., 299
Wallace, George C., 114, 129
Wallace, James N., 238
Wallace, Mike, 88
Wallace, Paul, 243
Wallace, R. A., 170
Wallich, Henry C., 238
Walt, Lewis W., 284
Walter, J. Jackson, 77–78
Walterhouse, Harry F., 254
Walton, Richard J., 43
Ware, Alan, 94
Wagner, Denis, 272, 284, 290
Warner, Geoffrey, 272
Warner, Robert M., 152
Warner, Sam Bass, Jr., 201
Warnock, Charles F., 192
Warren, Earl, 164, 198
Wahsburn, Michael A., 238, 272
Washington, D.C. Inaugural Committee, 43, 58, 152

INDEX 361

Waskow, Arthur, 143, 299
Waterman, Kenneth, 222
Waters, G. E., 164
Watson, H. Lee, 47
Watters, Pat, 164
Watterson, Joseph, 320
Watts, Sarah Miles, 88
Waxman, Chaim Issac, 222
Way, Frank H., Jr., 104, 116
Wayne, Stephen J., 45
Ways, Max, 58, 143–144, 238
Weaver, Gary Rodger, 310
Weaver, John D., 198
Weaver, Robert C., 70, 144, 201
Webb, William R., 182
Weber, Janice, 320
Wechsler, James A., 60, 94, 129, 272, 299
Weeks, Christopher, 222
Weeks, Oliver Douglas, 18, 25, 34
Weeks, Stanley B., 249
Weidenbaum, Murray L., 192, 310
Weihmiller, Gordon R., 249
Weinberger, Bernard, 222
Weintraub, Arnold Norman, 276
Weisbrod, Burton A., 144
Weisbrod, Carol, 196
Weisner, Jerome, 225
Weissman, Stephen R., 258
Welch, June Rayfield, 19
Welch, Wayne, 222
Wells, John M., 299
Wells, Paul, 222–223
West, J. Bernard, 319
West, Thomas R., 39–40, 89
Westin, Alan F., 144
Westin, M., 323
Westly, David L., 144
Westmoreland, William C., 261, 269–270, 272, 276
Whalen, Barbara, 164
Whalen, Charles, 164
Whalen, Richard J., 249

Wheaton, William L. C., 201
Wheeler, Earle G., 70, 284–285
Whetten, Lawrence L., 259
White House Conference on Education, 169–170
[White House Conference on Public Health], 185
White House Conference ["To Fulfill These Rights"], 164
White, Daniel Ernest, 47
White, Ralph K., 273
White, Theodore H., 114
Whiting, Allen S., 243
Whitman, Arthur, 51
Whitnah, Donald R., 228
Whitney, David C., 9
Wick, James L., 25, 34, 39
Wickenden, Elizabeth, 223
Wicker, Tom, 88, 153, 249
Widener, Alice, 130, 144
Widick, B. J., 130
Widner, Ralph R., 223
Wiegand, G. C., 144
Wiener, Leonard, 114
Wilcox, Francis O., 238
Wilcox, Walter W., 228
Wildavsky, Aaron B., 31, 94, 111, 125, 182, 217
Wilgus, A. Curtis, 254
Wilheim, Maria, 299
Wilkins, Lillian Claire, 299
Wilkins, Roy, 144
Wilkinson, Kenneth P., 153
Williams, G. Mennen, 259
Williams, Geoffrey, 290
Williams, John, 25, 58, 153
Williams, Roger N., 310
Williams, Whiting, 153
Williams, William A., 273
Willis, Benjamin C., 170
Willis, John M., 310
Willmann, John B., 70, 202
Wilmer, Harry A., 273
Wilson, Amy, 325
Wilson, Beclee Newcomer, 223

Wilson, Bob, 88
Wilson, Dick, 243
Wilson, George C., 193, 285, 310
Wilson, James Q., 202
Wilson, Larman C., 254–255
Wilson, Melford A., Jr., 285
Wilson, Richard W., 9
Wilson, Richard, 130
Windmiller, Marshall, 310
Windsor, Philip, 240
Wise, David, 130
Witcover, Jules, 130, 223
Witkin, Gordon, 153
Woelflein, Kevin G., 182–183
Wolanin, Thomas E., 82
Wolf, Eleanor P., 202
Wolfenstein, Eugene Victor, 144, 223, 273
Wolfinger, Raymond E., 102
Wolin, Sheldon S., 306
Wood, Robert C., 202
Woodward, C. Vann, 58
Woolley, John T., 170
Wormuth, Francis D., 299
Worsnop, Richard L., 223, 299
Wright, Deil S., 82
Wright, Lawrence, 58
Wright, Quincy, 299
Wrigley, Robert L., Jr., 223

Wrong, Elaine Gale, 164
Wyschogrod, Michael, 310

Yarmolinsky, Adam, 153
Yim, Kwan H., 243
Yoder, Jess, 310
Yost, Charles W., 238
Young, Whitney M., 223
Younger, George D., 224

Zacharias Report, see President's Science Advisory Board, Panel on Education Innovation
Zant, Thomas, 285
Zarefsky, David H., 164, 185, 224
Zaroulis, Nancy, 311
Zeidenstein, Harvey G., 102
Zeiger, Henry A., 44, 94, 130, 299
Zeitlin, Maurice, 311
Zhukov, G., 193
Zikmund, Joseph II, 34, 114
Zimbalist, Sidney E., 224
Zinn, Howard, 273
Zuckert, Eugene M., 70
Zurcher, Louis, Jr., 224
Zwikl, Kurt D., 34